The Political Economy of Stalinism
Evidence from the Soviet Secret Archives

This book uses the formerly secret Soviet State and Communist Party archives to describe the creation and operations of the Soviet administrative-command system. It concludes that the system failed not because of the "jockey" (i.e., Stalin and later leaders) but because of the "horse" (the economic system). Although Stalin was the system's prime architect, the system was managed by thousands of "Stalins" in a nested dictatorship. The core values of the Bolshevik Party dictated the choice of the administrative-command system, and the system dictated the political victory of a Stalin-like figure. This study pinpoints the reasons for the failure of the system – poor planning, unreliable supplies, the preferential treatment of indigenous enterprises, the lack of knowledge of planners, etc. – but also focuses on the basic principal–agent conflict between planners and producers, which created a sixty-year reform stalemate. Once Gorbachev gave enterprises their freedom, the system had no direction from either a plan or a market, and the system imploded. The Soviet administrative-command system was arguably the most significant human experiment of the twentieth century. If repeated today, its basic contradictions and inherent flaws would remain, and its economic results would again prove inferior.

Paul R. Gregory is Cullen Professor of Economics at the University of Houston and currently serves as a Research Fellow at the Hoover Institution, Stanford University. He is also a research professor at the German Institute for Economic Research (DIW) in Berlin. Professor Gregory has published widely in the field of Russian and Soviet economics for more than thirty years and served as a visiting professor at Moscow State University. Among his numerous books are *Restructuring the Soviet Economic Bureaucracy* (1990), *Before Command: The Russian Economy from Emancipation to Stalin* (1994), and *Russian National Income, 1885–1913*. He is the co-author (with Robert Stuart) of *Russian and Soviet Economic Structure and Performance*, now in its seventh edition. Professor Gregory received his Ph.D. in economics from Harvard in 1969.

The Political Economy of Stalinism

Evidence from the Soviet Secret Archives

PAUL R. GREGORY

University of Houston
Hoover Institution

CAMBRIDGE
UNIVERSITY PRESS

PUBLISHED BY THE PRESS SYNDICATE OF THE UNIVERSITY OF CAMBRIDGE
The Pitt Building, Trumpington Street, Cambridge, United Kingdom

CAMBRIDGE UNIVERSITY PRESS
The Edinburgh Building, Cambridge CB2 2RU, UK
40 West 20th Street, New York, NY 10011-4211, USA
477 Williamstown Road, Port Melbourne, VIC 3207, Australia
Ruiz de Alarcón 13, 28014 Madrid, Spain
Dock House, The Waterfront, Cape Town 8001, South Africa

http://www.cambridge.org

First published 2004

Printed in the United States of America

Typeface Sabon 10/13pt. *System* LATEX 2$_\varepsilon$ [TB]

A catalog record for this book is available from the British Library.

Library of Congress Cataloging in Publication Data
Gregory, Paul R.
The political economy of Stalinism : evidence from the Soviet secret
archives / Paul R. Gregory.
p. cm.
Includes bibliographical references and index.
ISBN 0-521-82628-4 – ISBN 0-521-53367-8 (pbk.)
1. Soviet Union – Economic conditions – Sources. 2. Soviet Union – Politics
and government – Sources. 3. Bureaucracy – Soviet Union – History – Sources.
1. Title.
HC335.3.G74 2003
330.947'084–dc21 2003043586

ISBN 0 521 82628 4 hardback
ISBN 0 521 53367 8 paperback

Contents

Illustrations

Tables

Preface

The collapse of the Soviet Union in December of 1991, in some sense, also signaled the end of scholarly study of the Soviet administrative-command economy by economists. As a long-term student of this economy, I was acutely aware that our lack of knowledge about this economy remained considerable. This ignorance was not due to the lack of acumen or effort but to the veil of secrecy that had been erected by Soviet leaders around this system. As Mikhail Gorbachev began his policy of Glasnost in the mid-1980s, the barriers of secrecy began to fall, but the scholarly community had by then turned its attention to more pressing agendas, such as the Soviet system in collapse and then the fundamental issue of its transition. Specialists on the Soviet economy turned primarily to transition as did numerous newcomers to the field, attracted by the challenge of transitioning a planned socialist economy into something resembling a market economy. Few continued to study the fundamental nature of the Soviet administrative-command economy either due to the conviction that we already knew all we needed to know or the belief that there were better uses of our time.

This book studies the creation of the Soviet administrative-command economy in the 1930s. I have written it for three reasons: First, only now is it possible to study the Soviet economic system without the barrier of secrecy. The Soviet State and Party Archives were opened to scholars in the early 1990s, and it is now possible to study the Soviet economy using the very records that its administrators used many years earlier. Moreover, we can read the candid memoirs of actual participants that can now be published with few restrictions or interview those persons who managed the system prior to its demise. Second, I regard the Soviet Union's experience with the planned socialist system as the most important social, political, and economic experiment of the twentieth century. This system continues to have considerable emotional appeal throughout the world to those who believe that it offers economic progress and fairness, free of chaotic market forces. Despite its demise, the Soviet system continues to have its apologists, who argue that it failed because of the wrong people and the wrong policies. It is therefore vital to have a conclusive and definitive record of how it operated in reality, not in stereotypic form, for its devotees and enemies alike. Third, we cannot understand the transitions taking place in the fifteen republics that once constituted the Soviet Union without understanding their initial conditions. We must know what features of these transition economies are deeply rooted in the Soviet past and which are new (and hopefully transitory) phenomena associated with the unique circumstances of transition.

The material presented in this book represents a substantial collaborative effort. I assembled a team of researchers who began the work in 1996. We were fortunate to receive financial support from the National Science Foundation, which carried us through the first four years of the project. We were then particularly grateful to receive not only the financial support of the Hoover Institution but also access to its growing collection of Soviet archives and support from its archival staff to carry the work through to the present. The research team consists of, in alphabetical order, Eugenia Belova, Valery Lazarev, Andrei Markevich, and Aleksei Tikhonov. Our talented young researchers and scholars worked in the Soviet archives both in Moscow and at the Hoover Institution, producing the studies, articles, and research notes that serve as the core of this work. The wider research team consists of the dedicated senior scholars, both inside and outside of Russia, who have produced the invaluable research articles and monographs that are used and widely cited throughout this book. They are too numerous to mention, but I would single out R. W. Davies, Mark Harrison, Oleg Khlevnyuk, E. A. Rees, Elena Osokina, and Nikolai Simonov. Fortunately, we constitute a cooperative group of scholars, who meet periodically to exchange results and organize our cooperation. Our Website, www.Soviet-archives-research.co.uk, is maintained by Mark Harrison. This book also owes a strong debt to the editors of the annotated collections of archival documents, which are also used intensively, such as Oleg Khlevnyuk, V. P. Danilov, A. Berelovich, Lars Lih, and Oleg Naumov. Following R. W. Davies's admonition to archival scholars to avoid reinventing the bicycle, I should also state a debt of gratitude to those scholars who so effectively culled material from official Soviet publications from the 1950s and 1960s, in particular Eugene Zaleski, Abram Bergson, Holland Hunter, Naum Jasny, Joseph Berliner, and David Granick.

This book was made possible by many persons and organizations. I hesitate to name them in fear of leaving someone out. This book and much of the research was made possible by the financial support of the Hoover Institution as represented by John Raisian and Charles Palm and by the assistance of its archival staff directed by Elena Danielson. The work could not have been initiated without a grant from the National Science Foundation. I received advice and comments from many colleagues whom I mention in random order: R. W. Davies, Mark Harrison, Valery Lazarev, Eugenia Belova, Sergei Afontsev, Wolfram Schrettl, Irwin Collier, Leonid Borodkin, Peter Boettke, Carol Leonard, Andrei Markevich, Dale Steinreich, and Andrei Sokolov. I also must thank Natalie Volosovych for patient editorial assistance in navigating this manuscript through many drafts. I would also like to thank Nancy Hulan and her associates at TechBooks for their skillful and professional editorial assistance.

PAUL R. GREGORY

I

The Jockey or the Horse?

The Soviet administrative-command economy was the most important social and economic experiment of the twentieth century. Its failure continues to reverberate throughout those countries in Europe, Asia, and Latin America that adopted it, either forcibly or voluntarily. Its symbolic end dates to December 25, 1991, when the flag of the once-powerful Soviet Union was lowered over the Kremlin and replaced by that of the Russian Federation. The abandonment of the administrative-command economy began in the late 1980s in Central and Southern Europe, spread throughout the fifteen Soviet republics with the collapse of the USSR, and expanded into Asia.[1] The former administrative-command economies have had to confront their pasts as they make their transitions to market economies. Empirical studies show that the heavier the imprint of the administrative-command system, the more difficult has been the transition.[2]

The administrative-command economy was formed without a theoretical blueprint in the 1930s by a small coterie of revolutionaries with little or no economic or administrative experience. Their first experiment,

---

[1] China, of course, had begun a major reform of its former administrative-command economy in 1979.

[2] Robert Stuart and Christina Panayotopouolos, "Decline and Recovery in Transition Economies: The Impact of Initial Conditions," *Post-Soviet Geography and Economics* 40, no. 4 (1999): 267–80; James Millar, "The Importance of Initial Conditions in Economic Transitions: An Evaluation of Economic Reform Progress in Russia," *Journal of Socio-Economics* 26, no. 4 (1997): 359–81; Gary Krueger and Marek Ciolko, "A Note on Initial Conditions and Liberalization During Transition," *Journal of Comparative Economics* 1, no. 4 (December 1998): 718–34.

called War Communism, was motivated by ideology but later blamed on wartime emergency; it caused a severe economic collapse, and a retreat was sounded to the mixed economy of the New Economic Policy (NEP). After resolution of a brutal power struggle over the succession to Lenin's mantle, the victorious Stalin and his allies embarked in 1929 on a course of rapid industrialization and forced collectivization, which required the creation of a new command system. This "Team Stalin" had fashioned, by the mid-1930s, an economy of full state ownership run by administrative resource allocation. As Stalin consolidated power, the team carried less weight than did Stalin the dictator, but they remained important cogs in the economic administration. Planning was carried out primarily by the State Planning Commission (Gosplan), but production was the responsibility of industrial ministries, which managed state enterprises and collective farms. The Soviet state was a close amalgam of the Politburo of the Communist Party and the Council of People's Commissars, the highest state body. This "administrative-command system," to use the pejorative term later coined by Mikhail Gorbachev, remained remarkably unchanged until its final collapse.

Blame the Jockey or the Horse?

Some contend that the Soviet system was doomed from the start. Ludwig von Mises and F. A. Hayek, in their classic critique of planned socialism written in the 1920s and 1940s, outlined the system's many Achilles' heels.[3] They contended that socialism would fail in the end. Lacking markets, there could be no rational economic calculation, and no economy can function if it does not know what is abundant and what is scarce. With state ownership, there would be little incentive to use resources rationally, and even dedicated state managers would be left without operating rules. A central planning board, charged with managing an entire economy, would find itself overwhelmed by the complexity of planning. In a word, Hayek and Mises insisted on the inevitable unfeasibility of planned socialism – the first prognosticators of its collapse. At best, the system would operate at low levels of efficiency and would clearly be inferior to market economies. The contemporary literature on the inefficiency of

---

[3] Ludwig Mises, *Socialism: An Economic and Sociological Analysis*, trans. J. Kahane (London: Jonathyn Cape Ltd., 1936); F. A. Hayek, "The Use of Knowledge in Society," *American Economic Review* 35 (1945): 510–50; F. A. Hayek, "Socialist Calculation: The Competitive Solution," *Economica*, n.s., 7 (May 1940): 125–49.

bureaucratic governance of state enterprises validates Hayek and Mises's conclusions, especially given that, in the Soviet case, the public sector encompassed the entire economy.[4]

Contemporary defenders of the administrative-command economy, however, argue that the Soviet system, which transformed Russia from backwardness to industrial power, failed because of *inept policies* and *incompetent administrators*, not because of its fundamental flaws. They cite that, up to its end, the Soviet economic system was not unpopular among the citizenry and that most Soviet officials and Western experts felt that the status quo could have been continued, albeit at relatively low rates of growth.[5] Advocates also argue that if only someone other than Stalin had won the power struggle or if policy mistakes had been avoided, the system's soundness would have been demonstrated.

The worldwide appeal of Marxism, communism, or the Radical Left remains remarkably unaffected by the collapse of communism.[6] Some avoid the implications of the collapse entirely by arguing that the Soviet Union and Eastern Europe were simply "posing as 'socialist' or 'command' economies"[7] and were "tragic or misunderstood embodiments of good intentions."[8] Leading leftist intellectuals argue that "the tragic abortive attempt [in the former Soviet Union] proves nothing about the impossibility ... of building socialism." And "Marxist thought becomes even more relevant after the collapse of communism in the Soviet Union and Eastern Europe than it was before."[9] Although contemporary socialists focus on the coming crisis of capitalism, they do little to explain how a "new" communist system would work differently. Some advance a pragmatic market socialism, which will avoid dictatorship and use

4 W. A. Niskanen, *Bureaucracy and Public Economics* (Aldershot, England: Edward Elgar, 1994); W. A. Niskanen, *Public Analysis and Public Choice* (Cheltenham, England: Edward Elgar, 1998).
5 This is the conclusion reached based on interviews with former Soviet officials and advisors in Michael Ellman and Vladimir Kontorovich, *The Destruction of the Soviet Economic System* (Armonk, New York: Sharpe, 1998), 3–29.
6 Currently, there are more than five hundred leftist parties of different persuasions in Europe alone, with the numbers of leftist parties in France and Italy exceeding one hundred each. Argentina and Brazil have nearly fifty leftist parties each, and the number of parties of the left appears to grow each month according to *www.broadleft.com*.
7 Platform of the International Bureau of the Revolutionary Party, available from *http://www.geocities.com/leftcom.html*.
8 Paul Hollander, "Which God Has Failed," The New Criterion on Line, April 15, 2002, p. 2; available from *www.newcriterion.com*.
9 Statements of Daniel Singer, Cornel West, and John Cassidy cited in Hollander, "Which God Has Failed."

market forces, but preserve state ownership.[10] The continued appeal of
the communist system is easy to understand. It promises fairness and the
elimination of the anarchy of the market – business cycles, poverty, unemployment, inflation, and currency crises. To those living in poor countries,
this is a powerful message. The Bolshevik leadership promised to create
such a fair, prosperous, and orderly system in 1917. They had some sixty
years to deliver on this promise. How and why they went wrong cannot
be ignored; it is one of the most significant questions of history.

The late Joseph Berliner used an analogy to characterize the debate.[11]
Did the administrative-command economy fail because of a bad jockey or
a bad horse? If it had been directed by smarter leaders, would it have been
a success, or were Mises and Hayek correct that the system's collapse was
inevitable? This book seeks to answer Berliner's jockey or horse question.

This book describes the first two and a half decades of the world's first
administrative-command economy, under the tutelage of an increasingly
brutal dictatorship. The Soviet command system remains the most complex organization ever constructed by mankind. How it really operated
was kept from public view by pervasive secrecy. Official Soviet writings
emphasized the fable of "scientific planning," a mythical economy run
according to harmonious mathematical balances prepared by omniscient
planners and executed by selfless producers. Throughout the Soviet period, we lacked open records, candid memoirs of officials, and a free
press to inform us how and how well the system operated. We had to rely
on a controlled press and a muzzled statistical office, émigré interviews,
and rare serendipitous behind-the-scenes glimpses of the system's workings.[12] The published Soviet literature permitted only tantalizing hints of
massive "political-economy–type" negotiations, strategic behavior, and

---

[10] James Junker, *Socialism Revised and Modernized: The Case for Pragmatic Market Socialism* (New York: Praeger, 1992).

[11] Joseph Berliner, "Soviet Initial Conditions: How They Have Affected Russian Transition," paper presented at the International Conference sponsored by Moscow University, Harvard Davis Center, and University of Houston International Economics Program,
entitled "Soviet Economy in the 1930s–1970s," Zvenigorod, Russia, June 22–24, 2001.

[12] Joseph Berliner, "The Contribution of the Soviet Archives," in Paul Gregory (ed.), *Behind
the Facade of Stalin's Command Economy* (Stanford, Calif.: Hoover Institution Press,
2001), 1–10. The most notable émigré research projects were the famous Harvard Interview Project of the 1950s and the Soviet Interview Project and Israel Soviet Interview
Projects of the 1980s. Representative publications are Alex Inkeles and Raymond Bauer,
The Soviet Citizen (Cambridge, Mass.: Harvard University Press, 1959) and James Millar
(ed.), *Politics, Work and Daily Life in the USSR: A Survey of Former Citizens* (Cambridge:
Cambridge University Press, 1987).

opportunism taking place out of sight of Western observers.[13] Thwarted by this veil, we came to rely on convenient textbook stereotypes,[14] despite a number of scholarly efforts to probe for the real workings of the system.[15] As the postwar Soviet leadership, disappointed by economic performance, opened the door for discussion of economic reform, we learned more about the weaknesses of the system.[16] The system's inability to reward risk takers meant limited technological progress.[17] Unable to calculate rates of return, planners could not make rational investment choices.[18] One reform initiative after another was aborted, placing the system on a "treadmill of reform."[19]

We cannot answer Berliner's jockey-versus-horse question without a clear understanding of how the system really worked, both formally and informally. We must obviously move beyond the convenient textbook generalities into the real world of the Soviet system. What we know for certain is that the administrative-command system survived longer than Mises and Hayek would have expected and, at its peak in the 1960s and 1970s, it constituted a credible military threat as a world superpower. These facts alone suggest that the real workings of the administrative-command economy were complex and subtle. Mises and Hayek's critiques of a "pure" planned economy are undoubtedly valid: The center cannot plan and price millions of goods and services; the coordination and incentive problems of such a complex organization would have been overwhelming; extracting reliable information from reluctant subordinates must have been a nightmare. Yet this system survived for more than sixty years!

---

[13] D. V. Averianov, *Funktsii i Organizatsionnaia Struktura Organov Gosudarsatvennogo Upravleniia* (Kiev: Nauka, 1979).

[14] Paul Gregory and Robert Stuart, *Russian and Soviet Economic Structure and Performance*, 6th ed. (Reading, Mass.: Addison Wesley, 1998). Alec Nove, *The Soviet Economic System* (London: Allen & Unwin, 1977).

[15] Peter Rutland, *The Myth of the Plan* (LaSalle, Ill.: Open Court, 1985). E. A. Hewett, *Reforming the Soviet Economy: Equality Versus Efficiency* (Washington, D.C.: Brookings Institution, 1988).

[16] Alec Nove, "The Problem of Success Indicators in Soviet Industry," *Economica* 25 (1985): 97; Paul Gregory, *Restructuring the Soviet Economic Bureaucracy* (Cambridge, England: Cambridge University Press, 1990).

[17] Joseph Berliner, *The Innovation Decision in Soviet Industry*, (Cambridge, Mass.: The MIT Press, 1976).

[18] Gregory Grossman, "Scarce Capital and Soviet Doctrine," *Quarterly Journal of Economics* 67, no. 3 (August 1953): 311–43.

[19] Gertrude Schroeder, "The Soviet Economy on a Treadmill of Reforms," U.S. Congress Joint Economic Committee, *Soviet Economy in a Time of Change* (Washington, D.C., 1979).

The first studies of Soviet managers suggested an answer to the apparent puzzle of the system's durability.[20] At the microeconomic level, managers, chief engineers, and accountants had an unexpectedly wide range of discretion outside of the planning system. Vast expanses of unplanned actions existed in the planned economy. Enterprises supplied themselves, concealed information from superiors, and formed opportunistic alliances with their immediate superiors. Studies from the postwar period, in turn, disclosed a massive "second economy" existing alongside the official economy, which provided businesses and consumers the goods and services that planners could not.[21]

Managerial discretion and the second economy relate to actions taken at relatively low levels. They do not explain how resources were allocated in the real world of high-level decision making. My earlier study of the "mature" Soviet economy concluded, based on interviews with former officials, that we still knew relatively little about how *central* institutions actually worked.[22] We did not know how central authorities dealt with each other, how they coaxed information from subordinates, how they managed the complex problem of planning, how they shared responsibility, what incentives were used, what areas were planned and what areas remained unplanned, and what the true goals of the leaders were. These are only a few of the questions that remained unresolved as of the late 1980s.

Raymond Powell, in an overlooked article written in 1977, attempted to explain the puzzling durability of the Soviet system. He proposed that the system could indeed generate enough information to be "workable,"[23] by utilizing unorthodox sources of economic information that are of secondary importance in market economies. State and party officials could tune in on the thousands of petitions, complaints, emergency telephone calls, and other appeals from subordinates to determine what must be done and what could be put aside. Powell's theoretical hunch was that the Soviet system survived so long because its officials learned how to use

---

[20] Joseph Berliner, *Factory and Manager in the USSR* (Cambridge, Mass.: Harvard University Press, 1957); David Granick, *Management of Industrial Firms in the USSR* (New York: Columbia University Press, 1954).

[21] Gregory Grossman, "The Second Economy of the USSR," *Problems of Communism* 26 (September–October, 1977): 25–40; Vlad Treml, "Production and Consumption of Alcoholic Beverages in the USSR: A Statistical Study," *Journal of Studies on Alcohol* 36 (March 1975): 285–320.

[22] Paul Gregory, *Restructuring the Soviet Economic Bureaucracy*, 146–67.

[23] Raymond Powell, "Plan Execution and the Workability of Soviet Planning," *Journal of Comparative Economics* 1, no. 1 (March 1977): 69–73.

unconventional information for decision making. He did not argue that such "nonprice signals" made the system work well, only that they made the system work.

The Soviet State and Party Archives

Ironically, it was the collapse of the administrative-command system that made this study possible. With the lifting of the veil of secrecy, two new research approaches were opened. First, persons who had worked at high levels within this system could either be interviewed or their increasingly candid memoirs could be read. Starting with the *Glasnost* initiated by Gorbachev in the mid-1980s, former high-level actors could serve as "expert informants."[24] Officials and managers who occupied responsible positions in the 1970s and early 1980s should still have vivid memories of how things were done. One drawback is that living participants could provide information only about the mature system, not about its origins. The administrative-command economy was founded in the early 1930s; even young administrators at the time would have been in their late eighties or early nineties when they were allowed to speak freely. The demographic odds of such high-level administrators being alive in the 1990s would have been relatively slim, given the hard times of the 1930s and the war years of the 1940s. Moreover, few of the founding fathers survived the Great Purges of 1937–8. Fortunately, three of the highest-level surviving founders did leave behind fragments of memoirs in the early 1990s.[25]

The search for the origins of the administrative-command economy leads us to the Soviet State and Party Archives, which were opened to scholars in the 1990s. This book deliberately focuses on the first two and a half decades of the administrative-command economy because we are

---

[24] Yuly Olsevich and Paul Gregory, *Planovoia Sistema v Retrospektive: Analiz i Interviiu s Rukovoditeliami Planirovaniia SSSR* (Moscow: Teis, 2000).

[25] Of Stalin's original team, which numbered more than twenty, only four survived the Great Purges: Lazar Kaganovich, Vyacheslav Molotov, Anastas Mikoian, and K. E. Voroshilov. The first three lived to advanced ages, as did the former minister of oil and Gosplan chairman, N. K. Baibakov. Molotov and Kaganovich were interviewed by Chuev in F. I. Chuev, *Sto Sorok Besed s Molotovym* (Moscow: Terra, 1991), and F. I. Chuev, *Tak Govoril Kaganovich* (Moscow: Otechestvo, 1992). Baibakov was interviewed in Olsevich and Gregory, *Planovoia Sistema.* Another founder's (Anastas Mikoian) memoirs were published as A. I. Mikoian, *Tak Bylo. Razmyshleniia o Minuvshem* (Moscow: Vagrius, 1999). Voroshilov died in 1960.

keenly interested in how its institutions were created. Russian archivists have placed virtually no restrictions on the use of documents for this early period. The Soviet State and Party Archives constitute a treasure of records of the founders. The administrative-command system was run by written decrees, instructions, reports, and studies, although many key decisions were made in Stalin's private study and not recorded. Most actions, however, were recorded on paper, and these records were meticulously maintained by generations of archivists. Officials and archivists were loathe to discard documents; hence, the archives reveal both the light and dark sides of the system. Unlike the Nazi regime, which carefully avoided written records of its crimes, the Soviet archives speak frankly about persecutions, purges, terror, executions, and the infamous gulag system. Stalin's correspondence is interspersed with terse orders to send opponents of collectivization to concentration camps, to execute those stealing property, and to shoot political opponents:[26] "Kondratieff, Groman [two prominent nonparty economists, especially reviled by Stalin], and a few other scoundrels must definitely be shot."[27] Stalin's signature appears on documents authorizing mass executions.[28] Stalin could casually order the resettlement of thirty thousand peasant families to desolate regions where they stood little chance of survival.[29] The archives also do not whitewash the misdeeds of party officials, all supposedly dedicated to building a better world of socialism. Thousands of party investigations of criminal wrongdoing by party members are carefully filed in the archives awaiting investigation by scholars. These documents show party officials stealing millions of rubles, constructing massive bribery networks, and selling party memberships to the highest bidder.[30]

This book uses materials from the formerly secret Soviet State and Party Archives, in particular from the Russian State Archive of the Economy (RGAE) and the State Archive of the Russian Federation (GARF).[31] These

---

[26] Oleg Khlevnyuk et al., *Stalin i Kaganovich. Perepiski. 1931–1936 gg.* (Moscow: Rosspen, 2001), 235.

[27] Lars Lih, Oleg Naumov, and Oleg Khlevniuk, *Stalin's Letters to Molotov, 1925–1936* (New Haven, Conn.: Yale University Press, 1995), 165–7, 200–1.

[28] J. Arch Getty and Oleg Naumov, *The Road to Terror: Stalin and the Destruction of the Bolsheviks, 1932–1939* (New Haven, Conn.: Yale University Press, 1999), 25.

[29] Khlevnyuk et al., *Stalin i Kaganovich. Perepiski*, 316.

[30] For an analysis of economic crimes committed by party members, see Eugenia Belova, "Economic Crime and Punishment," in Paul Gregory (ed.), *Behind the Facade of Stalin's Command Economy* (Stanford, Calif.: Hoover Institution Press, 2001), 131–58.

[31] Readers interested in learning more about these archives should start with the thorough guides to the Soviet State and Party Archives, such as *Kratkiy Putevoditel': Fondy i*

archival materials were studied both in Moscow and at the Hoover Institution. The original archival material is drawn from the various archival "funds" (*fondy* in Russian) described in Appendix A. We also draw heavily from annotated collections of archival materials[32] and from the various monographs based on archival research cited throughout this book.

Models of Dictatorship

The Soviet system is one of many in a long line of brutal dictatorships, dating from the Egyptian pharaohs to the latest African or Middle Eastern despot. Stalin has earned the dubious record as Hitler's rival as measured by the sacrifice of innocent lives. Scarcely a Russian, Ukrainian, or Central Asian family was spared his cruelty either in the form of executions and deportations of peasants or in purges of officials, managers, and military personnel. This book has more to say about an *economic* dictatorship than of a *political* one, although the two are closely intertwined. It describes an economic system where the dictator strives to gain full control of the economy through an extreme concentration of power. Other dictators have had different goals: in Pinochet's Chile, the dictator used political power to establish market allocation and private ownership.[33] Hitler's dictatorship was based on nationalism, state control, ethnic hatred, and the push for territorial expansion, but it preserved the property rights of ethnic Germans. Iraq's Saddam Hussein used the control of economic resources to suppress opposition, eradicate ethnic groups, and reward loyalty. Clearly, the Soviet dictatorship was unique in a number of respects; nevertheless, we must consider whether general principles can be gleaned that apply to other dictatorships, motivated by other principles and pertaining to different circumstances.

All economic dictators presumably face common problems: they cannot decide and control everything themselves. They must, therefore, use an administrative structure in which subordinates are delegated authority.

Kollektsii Sobrannye Tsentral'nym Partiinym Arkhivom (Gosudarstvennaia Arkhivnaia Sluzhba Rossiiskoi Federatsii) (Moscow: Blagovest, 1993); William Chase and Jeffrey Burds (eds.), *State Archival Service of the Russian Federation, A Research Guide: I. Guide to Collections* (Moscow: Blagovest, 1994).

[32] Three annotated document collections cited frequently in this book are Lih et al., *Stalin's Letters to Molotov;* and O. V. Khlevnyuk, A. V. Kvashonkin, L. P. Kosheleva, and L. A. Rogovaia (eds.), *Stalinskoe Politburo v 30-e gody* (Moscow: AIRO-XX, 1995); and Khlevnyuk et al., *Stalin i Kaganovich. Perepiski.*

[33] Carmelo Mesa-Lago, *Market Socialist and Mixed Economies: Comparative Policy and Performance, Chile, Cuba, and Costa Rica* (Baltimore: The Johns Hopkins Press, 2000).

The dictator must control these subordinates by incentives and threats – carrots and sticks, if you will. Some subordinates will be closer to and more trusted by the dictator. Others will possess skills necessary to the dictator, such as the ability to manage production facilities or to plan, but may be remote from or even inimical to the dictator. The performance of all subordinates, both from the dictator's immediate circle and from outside, must be monitored and evaluated. Subordinates, seeking to avoid the dictator's wrath, will be inclined to report only positive information, concealing unfavorable information from the dictator's view.

How a socialist economic dictator would organize and control this inevitable administrative hierarchy was an issue into which Mises and Hayek did not delve deeply. They wrote vaguely of a Central Planning Board or euphemistically of "the center," but a command economic dictatorship requires a massive administrative apparatus, whose workings must be understood. Organization theory, information economics, and the new institutional economics provide templates for studying complex organizations, such as corporations, industrial ministries, or even entire administrative-command economies.[34] These literatures share common features: they stress that the dealings of the superior (such as the dictator), or *principal*, with subordinates, or *agents*, can be explained by transaction and information costs. When it is too costly to use the agent to carry out an action, the dictator will execute the action himself. Agents will not faithfully interpret and execute the directives of principals because their goals typically diverge. Agents possess more information about their local circumstances; therefore, they engage in opportunistic behavior, taking advantage of the dictator's information disadvantage. The dictator must establish checks and balances to limit such opportunism and must devise appropriate incentives and punishments. The new institutional economics particularly focuses on the dictator's problems with organized groups of agents – industrial, regional, or other lobbies formed to elicit actions favorable to the narrow group but against encompassing interests.[35]

[34] See, for example, Ronald Coase, "The New Institutional Economics," *American Economic Review* 88, no. 2 (May 1998), 72–4; D. C. North, "Institutions and Economic Performance," in *Rationality, Institutions, and "Economic Methodology"* (London: Routledge, 1993), 242–63; O. E. Williamson and S. G. Winter (eds.), *The Nature of the Firm* (Oxford: Oxford University Press, 1993); and Oliver Williamson, "The Institutions of Governance," *American Economic Review* 88, no. 2 (May 1998), 75–9.

[35] The two most relevant works are Ronald Wintrobe, *The Political Economy of Dictatorship* (Cambridge: Cambridge University Press, 1998), and Mancur Olson, *The Logic of Collective Action: Public Goods and the Theory of Groups* (Cambridge, Mass.: Harvard University Press, 1971).

The Stalin dictatorship, like any other dictatorship, could not have been immune to such principal–agent problems, although socialist theory predicted that a "new Soviet man" would emerge who would place the interests of society above his own. How the Stalin dictatorship coped with agents should provide general lessons that transcend time and geographical boundaries. We must particularly study how the dictator managed subordinates, differentiating between his natural "functional" allies, such as the planning agency, and those agents whose narrow goals diverged from those of the dictator, such as producers.[36]

This book asks another core question: What truly motivated the Soviet dictatorship? What was the dictator's objective function? What did Stalin and his allies most want to accomplish above all other things? We posit and test four alternative models of economic dictatorship. Our first model is the "scientific planner" – a benevolent dictator prepared to turn resource allocation over to planning experts, content to set only general rules and guidelines. The scientific planning model is that heralded in the official Soviet literature. An all-knowing party (the dictator) plays its leading role but leaves the concrete decisions to scientific planners. The planners follow the general principles and guidelines of the party and plan outputs and inputs using scientific norms and mathematical balances to achieve the best results for society.[37]

The second model is Mancur Olson's "stationary bandit," based on Stalin as the exemplar.[38] A stationary bandit is characterized by a long time horizon. No matter how ruthless, despotic, or evil-intentioned, the stationary bandit must maximize growth and development in his own selfish interest. A reasonably efficient, growing economy is necessary to maximize long-run tax revenues, achieve military power, and accumulate resources to reward political allies. The stationary-bandit model suggests that the growth-maximizing policies of the 1930s would have been pursued by any person in Stalin's shoes. The stationary bandit is, in effect, a development planner. Given that the Soviet Union was backward and

[36] The distinction between functional agents and production agents was suggested in Gregory, *Restructuring the Soviet Economic Bureaucracy*, chapters 2–3.
[37] See, for example, *Ekonomicheskaia Entsiklopedia: Promyshlennost' i Stroitel'stvo* (Moscow: Gosudarstvennoe Nauchnoe Izdatel'stvo, 1962), 327–30; *Gosplan USSR, Metodicheskie Ukazania k Rasrabotke Gosudarstvennykh Planov Ekonomicheskogo i Sotsial'nogo Razvitiia SSSR* (Moscow: Economika, 1980).
[38] Mancur Olson, "The Devolution of Power in Post-Communist Societies," in *Russia's Stormy Path to Reform*, ed. Robert Skidelsky (London: The Social Market Foundation, 1995), 9–42. See also Peter Murrell and Mancur Olson, "The Devolution of Centrally Planned Economies," *Journal of Comparative Economics* 15, no. 2 (June 1991), 239–65.

surrounded by capitalist enemies, the stationary bandit's best strategy was to aim for rapid industrialization, high investment rates, and autarky.

A third model is the "selfish dictator," whose primary goal is the accumulation of political power, which is achieved by strategic gift giving and the buying of political loyalty. The selfish dictator is driven not to maximize growth or welfare but to consolidate totalitarian control. When confronted with choices, the selfish dictator allocates resources to maximize political power not to achieve the best economic results. The selfish dictator gains allies and political support by distributing the economic rents extracted from ordinary citizens. Insofar as citizens will not part with their economic resources voluntarily, the dictator must apply force and coercion.[39] Indeed, Stalin carefully chose and cultivated allies; he reacted with fear and panic to threats to his political power, no matter how small; he bullied and bribed associates.[40] Selfish dictators, who sacrifice economic performance for political power, are not rare. Examples would be those who initiated the Chinese Cultural Revolution, Pol Pot in Cambodia, Mugabe in Zimbabwe, and Castro in Cuba.

The fourth model is the "referee–dictator," who mediates among the powerful vested interests that constitute the real sources of power. The referee–dictator model would be expected at a mature phase of dictatorship, when the stationary bandit or power-maximizing dictator is no longer able to dominate, but falls under the influence of industrial and regional elites.[41] In market economies, the domination of the political process by interest groups may emerge slowly due to free riding and the difficulty of organizing effective lobbying.[42] Mancur Olson and others have characterized the mature Soviet economy as dominated by interest groups pulling the leadership in different directions and giving it a lack of coherence.[43] Interest groups, however, might form more quickly

---

[39] These alternate models are elaborated in Valery Lazarev, "Initial Conditions and the Transition Economy in Russia," paper presented at the Evolution of the Soviet Elite and its Post-Communism Transformation Conference; University of Houston; Houston, Texas; April 19–21, 2001. Alternate models are also discussed in Valery Lazarev and Paul Gregory, "Commissars and Cars: The Political Economy of Dictatorship," *Journal of Comparative Economics*, 31, no. 1, 1–19.

[40] Getty and Naumov, *The Road to Terror*, 53–8, demanded the death penalty for M. N. Riutin in 1932 for distributing a pamphlet calling for Stalin's overthrow, a move Stalin's team failed to support.

[41] See E. A. Rees (ed.), *Decision Making in the Stalinist Command Economy, 1932–37* (London: MacMillan, 1997), 6–7, for a brief summary of these "interest–group" models.

[42] Mancur Olson, *The Logic of Collective Action: Public Goods and the Theory of Groups* (Cambridge, Mass.: Harvard University Press, 1971).

[43] Mancur Olson, *The Rise and Decline of Nations: Economic Growth, Stagflation, and Social Rigidities* (New Haven, Conn.: Yale University Press, 1982), has argued that the

in young administrative-command economies because of the ready-made concentration of economic power in industrial ministries and regional authorities. Unlike others who relate interest-group power to the mature Soviet system, historian J. Arch Getty has suggested that even Stalin had to bow to lobbies in key decisions in the 1930s.[44]

The first two models, at least, incorporate the intent to produce good economic performance. Scientific planning is implicitly an optimizing model but is subject to the information and computation problems raised by Mises and Hayek. The stationary-bandit model at least aims at rapid growth and development. The selfish dictator drops all pretense of economic goals. The referee–dictator model implies poor economic performance. Resource allocation disintegrates into an incoherent battle among interest groups over economic rents; encompassing interests are overlooked.

We would like to test which model best describes the Soviet Union of the 1930s. We lack the quantifiable data usually required for hypothesis testing; we have, instead, observations of the dictator's behavior in concrete situations. Anecdotal information makes hypothesis testing more difficult but not impossible. Some activities, such as direct loyalty buying, might not be recorded. A selfish dictator would characterize political bribery as an act of economic rationality. Both a stationary bandit and a power-maximizing dictator would place the most trusted allies in charge of key industries. Concessions to industrial or regional lobbies could be the acts of a referee–dictator, a stationary bandit, or a power maximizer.

The personal role of Stalin constitutes a complication. Economists prefer models in which personalities are not particularly important, as opposed to historians who often emphasize the unique roles of individuals. We like to think that our general models explain how any dictator, with a defined objective function, behaves under a given set of circumstances irrespective of time and place. The first three models assume a "rational" dictator, who maximizes his objectives subject to economic and political constraints, but can we apply rationality assumptions to a dictator whose acts appear to be irrational? Was Stalin's annihilation of his own

---

long-term decline of the Soviet economy can be attributed to the growing strength of special interests, just like the long-run decline of Europe (Eurosclerosis) explains declining economic performance in Europe. Peter Boettke, *Calculation and Coordination: Essays on Socialism and Transitional Political Economy* (London: Routledge, 2001), makes similar arguments about the mature Soviet economy under Brezhnev.

44 J. Arch Getty, *Origins of the Great Purges* (Cambridge, England: Cambridge University Press, 1985). Getty and Naumov repeat this claim in a more careful tone in the preface to their *The Road to Terror*.

military staff and of leading managers and specialists during the Great Purges of 1937–8 before the Nazi invasion the actions of a rational dictator? The same can be asked of his imprisonment of returning POWs in the vast gulag system. Stalin appeared to believe some of the more bizarre stories of wrecking and sabotage, and he harbored paranoid fears of contagion of loyal party members by nonparty specialists.[45] However, irrationality may be a rational strategy to intimidate opponents or to ensure loyalty. Ronald Wintrobe writes,

Stalin may have been extraordinarily ruthless but was not irrational if we look at the effects of terror from his point of view. He transformed the Communist Party of the Soviet Union, especially its upper echelons, from an organization dominated mainly by old Bolsheviks whose loyalties were primarily to the Party itself (or to each other) into an elite which was entirely of Stalin's own making.[46]

On strictly economic matters, the archives show Stalin to be well informed and consistent. He had well-defined goals, he gathered his facts carefully, and he listened to advice and sometimes changed his mind as a consequence of such advice.[47] Stalin's penchant to swing between paranoia and rationality is illustrated in a routine letter to his trusted deputy, V. Molotov, dated approximately August 6, 1929:

1. Transfer Comrade Mirzoian to the Trade Union International. 2. Purge the finance ministry and state bank of wreckers despite the wails of dubious communists and definitely shoot two or three dozen wreckers from these *apparaty*, including several dozen common cashiers. 3. Kondratieff, Groman and a few other scoundrels must definitely be shot. 4. A whole group of wreckers in the meat industry must definitely be shot. 5. It is a mistake to issue nickel coins now. 6. It is a mistake to import shoes from England. 7. It is good that the United States has allowed the importation of our timber. 8. How are things with German credits? 9. Force grain exports; credits will come. 10. Pay attention to the Stalingrad and Leningrad tractor factories. Things are bad there.[48]

This letter could be either that of a paranoid person or a calculating totalitarian ruler bound by no moral constraints. Stalin's role is clearly pivotal in deciding the jockey-or-horse issue. Clearly, the Soviet Union would have been better off without Stalin. Yet, the purpose of modeling dictatorship is to posit behavior that is independent of personalities. In

---

[45] These conclusions are drawn in Khlevniuk et al., *Stalinkkoe Politburo*, and in Lih et al., *Stalin's Letters to Molotov*, 50; also see Getty and Naumov, *The Road to Terror*, 26–8.

[46] Wintrobe, *The Political Economy of Dictatorship*, 227.

[47] For examples of Stalin's economic policy making, see R. W. Davies, "Making Economic Policy," in Gregory (ed.), 61–80.

[48] Lih et al., *Stalin's Letters to Molotov*, 200–1.

effect, the models suggest that the system itself predestines the personality of the dictator.

Was Stalin Inevitable?

Alec Nove's famous query "Was Stalin necessary?" can be rephrased as "Was Stalin *inevitable?*" Are administrative-command economy and brutal dictatorship inexorably linked like Siamese twins? Does the administrative-command economy automatically breed totalitarianism or does totalitarianism breed this type of economic system?

Obviously, the world's first administrative-command economy was created by more than one person. In the mid-1920s, Stalin joined the "moderate" Politburo majority and was far from the dominant political figure. After defeating his former moderate allies in 1929, Stalin was first among equals in the ruling elite. It was not until the mid-1930s that Stalin became "master of the house," a moniker used by his Politburo associates. Stalin, despite his growing absolute power, continued to involve his immediate associates in decision making, was influenced by their arguments, and insisted on the appearance of collective decision making, even when this became a formality. Stalin could make few of the thousands or hundreds of thousands decisions that had to be rendered each month, quarter, and year. He was troubled by the shortage of executive talent among those he trusted and used solicitous flattery, pleading, and bargaining to keep key persons on his team. Yet, I attribute the creation of the administrative-command system more to Stalin than to any other person because of his clear conception of how power should be exercised.[49] He scarcely participated in the intellectual debates over development policy of the 1920s. Stalin and his team won the support of the majority of the party in a relatively open power struggle in the late 1920s (see Chapter 3). His allies accepted him as their leader because of his superior leadership skills and his innate expertise on raw political power. Stalin crafted and maintained the fateful Politburo coalition through cunning, threats, manipulation, blackmail, and an iron determination that made the fateful decisions for forced collectivization and superindustrialization. Stalin's political victories were the result of better preparation and harder work, the willingness

---

[49] For documentation of the fact that Stalin alone had a firm conception of how the Soviet system should be formed, see Oleg Khlevnyuk, *Politburo: Mekhanizmy Politicheskoi Vlasti v 1930-e gody* (Moscow: Rosspen: 1996). This conclusion is also shared by Lih et al., in *Stalin's Letters to Molotov*, introduction, 17.

to employ extreme and brutal methods, and a ward boss's knowledge of the people with whom he was dealing.

The Bolshevik Party was designed by V. I. Lenin as an elite group of revolutionaries whose goal was to gain political power by socialist revolution and to maintain power using any means necessary. As long as the Bolsheviks remained in control, there would be no consideration of democracy. The elections to the Constitutional Assembly, held on November 26, 1917, showed that the Bolsheviks could command only a quarter of the votes in a democratic election.[50] Democracy was out of the question for the Bolshevik leadership; the sole issue would be the degree of democracy within the ruling party. Would power be exercised by party democracy, by a relatively small group of top party officials such as a Politburo, or by one person? Indeed, this was the fundamental political issue that had to be resolved in the late 1920s and early 1930s.

The next chapter explains that these Bolshevik leaders would inevitably choose a planned economy. Dedicated to preserving dictatorial political control, they could not tolerate market allocation as an alternative source of power in society. Hence, the choice of planning was inevitable. Would Bolshevik leaders be inclined to turn resource-allocation authority over to experts? Would they put economic interests above the consolidation of political power? Would they be able to control industrial and regional lobbies? If a command economic system was inevitable, what kind of leaders would it breed?

F. A. Hayek contends that a dictator or dictators operating an administrative-command system would be particularly skilled in political intrigue and infighting.[51] Resources cannot be administratively allocated without the exercise of extreme political power. Administrative orders must be backed by the threat of punishment and coercion. Resource allocation, by definition, means taking from one to give to another. Only those with unscrupulous and uninhibited moral behavior will advance in the political apparatus.[52] As Hayek wrote, although there may be no original intent to exercise political power over people, "planning leads to dictatorship because dictatorship is the most effective instrument of coercion and enforcement of ideals and, as such, essential if central planning on a large scale is to be possible."[53] "In order to achieve their

---

[50] *Encyclopedia of Russia and the Soviet Union* (New York: McGraw-Hill, 1961), 114.

[51] F. A. Hayek, *The Road to Serfdom*, 50th Anniversary Edition (Chicago: Chicago University Press, 1994), chapter 10.

[52] Boettke, *Calculation and Coordination*, 52–6.

[53] Hayek, *Road to Serfdom*, 78.

end, collectivists must create power – power over men wielded by other men – of a magnitude never before known, and … their success will depend on the extent to which they achieve such power."[54] Hayek writes further that "the unscrupulous and uninhibited are more likely to be successful" in a totalitarian society.[55] Hayek's conclusion is echoed by Frank Knight, who argued that planning authorities would have to "exercise their power ruthlessly to keep the machinery of organized production and distribution running" and "They would do these things whether they wanted to or not; and the probability of the people in power being individuals who dislike power is on the level with the probability that an extremely tender-hearted person would get the job of whipping-master on a slave plantation."[56] Hayek further contends that the moral and economic behavior of dictators would be unconstrained by laws and rules because a dictatorship "cannot tie itself down in advance to general and formal rules that prevent arbitrariness.... It must constantly decide questions which cannot be answered by formal principles only."[57]

Brutality was indeed a valued trait of the Bolshevik leadership. Stalin's first deputy throughout the 1930s, L. M. Kaganovich, was selected for his personal brutality. He ordered thousands to be executed during the collectivization drive and personally ordered thirty-six thousand executions, largely of his own subordinates, during the Great Purges.[58] Nikolai Bukharin (a leader of the opposition to Stalin in the late 1920s) was chastised for lack of brutality by one of Stalin's henchmen (K. E. Voroshilov) in the following telling words: "Bukharin is a sincere and honest person, but I fear Bukharin no less than Tomsky and Rykov [two other leaders of the opposition]. Why do I fear Bukharin? Because he is a soft-hearted person."[59] Softness was a sign of weakness. One of Stalin's closest friends (A. S. Yenukidze) was ostracized for showing pity on discredited party members and their families.[60] Destitute widows of expelled leaders were told to get jobs and stop complaining.[61] Discredited party leaders were set upon by their former friends and associates with the brutality of sharks

[54] Hayek, *Road to Serfdom*, 159.
[55] Hayek, *Road to Serfdom*, 149.
[56] F. Knight, "Lippmann's The Good Society," *Journal of Political Economy* (December 1936): 869, cited in Boettke, *Calculation and Coordination*, 53.
[57] Hayek, *Road to Serfdom*, 82.
[58] Khlevnyuk et al., *Stalin i Kaganovich, Perepiski*, 28.
[59] Getty and Naumov, *The Road to Terror*, 102.
[60] Ibid., 161–71.
[61] Ibid., 291.

circling a bleeding swimmer. There was open discussion of "working over" (torturing) political opponents.

Stalin was clearly an expert on brutality. As the party's General Secretary, Stalin knew the party leadership inside out, and he was able to tick off the names and backgrounds of all regional and local leaders. Stalin's correspondence reads like that of a party boss in Chicago or New Jersey – full of recommendations and suggestions and discussions of strengths and weaknesses of local party leaders. Stalin read all documents, including articles written by friends and foes alike, and took meticulous notes to later prove ideological violations. He was well prepared for meetings and spent considerable thought in devising strategy. He was patient and chose the right moment for his political maneuvers. He had few rivals in terms of personal ruthlessness. Stalin was hateful and spiteful, as in his angry denunciations of nonparty specialists who should be "hounded out of Moscow." Stalin organized clandestine intrigues against other Politburo members, despite rules against informal Politburo meetings, while his opponents obeyed party discipline and did not speak out publicly against party decisions they opposed. True to Hayek's predictions, those who obeyed moral rules lost. Stalin abandoned ardent supporters, such as Sergo Ordzhonikidze, when he (as Minister of Heavy Industry) defended besieged managers. Stalin had been close to Nikolai Bukharin (their families had even vacationed together) but he could tell Bukharin that a decision to shoot him was "nothing against you personally."[62] Stalin instructed his faithful henchman, L. M. Kaganovich, how to interrogate the wife of a political opponent: "It is necessary to bring her to Moscow and subject her to careful interrogation. She could reveal much of interest."[63] Stalin could turn against his oldest friends on a moment's notice: "Enukidze is a foreigner to us. It is strange that Sergo [Ordzhonikidze] continues to associate with him."[64] Stalin's pettiness was without limits; when a famous academician (Pavlov) was nominated for a medal in honor of his eighty-fifth birthday, Stalin responded: "No medal; he is not one of us."[65] During Politburo meetings Stalin doodled sadistic cartoons depicting the intended fate of perceived opponents.[66]

---

[62] Getty and Naumov, *The Road to Terror*, 25.
[63] Khlevnyuk et al., *Stalin i Kaganovich Perepiski*, 643.
[64] Ibid., 558.
[65] Ibid., 497.
[66] Mark Franchetti, "Stalin Drew Cartoons of His Victims' Fate," *London Sunday Times*, July 8, 2001. In one cartoon attributed to Stalin (around 1930), he drew a picture of his finance minister, Nikolai Briukhanov, depicting him naked and hanging by his genitals.

By the late 1920s, potential Stalin rivals were no longer in the picture: Lenin had died in January 1924 and Leon Trotsky was exiled in 1927. Most of the remaining "old Bolsheviks" were a poor match for Stalin, and he crushed newcomers with ease. Any Stalin associate who showed initiative and independence did not last long: Stalin's fellow Georgian, Sergo Ordzhonikidze, was hounded into suicide for his streak of independence.[67] The later Chairman of the State Planning Commission and Deputy Prime Minister, N. A. Voznesensky, noted for independent thinking, was executed. Stalin's telling praise of Voznesensky reveals the reason for his fate:

Unlike other associates who mask disagreements by either agreeing or pretending to agree among themselves before coming to me, Voznesensky, if he is not agreed, does not agree on paper. He comes to me and expresses his disagreement. They understand that I can't know everything and they want to make of me a rubber stamp. I pay attention to disagreements, to disputes, why they arose, what is going on. But they try to hide them from me. They vote and then they hide.... That is why I prefer the objections of Voznesensky to their agreements.[68]

Stalin readily acceded to Voznesensky's execution when his Politburo colleagues fabricated charges of treason against him in 1949.[69]

Notably, the few survivors from Stalin's inner circle (i.e., Kaganovich, Molotov, and Mikoian) shared the common characteristics of blind obedience, loyalty, sycophantism, and lack of imagination and initiative. Kaganovich served as Stalin's deputy throughout most of the 1930s. In his massive correspondence with Stalin, his most repeated phrases are "You are absolutely correct" and "I am in perfect agreement with you."[70] Kaganovich's flattery knew no limits. Declaring himself Stalin's "student," Kaganovich wrote: "You, Comrade Stalin, so broadly and clearly stated the issue from the point of view of the Party that there can be no hesitation."[71] Notably, Kaganovich showed no loyalty to other Stalin team members, passing up few opportunities to point out their flaws to Stalin.

The accompanying note reads: "To all members of the Politburo, for all present and future sins, Briukhanov should be hung by his balls. If they should hold up, he should be considered not guilty as in a court of law. If they give way, he should be drowned in a river."

[67] O. V. Khlevnyuk, *Stalin i Ordzhonikidze: Konflikty v Politburo v 30-e gody* (Moscow: Izdatel'skiy Tsentr Rossiia Molodaia, 1993).

[68] O. V. Khlevnyuk, *Sovetskaia Ekonomicheskaia Politika na Rubezhe 40-50 Godov i Delo Gosplana* (working paper, Florence, Italy, March 2000), 13.

[69] Ibid., 13.

[70] Khlevnyuk et al., *Stalin i Kaganovich. Perepiski*, 333.

[71] Ibid., 284.

Conversely, when Kaganovich knew that another official was in Stalin's favor, he did not hesitate to heap praise, "Things are going well with Comrade Ezhov [NKVD minister from 1936 to 1938]. He is firmly and energetically eradicating counter-revolutionaries and is conducting inter-rogations brilliantly and thoughtfully."[72] Ezhov's high standing was tem-porary and did not prevent his execution in 1940. Stalin's faithful sup-porters fit Hayek's description:

The chances of imposing a totalitarian regime on a whole people depends on the leader's first collecting around him a group which is prepared voluntarily to submit to that totalitarian discipline which they are to impose by force upon the rest ... He [the dictator] will be able to obtain the support of all the docile and gullible, who have no strong convictions of their own but are prepared to accept a ready-made system of values.[73]

Some Conclusions

Alec Nove's question "Was Stalin necessary?" was answered long ago. Collectivization ruined agriculture's long-run chances; the imposition of force in the countryside did not transfer net resources from agriculture to industry. Superindustrialization created a massive industrial capital stock that was either poorly selected or misused, and high investment rates gen-erated only a temporary spurt in economic growth, followed by protracted decline and stagnation. Stalin's purges of the military and industrial elite cost the country its best and brightest. Gulag labor proved to be ineffi-cient, and the gulags spawned a professional criminal class that continues to plague Russia even today.[74] "Was Stalin inevitable?" can be answered in the affirmative if we refer to a Stalin-like figure. After Lenin's death, Stalin had the greatest comparative advantage among the old Bolsheviks in the exercise of political power and brutality. If there had been someone with greater skills, that person would have been the "Stalin." Oleg Khlevnyuk's authoritative account demonstrates Stalin's personal inevitability as of the late 1920s.[75] Had Stalin had a better organized, more cunning, and more brutal rival, that rival would have beaten out Stalin.

---

[72] Ibid., 702.
[73] Hayek, *Road to Serfdom*, 151–3.
[74] Oleg Khlevnyuk, "The Economy of the Gulag," in *Behind the Facade of Stalin's Com-mand Economy*, ed. Paul Gregory (Palo Alto, Calif.: Hoover Institution Press, 2001), 111–30.
[75] Khlevnyuk, *Politburo: Mekhanizmy Politicheskoi Vlasti*, chapters 1–2.

Political and (ultimately) personal survival in the administrative-command system required blind loyalty and a lack of initiative. This does not mean that the Soviet dictatorship of the 1930s consisted of one dictator. Rather, it consisted of hundreds or thousands of dictators. Just as Stalin demanded fawning and obsequiousness, his immediate associates demanded the same from their subordinates, and so on down the line. Kaganovich's handling of his subordinates was no less brutal than Stalin's treatment of Kaganovich, who rivaled Stalin in brutality but not in cunning or resolve.

Berliner's jockey-versus-horse question thus proves to be relatively complicated. The jockey and horse are not selected independently. The next chapter shows that the jockey (Stalin or the Bolshevik elite) inevitably would have chosen only one kind of horse (the administrative-command system). Likewise, the administrative-command system breeds a particular type of jockey – a specialist in brutality and the exercise of raw political power. This insight appears to rule out one dictatorial model – the scientific planner, content to let experts make the key decisions. As long as the dictator exercises power effectively, the dictator–referee model is also ruled out. This fourth model would come into play only when the brutal dictator begins to lose control. Throughout the 1930s, the dictator's power and brutality appeared to strengthen rather than weaken.

The next chapter deals with the collectivization and industrialization decisions of the late 1920s, and it shows that the choice of a market economy was ruled out by the core values of the Bolshevik Party. The chapters that follow describe the building blocks of the Soviet administrative-command system, beginning with the fateful decision to embark on the course of creating a command system – a decision that could not be made prior to Stalin's victory in his power struggle against his political opponents.

2

Collectivization, Accumulation, and Power

My grandfather grew up in a village where he cultivated the land with his brother and their children. His neighbor, Petya, was a ne'er-do-well, who slept on the porch of his ramshackle hut and spent his evenings drinking and beating his miserable wife. He would watch in disdain as we sweated in the hot sun building a new barn or brought home a new cow. During hard times, Petya would appear at our door asking for a handout. In 1929, Petya appeared at my grandfather's door accompanied by a handful of thugs, sporting a military uniform and cap bearing a red star, and declared: "In the name of Soviet power, I order you to hand over all your property and land to the collective." This is why my grandfather hated communism and Soviet power all his life.

(Story told to the author in Moscow by a seventy-five-year-old Russian.)

This book describes how and why a small group of socialist revolutionaries, led by one of history's worst tyrants, Josef Stalin, created the world's first administrative-command economy. The story is told from the records of the formerly secret Soviet archives from the same documents these "founders" used more than a half century earlier. This chapter describes the background of the 1929 decision to abandon the New Economic Policy (NEP) for a never-before-tried feat of social engineering: An entirely new system of economic and political management was to be created in short order, founded on the principles of the "leading role of the party" (read: dictatorship of the Communist Party), complete state ownership, and elimination of private economic activity. Stalin termed the fateful decision to create the administrative-command economy the *Great Break-Through (Velikii Perelom)*.

The Great Break-Through began with the Sixteenth Party Congress's approval of the maximum variant of the first Five-Year Plan in April of 1929 and was sealed by the Politburo's approval of Stalin's "On Grain Procurements" on August 15, 1929. The first action signaled not only Stalin's victory over his "right deviationist" opponents, but also the beginning of a massive industrialization drive. "On Grain Procurements" firmly ensconced the principle of compulsory agricultural deliveries from a peasantry entrapped in collective farms.[1]

The decision to collectivize agriculture by force was far from settled as of April 1929. The Sixteenth Party Congress projected that three quarters of the peasant population would still be in private households in 1933.[2] Collectivization was enshrined with the November 1929 Central Committee decision to force peasant households into collective farms.[3] The declaration of war against the more prosperous peasants, the kulaks, was issued by Stalin's January 5, 1930, declaration: "We have gone over from a policy of limiting the exploiting tendencies of the kulak to a policy of liquidating the kulak as a class."[4] Thus, in the eight months between April and November of 1929, Stalin succeeded in emasculating opposition to collectivization within the party's ruling bodies, the elite Politburo, and the larger Central Committee. The industrialization and collectivization decisions of 1929 resolved once and for all the debate between the party's right wing and Stalin and his allies. The Soviet Union would thereafter be directed by a national plan to create an industrialized economy in the shortest possible time, characterized by collectivized agriculture, state ownership, and a dictatorship by the Communist Party, which would speak with one voice and would allow no internal opposition.

The official history of the Soviet Communist Party maintains that the decisions of 1929 were preordained by two earlier failures; namely, the failure of capitalism in Russia prior to the 1917 revolution and the failure of the NEP of 1921 to 1928.[5] The aborted attempt to achieve full

---

[1] These events are described in considerable detail in R. W. Davies, *The Socialist Offensive: The Collectivization of Agriculture*, vol. 1 (Cambridge, Mass.: Harvard University Press, 1980), chapter 3.

[2] Ibid., 112.

[3] *Bolshaia Sovetskaia Entsiklopedia*, vol. 21 (Moscow: Sovetskaia Entsiklopedia, 1975), 616; *Kratkaia Istoria SSSR* (Moscow: Nauka, 1972), 232.

[4] Davies, *The Socialist Offensive*, 197.

[5] *Istoriia Kommunisticheskoi Partii Sovetskogo Soiuza* (Moscow: Polizdat, 1959), chapters 1–12.

communism immediately, the War Communism system of 1918 to March 1921, is dismissed as an emergency measure brought on by the civil war. The English socialist, Maurice Dobb, bought the official Soviet explanation, which was then widely accepted in the West as a consequence of Dobb's influential texts first published in the late 1920s.[6] NEP, in particular, was represented as a crisis-ridden system that had to be replaced. Yet, by all normal indicators, NEP was a resounding success. The economic recovery that began in 1921 was one of history's most rapid. NEP's mix of state and private ownership and market allocation and its apparent success pose one of history's great counterfactual questions: What would have happened had the Soviet power struggle been won by the pro-NEP right wing of the Bolshevik Party? A persuasive econometric study of this counterfactual scenario suggests much more favorable economic outcomes and the avoidance of the cataclysmic losses of forced collectivization.[7] Yet, official Soviet doctrine states that a continuation of NEP was not an option.

The Prerevolutionary Failure Story

With the exception of the fleeting attempt to create a command system during War Communism, the period 1885 to 1929 was one in which administrative commands played a relatively minor albeit growing role. The Russian economy in 1913 was much poorer than its neighbors to the West, and it shared many of the same institutional flaws with other relatively backward market economies of the time. Corporate law was weak, but there was an active Russian equity market in which private stocks and bonds and government debt traded.[8] Bureaucratic interference was strong but not paralyzing. Agriculture was divided between peasant and gentry lands, with the latter declining in share. Peasants were organized into traditional communes and village self-governments, but the Russian grain market was integrated into the world grain market, transportation costs were falling, and peasants had finally gained the right to exit the commune as a consequence of the Stolypin Reforms of 1906 and 1911. Russia was a major player in international trade, as the world's second

[6] Maurice Dobb, *Soviet Economic Development Since 1917*, 5th ed. (London: Routledge & Kegan Paul, 1960). The first edition was published in 1928.

[7] Holland Hunter and Janusz Szyrmer, *Faulty Foundations: Soviet Economic Policies, 1928–1940* (Princeton, N.J.: Princeton University Press, 1992), chapters 13–14.

[8] Thomas Owen, *The Corporation Under Russian Law, 1800–1917* (Cambridge: Cambridge University Press, 1991).

largest agricultural exporter, although its trade was restricted by relatively higher tariffs. Russia was a remote and forbidding place, but its natural wealth and massive population attracted huge amounts of foreign capital by offering relatively high rates of return.[9] Russia was the world's largest debtor nation on the eve of World War I. Russia's 1918 default set off repercussions in world financial markets that eclipsed subsequent defaults up to the present day.

Prerevolutionary Russia was a market economy in which economic decisions were made primarily by individual businessmen, tradespersons, and farmers; prices were dictated by markets; and state planning was absent, despite a substantial Russian-Nationalistic and Marxist literature proclaiming the uniqueness of the Russian economic experience. The Russian market economy was relatively successful, despite a political and scholarly consensus that it failed. Writers as disparate as V. I. Lenin and Alexander Gerschenkron, the Harvard economic historian, agreed on this failure story, for quite different reasons. Lenin used the image of failure to bolster his claim that the socialist revolution should start in Russia as the "weakest link in the capitalist chain." Gerschenkron argued that the 1917 revolution was a result of policy errors and could easily have been averted. The fateful delay of agricultural reform meant the loss of a Westernized Russia, integrated into the Western world.[10]

My earlier book, *Before Command*, painted a picture of relative economic success: Russian agriculture, despite its serious institutional problems, grew as fast as European agriculture (during a period of relatively rapid agricultural progress throughout the industrialized world), and Russia's total output grew more rapidly than Europe's did.[11] If one projects forward this growth, Russia was several decades away from developing into a middle-income, European economy when the massive shock of World War I destroyed the institutions and much of the human and physical capital that had created this impressive growth. These conclusions, which have not been seriously challenged, dispel the myth of Russian economic failure prior to 1917 and of the futility of pursuing a capitalist path in Russia after World War I.

---

[9] John McKay, *Pioneers for Profit: Foreign Entrepreneurship and Russian Industrialization, 1885–1913* (Chicago: University of Chicago Press, 1970).

[10] V. I. Lenin, *The Development of Capitalism in Russia* (Moscow: Progress, 1977); Alexander Gerschenkron, *Economic Backwardness in Historical Perspective* (Cambridge, Mass.: Harvard University Press, 1962).

[11] Paul Gregory, *Before Command: An Economic History of Russia from Emancipation to First Five-Year Plan* (Princeton, N.J.: Princeton University Press, 1994).

Russia, despite its impressive growth, was an economy that was relatively backward on the eve of the 1917 revolution. Its per capita income was less than one third of France or Germany and was 60 percent of the less-developed Austro-Hungarian Empire.[12] The leaders of the new socialist state, therefore, would have been concerned by encirclement by hostile states whose economics were much more advanced.

The Communist victory over white forces in the Russian civil war eliminated the option of market-economy development in Russia. From late 1917 until 1991, the political monopoly of the Communist Party of the Soviet Union (CPSU)[13] was not challenged, and the party leadership, throughout this entire period, adhered to three core ideological principles: complete state ownership, a planned economy to replace the "anarchy of the market," and the "leading role of the party." Underlying these core principles was the notion that the socialist cause was more important than any individual (except Stalin, who was the socialist cause). In Stalin's words, "Don't spare the individual; spare only the cause."[14]

These core principles clearly ruled out a market capitalist economy and were also incompatible with NEP's mix of private and state ownership and planned and market activity, as will be shown. The choice of the administrative-command system, or a close substitute, would have been inevitable, given the facts of party control and its three core principles.

The Experiments

Lenin was the consensus leader of the Bolshevik Party; during his lifetime, there would be no real challenge to his authority. He dominated not only the rule of the Soviet Union, but also its ideology. The struggle among various factions of the party had to wait his incapacitation in March 1923 and his subsequent death on January 21, 1924. Lenin taught that revolution could be sparked only by dedicated professional revolutionaries: hence, the Bolshevik Party limited its ranks to a small group of activists. The "old Bolsheviks" joined the party between 1898 and 1906.[15] The Bolsheviks gained power in 1917 due not to their popularity

[12] Paul Gregory, *Russian National Income, 1885–1913* (New York: Cambridge University Press, 1982), 156.

[13] Throughout most of the 1930s, the CPSU was actually called the Great Communist Party of Russia and then of the Soviet Union. Its acronym was VKP.

[14] Lih et al., *Stalin's Letters to Molotov* deals with these ideological principles in the introduction.

[15] A convenient list of short biographies of top party and state officials is found in Khlevnyuk et al., *Stalinskoe Politburo,* 259–321.

but to the ineptitude of the hapless provisional government, which neither pulled Russia out of the war nor promised land and bread as did Lenin. It was Lenin's small group of revolutionaries, probably to their great surprise, who took over the running of the country endowed with the world's largest land mass and a population (130 million) twice that of its largest European neighbor (Germany).

As former outcasts and, in most cases, fugitives, no old Bolshevik had appreciable administrative experience. Vladimir Lenin had written extensively but in a theoretical vein on Russian capitalism and on revolutionary strategy. Leon Trotsky was a charismatic leader able to marshal the Red Army to its eventual civil war victory. Nikolai Bukharin was an intellectual who had written extensively on socialist theory but lacked practical experience. Josef Stalin had joined the Bolshevik Party in 1898, was educated in a Georgian seminary, and trained as a journalist, but worked as an underground revolutionary most of his adult life. None had a reasonable knowledge of conventional economics, as it was understood at the turn of the century, and none had ever met a business payroll or run a government department. The top leaders were in their thirties and early forties when they came to power. They had to decide Lenin's famous question, "What is to be done?"

Their first step, the Land Decree of 1917, confiscated the land of the remaining large estates and redistributed it to peasant households. Lenin had little choice but to formalize the spontaneous peasant confiscations that were going on in the countryside. The Land Decree eliminated the remaining large estates and left Russian agriculture in the hands of peasant households, who continued to maintain their traditional forms of village self-government.

War Communism: The Founders' Original Intent. War Communism has been widely interpreted as forced upon the Bolshevik leadership by the Russian civil war.[16] Yet, there is contrary evidence of an original intent to introduce a communist society immediately without going through preparatory stages.[17] The writings of the Bolshevik founders, both prior to and during War Communism, reveal a clear desire to create an economy based on a "settled" plan and abolition of private property – tasks that they enthusiastically embraced upon seizing power. The Bolsheviks

---

[16] Silvana Malle, *The Economic Organization of War Communism, 1918–1921* (Cambridge: Cambridge University Press, 1985).

[17] Paul Craig Roberts, *Alienation and the Soviet Economy* (Albuquerque: University of New Mexico Press, 1971), chapter 2; Peter Boettke, *Calculation and Coordination*, chapters 6 and 7.

nationalized virtually all enterprises including those employing only one or two persons, banned all private trade, abolished money, and confiscated what they termed "agricultural surpluses." That wholesale nationalizations were carried out in mid and late 1917 before the outbreak of civil war and the most extreme nationalization decree was passed in November 1920 after the civil war had largely ended refute the official position that War Communism was simply a reaction to wartime emergency.

War Communism's result was once described as "the greatest failure in economic history."[18] Output collapsed, and there was massive deurbanization as people fled the cities. Industrial production fell to one fifth of its prewar level in 1920. It is no surprise that such an abortive attempt to create a money-less, market-less, private-property-less economy overnight under precarious political conditions would be disastrous. The War Communism fiasco shows, however, both the inclination of the new leadership to bow to ideological goals and their extreme ineptitude, naiveté, and unpreparedness to govern.

NEP: Could Communists Tolerate Markets?   Lenin announced the NEP in March 1921 following the ominous Kronstadt Rebellion of sailors, who only a few years earlier had counted among the Bolsheviks' strongest supporters. On March 23, 1921, Lenin announced a proportional tax on agriculture to replace the confiscation of grain. Private trade was again legalized, although large state-run organizations continued to dominate wholesale trade. A monetary reform introduced a new stable currency, the *chervonets*, which was even quoted in international foreign exchange markets. Although Lenin stuck with his fateful February 10, 1918, decision to repudiate foreign debt, attempts were made to entice foreign concessionaires back to Russia along with previous owners.[19] The Supreme Council of the National Economy tried to manage large state enterprises but did not attempt to compile national plans. The finance ministry exercised more influence on the economy through its direction of credit "limits" than did any planning agency.

Peasants responded to NEP's liberalization by sowing more grain, empty shops were again stocked with goods, and people returned from

---

[18] Quotation of William Chamberlin cited in Boettke, *Calculation and Coordination*, 78.
[19] Paul Gregory, "Russia and Europe: Lessons of the Pre-Command Era," in *European Economic Integration as a Challenge to Industry and Government*, eds. R. Tilly and P. Welfens (Berlin: Springer, 1996), 461–96.

the countryside to abandoned towns and cities. Industry and transportation, which had produced only one fifth of their prewar levels in 1920, reached prewar production levels by 1926. Agriculture, which had fallen to 60 percent of its prewar level, also recovered by 1926.[20] Despite the inducements to join collective and state farms, peasants were content to farm their own plots within the familiar setting of the commune and village self-government.[21] Despite massive propaganda efforts, less than 2 percent of peasant households had joined collectives by 1928.[22]

Could the conspiratorial Bolshevik Party accept an economic system in which major decisions were made by impersonal grain markets, middlemen, and peasant households? The opening of the archives allows us to shed more light on this issue. The story of the end of the NEP and the Great Break-Through can be told largely in terms of the battle over grain – who should market it, to whom should it be sold, and at what prices?

Grain and Accumulation

So far, we have listed three core values of the Communist Party: state ownership, a planned economy, and the leading role of the party. There was a fourth value, based on Marxist thought, that was used so persistently and consistently that it also qualifies as a core value: capital accumulation. The effect of this fourth core value can be seen in the rapid increases in the investment rate in the 1930s and the extraordinarily high investment rates of administrative-command economies throughout the world.[23] Nikita Khrushchev won the post-Stalin power struggle in the early 1950s by his adherence to the principle of priority of heavy industry. The strategy of the Great Break-Through was clearly guided by the forced capital accumulation strategy laid out in the mid 1920s by Leon Trotsky's left deviationists.[24] It was Trotsky's theorists who explained the

[20] G. W. Nutter, "The Soviet Economy: Retrospect and Prospect," in *Political, Military, and Economic Strategies in the Decade Ahead*, eds. S. Abshire and R. V. Allen (New York: Praeger, 1963), 165.

[21] V. P. Danilov, *Rural Russia under the New Regime* (Bloomington: Indiana University Press, 1988).

[22] Lazar Volin, *A Century of Russian Agriculture* (Cambridge, Mass.: Harvard University Press, 1970), 211.

[23] Paul Gregory and Robert Stuart, *Soviet Economic Structure and Performance*, 2nd ed. (New York: Harper and Row, 1981), 381–5.

[24] Alexander Erlich, *The Soviet Industrialization Debate, 1924–28* (Cambridge, Mass.: Harvard University Press, 1960); Nicholas Spulber, *Soviet Strategy for Economic Growth* (Bloomington: Indiana University Press, 1964).

principles of forced accumulation. It was Stalin who created the instruments of force to gather this surplus.

Marx had little practical economic advice to offer the leaders of the world's first socialist state, other than primitive capital accumulation. Primitive accumulation argued that relatively poor societies accumulate their initial capital by force. The first capitalists accumulated capital by stealing from weaker elements of society or as wartime booty. The first capital was raised not by patient saving (refraining from consumption) or plowing back profits but by taking "surpluses" from someone else. Hence, the Bolshevik leaders had to consider from whom to extract capital in a new socialist state.

One of Stalin's winning strategies was to control the rhetoric of discussion. Those opposed to his ideas represented a deviation (*uklon*) from true Marxist–Leninist principles.[25] Trotsky's left deviationist strategy was spelled out by his chief theoretician, E. A. Preobrazhensky,[26] who argued in the mid-1920s that peasant agriculture should be the source of primitive capital accumulation. Preobrazhensky's reasoning was that industrialization required labor to move from the countryside to the city, where industrial workers had to be fed with agricultural surpluses. In a world of static agricultural production, such a transfer would occur only if peasants consumed less (their standard of living fell) in order for the growing city population to be fed more. According to Preobrazhensky, Russian peasants had been accustomed to lower living standards before the revolution, to which they could return without a loss of agricultural output.

Preobrazhensky identified the source of primitive capital accumulation, but he could not identify the transfer mechanism. He proposed that the state establish a grain-purchasing monopoly, which would set low purchase prices to drive down peasant income, resell at higher retail prices, and use the trading profit to finance industrial investment. If private markets set agricultural prices, the gap between wholesale and retail prices would narrow to a competitive trading margin, the state would lose its profits, and peasant income would not fall. In effect, Preobrazhensky proposed a massive income-redistribution scheme, which would transfer income from agriculture to industry. He failed to answer the most important question: If peasants are offered low prices, what will motivate

[25] Getty and Naumov, *The Road to Terror*, 20–2.
[26] E. A. Preobrazhensky's book from 1926 has been translated and published as *The New Economics*, trans. Brian Pierce (Oxford: Oxford University Press, 1964).

them to deliver their products to the state? They could either eat the grain themselves, feed it to their livestock, or cut back on production. It was Stalin who provided the mechanism to force deliveries at low prices.

The fate of the left deviationists is well known. Stalin allied himself with the moderate majority in the Politburo to remove Trotsky from the party in 1926. One year later, Stalin began to embrace the very principles for which the left deviationists had been discredited. It is not known whether Stalin opposed the left-deviation program for political gain only or whether he later converted to their thinking. In either case, the practice of compiling balances of oil, steel, and grain contributed to a growing sense of emergency. As state planners began to prepare "balances" of steel, oil, and notably grain, attention was directed to how much grain the state was collecting for transfers to the city. This balance mentality suggested that the state be both the collector (buyer) of goods and their distributor.[27] Important goods like grain should not be left to the "anarchy of the market." The proper distribution of grain to city dwellers and for export could only be assured if the state was the purchaser. Agricultural goods that disappeared into the private economy were regarded as lost, even if the private market eventually sold these goods in urban markets. The terminology is instructive: instead of state grain purchases, the state collects or procures grain through "campaigns." The state agency that obtains grain from the agricultural population is not a purchasing agency but a procurement agency. An integral part of the grain balance was the grain-collection "target" to be purchased at state delivery prices. If these targets were not met, a grain-collection crisis was declared.

The Grain-Collection Crises Revisited. The events of 1927 and 1928 leading up to forced collectivization have been well chronicled.[28] Throughout the early years of the NEP, agricultural producers had the right to sell either to private traders (called Nepmen) or to state procurement organizations, the three most important being "Central Union" (*Tsentrosoiuz*), "Grain Central" (*Khlebotsentr*), and "Union Grain" (*Soiuzkhleb*), all of which fell under the supervision of Anastas Mikoian, the Commissar of Trade. Each year, the party's Politburo set grain-collection targets for the procurement campaign and anxiously followed

---

[27] Gregory, *Restructuring the Soviet Economic Bureaucracy*, 156–8.
[28] Moshe Lewin, *Russian Peasants and Soviet Power* (London: Allen & Unwin, 1968); Davies, *The Socialist Offensive*, 112; Stephan Merl, *Der Agrarmarkt und die Neue Ökonomische Politik* (Munich: Oldenbourg, 1981).

the course of grain collections via reports from procurement agencies and its informer network in the countryside.[29] According to official statistics, state grain purchases fell from 10.6 million tons in 1926 to 1927 to 10.1 million in 1927 to 1928 and then to 9.35 million tons in 1928 to 1929.[30] This 12 percent reduction forced the Soviet state to import grain for the first time in Russian history.[31] Alarm bells were sounded in the Kremlin, which declared a grain-procurement emergency.

The grain-procurement crises provided Stalin with ammunition to move against the more prosperous peasants – the kulaks and middle peasants. Stalin, in a May 1928 report, cited data showing that grain output had regained prewar levels but that grain marketings were only half their prewar level.[32] He blamed the middle and prosperous peasants; his figures showed that poor peasants were marketing the same percentage of output as before.[33] The Politburo used these figures to justify the collection of grain by "extraordinary *(chrezvychainye)* measures," as police and militia grain confiscations were euphemistically called. The first extraordinary grain collections were conducted on a large scale in October 1927. Party officials, police, and secret police were dispatched to grain-producing regions. Regional and local party authorities were made personally responsible for procurement targets, roadblocks were set up, grain selling on local markets was confiscated, and prison sentences were handed down for grain burning and private grain trading.[34] Stalin personally supervised extraordinary measures in the Urals and Siberia. Some argue that Stalin's epiphany in favor of forced collectivization occurred during his supervision of extraordinary measures. Stalin's conclusion, which became official Soviet doctrine, was that as long as peasants remained free, they could sabotage any industrialization effort by withholding their grain. The reduced grain collections of the late 1920s were depicted as intentional acts of defiance of Soviet rule.

Starting in the 1960s, economists began to question the official Soviet version of events. Jerzy Karcz showed that Stalin's figures on the peasant marketing "boycott" were distorted and perhaps doctored to bolster

---

[29] A. Berelovich and B. Danilov, *Sovetskaia Derevnia Glazami VChK-OGPU-NKVD*, vol. 1, 1918–1922 (Moscow: Rosspen, 1998); vol. 2, 1923–1929 (Moscow: Rosspen, 2000).

[30] Davies, *The Socialist Offensive*, 427.

[31] Lewin, *Russian Peasants*, 214–44.

[32] J. Karcz, "Thoughts on the Grain Problem," *Soviet Studies* 18, no. 4 (April 1967): 399–402.

[33] For Stalin's figures, see Merl, *Der Agrarmarkt*, 446.

[34] Ibid., 313–67.

TABLE 2.1. *Output, State Purchase, and Prices of Grain*

	Year		
	1926/1927	1927/1928	1928/1929
Grain production (million tons)	74.6	72.8	72.5
Grain collection (million tons)	11.6	11.1	9.4
Price of wheat in private market (kopeks per centner)	861	892	1120
State wheat prices (kopeks per centner)	648	622	611
Ratio of state to private grain prices (1913 = 100)	0.89	0.79	0.45

Source: M. Lewin, *Russian Peasants and Soviet Power* (London: Allen & Unwin, 1968), 241–4; R. W. Davies, *The Collectivization of Soviet Agriculture*, vol. 1 (Cambridge, Mass.: Harvard University Press, 1980), 419; Tsentral'noe Statisticheskoe upravlenie, *Statisticheskii Spravochnik 1928* (Moscow: Izdatel'stvo Ts.s.u, 1929), 723–30.

the case against the kulak. The procurement crisis was limited to *state procurements*, not to overall agricultural marketings, and it was caused by state pricing policy, not by a conspiracy to destroy Soviet power.[35] Mark Harrison, examining more extensive data almost twenty years after Karcz, concluded that peasants were retaining more grain and selling less in the late 1920s because of the loss of large estates, unfavorable prices, and increased production of nongrain crops, not as acts of political defiance.[36] Given the confusion surrounding agricultural marketings in a mixed system that discourages sales to private traders, we shall never know the exact figures. With entirely new conditions in agriculture after the revolution, changes in marketing rates and production patterns would not be surprising, but was this crisis grounds for the end of private agriculture? What was the true cause of the crisis: a purely political action by enemies of the state or conventional economic factors?

Table 2.1 shows that state grain purchase prices declined as ratios of market prices throughout the late 1920s. By the 1928 to 1929 agricultural

[35] Much of this discussion is based on an earlier joint work: Manouchehr Mokhtari and Paul Gregory, "State Grain Purchases, Relative Prices, and the Soviet Grain Procurement Crisis," *Explorations in Economic History*, 30 (1993): 182–94.
[36] Mark Harrison, "The Peasantry and Industrialization," in *From Tsarism to the New Economic Policy*, ed. R. W. Davies (Houndsmills, England: MacMillan, 1990), 109–17.

year, state prices were less than half of those offered in private markets. These relative prices explain eloquently the grain-collection crises of 1927 and 1928. Grain producers preferred to sell at the full price to private traders rather than at half price to the state, as long as the choice was voluntary. State procurement prices offered little incentive to farmers. After 1927, they failed to cover average costs,[37] and many peasants chose symbolically to burn grain rather than turn it over to the state. State grain prices were set low relative to industrial crops and to meat and dairy products so that peasants switched to industrial crops or to feeding grain to livestock.[38] As long as sales were voluntary, peasant sales should be explained by economic factors such as relative prices. With higher private prices, grain would be sold to private buyers. With grain prices low relative to livestock and dairy products, peasants would feed their grain to livestock rather than sell. When only the choice of selling to the state at prices below production costs remained, peasants would rather eat their grain or burn it. These choices are clearly economic, not political.

Figure 2.1 shows the impact of extraordinary measures on state grain collections by contrasting the normal periodicity of state grain purchases in 1926/1927 with the crisis collections of 1927/1928. In 1926/1927, most grain was purchased between August and December. However, when the state announced a reduction in its grain procurement prices in late August 1927, procurements dropped sharply during the very period when grain purchasing was normally at its peak. Extraordinary measures were applied in late October to counter the decline in state procurements. Police and party commissars were sent to the countryside to organize collections and to punish peasants who sold to private traders and to arrest speculators. Their effects began to be felt in January 1928 with the partial recoupment of procurements lost between September and December of 1927. The state's inability to procure grain from private peasants at the prices it dictated was the primary rationale for forced collectivization. "If peasants do not hand over grain voluntarily, we must take it by force" was the thinking.

Interpreting Stalin Correctly. The grain-collection crisis was caused in large part by state pricing policy, not by the hostile political actions of recalcitrant peasants. If the state's purchasing agents had competed in price with private traders, grain purchases would have fluctuated with harvests

---

[37] Merl, *Der Agrarmarkt*, 137–9.
[38] Davies, *The Socialist Offensive*, 39–41.

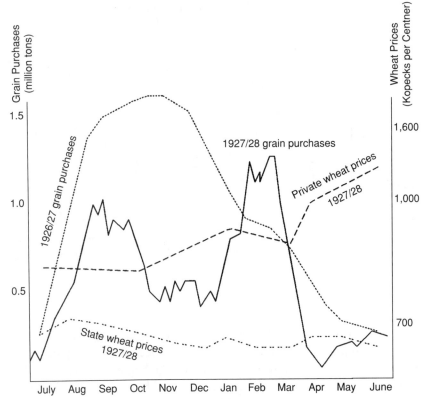

FIGURE 2.1. Soviet grain-procurement crisis.
Source: Stephan Merl, *Der Agrarmarkt und die Neue Oekonomische Politik* (Munich: Öldenbourg, 1981), 322.

and with relative prices of various farm products. In fact, state agencies could perhaps have offered somewhat less because of their superior distribution, transportation, and storage facilities.

One interpretation of the grain-collection crises is that Stalin and his allies were economic illiterates, who expected peasants to sell to them at half price! This explanation ignores the Bolshevik's fundamental goal of primitive accumulation – the collection of "tribute" from peasants to finance industrialization. According to the Preobrazhensky model, peasants had to deliver grain in the quantities targeted by the state *and* at low prices. It was the low prices that would create the surplus when the state resold the grain at higher retail prices. If the grain went to private traders, the state would lose both physical control of its allocation and its profits. Figure 2.2 illustrates the grain-procurement problem. The state wished to procure (purchase) *OT* units of grain at the low state price but, at that

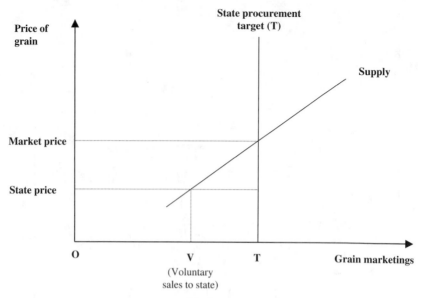

FIGURE 2.2. Markets vs. coercion.

price, only *OV* units would be sold to state organizations voluntarily. The difference (*VT*) would either be sold at prices above the state price to private traders or fed to livestock, eaten, or burned, especially if the state price was below the cost of production. The message is clear: The state cannot procure its targets if the price is not high enough to elicit that volume of sales *except by force*. There must be some mechanism to force peasants to sell the targeted amount. The lack of such a mechanism of force in the mid-1920s was the weak link in Preobrazhensky's program. Stalin's forced collectivization supplied the coercive force that would extract the surplus from the reluctant countryside.

Stalin's letters (to his Prime Minister Molotov) and other records clearly reveal Stalin's logic in combining low prices with force. Stalin was no economic illiterate; he had a reasonable understanding of how agricultural markets worked and preferred to base his decisions on the logic of things rather than on intelligence reports or the advice of others.[39] Stalin was well aware that higher grain prices would elicit more sales. In September 1934, he ordered a 15-kopek increase in the purchase price of wheat to stimulate sales.[40] He was knowledgeable about world grain markets,

[39] Lih et al., *Stalin's Letters to Molotov*, 47.
[40] Khlevnyuk et al., *Stalin i Kaganovich. Perepiski*, 478.

stating in a letter to Molotov dated approximately August 23, 1930, that, "We have one and a half months left to export grain: starting in late October (perhaps even earlier), American grain will come on the market in massive quantities, and we won't be able to withstand that. If we don't export 130–150 million puds of grain in these six weeks, our hard currency situation could become really desperate."[41] Stalin based the entire success of his economic program on the fulfillment of state grain collection targets. In a letter to Molotov he states, "If we can beat this grain thing, then we'll prevail in everything, both in domestic and foreign policies."[42] Stalin's mood became jubilant upon learning in December 1929 that grain collections were improving and that the stocks of grain in cities were growing. "The eyes of our rightists are popping out of their heads in amazement."[43] What counted was grain in the hands of the state, not total grain production. As stated later in 1934 by a Stalin deputy (Zhdanov), referring to the elimination of rationing, "What determines our welfare, our equilibrium with relation to grain... is the quantity of grain *in the hands of the state* [author's italics]. This matter is of the highest importance and we cannot lose sight of it for one minute."[44] Stalin stressed the importance of a single (low) grain-procurement price and railed against "the presence of a large number of urban speculators at or near the grain market who take the peasants' grain away *from the government* [author's italics] and – the main thing – create a wait-and-see attitude among the grain holders."[45] Stalin branded private traders as "vile," "criminals and bandits," and "enemies of the state." In a letter dated September 1, 1929, Stalin argued that there must be a monopoly state purchaser of grain (instead of three state agencies): "Without such a reform, competition among us is inevitable and its consequences are inevitable."[46] A Stalin deputy (Zhdanov) reiterated this position, "We cannot allow the presence of a large number of buyers in one region, because where there is overlap, there is competition, which raises prices."[47]

Stalin's correspondence demonstrates an intimate knowledge of the course of procurement campaigns. He personally set grain-collection

[41] Ibid., 203.
[42] Ibid., 175–6.
[43] Ibid., 183.
[44] This statement of Zhdanov is from a rare stenographic report of a Politburo meeting of November 21, 1934, from Khlevnyuk et al., *Stalinskoe Politburo*, 51–3.
[45] Lih et al., *Stalin's Letters to Molotov*, 165.
[46] Ibid., 176.
[47] This statement of Zhdanov is from a rare stenographic report of a Politburo meeting of November 21, 1934, from Khlevnyuk et al., *Stalinskoe Politburo*, 51–3.

targets: Stalin (August 22, 1931) to Kaganovich: "It is necessary to lower the plan of the Siberians and Middle Volgans. I fear it is necessary to lower the Lower Volgans a little. It is possible to give Middle Volga 100 million puds, and Western Siberia 85, but then Lower Volga will raise the question – to give it 100 million. It would then be necessary to lower the animal grain fund from 100 to 60 or 50 million puds."[48] Throughout the 1930s, Stalin received petitions from regions to lower their procurement targets. He denied most but granted some. In fact, by the mid-1930s, Stalin's correspondence with his deputy Kaganovich was dominated by this issue. Kaganovich would usually pass petitions to Stalin with the query: "Your opinion?"[49] Stalin kept exact track of how much was being collected, from whom, and who needed to be punished for failure. In his August 29, 1929, letter to Molotov, he wrote: "The grain procurements have gone well. Stick to a firm policy regarding Siberia, Kazakhstan, Bashkiria. No concessions to Eikhe and other comrades wishing to shirk difficult responsibilities. We must and can accumulate 100 million puds of emergency reserves, if we are really Bolsheviks and not full of hot air."[50] A rare verbatim report of a plenary meeting of the party Central Committee on October 1, 1931, shows Stalin's handling of petitions.[51] The party secretaries of the Central and Lower Volga regions pled for lower grain targets due to drought: "I must declare directly at this plenum that in view of the bad harvest resulting from the drought in the Lower Volga we cannot fulfill the plan issued to us." After Stalin's afternoon meeting with the party secretaries, Anastas Mikoian, Stalin's commissar for trade, announced reductions in some regions and increases in others. The party secretary of Kazakhstan, a Comrade Goloshchekin, objected to his increased quota: "In any case, I must say that 55 million is impossible," to which Mikoian retorted, "I have read out to you an official document, a decision of the Politburo, 55 million without rice. This is absolutely precise. I do not know why you are confusing things." Stalin was particularly incensed when high party leaders, assigned to grain-producing regions, were unable to meet their quotas.[52]

Stalin was convinced that little could be accomplished without force and punishment. His directives are interspersed with terse orders to "start

[48] Khlevnyuk et al., *Stalin i Kaganovich. Perepiski.* 59.
[49] Ibid., 632, 639, 688, 696.
[50] Lih et al., *Stalin's Letters to Molotov*, 175.
[51] This and following citations are taken from R. W. Davies, "Making Economic Policy," 69–70.
[52] Khlevnyuk et al., *Stalin i Kaganovich. Perepiski*, 74, 164, 225.

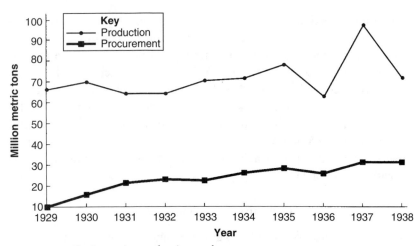

FIGURE 2.3. Soviet grain production and procurement.
Source: P. Gregory and R. Stuart, *Russian and Soviet Economic Structure and Performance* (Boston: Addison Wesley Longman, Inc., 2001), 77.

punitive measures," "turn over to the courts," or "fight the vile wreckers." In a September 16, 1926, letter to Molotov, he ordered that "violators of the pricing policy on state procurements must be removed and turned over to the courts and their names published."[53] On August 10, 1929, Stalin instructed Molotov "to expose and hand over immediately to the courts (with immediate dismissal from their posts) all those procurement officials caught trying to obtain grain by competing with other state officials."[54]

Collectivization was an institutional mechanism to control grain collections. If peasants had been willing to sell to the state at its prices, collectivization would not have been necessary, as a June 1929 statement by Mikoian attested, "I fear my statement will be considered heretical, but I am convinced that, if there were no grain difficulties, the question of strong collective farms ... would not have been posed at this moment with such vigor, scope, and strength. ... If grain were abundant, we would not at the present time have set ourselves the problems of kolkhoz and sovkhoz [state farms] construction in such a way."[55]

Collectivization achieved Stalin's main economic goal: secure supplies of grain at low prices. Figure 2.3 shows that, between 1929 and 1938,

[53] Lih et al., *Stalin's Letters to Molotov*, 127–8.
[54] Ibid., 166.
[55] Mikoian's statement was published in *Pravda* on June 27, 1929. It is quoted in Davies, *The Socialist Offensive*, 120.

state grain collections rose steadily despite no increase in output. Collectivization indeed placed the control of grain output directly in state hands. Preobrazhensky, in a failed attempt to rehabilitate himself, enthused, "Collectivization – this is the crux of the matter. Did I have this prognosis of collectivization? No, I did not."[56] To which a thoughtful scholar added, "[Preobrazhensky] was careful not to add that neither did Stalin at the time when the industrialization debate was in full swing. And he was wise not to point out that the decision to collectivize hinged not on superior intellectual perspicacity but on the incomparably higher resolve to crush the opponent."[57]

Collective Farms and Politics

Forced collectivization set off a rural war against Soviet power. Secret police reports listed 1,300 peasant mutinies in 1929; February alone saw 736 mass peasant demonstrations of a quarter million peasants. New governments, independent of Soviet power, were set up in western Ukraine. In 1930, the interior ministry (OGPU) alone executed more than twenty thousand peasants.[58] Figure 2.3 shows that grain production dropped in 1930 and 1931, whereas grain collections increased. With grain production down and collections up, famine spread. The Politburo reacted to famine with Draconian measures. Regions in which starvation was rampant were ordered to deliver their quotas under the threat of extreme punishment. Starving families were executed for stealing grain, and penalties were imposed for feigning hunger. Politburo members who recommended assistance to starving regions were ridiculed by Stalin as being soft. Figure 2.3 captures the enormous loss of foregone grain production. Grain production in 1938 was not appreciably above that at the start of collectivization.

The ability of Stalin and the Politburo to extract grain collections at low delivery prices, despite massive unrest and starvation, underscores what Stalin may have regarded as his greatest achievement: the imposition of Soviet power in the countryside on his natural enemies – the peasant class. Clearly, such a show of force would have failed at the time of the revolution. In 1917, the USSR's population was 163 million, of which 134 million lived in rural areas.[59] Thus, slightly more than four of every

[56] Quoted in Erlich, *The Soviet Industrialization Debate*, 177.
[57] Ibid., 144.
[58] These figures are cited by O. Khlevnyuk, *Politburo*, 17–19.
[59] *Narodnoe Khoziaistvo SSSR za 70 Let* (Moscow: Finansy i Statistika, 1987), 5.

five subjects lived in the countryside. The Bolshevik party was an urban organization. Only 494 peasants belonged to the party in 1917 and before 1917 only four rural party cells existed. On October 1, 1928, out of the 1.4 million party members and candidate members, only 198,000 were classified as peasants or agricultural workers. There was one peasant party member in every 125 peasant households. According to E. H. Carr, "Many villages can never have seen a communist except in the guise of an occasional visiting official."[60] Stalin, as the architect of the Soviet dictatorship, could not have been content with four out of every five of his subjects effectively outside of his control.

Nor did Stalin like what he saw in the countryside. The party's window to the countryside was provided by the Ministry of Interior's (called first VchK, or Cheka, then OGPU, then NKVD, and then MVD) secret reports on the Soviet countryside.[61] As noted by the first head of the Soviet secret police, Feliks Dzerzhinsky, these reports "give a one-sided picture – only black – without correct perspective."[62] The OGPU/NKVD chose their coverage to suit party leaders. Prior to Trotsky's expulsion, peasants were reported as declaring, "Trotsky is our leader."[63] After the break with right deviationists, reports spoke of "peasant-union slogans to cover the flag of the right."[64] At best, peasants were "indifferent to political questions."[65] In 1928, an antireligion campaign was resisted by peasants: "Beat us, but we'll not let you close the church."[66] As forced collectivization accelerated in 1930, peasant resistance became the primary theme of reports replete with statistics on kulak resistance, de-kulakization norms, arrests, banishments, transit to relocation centers, and peasants killed or injured in the course of fleeing. Peasants were threatened: "If you do not deliver grain, you'll be considered an enemy of Soviet power, and we'll enter your name on the black board."[67] Table 2.2 is a summary table prepared by the secret police on the fourteen thousand peasant uprisings of 1930. The accompanying note provides a flavor of individual reports.[68]

---

[60] These statistics and the quote from E. H. Carr are cited in Davies, *The Socialist Offensive*, 51–2.

[61] A. Berelovich and B. Danilov, *Sovetskaia Derevnia Glazami*, vols. 1 and 2.

[62] Ibid., 16–31.

[63] Ibid., 611.

[64] Ibid., 1019.

[65] Ibid., 668.

[66] Ibid., 825.

[67] Ibid., 328.

[68] These cases are from Berelovich and Danilov, *Sovetskaia Derevnia Glazami* vol. 1, 705–16.

TABLE 2.2. *Mass Peasants' Demonstration, 1930[a] (in USSR Territory)*

Month of Mass Demonstrations	Total Number of Mass Demonstrations	Demonstration with Female Predominance	Collectivization	Disruptions by Anti-Soviet Elements	Closing of Churches, Dismantling of Bells	Sowing and Harvesting Campaign	State Grain and Meat Procurements	Tax Campaign	Food Shortage	Shortage of Manufactured Goods	Others
January	402	229	158	68	159	7	2		4		4
February	1,048	379	723	178	103	19	2	1	9		13
March	6,528	1,172	5,010	749	514	160	2	5	65		23
April	1,992	550	789	457	391	147		2	172		34
May	1,375	486	284	338	126	154	3	1	433	3	36
June	886	301	175	214	69	37	4	1	348		35
July	618	167	170	177	38	9	29	2	141	5	47
August	256	105	50	61	25	7	73	1	17	3	19
September	159	82	12	40	10	2	65	3	9	7	11
October	270	141	6	33	23	1	173	11	9	2	12
November	129	56	3	17	12	1	67	3	10	6	10
December	91	44	2	7	17		36	11	3	1	14
Total in 1930	13,754	3,712	7,382	2,339	1,487	544	456	41	1,220	27	258

[a] Central Archive FSB RF. Secret-political department OGPU. Memorandum about forms and dynamics of class struggle in countryside in 1930. S.32.

Source: A. Berelovich and B. Danilov, *Sovetskaia Derevnia Glazami VChK-OGPU-NKVD, 1923–1929, vol. 2.* (Moscow: Rosspen, 2000), 18.

Peasant resistance to Soviet power was a fact of life and was brought to life by these secret reports. Hence, the forced collectivization drive would have been viewed by the Soviet leadership as a way to gain control of a hostile countryside. The Bolshevik leadership had hoped that it could find allies among the poorer peasants by turning them against the rich kulaks. In fact, the party debated the fate of the kulaks more than one year. Most presumed that they would lose their property but would be admitted to collective farms. Stalin rendered his decision in an electrifying speech at the Communist Academy on December 27, 1929: "When the head is cut off, you do not weep about the hair. . . . Can kulaks be admitted to the collective farms? Of course it is wrong to admit the kulak into the collective farms. It is wrong because he is the accursed enemy of the kolkhoz movement."[69] The exclusion of kulaks from collective farms meant their deportation, execution, or, in the most fortunate cases, flight to the anonymity of the city. Collectivization created the first major influx into the gulags. As of January 1, 1933, the camps housed 334,000 inmates

Smolensk Province, November 16: "Bands consisting of 100 and 200 peasants are agitating against communists and attacking Soviet establishments."

Moscow Province, November 20: "Communist candidates from the Russian Communist Party were thrown out and as a result one communist was elected to the regional Soviet, four nonparty candidates, and one candidate agitating against the Russian Communist Party. Kulaks agitating against the agricultural tax and a tax collector murdered."

Novonikailovsky Province, November 21: "The head of the provincial revolutionary tribunal has gone on a drunken spree, buying liquor from peasants with flour from army supplies."

Tambov Province, November 22: "Peasants are indifferent to the Russian Communist Party. Voluntary peasant committees are being formed."

Tiumen Province, November 11: "In Ialutrvorovsky, kulaks are agitating against Soviet power."

Novgorod Province, November 24: "Six sessions of the people's courts and two sessions of the revolutionary tribunal are working in the province. Since the beginning of the campaign, 3064 persons have been arrested . . . 620 were turned over to the people's court and 161 were turned over to the revolutionary tribunal."

Tver Province, December 2: "Several groups are refusing to participate in the election, saying that agricultural Soviets are not necessary."

Ryazan Province, December 11: "Peasants are indifferent to the Russian Communist Party due to the lack of political workers . . . they are also indifferent to the cooperatives [collective farms] because the cooperatives don't fulfill their needs. For non-payment of taxes 1699 persons were arrested – including nine people occupying responsible administrative positions."

Armenia, December 25: "Peasants are refusing to pay their taxes, declaring that they do not recognize the government of Armenia."

[69] Stalin's speech was published in *Pravda* on December 29, 1929. It is quoted in Davies, *The Socialists Offensive*, 197–8.

and 1,142,000 were located in special settlements. The majority of these were the victims of collectivization.[70]

To strengthen Soviet power in the countryside, Stalin appointed the former deputy head of the much-feared Worker-Peasant Inspection (Y. A. Yakovlev) as Commissar of Agriculture. His trusted but beleaguered Politburo associate (A. Mikoian, Commissar of Trade) oversaw grain collections. Politburo members bombarded these agricultural organizations with instructions.[71] Politburo members were made personally responsible for collections in specific regions.[72] Thousands of party activists were sent to the countryside. Police, militia, and OGPU/NKVD forces were everywhere. After initially limiting authority to order executions to the Central Committee on April 20, 1931,[73] authority to impose the death penalty was extended to include the OGPU and courts of republics. A Politburo Decree of September 16, 1932, required that death sentences be carried out immediately.[74] By March 1930, the Politburo was authorizing specific officials to order the death penalty.[75]

Concluding Comments

This chapter relates the logic of forced collectivization, a decision that doomed Soviet agriculture to mediocre performance until the end of the Soviet Union in 1991. A country that was the world's second largest agricultural producer and exporter could no longer feed itself by the 1960s and had to turn to grain imports from its arch rival, the United States. It was Stalin's indifference to rural suffering that led him to dismiss earlier calls for grain imports as a "political minus" that would be used by foreigners "crying about the lack of grain in the USSR."[76] But by Stalin's and his Politburo's calculations, the benefits of the introduction of force into the countryside outweighed these costs. The economic logic of collectivization was enunciated by Preobrazhensky in his "primitive capital accumulation" model, which advised to sacrifice agricultural living

---

[70] Khlevnyuk, "The Economy of the Gulag," 116.

[71] R. W. Davies, *The Soviet Collective Farm, 1929–1930* (Cambridge, Mass.: Harvard University Press, 1980), 7–8.

[72] Khlevnyuk et al., *Stalinskoe Politburo,* 115.

[73] Ibid., 59.

[74] Ibid., 61.

[75] Ibid., 63, 65. Comrades Belitsky, Karlson, and Leplersky in Ukraine, and Eikhe in Western Siberia were authorized to pronounce death sentences.

[76] Khlevnyuk et al., *Stalin i Kaganovich. Perepiski,* 462.

standards to achieve a surplus for industrial investment. When proposed by Preobrazhensky in the mid-1920s, this scheme was unworkable. Peasants would not voluntarily hand over their grain to the state at prices below cost of production. Stalin's contribution to primitive accumulation was to create the institutions of force to extract the surplus from peasants. Adherence to primitive accumulation was so consistent that we elevate it to a core principle of Soviet power along with state ownership, planning, and the leading role of the party.

Collectivization and the introduction of a network of force into the countryside could be interpreted as actions either of a stationary bandit or a power-maximizing dictator. A stationary bandit, convinced – rightly or wrongly – that an investment surplus must be extracted from agriculture for industrialization, would call for maximum political power in the countryside. A selfish dictator, irrespective of economic objectives, could not accept a political system that does not control three quarters of the citizenry. Collectivization and the extreme pressure it placed on powerful regional party leaders were not the actions of a referee–dictator responding to pressures from interest groups. Collectivization did not originate as a consequence of powerful lobbies; rather, it was an action conceived and executed at the highest levels.

Figure 2.2 brought home the contradiction between primitive accumulation and the NEP. As long as private property rights remained and peasants made market-based decisions, the state could not procure grain at the low prices it wished. The so-called grain-collection crises, which served as the official rationale for collectivization, cannot be considered "failures" of private agriculture. Soviet agriculture, as it was constituted during the NEP, grew at a rapid pace, slowing down only with increasing state intervention. Although it is difficult to obtain accurate measures, it is likely that peasants were producing more, eating more, and feeding more grain to their livestock during the NEP than ever before. Their real incomes were rising. What they were not doing was selling their grain to the state at low prices. Extraordinary measures and then forced collectivization provided the venue for an immense battle over the distribution of income. The communist leadership believed that the NEP gave too much to the peasants (in terms of income from sales and from consumption of own production) and too little to the city. The Great Break-Through put in place a totalitarian system to change the distribution of income to the disadvantage of the peasantry.

The core values of the Bolshevik Party consisted of state ownership, a planned economy, and the leading role of the party. These three principles were in direct conflict with the NEP, and any decision in favor of the NEP agriculture would have required an eventual dropping of these core values. The right deviationists favored the NEP mixed economy. Had they been victorious and carried through on their pledge to continue the NEP system, the administrative-command system would not have been created. The result would have been, at least for a time, a highly regulated market economy operated by a political system that tolerated different points of view. The long-term outcome would have been an economic system not much different from that of the more highly regulated European economies on the eve of World War II. Hence, it was not only Stalin's greater political skill and brutality that carried the day. The right deviationists were out of line with the core values of the Bolshevik Party, whose rank and file supported these principles. Stalin won because he understood this simple fact.

Collectivization was carried out following the logic of primitive accumulation. The Soviet leadership presumed that, by buying grain at low prices and selling at higher prices, budget surpluses would be generated for investment finance. According to Marx's model of expanded reproduction, a poor country must create capital at as fast a pace as possible. From a simplistic point of view, any strategy that reduces consumption (e.g., by reducing peasant incomes) increases saving, which is the difference between output and consumption. Primitive accumulation appeared to work insofar as the investment rate doubled between 1928 and 1937, but was this increase a consequence of collectivization's depression of rural living standards or did everyone's consumption fall to accommodate more investment? Abram Bergson, the most noted student of Soviet growth, answers as follows: "Contrary to a common supposition, the industrial worker fared no better than peasants under Stalin's five-year plans."[77] In other words, something went wrong in Stalin's execution of primitive accumulation!

Grain is produced by land, labor, and capital, where agricultural capital consists of buildings, inventories, farm equipment, and animals, such as horses and oxen that provide tractive power. If forced collectivization were to cause a loss of labor effort or capital stock, the reduced standard of living need not create a surplus if output itself is reduced. One of the best documented costs of collectivization was the wholesale slaughter of

---

[77] Abram Bergson, *The Real National Income of Soviet Russia Since 1928* (Cambridge, Mass.: Harvard University Press, 1961), 257.

livestock, including the horses and oxen that were the traditional source of tractive power in Russian agriculture. The loss of livestock was severe. Agriculture's stock of livestock in 1933 was 40 percent of its 1928 level.[78] Given the widespread peasant opposition to collectivization, labor effort must have declined as well. Whereas secret-police reports fabricated left deviationist and right deviationist plots in the countryside in the mid-1920s, they could now document the real outrage of peasants as they fought against collectivization. If collectivization, therefore, destroyed agricultural capital stock and reduced labor effort, it is unclear whether the reduced peasant living standards produced any kind of a surplus. The most direct test of agriculture's surplus contribution is to subtract the flow of industrial goods to agriculture from the flow of agricultural goods to the city – a kind of balance of payments for agriculture vis-à-vis industry. Such calculations, made by James Millar, Michael Ellman, and the Soviet economist A. A. Barsov, conclude that there was virtually no surplus.[79] This finding is puzzling in light of the growing deliveries of grain to the city shown in Figure 2.3. The answer to this puzzle is that industry had to make up for the loss of animal power by producing tractors and combines for agriculture – a reverse flow of products back into agriculture. The increase in the investment rate, therefore, was paid for by general reductions in living standards of both farm and industrial workers.

What appeared to be a simple and decisive strategy – gather tribute from agriculture to pay for industrial investment – turned into a complex equation with unanticipated consequences. The story related at the beginning of the chapter eloquently explains what must have been the impact of collectivization on incentives, even ignoring the fact that the most able farmers were largely liquidated in an incredible loss of human capital. Even Stalin recognized that agriculture cannot operate without positive incentives. By June 1932, Stalin was ordering to send a "maximum of manufactured consumer goods to the grain-, sugar-, and cotton-producing regions" to stimulate production.[80] By September 1934, Stalin was

---

[78] Hunter and Szyrmer, *Faulty Foundations*, 228.

[79] James Millar, "Soviet Rapid Development and the Agricultural Surplus Hypothesis," *Soviet Studies* 22, no. 1 (July 1970); Michael Ellman, "Did the Agricultural Surplus Provide the Resources for the Increase in Investment in the USSR During the First Five-Year Plan?" *Economic Journal* 85, no. 4 (December 1975); A. Vyas, "Primary Accumulation in the USSR Revisited," *Cambridge Journal of Economics* 3, no. 3 (1979), 119–30.

[80] Khlevnyuk et al., *Stalin i Kaganovich. Perepiski*, 162.

ordering "to raise the purchase price of grain in comparison to the current price by 15 kopeks for grain and 10 kopeks for rye."[81] Stalin and the Politburo, who earlier had argued against any limits imposed by economic laws, now found themselves constrained by the most basic of economic laws – the need to provide economic incentives to encourage production and effort.

[81] Ibid., 478.

3

The Principles of Governance

Excerpts (condensed) from transcript of interrogation of S. I. Syrtsov, Chairman of the Council of People's Commissars of the Russian Republic and Candidate Member of the Politburo on October 23, 1930, accused of criticizing the Politburo and Stalin, S. Ordzhonikidze presiding:

Syrtsov: "It seems abnormal that Politburo decisions are predetermined by a leading group. I can completely understand when someone who has followed an incorrect political line is excluded. But, as I see it, there are mechanical members of the Politburo, like Kuibyshev, Rudzutak, and Kalinin, who do not participate at all, which creates a situation . . ."
Ordzhonikidze (interrupting): "Who makes up this leading group?"
Syrtsov: "The other Politburo members, of course, or part of them."
Ordzhonikidze: "You say so. You are the one who should know."
Syrtsov: "I am explaining to you that if all members of the Politburo were not bound by preliminary decisions, issues would be discussed in a different way."[1]
From transcript of Syrtsov's expulsion on November 4, 1930:
Ordzhonikidze: "Every member of the party must come to his party if he has doubts. The party should help such a comrade resolve his own doubts, to save him, and set him on the right course. If he does this, no one will call him to his party responsibility. But when he does these things in secret, this becomes an anti-party matter. Can we have such people in our leadership who try to tear it down?"
Stalin: "It is impossible!"[2]

---

[1] Statement of Syrtsov before the Central Control Commission chaired by Ordzhonikidze in Khlevyuk et al., *Stalinskoe Politburo*, 99–100.
[2] The protocol of this joint meeting is in Khlevnyuk et al., *Stalinskoe Politburo*, 103–5.

The Power Struggle

This chapter describes the power struggle following Lenin's death in January 1924 that established the principles of governance of the administrative-command system. The power struggle was for control of the party's highest governing body, the Politburo, which in December 1927 had a membership of nine full voting members: Josef Stalin served as General Secretary. N. I. Bukharin, A. I. Rykov, and M. P. Tomsky formed the right opposition that favored continuation of NEP policies. The five other members were V. V. Kuibyshev (party member since 1904), V. M. Molotov (party member since 1906), K. E. Voroshilov (party member since 1903), M. I. Kalinin (party member since 1898), and Y. E. Rudzutak (party member since 1905). Of these five swing votes, the alcoholic Kuibyshev served primarily as an economic administrator, heading at the time the Supreme Economic Council, before being transferred to head Gosplan. The innocuous Kalinin headed the Central Executive Committee of the government, Voroshilov was the minister of Military and Naval Affairs, and Rudzutak was deputy chairman of the Council of People's Commissars and chairman of the Worker-Peasant Inspection. Stalin needed the support of these five Politburo members to vanquish the right opposition. Three short years later (December 1930), the Politburo had ten members. No one from the right opposition remained. Bukharin, Rykov, and Tomsky had been replaced by Stalin loyalists, L. M. Kaganovich, former Caucasian Party leader G. K. (Sergo) Ordzhonikidze, and by two regional party bosses – S. M. Kirov from Leningrad and S. V. Kosior of Ukraine. This dramatic change between 1927 and December 1929 formed the Politburo that approved the Great Break-Through.

Stalin's path to political victory illustrates F. A. Hayek's notion that the leader with a comparative advantage in brutality would emerge the victor. Although Stalin was recognized by the mid-1920s as a master of detail, cunning, and a controller of appointments – far from the nonentity depicted in earlier literature – the odds seemed to favor his better-known rivals:[3] Rykov (party member since 1898) had replaced Lenin as head of government and controlled the levers of government; Bukharin (party member since 1906) was viewed as the chief "theoretician" and served as editor of the government's official newspaper; Tomsky (party member since 1904) had strong backing from the trade unions. Stalin faced a tough

---

[3] E. A. Rees, "Leaders and Their Institutions," in *Behind the Facade of Stalin's Command Economy*, ed. Paul Gregory (Stanford, Calif.: Hoover Institution Press, 2001), 35–60.

challenge in winning support against these three. Politburo members were on cordial terms; their families lived together in the Kremlin. Earlier, it had been easy to recruit support against Trotsky whom the other Politburo members despised.

Stalin's opponents did not know then that the succession was literally a matter of life or death. Of the nine Politburo members in December 1927, four were executed; one died a natural death in 1935. Bukharin portended his fate in an emotional letter to Stalin dated October 14, 1930, (seven years before his eventual execution):

Koba: [Stalin's nickname to his immediate associates] After our telephone conversation I am in a condition of dismay. Not because you frightened me – you cannot frighten me and do not frighten me. But because your bizarre accusations [that he was plotting Stalin's assassination] clearly show a diabolical, vile, and low provocation in which you believe, which will lead to no good, as if you are destroying me politically as well as physically.[4]

Stalin's brutality, cunning, and knowledge of people served him well in this final power struggle. He responded with outrage to any informal meeting of Politburo members (even though he arranged earlier for the Politburo to meet without Trotsky),[5] while he privately lobbied Politburo members and encouraged his allies to do the same. Stalin to Molotov in August 1928:

I was with Sergo [Ordzhonikidze]. His mood is good. He stands firmly behind the party line of the Central Committee, against those who are wavering.... Andreev [a candidate member of the Politburo] apparently visited Sergo and talked with him. According to Sergo, Andreev firmly supports the party line. Tomsky it appears tried to turn him (during the Plenum), but did not succeed. Under no circumstances can we allow Tomsky or any one else to turn Kuibyshev or Mikoian. Is it not possible to send Tomsky's letter against Kuibyshev?[6]

Stalin parsed innocuous articles of Bukharin (that had been approved in advance) to uncover ideological "mistakes." Any informal meeting could be interpreted as a violation of party discipline. Stalin used a casual meeting between Kalinin and the discredited economist N. D. Kondratiev to keep his frightened colleague in line.[7] Any informal discussion of party policy could be labeled as "weakening party discipline" and "turning

---

4 Bukharin's letter of October 14, 1930, is quoted in Khlevnyuk, *Politburo*, 38.
5 E. A. Rees and D. H. Watson, "Politburo and Sovnarkom," in *Decision Making in the Stalinist Command Economy*, ed. E. A. Rees, 1932–1937 (London: MacMillan, 1997), 11.
6 Khlevnyuk, *Politburo*, 22.
7 Ibid., 35–6.

the party into a discussion club."[8] Stalin intimidated Voroshilov with a fabricated plot to create a military dictatorship.[9] He branded out-of-favor party members as "weak," "rotting," "not one of us," or "bureaucrats with high opinions of themselves."[10]

Stalin's conclusive victory came in April 1929, when he mustered a Politburo majority against the right deviationists on charges of factionalism.[11] Bukharin was expelled from the Politburo in November 1929, for the offense of (in the words of the Politburo resolution of July 22, 1929): "making indirect sorties against decisions of the Central Committee (in conversations with Comrade Kamenev and Platonov)."[12] Tomsky was not reelected by the July 1930 Party Congress. Rykov was reelected to the Politburo in July 1930, but was expelled in December 1930.[13] The right deviationist purge was not limited to its three leaders; between 1929 and 1931, 250,000 party members were expelled for right deviationist associations.[14]

The Five Issues of Governance

The party power struggle was fought over five fundamental issues: First, what economic system should be chosen? The outcome of this debate – superindustrialization, forced collectivization, and the annihilation of the kulaks – was discussed in the previous chapter. Second, was the Communist Party to follow one common policy – the general line (*general'naia liniia*) – or tolerate different viewpoints? Would the party allow factions or be united by one common policy? Third, would the state have a power base separate from the party, or was there to be no essential difference between the state and party? Given Lenin's dominant status during his lifetime, the issue of state/party separation had not been raised. Lenin headed the government and also the party. For Stalin, the division of power between the state and party was an intense concern because one of his

---

[8] Lih et al., *Stalin's Letters to Molotov*, 162.
[9] Letter from Stalin to Ordzhonikidze dated September 24, 1930. Cited in Khlevnyuk, *Politburo*, 37. In a confidential letter to his confidant (Ordzhonikidze), Stalin indirectly admitted the fabrication: "It seems to say that [Marshall] Tukhachesvsky is a prisoner of anti-Soviet elements.... Is this possible? Of course, it is possible, as long as it is not ruled out."
[10] Stalin's description of Mikoian in Khlevnyuk et al., *Stalin i Kaganovich. Perepiski*, 52.
[11] Ibid., chapters 1–2.
[12] Lih et al., *Stalin's Letters to Molotov*, 134.
[13] Khlevnyuk, *Politburo*, 24.
[14] Ibid., 21.

chief rivals controlled the reins of government. Fourth, how much party democracy should be allowed? To what degree could the rank and file of the party influence the central party apparatus? Fifth, was there to be a collective or single dictator?

These five separate points ultimately speak to the same issue: the degree of centralization of power. The NEP system was characterized by uncon-centrated economic power controlled largely through indirect regulation and the forging of political consensuses. The open industrialization debate of the mid-1920s demonstrates a toleration of different points of view. Neither economic nor political institutions were highly concentrated, an arrangement that was consistent with the NEP. The NEP implicit con-tract was, in effect: "As long as you do not oppose us, you can be one of us." As the NEP began to be replaced by the administrative-command system, new governance arrangements required an extreme centralization of power. No longer would passive support of Politburo decisions be tol-erated. Under this type of political regime, political leaders were to be judged not on the basis of their actions, such as support of collectiviza-tion, but according to their perceived innermost thoughts. "If you are not enthusiastically with us, you are against us." Given that one's thoughts are not known to others, life became dangerous for the Soviet elite. They could be accused of wrong thinking, not merely of wrong behavior.

The Choice of Economic System. During the annihilation of the left devi-ationists, Stalin joined the Politburo majority, along with Rykov, Tomsky, and Bukharin, who favored moderate policies and opposed the revolution from above advocated by the left wing. The moderates won the industri-alization debate with the expulsion of Trotsky, but lost the war three years later when Stalin expelled them and enacted the very policies of the discredited left.[15] The Great Break-Through was approved by the new Politburo majority cobbled together by Stalin. Collectivization, natio-nalization, and forced industrialization signaled the emergence of an administrative-command system that required the new principles of gov-ernance described in the following.

Rivalry and Political Competition. The defeat of the left deviationists dispatched Stalin's most formidable political enemies, but left open the is-sue of political competition within the ruling elite of the party. Members of the right wing of the party staked out a clear ideological position. They

---

[15] Moshe Lewin, *Russian Peasants*, 214–44; Stephan Merl, *Der Agrarmarkt*, 313–88.

favored a mixed economy, balanced growth, and a continuation of private peasant agriculture. Stalin initially expressed no personal opinions but became convinced (as described in the previous chapter) that agriculture must be collectivized, kulaks must be brought under control, and force must be introduced into the countryside. With these growing differences on fundamental issues, the party had to decide how to deal with conflict. The earlier conflict with the left opposition was dealt with via fairly open discussion. Each side expressed its opinion in the press and in meetings (although Trotsky felt that Politburo meetings were rigged in advance). In the mid-1920s, there was no pretense of party unity. There was an open tooth-and-nail brawl from which the moderate Politburo majority emerged victorious. Trotsky went first into internal exile and then to Mexico, where he fell victim to a Stalin assassin. A disparate group of Politburo members, ranging from party ward boss (Stalin), educated bureaucrat (Rykov), alcoholic pencil-pusher (Kuibyshev), intellectual (Bukharin), and nonentity (Kalinin), had to make the key decisions for society and the economy.

The nine members of the ruling elite would not be expected to see eye to eye. They would naturally disagree on many issues. The rule of party discipline provided a temporary compromise. Politburo members were allowed to have different views, but once a decision was rendered, all Politburo members were supposed to fall into line and publicly support a single general line. Indeed, Bukharin, Rykov, and Tomsky followed party discipline as good soldiers and supported Politburo decisions, which they personally opposed. Rykov, as the head of government, enforced the Great Break-Through, which he opposed. For Stalin, party discipline was an unacceptable long-run solution. It tolerated independent thinking within the Politburo, and it left in place high officials, such as Rykov, to enact policies for which they had limited sympathy. Stalin could stomach only like-thinkers, who accepted the general party line without reservation.

Under the rules of party discipline, those with reservations publicly supported party policies. To remove them from office, Stalin therefore had to manufacture deviations from the general line from their articles or public statements. The incredulous Bukharin was expelled in November 1929 for the offense of (in the words of the Politburo resolution of July 22, 1929) "making masked attacks against the party line in speeches and articles."[16] Rykov was still prime minister when Stalin arranged for

---

[16] Lih et al., *Stalin's Letters to Molotov*, 134.

him to be accused in Sverdlovsk in June 1930 of organizing an opposition group. Rykov vigorously defended his loyalty with the following statement:

Comrade Rumiantsev [Rykov's accuser] is no common member of the Party. He should weigh his words. We are members of the ruling party. I am chairman of the Council of People's Commissars and a member of the Politburo. I voted for the resolution and am one of the few that participated in the decision.... If after seven months of my political, economic, and Soviet work, someone asks: how do I stand to the general line of the Party? I can answer only thus: I decisively do not understand the basis for such a question! The fact that someone is accusing me of being a leader of some kind of faction suggests a certainty that such a grouping, created with my participation, exists. Why sow such doubts? Therefore I must demand an explanation of how and why and on the basis of what information Comrade Rumiantsev can ask me how I, as a leader of a substantial organization, relate to the general line of the Party?[17]

Stalin's fixation on party unity continued after the dispatch of the right deviationists. The nine other fellow Politburo members that constituted Stalin's team as of December 1929 were compliant but human. They clashed with one another regularly over large and small matters. These frictions could escalate into real rifts. Stalin, not the most solicitous of persons, had to spend considerable time soothing egos and refereeing disputes. He eventually turned against fellow Georgian, Ordzhonikidze, because of his habit of clashing with other party leaders. One such confrontation was so rancorous that Kuibyshev insisted on resigning. The vacationing Stalin assigned the loyal Kaganovich to mend the rift: "Comrade Ordzhonikidze is behaving even worse. He does not consider that his behavior (his attacks on Molotov and Kuibyshev) objectively leads to the rift of our ruling group, creating a danger of its destruction."[18]

To preserve the single party line, a mechanism for resolving disputes among Politburo members was required. Party rules dictated face-to-face meetings of conflicting parties, a rule Stalin conveniently ignored in his conflict with Bukharin. Special sessions of the Politburo were called to deal with high-level disputes. There are no records of such dispute-resolution sessions, but it appears that Stalin himself acted as mediator. A December 1931 Politburo meeting provides a hint of how this worked: Ordzhonikidze, then-chairman of the Supreme Economic Council, threatened to resign over Molotov's proposal to divide his organization into

---

[17] Rykov's speech is quoted in Khlevnyuk, *Politburo*, 26.
[18] Khlevnyuk et al., *Stalin i Kaganovich. Perepiski*, 51.

three industrial ministries. The Politburo appointed a commission including the two protagonists, as well as Stalin and the second secretary of the
Politburo (Kaganovich), to draft a reorganization decree for the Supreme
Council and to reject Ordzhonikidze's resignation. A special session of
the Politburo was then called to resolve the personal dispute between
Molotov and Ordzhonikidze. There is no record of this meeting; probably
none was kept.[19] What is known is that Ordzhonikidze did not resign and
the Supreme Council was subdivided into ministries with Ordzhonikidze
taking the office of heavy industry ministry.

Independent State Power? Rykov, the prime minister, and Stalin's last
remaining rival, survived the first round of expulsions and remained the
head of government, the chairman of the Council of People's Commissars,
until his dismissal and expulsion from the Politburo in December 1930.
Stalin, as the party general secretary, feared that the government, under
Rykov, posed a real challenge to the leading role of the party. The Meeting
of Deputies (*soveshchanie zamov*), which set its own agenda and gathered
together all top government ministers, was particularly feared as an alternative to party power. Rykov did not pose the first such threat. Trotsky
had been highly critical of "the regime of professional [party] secretaries,
cut off from the masses and enjoying their bureaucratic privileges."[20]

On September 22, 1930, Stalin sent the following top-secret letter to
Molotov, written in his usual canonical style:[21]

Vyacheslav: 1) It seems to me that it is necessary by fall to decide conclusively
about the Soviet leadership (*verkhuska*). We must resolve the general question of
the interrelationship between party and state (Soviet) power, not divided one from
the other. My opinion on this matter: a) It is necessary to relieve Rykov and drive
out his bureaucratic and consultative-secretarial apparatus. b) You will be required
to replace Rykov as the chairman of the Council of People's Commissars. This is
necessary. Otherwise there will be *a break between party and Soviet leadership*
[author's italics]. With such a combination, we can have *a full unity of the Party
and Soviet leadership* [author's italics], which necessarily doubles our power.[22]

Rykov's grip on power was already visibly slipping. On November 29,
1930, the Politburo's military commission met without him to discuss

---

[19] O. Khlevnyuk, "The People's Commissariat of Heavy Industry," in *Decision Making in
the Stalinist Command Economy, 1932–37*, ed. E. A. Rees (London: MacMillan, 1997),
104.

[20] Getty and Naumov, *The Road to Terror*, 38.

[21] Khlevnyuk et al., *Stalinskoe Politburo*, letter from Stalin to Molotov, Document 88,
96.

[22] Ibid., 96.

military equipment orders. Stalin's plan was executed at an evening meeting on December 19, 1930, of the Central Committee and the Central Control Commission (Stalin arranged for the latter to vote as an exception), called ostensibly to discuss the national economic plan. Kuibyshev departed from his expected presentation of the economic plan to call for Rykov's dismissal:

> I consider that, in order to fulfill this difficult plan for 1931, there must be complete unity. The fact that Comrade Rykov has not been among the active fighters for the general line, has not battled against those views, the harm of which he has recognized, demonstrates that such a division exists as long as Comrade Rykov heads the state apparatus. And this harms the entire Soviet apparatus. The consequence is that we have a Central Committee and its leadership in the form of the Politburo and its Plenum occupied with the magnificent creation of socialism, leading the proletariat into new battles, fighting against class enemies while we have a state (Soviet) leadership which "does what it can." This cannot continue.[23]

Kosior's (party leader from Ukraine and soon-to-be Politburo member) proposal to "free Rykov from his responsibilities as Chairman of the Council of People's Commissars and from the Politburo to be replaced by Molotov as Chairman and Ordzhonikidze as Politburo member" was accepted unanimously. The complete control of both government and party fell to Stalin and his team. Prior to that time, Molotov had held no significant administrative posts, but he had a record of extreme loyalty to Stalin.

The unification of the state and party into one interlocking directorate was affirmed by the bureaucratic procedures subsequently put in place. Politburo decrees were henceforth issued either in the name of the Central Committee or as directives of the Council of People's Commissars, signed by Molotov, by one of his deputies, or by the chancellery office. The practice of joint issuance of key decrees meant that the state could take no actions without Politburo clearance. Notably, most decrees (more than five thousand) were classified as top secret and far exceeded the number of published decrees.[24] The interlocking directorate became a

---

[23] Quoted in Khlevnyuk, *Politburo*, 51–2.
[24] Party decrees were sent to party committees as statements of intent before being "legalized" as Council of People's Commissars decrees. Politburo approval of decrees assured a Stalin confidante sign-off: A short explanation signed by Molotov accompanied all draft decrees. Copies were filed in the secret department of the chancellery, which was responsible for correspondence with the Politburo. After Politburo confirmation, the originals were filed as materials to the protocols of the Politburo. The secret department circulated Politburo decrees to a specified list of recipients through the interior ministry's communication system according to special instructions. Davies, "Making Economic Policy," 63; Khlevnyuk et al., *Stalinskoe Politburo*, 17.

decree-producing machine. In the period from January to September 1932, between 1,500 and 6,100 documents were dispatched monthly through secret-police channels. According to published procedures, secret decrees were to be handled with care, especially the most confidential "special file" (*osobaia papka*) cases; however, officials, faced with an avalanche of decrees, often ignored these safeguards.[25]

The Politburo's ability to reject Council of People's Commissars' decrees revealed it as clearly superior. A decree concerning the financing of party schools was rejected by Stalin: "I am not able to approve; the proposal is not justified."[26] In another case, Stalin denied a decree to import equipment, declaring that the USSR is able to produce that equipment itself.[27] In another case, Stalin rejected a decree prepared for credits to Mongolia: "I am against. Mongolia can buy 200 trucks paying us in meat or wool."[28]

The unity of state and party masked a hierarchy of authority with the Politburo being superior to the Council of People's Commissars. An order issued by the Central Committee (Politburo) carried more authority than one issued by the Council of People's Commissars. At times, Stalin himself was confused as to which organization should issue a decree. Stalin to Kaganovich (September 14, 1931):

You can issue the decree (about wages in metallurgy and coal) in the name of the Supreme Council of the National Economy and the All Union Council of Trade Unions. If you need the signature of the Central Committee, then it is necessary to publish it in the name of the Central Committee and the Council of People's Commissars. In that case, I ask you to send the text for my review.[29]

Stalin was particularly incensed by ministries trying to issue decrees in the name of the Central Committee (Politburo), to enhance their authority. Stalin to Kaganovich (September 9, 1931):

The headline in *Pravda* that a decree of the Supreme Council has been approved by the Central Committee creates a strange impression. Why were all these approved

---

[25] A survey of 1933 showed that only 40 percent of secret documents were actually returned on time. For example, the deputy minister of heavy industry (NKTP) had received eighteen copies but had returned only five. The Politburo imposed sanctions on the most negligent recipients, such as withdrawing the right to receive further documents. A Central Asian party official (Ikraimova), for example, was punished for leaving protocols in his room in Hotel National and was deprived of the right to receive documents for three months (Khlevnyuk et al., *Stalinskoe Politburo*, 78).

[26] Ibid., 18.

[27] Ibid., 18.

[28] Ibid., 38–9.

[29] Khlevnyuk et al., *Stalin i Kaganovich. Perepiski*, 102–3.

by the Central Committee and not the Council of People's Commissars? Why do they want to make the Central Committee a participant, but ignore the Council of People's Commissars? This maneuver is turning the Politburo into a rubber stamp.[30]

Plenums of the Central Committee, such as the one of December 19, 1930, that dismissed Rykov, carried the highest weight because they were usually called to make major personnel changes or to discuss major issues, such as Stalin's order to Kaganovich (September 26, 1931) to call a plenum on transportation, trade, and grain collections.[31] Plenum decrees and reports were prepared with great care because they were widely distributed to the party rank and file.[32]

Party Democracy. Rituals and myths played an important role in the administrative-command system. Five-year plans, May Day parades, and Lenin's mausoleum served the ceremonial role of inspiring the population and legitimizing those in power. With the extreme centralization of power in the hands of the Politburo or Stalin personally, there could be no questioning the legitimacy of coercive orders. Even the smallest hints of illegitimacy would be met with alarm and concern. Politburo orders were issued, in Stalin's words, to protect the interests of "the working class."[33] The dictator's ultimate legitimacy rested on the claim of being the true representative of the working class.

The Communist Party was, on paper, organized on a democratic basis. Formally, the highest authority was the Party Congress, which met periodically to choose the leadership and discuss major issues, such as confirming a five-year plan. Up until the end of the Soviet Union, the practice of using Party Congresses to affirm changes in leadership and major policy changes continued. Nikita Khrushchev, for example, used the Twentieth Party Congress of 1956 to deliver his famous anti-Stalin speech. Thus, in theory, the party's rank and file were empowered to change the leadership. The Communist Party had a complex regional hierarchy. Republican party organizations from large republics, such as the Ukrainian Communist Party or the Caucus Communist Party, and from the major cities, such as Moscow and Leningrad, stood at the apex of the regional hierarchy; leaders of the most powerful republican and city

---

[30] Ibid., 93.
[31] Ibid., 121.
[32] Getty and Naumov, *The Road to Terror*, 230.
[33] Khlevnyuk et al., *Stalin i Kaganovich. Perepiski*, 72.

party organizations were members of the Central Committee and often of the Politburo itself. Regional and district party organizations occupied intermediate positions, while the lowest level was occupied by Primary Party Organizations attached to factories and to other organizations.

Between 1929 and 1932, the ranks of the party swelled from 1.2 million to 3.5 million. Whereas the Bolshevik Party began as a small revolutionary party, this tripling in size increasingly populated it with relatively unknown persons whose loyalty was not certain. If these 3.5 million rank and file party members turned against the leadership, the consequences could be disastrous.

Stalin and the Politburo had to resolve two issues with respect to the party's regional leadership and its rank and file members. First, they had to be wary of any tendencies on the part of lower-level party members to conclude that they were the true representatives of the working class. Second, the top party leadership had to worry about outbreaks of democracy, particularly those engineered by formidable enemies, such as the exiled Trotsky. The Politburo had an arsenal of weapons to combat such unhealthy tendencies. All party members were controlled by various party control commissions, beginning with the Worker-Peasant Inspection in the late 1920s. Insofar as virtually all substantive positions were occupied by party members, the party played a judiciary role by resolving disputes among party members and punishing errant party members.[34] Any party members ailing from fits of democracy or illusions that they represented the proletariat could be brought to their "party responsibility" by such control commissions. A rigid, formal structure was put in place to ensure that all party officials faithfully executed the party line. Each local, regional, and republican party office was ordered "to place the responsibility on one of its secretaries for monitoring the fulfillment of directives of the Central Committee and the responsibility for timely responses to related questions."[35] In a typical case from 1930, Stalin sent a telegram to Urals and Siberian party committees demanding that they report within three days why the flax and cotton plan were not fulfilled and to report measures taken.[36] The party first secretary was obligated to respond prior to the official report, namely within two days. A third weapon against party democracy was the careful staging of Party Congresses or Central Committee Plenums. They were called only after internal leadership disputes had been resolved, and the party leadership could present a

[34] Belova, "Economic Crime and Punishment," 131–58.
[35] Khlevnyuk et al., *Stalinskoe Politbiuro*, 83–5.
[36] Ibid., 82–3.

united front. For example, Stalin had to delay the fateful December 1930 Central Committee Plenum that discharged Rykov until he was sure of unanimous Politburo support. The first postwar Party Congress was delayed two years, pending conclusion of the postwar power struggle.

The first crises of the Great Break-Through – famine, budget crisis, and failed investments – tested the relationship between Moscow and lower party organizations.[37] The economic and social crisis spilled over into the political arena as a crisis of confidence in the leadership of Stalin's team. Letters of support for the ousted Rykov appeared even in the party press. Ominously, a secret letter circulated in party circles calling for Stalin's replacement by Leningrad party leader, S. M. Kirov. The Politburo responded with a diversionary campaign against "wreckers" and nonparty "specialists" who were blamed for the economic crisis. Managers were dismissed, and specialists were accused of sabotage in campaigns orchestrated by Moscow but carried out by local party officials and militia.[38]

The local excesses of the 1929 to 1930 purges taught that Moscow could not rely on local party officials, despite the clear line of communication. The campaign against managerial and specialist wreckers originated with Stalin and was enthusiastically supported by key Politburo allies. Local party officials, in their zeal to oust wreckers, took over management of local enterprises. Managers from the Donbass region complained that more than half of their specialists were in prison. As the campaign's disastrous effect on production became apparent in 1930, the Politburo took steps to stop it in its tracks. Ordzhonikidze, as the new chairman of the Supreme Economic Council, an early supporter of the purge, now sought to return authority to "his" managers. At a conference of workers in January to February of 1931, attended by Stalin and Molotov, Ordzhonikidze declared that the mass of workers and managers were not wreckers, a retreat supported by Stalin (the archives contain Stalin's margin notes on Ordzhonikidze's draft). The Politburo, on January 20, 1931, instructed local party organizations not "to remove directors of works of all-union significance without the approval of the Central Committee and of the Supreme Economic Council."[39]

Despite clear-cut instructions from Moscow, local party organizations, local militia, and even local OGPU continued their harassment of managers. In March 1931, Ordzhonikidze censured the Rostov party

37 R. W. Davies, *Crisis and Progress in the Soviet Economy, 1931–1933* (Basingstoke, England: MacMillan, 1996), chapters 3–10.
38 Khlevnyuk, *Politburo*, 33.
39 Khlevnyuk, "The People's Commissariat of Heavy Industry," 98.

organization for turning his manager over to the OGPU and taking charge
of the factory. In the spring of 1931, the Politburo had to assure a plant
director in the North Caucus of "normal working conditions . . . and that
the local party organization, militia, and OGPU would end the practice
of interrogating specialists without the authorization of the enterprise directorate or of higher authorities."[40] On June 22–23, 1931, the Central
Committee again had to order that no director be arrested without the
agreement of the ministry. In August 1931, the Politburo had to fire a
local party leader for replacing local managers with local party officials.
As late as April 1933, more than two years after the Politburo had called
off its campaign, the Central Committee had to rebuke local party organizations for interfering in managerial affairs. Such disobedience indicates
an ongoing power struggle between Moscow and local party officials who
concluded that they, not Moscow, represented the interests of the proletariat. Their unwillingness to bend to central orders for more than two
years illustrates the ferocity of this dispute.

Local disobedience represented a lesser threat than party democracy.
The party elite numbered in the hundreds or low thousands, whereas party
members numbered 3.5 million. Stalin's most violent tirades occurred
when rivals threatened to take disputes directly to the party membership.
When M. N. Riutin distributed a platform calling for Stalin's ouster in
1930, Stalin demanded (but did not get) his execution. He had to be satisfied with Riutin's expulsion from the party.[41] Stalin feared Trotsky, even
in exile, because of his threats to take issues directly to the rank and file.[42]

The lesson of the early 1930s was that the party's grassroots represented
a threat to the monopoly party line. They could respond with too great
enthusiasm to party campaigns and, once campaigns were started, they
were difficult to restrain. Stalin's answer was centralization. The Politburo
established the USSR Procuracy on July 1, 1933, to replace republican
procurators.[43] By the mid-1930s, the power to punish factory directors
had been centralized in the Ministry of Interior and in the Procurator's office, the two offices that provided the venue for the Great Terror of 1937–
38. The dictator asserted control over party members by concentrating
punitive powers. Whereas in the early 1930s, local party officials and even
local OGPU officers could arrest, fire, and otherwise punish, this authority
was centralized by the mid-1930s.

[40] Ibid., 99–103.
[41] Getty and Naumov, *The Road to Terror*, 53.
[42] Ibid., 63.
[43] Ibid., 119.

Collective Leadership or Dictatorship? The "deal" that Stalin implicitly offered his Politburo allies in December 1930 was a political equilibrium of collective decision making. The Politburo was to be the supreme decision-making authority, and its decisions were to be made collectively, although Stalin was the first among equals. In the early 1930s, Stalin could dictate decisions he considered vital but, if he went too far, the Politburo could still rein him in. In violation of this implicit contract, the period 1932 to 1937 saw the marked decline of collective decision making. Politburo meetings declined from weekly meetings in 1929 to forty-seven meetings in 1932, twenty-four in 1933, eighteen in 1934, fifteen in 1935, and a mere nine in 1936. In 1938, there were four meetings, and in 1939 and 1940, just two meetings each.[44] By 1936, the Politburo was largely a consultative body. Politburo members now referred to Stalin as the "master of the house."[45] The Orgburo and Secretariat of the Central Committee were so much under Stalin's control by the mid-1930s that he did not even bother to attend their meetings.[46] Stalin's personal secretary (Poskrebyshev) counted among the most powerful figures in the Soviet administration.

The path from a collective to a personal dictatorship clearly can be explained in part by Stalin's thirst for absolute power. But, returning to the jockey-versus-horse issue, we must ask whether the same result would have occurred with an alternate Stalin-like figure. There are several theoretical arguments in favor of the evolution to a single dictator: Olson's stationary-bandit model (see Chapter 1) implicitly suggested that only a single person (or a very cohesive small group) could prevent the rise of vested interests. Only a supreme leader could consistently ensure development objectives. Hayek wrote of the tendency for collective decision making to transform into one-person rule under conditions of administrative allocation:

> But in a society which for its functioning depends on central planning this control cannot be made dependent on a majority being able to agree; it will often be necessary that the will of a small minority be imposed on the people because this minority will be the largest group able to agree among themselves on the question at issue.[47]

In fact, Hayek's view of decisions by ever-smaller groups is confirmed by the fact that by the mid-1930s, decisions were made by ad hoc groups of

---

44 Rees, "Leaders and Their Institutions," 11.
45 See, for example, the letter from Kaganovich to Ordzhonikidze in Khlevnyuk et al., *Stalinskoe Politburo*, 146–7.
46 Rees and Watson, "Politburo and Sovnarkhom," 13.
47 Hayek, *The Road to Serfdom*, 77.

Politburo members, which Khrushchev later called "decisions by quintets and sextets."[48] The Arrow Impossibility Theorem of Nobel Laureate Kenneth Arrow provides, surprisingly, a third rationale for the emergence of a supreme leader.[49] Arrow's theorem concludes that it is impossible to develop rules of social choice (should society choose policy A, B, or C) that meet necessary conditions when the only information present is the rankings of various alternatives by different individuals.[50] Public choices may not be transitive (A is preferred to B, and B is preferred to C, but C is preferred to A) in such a setting. Decisions among alternatives, therefore, require some established procedure – such as a fixed criterion, a random device (e.g., the roll of a dice), or recourse to an arbiter – when two alternatives tie for first place. The Soviet Union, of course, was not a democracy in December 1930, but it had ten decision makers with differing preferences. The democracy-advocate Arrow explicitly ruled out the selection of a dictator, whose preferences dominate, to resolve his paradox. Hayek ruled out a rules-based resolution, arguing that an administrative system "cannot tie itself down in advance to general and formal rules that prevent arbitrariness.... It must constantly decide questions which cannot be answered by formal principles only."[51] The arguments of Olson, Hayek, and Arrow, therefore, seem to provide reasons why an administrative-command economy will evolve into a single-person dictatorship. In fact, a collective dictatorship may be unstable and may yield inferior results.

Indeed, Stalin's candid correspondence reads like that of a stationary bandit. Stalin argued that only a bold leader could take actions that were unpopular but necessary. When the Ukrainian party branded the grain-collection plan as unrealistic in 1932, Stalin wrote: "This is not a party, but a parliament or a caricature of a parliament. Lenin was correct that a man not having the courage to swim against the current at the right time cannot be a leader."[52] He insisted on "encompassing" economic decisions and railed against narrow rent-seeking activities, particularly by other Politburo members. He complained regularly about the "selfishness" of Ordzhonikidze (Minister of Heavy Industry) and Mikoian (Minister of Trade). He accused Ordzhonikidze "of pressing on the state budget on

[48] Rees and Watson, "Politburo and Sovnarkom," 11.
[49] Kenneth J. Arrow, "Little's Critique of Welfare Economics," *American Economic Review*, 41 (December 1951), 213–19.
[50] William Vickrey, *Microstatics* (New York: Harcourt, Brace and World, 1964), 272–3.
[51] Hayek, *The Road to Serfdom*, 82.
[52] Khlevnyuk et al., *Stalin i Kaganovich. Perepiski*, 273.

the working class, making the working class pay with its currency reserves for his own inadequacy."[53] The "selfish" requests of the Deputy Minister of Heavy Industry (Piatakov, whom Stalin particularly loathed) were especially irritating:

Bolsheviks cannot take this path if they wish to avoid turning our Bolshevik party into a conglomerate of branch groups.... What is better: to press on the government's currency accounts, allowing the economic bureaucracy a quiet life, or to press on the economic bureaucracy and protect the interests of the state?[54]

Stalin berated Mikoian for proposing a grain reserve for his trade ministry: "Why such unlimited faith in the trade ministry and such limited faith in the government?"[55] Stalin's anger at Ordzhonikidze rose to accusations of deceit: "[Ordzhonikidze] is trying to rob state coffers by misusing metals imported for Cheliabinsk construction and selling them. Scoundrel!"[56] More on Ordzhonikidze: "It is bad when we begin to deceive each other."[57] Again, Stalin on Ordzhonikidze's grab of scarce foreign exchange: "The use of these funds must be discussed in the interests of the state as a whole, not only in the interests of [Ordzhonikidze]."[58]

Stalin could count on relatively few allies to fight against narrow interests. Most Politburo members had specific regional or industrial responsibilities. Few, like Molotov, could see the whole picture. Consider Kaganovich's complaint (written long after Stalin had died):

When we worked together in the Central Committee, we [Molotov and Kaganovich] worked in a friendly manner, but when he became Chairman of the Council of People's Commissars and I Minister of Transport we argued.... I demanded more rails, investment, Gosplan did not give and Molotov supported them.[59]

Such quotes show Stalin attempting to restrain interest groups to force actions in favor of encompassing interests. They do not tell the full story, however. The Politburo and Central Committee were torn by conflicting

---

53 Ibid., 72.
54 In both cases, the Ministry of Heavy Industry attempted to reduce the plan targets through imports. The first case involved Ordzhonikidze's attempt to push an increase in steel imports through the Politburo (Rees and Watson, "Politburo and Sovnarkhom," 16). The second case involved the Deputy Minister of Heavy Industry's attempt to force the currency commission to allot additional currency for imports of wagon axles.
55 Khlevnyuk et al., *Stalin i Kaganovich. Perepiski*, 80.
56 Ibid., 101.
57 Ibid., 80.
58 Ibid., 88.
59 F. Chuev, *Tak Govoril*, 61.

interests: with limited investment resources, they had to decide which industries and regions would receive investment. Should national or regional organizations be given priority? How should skilled labor be divided between civilian and military activities? Each distribution of resources had its supporters and opponents within the Politburo and Central Committee. A power-maximizing dictator could play these conflicting interests to solidify political power and might sacrifice economic considerations along the way.

Indeed, Stalin's correspondence with his faithful Kaganovich is full of orders for what could be political payoffs. Kaganovich himself was called to Moscow as a reward for supporting Stalin's policies in Ukraine.[60] When Stalin gave personal orders distributing typewriters and a Ford to deserving parties, it is unclear whether these were political rewards or rewards for good economic performance.[61] During the famine of 1932, Stalin suddenly decided to buy off Ukraine, writing: "We can lose Ukraine!" and stating his intention "to turn Ukraine into a model republic" and "not to spare money for this purpose."[62] These solicitous about-faces could be the action of a stationary bandit, whose economy requires continued support from Ukraine, or it could be that of a selfish dictator, making a political payoff to Ukrainian leaders. The Politburo and Stalin had to referee disputes among republics, such as a conflict between Kazakhstan and Western Siberia over ownership of eight state farms.[63] Molotov had to personally resolve conflicts among regional party bosses over who would get an imported car.

A politician of Stalin's caliber could not have been indifferent to political considerations. In the late 1920s, he had to garner the support of the Central Committee, composed of some forty regional and national leaders to expel the left deviationists (in 1926) and the right deviationists (in 1929 and 1930). He needed the support of the Fifteenth Party Congress, which convened in April 1929, to gain approval for the Great Break-Through. He distributed investment projects to his favored regional party bosses in the late 1920s, presumably to gain their support against the right deviationists.[64] Stalin feared opponents in the Central Committee because membership gave them residual power no matter how discredited.

[60] Khlevnyuk et al., *Stalin i Kaganovich. Perepiski*, 26.
[61] Ibid., 96.
[62] Ibid., 133.
[63] Ibid., 106.
[64] J. R. Harris, *The Great Urals: Regionalism and the Evolution of the Soviet System* (Ithaca, N.Y.: Cornell University Press, 1999), 4.

When his Politburo colleagues proposed to appoint the disgraced former transport minister (Rukhimovich) to a Moscow position, Stalin objected: "These people do not understand that Rukhimovich is more dangerous, because he regrettably is a member of the Central Committee."[65] Stalin devoted inordinate attention to personnel matters; he knew intimately the names, histories, and proclivities of all party leaders. Stalin was uncharacteristically concerned in 1931–32 that his native Georgia was "on the verge of hunger" and of "bread riots." Although he made "feigning hunger" a counter-revolutionary offense in other regions,[66] he charged that the trade minister (Mikoian) had lied to him about Georgian grain storage facilities, and ordered Mikoian "to send grain to western Georgia and personally see to its delivery."[67] Stalin's anger at Mikoian was so intense that Mikoian threatened to resign.[68] Stalin listened attentively to the lobbying of regional and local officials[69] and delayed the formation of separate union-republican ministries in Georgia, Armenia, and Azerbaijan to avoid ruffling the feathers of regional politicians, including his own supporter, L. P. Beria.[70]

The archives show Stalin, willingly or forcibly, being thrust into the role of arbiter or tie breaker in clashes within the ruling elite. Three party leaders nominated themselves to fill the vacant position of transport minister, leaving it up to Stalin to make the final choice.[71] Unresolved issues were turned over to Stalin. Kaganovich to Stalin (August 15, 1931): "We put off the question of grain procurements [provides details]. We decided to delay until the 20th in order to receive your opinion."[72] Stalin's answers would come back in the form of carefully numbered instructions. When Stalin feared that Kaganovich could not handle the matter, he would suggest a delay until he could be present: "I am against the import of steel pipes. If possible, delay the matter until autumn."[73] When Ordzhonikidze disputed a Stalin decision, Stalin sent him an ultimatum: "In the case of your disagreement, I propose a special meeting of the Politburo which requires both our presence."[74]

---

[65] Khlevnyuk et al., *Stalin i Kaganovich. Perepiski*, 126.
[66] Getty and Naumov, *The Road to Terror*, 69.
[67] Khlevnyuk et al., *Stalin i Kaganovich. Perepiski*, 44–51.
[68] Ibid., 52.
[69] Khlevnyuk, "Sovetskaia," 8–14.
[70] Khlevnyuk et al., *Stalin i Kaganovich. Perepiski*, 704.
[71] Ibid., 118.
[72] Ibid., 46.
[73] Ibid., 71.
[74] Ibid., 35.

A dictator–referee is unable to control vested interests. The archives provide little support for the revisionist view of Stalin proposed by historian J. Arch Getty that Stalin's major actions were decided by bottom-up influences of pressure groups.[75] In its most extreme form, this revisionist view suggests that the Great Terror itself was caused by pressure from below, although Stalin was a willing participant.[76] Our reading of the archives yields a quite different picture of Stalin as a master of orchestrating interest groups when their support was needed. He relied primarily on placing his own people in responsible positions, where he actively sought mediocre but brutal loyalists. Stalin clearly played the role of stationary bandit – particularly his willingness to take on his own rent-seeking allies. Stalin had the insight to understand that the greatest rent-seeking danger came from within. Of course, Stalin, as a master politician, distributed "gifts" to ensure political support when it was necessary, but the impression is that he sought to limit such gift-exchange activity.

The Dictator's Curse

We have focused on how a highly centralized political machine was created to execute the Great Break-Through. In reality, significant decisions were few and far between. The daily reality of Soviet political governance was grinding tedium and mental and physical exhaustion. Routine decisions that had previously been rendered at lower levels were pushed ever higher up the administrative hierarchy as centralization of power proceeded. The fact that a small group of political leaders (the Politburo) or one leader (Stalin) was making the key decisions sentenced them to a life of toil, drudgery, and boredom. Hayek and Mises, in their critique of planning, emphasized the information overload on a "Central Planning Board." In practice, this overload fell directly on the shoulders of overworked political leaders.

The daily routine of Stalin and other Politburo members was filled with endless meetings, petitions, consultations, reading of statistical reports, reviewing plans, distributing products, and, for a change of pace, inspection trips. During such trips, party plenipotentiaries met with regional leaders and enterprise managers, pressured regions to deliver grain

---

[75] Getty, *Origins of the Great Purges*.

[76] Valery Lazarev, "Evolution of the Soviet Elite," 1–23, describes an implicit contract between the dictator and potential supporters in which future promotion benefits are offered in return for regime loyalty.

despite local starvation, and met with agitated workers. Such excursions were far from pleasure trips. Party leaders were authorized to impose punishment, at times even the death penalty, for crimes they uncovered.

A letter from Kaganovich to Stalin describes two of his routine days (August 30 and 31, 1931).[77] On August 30, Kaganovich attended a Politburo meeting on the export–import plan; oil transportation; and state purchases of potatoes, vegetables, beef, and chicken. During this meeting, Mikoian lobbied to lower his plan, it was decided to buy an oil tanker, the poor financial results of the third quarter were analyzed, and the foreign minister's granting of an interview without permission of the Politburo was discussed. The next day, Kaganovich first attended a meeting on railroad ties with the main administration of forestry products, in which a ministry official was accused of manipulating figures and a special commission was formed to solve the problem of deficient ties. Kaganovich then arranged a transfer of tractors from the agricultural ministry to the timber industry, subject to Stalin's approval. Later that day, Kaganovich oversaw the formation of a three-person Politburo special commission to prepare directives for regional party authorities on grain shipments to ports with a detailed calendar of shipments. This schedule, broken down into thirty-four grain-producing regions, constituted a major planning task involving intense lobbying from each region.[78] Kaganovich concluded his day with a report to the absent Stalin on these activities plus notes on a speech held by Bukharin that failed to praise the party. This list of activities includes only those events important enough to bring to Stalin's attention. The time in between was spent talking on the telephone, meeting petitioners, and working on other commissions, such as the transportation commission, for which Kaganovich was responsible.

Absences of Politburo members had to be coordinated carefully. Some member always had to be available to deal with official business. Kaganovich to Stalin (October 5, 1931): "I leave today for Cheliabinsk-Novosibirsk. In light of the fact that there will be a meeting of the Commission on Purges during my absence, I ask you to place Comrade Zhdanov on this commission."[79] Absences threatened the completion of work, such as Kuibyshev's (Chairman of Gosplan) complaint of August 10, 1932:

The commission which was selected by the Politburo [to deal with the 1932 plan] effectively fell apart with the departure of Comrades Stalin and Molotov. The

[77] Ibid., 73–5.
[78] Ibid., 691.
[79] Ibid., 510.

TABLE 3.1. *Politburo Meetings, 1930–1936*

	1930	1931	1932	1933	1934	1935	1936
January	6	8	5	2	1	5	0
February	6	6	7	2	1	1	1
March	8	8	6	5	3	1	1
April	7	8	5	3	1	2	1
May	6	7	4	1	2	1	1
June	6	7	10	3	3	3	1
July	7	11	5	2	6	3	1
August	8	6	13	4	2	1	0
September	9	11	6	4	3	1	1
October	7	6	3	2	11	0	1
November	7	7	4	2	2	1	0
December	8	9	4	2	11	1	1

Source: O. V. Khlevnyuk, *Politburo: Mekhanizmy Politicheskoi Vlasti v 1930-e gody* (Moscow: Rosspen, 1996), 288–91.

exchange of opinions in the first meeting of the commission and the failure of the sub commission (representatives of the most important economic institutions did not show up) force me to make the following recommendations [Kuibyshev then requests a series of delays and a reduction of tasks]. I ask you to authorize a leave of absence from August 20 to October 5 on account of my illness. ... In light of the fact that I clearly cannot handle the responsibilities of the chairman of Gosplan, I ask you to free me from this work and give me work that is within my powers (preferably in the regions).[80]

The pressure of work was so intense that such threats of resignation and pleas for lengthy vacations were commonplace.

Of course, Politburo members were obliged to attend Politburo meetings, which usually began at 2 PM and often lasted into the night. Table 3.1 shows the number of Politburo meetings, which declined after 1934 as Stalin assumed more and more power. Politburo members attended an average of six to seven Politburo meetings per month, in addition to their work on the numerous ad hoc commissions that did most of the real decision making. Table 3.2 shows that the Politburo normally considered some three thousand issues on an annual basis. Numerous other participants were invited to Politburo meetings as discussants or reporters. A representative Politburo meeting, for example, on March 5, 1932, had 69 participants and 171 points on its agenda.[81]

[80] Ibid., 710.
[81] Khlevnyuk et al., *Stalinskoe Politburo*, 232.

TABLE 3.2. *Number of Issues Discussed at Politburo Meetings, 1930–1940*

Year	No. of Issues	Year	No. of Issues
1930	2,857	1936	3,367
1931	3,878	1937	3,775
1932	3,704	1938	2,279
1933	3,245	1939	2,973
1934	3,945	1940	3,008
1935	3,282		

Source: O. V. Khlevnyuk, *Politburo: Mekhanizmy Politicheskoi Vlasti v 1930-e gody* (Moscow: Rosspen, 1996), 288–91.

The greatest burden of all, however, fell on Stalin as he took over more and more decision-making responsibility. Virtually every communication from Kaganovich set out various options and then asked Stalin for his opinion (*vashe mnenie?*). Kaganovich's messages were replete with refrains like: "Without you we can't decide,"[82] "Your decision on machinery imports?"[83] "Your decision on whose grain procurement quotas should be cut?"[84] and so on ad nauseum. Stalin was even asked to check poetry and essays for their ideological purity. On rare occasions, even Stalin would explode at this torrent of paper work, demanding that his Politburo associates decide something themselves, such as his tirade of September 13, 1933: "I won't read drafts on educational establishments. The paperwork you are throwing at me is piling up to my chest. Decide yourself and decide soon!"[85] Yet, just a few weeks after this outburst, Stalin berated the Politburo for distributing tractors contrary to his personal instruction. Stalin to Kaganovich: "I insist on my opinion!"[86]

Stalin's correspondence mixes matters of great import with trivia. In one communication, Stalin would order officials shot, the minister of transport fired, issue instructions on foreign exchange, order vast organizational changes, cut back investment, or order major foreign policy initiatives. In another communication (or often the same), Stalin would discuss the production of vegetables near Moscow, whether a particular bridge should have one or two lanes, whether a Soviet author should write books about Soviet industry, whether to give a Ford automobile to

[82] Ibid., 238.
[83] Ibid., 253.
[84] Ibid., 632, 639, 688, 696.
[85] Ibid., 340.
[86] Ibid., 379.

a particular official, the depth of a canal, what products to send to Baku, which articles published in various journals and newspapers included ideological errors, the prices of bread in various regions, the fact that *Pravda* must report on a daily basis automobile and truck production, and the renaming of a square in Moscow. Table 3.3 displays Stalin's appointments calendar of private meetings in his personal office with his most frequent visitors. It shows that he spent the most face-to-face time with his two deputies – Molotov, the head of government, and Kaganovich, his first deputy. In 1933, for example, he met with Kaganovich for 415 hours and with Molotov for 435 hours. During the initial year of the Great Purges, 1937, Stalin spent more time with his purge executor, Ezhov (527 hours) than with his head of government or first deputy. In a typical year – 1934, for example – Stalin spent some one thousand seven hundred hours in private meetings, the equivalent of more than two hundred eight-hour days.[87]

The dictator's curse was that, having the power to decide all, his most trusted colleagues had the incentive to decide as little as possible. Such a strategy minimized their risks. The less they decided, the less blame they would have when things went wrong. The dictator, meanwhile, could not readily distinguish trivial from significant matters and was reduced to being asked to decide everything.

Concluding Thoughts

This chapter describes the creation of the highly centralized machine of force and coercion required to execute the extreme development strategies of the Great Break-Through; in particular, radical primitive accumulation. The five principles of governance – the choice of the command system, the common "general line," the interlocking party–state directorate, the repression of party democracy, and the evolution to one-person dictatorship – likely created the most highly centralized concentration of power ever. An extreme concentration of political power goes hand-in-hand with an administrative-command system. The grinding routine of top-level Soviet officials just described is exactly what one would expect of an administrative-command system. Whereas the market makes the millions of resource-allocation decisions in a market economy, they must be made by harried, overworked, and underinformed officials in a command

---

[87] Stalin's calendar is reproduced in Khlevnyuk, *Politburo*, 290–1.

TABLE 3.3. *Meetings of Politburo Members with Stalin, 1931–1939*

	1931		1932		1933	
	No. of Meetings	Total Hours	No. of Meetings	Total Hours	No. of Meetings	Total Hours
Andreev	18	22.45	15	28.15	18	34.55
Voroshilov	29	56.45	40	89.50	65	150.30
Kaganovich	73	167.00	106	246.30	122	415.20
Kalinin	11	22.40	10	22.30	21	45.00
Kirov	12	22.55	10	28.25	5	9.50
Kosior	8	19.05	5	5.05	11	27.05
Kuybyshev	14	29.45	45	104.55	24	70.35
Mikoian	16	36.00	34	81.25	40	82.20
Molotov	97	126.15	117	291.45	140	435.15
Ordzhonikidze	24	45.15	47	52.20	35	100.50
Petrovskiy	–	–	–	–	–	–
Postyshev	49	109.25	56	136.40	13	35.05
Rudzutak	2	8.15	14	36.15	6	23.20
Chubar'	1	0.30	–	–	–	–

	1934		1935		1936	
	No. of Meetings	Total Hours	No. of Meetings	Total Hours	No. of Meetings	Total Hours
Andreev	28	76.05	24	61.20	22	58.45
Voroshilov	79	166.30	70	198.15	76	292.15
Zhdanov	86	278.30	21	58.45	14	32.00
Ezhov	17	23.40	32	88.15	31	75.30
Kaganovich	103	323.10	92	261.20	57	161.55
Kalinin	31	70.40	35	76.00	18	42.10
Kirov	18	62.15	Assassinated on 12/1/34			
Kosior	10	22.50	8	23.55	6	13.05
Kuybyshev	49	152.30	5	15.05	Died 1/25/35	
Mikoian	43	104.35	30	71.15	31	70.00
Molotov	97	334.45	101	315.35	109	267.40
Ordzhonikidze	59	186.50	77	218.00	67	176.35
Petrovskiy	1	1.45	–	–	–	–
Postyshev	8	19.35	12	28.40	1	2.30
Rudzutak	9	42.15	4	14.25	2	6.00
Chubar'	18	58.15	23	62.25	28	64.05
Eykhe	4	3.45	3	6.40	2	4.20
Yagoda	53	73.15	36	56.25	20	32.10

(continued)

TABLE 3.3. *(continued)*

	1937		1938		1939	
	No. of Meetings	Total Hours	No. of Meetings	Total Hours	No. of Meetings	Total Hours
Andreev	53	135.45	33	68.35	34	80.20
Beria	2	1.30	32	45.25	108	184.45
Voroshilov	142	438.35	99	266.00	181	509.40
Zhdanov	61	146.25	82	203.55	93	226.05
Ezhov	174	527.55	104	305.50 Not reelected in 1939		
Kaganovich	128	406.10	74	200.45	90	240.30
Kalinin	20	32.30	11	20.15	9	15.45
Kosior	19	33.05	Arrested in 1938			
Malenkov	62	72.35	74	96.15	50	72.15
Mikoian	57	130.40	48	98.10	142	301.10
Molotov	213	601.20	170	470.25	274	659.30
Ordzhonikidze	22	71.55	Committed suicide 2/37			
Petrovskiy	–	–	3	2.50 Not reelected in 1939		
Postyshev	8	11.20	Expelled from Politburo on 1/14/38			
Khruschev	15	23.20	18	43.45	24	70.40
Chubar'	31	74.30	6	10.45 Expelled from Politburo on 1/14/38		
Eykhe	3	6.10	2	2.40 Arrested on 6/16/38		

Source: O. V. Khlevnyuk, *Politburo: Mekhanizmy Politicheskoi Vlasti v 1930-e gody* (Moscow: Rosspen, 1996), 288–91.

economy. Without extreme concentration of power and a general line, the administrative decisions made by tens, hundreds, or thousands of officials would be disjointed. There must be a semblance of order to prevent chaos. The decision to merge the government and party into an interlocking directorate and the clear subordination of government agencies to party agencies represent a clear-cut rejection of scientific planning. The technical experts were located in government agencies, such as the planning agency. The rejection of party democracy clearly aided the concentration of power. The disobedience of local party officials to orders to stop the persecution of industrial managers and experts was an alarming challenge to central authority. But the rejection of party democracy was more important in confirming the credentials of the center to act on behalf of the working class. Although local party officials were closer to actual production and working conditions and individual party members worked in real factories and institutions, it was the Politburo or Stalin, not they, who "represented the masses."

The transformation of this machine of political power from one directed by a small group of leaders (the Politburo) to one directed by one person, Stalin, may have had a logic of its own. Insofar as the party leadership itself was made up of industrial and regional lobbyists, only a single, strong leader could withstand the pressure to create a dictator–referee system. The records show that Stalin understood that the most significant danger from vested interests came from within the ruling elite, and he played the role of stationary bandit in resisting these pressures. If a one-person dictator was indeed required to prevent the system from collapsing into the confusion of squabbling vested interests, we must ask why the Soviet Union did not again revert to a one-person dictatorship after Stalin's death. One of Stalin's traditions was indeed passed on to later generations of Soviet regimes – the unquestioned decision-making power of the General Secretary. After Stalin, the decisions of the General Secretary were not to be challenged except by removal, such as the ouster of Khrushchev in 1964. This tradition carried through to Gorbachev, whose perestroika reform ideas were opposed by the party's top leadership, who went along following the tradition that the General Secretary has the final say.[88]

With the acceptance of the development strategy of primitive accumulation and the power to impose the strategy in place, we turn in the next chapter to investment.

---

[88] Ellman and Kontorovich, *Destruction*, N.Y., chapter 2.

4

Investment, Wages, and Fairness

"The USSR is a generous country. It sends grain abroad, but is itself hungry."
"Let those compete who are full."
"We can't do the five-year plan in four years. It should not be completed on the bones of workers."
"Welcome the Five-Year Plan with empty stomachs."
                    (Graffiti on factory walls in 1930)[1]

The Soviet dictator – the Politburo or (later) Stalin alone – had to define its goals, what economists call its "objective function." An objective function specifies the goals of a person or organization (e.g., an enterprise) along with the relative weights (importance) attached to each goal. Abram Bergson used the term *planners' preferences* as a convenient shorthand for the Soviet dictator's objective function, be it the objectives of the Stalin dictatorship or of the collective postwar leadership.[2] Planners' preferences refers to the fact that the administrative-command economy was directed by the general party line – unlike market economies that are ultimately directed by consumer sovereignty.[3]

Clearly, the Politburo had multiple objectives in the 1930s, but, despite rumors of ideological splits, there was indeed a basic consensus for a secure power base, maximum economic growth, investment in heavy industry, and transferring resources out of the countryside.[4] After embarking

[1] Elena Osokina, *Za Fasadom Stalinskogo Izobiliia* (Moscow: Rosspen, 1998), 81–2.
[2] Abram Bergson, *The Economics of Soviet Planning* (New Haven, Conn.: Yale University Press, 1964), 338–40, 350–2.
[3] Bergson, *The Real National Income*, 110.
[4] O. Khlevnyuk, *Politburo*, 70–2; Getty and Naumov, *The Road to Terror*, 137.

on the Great Break-Through, there was no turning back. The fate of Stalin and his Politburo team hinged on its success. Stalin and his compatriots truly believed their own propaganda: they were surrounded by antisocialist wreckers, antagonistic kulaks, and domestic and foreign enemies; immediate industrialization was required for survival. "One of the big surprises of these documents [the archives] is that the Stalinists said the same things to each other behind closed doors that they said to the public."[5] Everywhere they saw "counter-revolutionaries sitting in comfort," cattle-like local officials who do not see "kulaks and White Guards sitting in the collective farms," or "White Guards preparing terror actions."[6]

In carrying out its leading role, it was the job of the party to select the optimal economic policies for the country. The party had a choice of two basic instruments: It could set optimal physical output targets for products such as steel, coal, and machinery, usually called "control figures," an approach discussed in the next chapter. Alternatively, it could select the optimal amount of investment and its distribution among economic branches. In theory, the two were intertwined. The stereotype of the administrative-command economy is that the investment plan was derived from the output plan. The leaders supposedly first determined output and then calculated the investment required to produce this output.

Of the two approaches, investment optimization was more firmly grounded in ideology. Marx's law of expanded reproduction clearly stated that growth depends on capital formation. Preobrazhensky proposed to extract investment surpluses from agriculture, and a coercive system of governance was put in place to force surpluses from the peasantry. The core Politburo strategy for the 1930s was massive investments – the hydroelectric dams, the huge automobile and tractor works, the blast furnaces, the canals, and the machinery complexes – of the first two five-year plans. From a practical point of view, it was easier to plan investment than physical outputs. The investment plan was centralized in the state budget's "expenditures on the national economy" and was broken down by actual agency recipients. The investment budget was in rubles, not in the intractable tons or meters in which control figures were measured. Table 4.1 relates the second five-year (1933–37) investment plan as an illustration of the outcome of investment planning.

[5] Getty and Naumov, *The Road to Terror*, 22.
[6] Ibid., 311.

TABLE 4.1. *Second Five-Year Plan Investment Goals, 1933–1937, by Commissariat (Million Rubles, 1933 Plan Prices)*

Commissariat	1933 (1)	1934 (2)	1935 (3)	1936 (4)	1937 (5)
1. National economy, total socialist sector	17,989	25,111	27,991	30,309	32,000
2. Commissariat of Heavy Industry	7,700	9,290	9,880	10,060	9,830
3. Electric power	700	990	1,025	1,275	1,360
4. Coal	650	667	700	725	758
5. Petroleum	545	770	1,000	1,175	1,210
6. Ore mining	46	57	69	83	95
7. Ferrous metals	1,665	1,825	2,025	2,000	1,825
8. Nonferrous metals	690	705	800	800	796
9. Machine-building	1,280	1,495	1,800	1,750	1,735
10. Chemical and coke-chemical	800	1,049	1,050	940	931
11. Commissariat of Light Industry	580	1,031	2,605	2,900	2,084
12. Commissariat of Timber Industry	414	571	700	865	900
13. Commissariat of Food Supply	780	997	1,150	1,200	1,213
14. Commissariat of Foreign Trade	90	116	102	90	77
15. Commissariat of Agriculture	1,340	1,878	2,165	2,555	2,822
16. Commissariat of State Farms	650	747	835	865	893
17. Commissariat of Transportation	2,165	3,707	4,016	4,190	4,622
18. Commissariat of Water Transport	506	962	886	860	1,031
19. *Glavk* for Highways	375	542	676	1,020	1,387

20. *Glavk* for Civil Aviation	115	193	251	390	551
21. Commissariat of Communications	206	349	350	375	420
22. *Tsentrosoiuz*	265	293	297	303	352
23. Industrial Cooperatives	128	139	155	190	238
24. Housing Cooperatives	86	111	150	200	259
25. Housing fund of executive committees	140	182	220	290	362
26. Communal construction in cities (included subway)	725	1,323	1,450	1,600	1,802
27. Education	240	458	600	781	1,071
28. Public health	238	349	550	760	1,178
29. Committee for Procurements of Council of People's Commissars	175	315	180	150	120
30. *Glavk* for Photography and Films	35	74	138	200	228
31. *Glavk* for Northern Sea Route	26	29	50	65	80
32. Other central agencies	1,010	1,455	585	400	480

Source: Vtoroi Piatiletnii Plan Razvitia Narodnogo Khoziaistva SSSR (1933–1937), cited in *Stalinist Planning for Economic Growth, 1933–1952* by Eugene Zaleski. Copyright © 1980 by the University of North Carolina Press. Used by permission of the publisher.

With extreme centralization of power, Stalin and his allies must have entered the period of five-year plans with some confidence. They had the coercive power to force surpluses from agriculture. They had removed the naysayers from power, and they could now manage an economy that they supposed had no limits. They could double or triple the capital stock in a few years with determination, hard work, and ideological commitment.

The Politics of Investment

Limits or not, the distribution of investment resources was heatedly contested. The Urals, Siberia, and the Caucasus wanted to be centers of heavy industry. Ukraine and Russia wanted to preserve their dominance. A regional leader promoted his investment proposals with the following fervor: "There is only one solution – to push forward and overcome these difficulties at any cost. . . . If anyone announces that we need to slow down a bit because his head is spinning, then we'll have to replace him with someone whose head is not spinning."[7] Stalin's Great Break-Through was particularly appealing to regional leaders because it promised investment for everyone.

In the final power struggle, the right deviationists stood for moderation, equilibrium, and balanced growth, whereas Stalin and his allies increasingly advocated massive investment programs. Regional leaders made up the single largest bloc in the Central Committee, and their voice was particularly important when the Politburo itself was divided.[8] The Urals wanted massive new engineering complexes (e.g., Uralmash); the Far East wanted new silver and gold mining plants; Uzbekistan wanted irrigation projects; the Central Black Earth Region wanted metallurgical plants and tractor factories. Regional lobbyists were turned down by Rykov and Gosplan in the late NEP period in the name of responsibility and balance. Gosplan's NEP leadership accused irresponsible regions of "self-serving projections based on local interest, lack of objectivity, and inexact calculations that undermine the very foundations of planning."[9]

Stalin's embrace of heroic industrialization provided an appealing contrast. All regional plans could be funded. There should be no limits. In mid-1929, the OGPU began receiving denunciations of state officials from the

---

[7] Harris, *The Great Urals*, 94.
[8] Ibid., 4–6.
[9] Ibid., 95.

regions, and in Central Committee meetings, regional leaders denounced the right wing for "disorganizing the economy and slowing growth."[10] By the November 1929 Central Committee plenum, the right-wing opposition was in full retreat, and the most ambitious variant of the first five-year plan received enthusiastic acceptance. In effect, Stalin and his allies practiced communist pork-barrel politics to win over regional leaders. Notably, it was the head of the Urals party committee (a Comrade Kabakov) who formally led the ouster of one of the leading right opposition figures (M. Tomsky). The protocol of the Sixteenth Congress of the Central Committee held on July 13, 1930, records the prearranged sacking of Tomsky (via non-reelection) from the Politburo:[11]

Kalinin: The election of the executive organs of the Central Committee is the first order of business. Are there any proposals?

Kabakov: I propose ten persons for the Politburo.

Kalinin: Is there a desire to discuss the number of members of the Politburo? (Voices: Accept.) No? Those in favor of a ten-person Politburo raise their hands. Opposed? Measure passes.

Kabakov: For Politburo members: Stalin, Kalinin, Rudzutak, Kuibyshev, Voroshilov, Rykov, Kaganovich, Kosior, Kirov [no mention of Tomsky].

Kalinin: How do we propose to vote, separately or all at once (Voices: At once.) We'll vote *en bloc*. (Laughter.) (Voroshilov: Explain what this means?) Because Comrade Voroshilov asks for an explanation, I take it that not everyone understands what *en bloc* means. It means together, as a whole. Those who are for the proposal raise their hands. Against? The proposal is upheld. Accepted unanimously.

Seconds later, Kalinin asks Kabakov for his nomination for the post of General Secretary (Stalin's position):

Kabakov: General Secretary, Comrade Stalin. (Voices: Of course.)

The "heroic" investment plans that gained the support of regional leaders were soon proven to have their own limits. Regional and industrial leaders still had to fight among themselves for investment; some national leaders argued for moderation, much as the discredited right deviationists had done only a few years earlier. The seesaw battles can be seen in the dramatic changes in the investment budget from one plan variant to the next, often separated by a week or even a day or two. Table 4.2 shows the ebb and flow of the 1935 and 1936 investment plans, with figures varying from a low of 18 billion rubles to a high of 27.1 billion rubles for 1935, and an even more extreme variation (from a low of 17 billion rubles to a

[10] Ibid., 96–8.
[11] Khlevnyuk et al., *Stalinskoe Politbiuro*, 94–5.

TABLE 4.2. *Alternate Investment Plan Drafts, 1935 and 1936 (Million Rubles)*

Plan Name	Amount
Five-year plan target 35	22,285
Claims of Gosplan sectors 35	33,768
Gosplan ceiling 25	26,537
Gosplan second ceiling 35	23,500
Politburo, July 1934	18,000
1935 plan, end of 1934	21,190
1935 actual plan	27,157
1936 plan (7.19.35)	17,700
1936 plan (7.21.35)	19,000
1936 plan (7.26.35)	22,000
1936 plan (7.28.35)	27,341
1936 plan (5.29.36)	35,053

Source: R. W. Davies, "Why Was There a Soviet Investment Cycle in 1933–37?", University of Warwick Summer Workshop, July 16, 1999, available as PERSA Working Paper No. 16 (Version 17, December 2001), 5.

high of more than 35 billion rubles) for 1936. Rejections of appeals for more investment were met with dismay, such as Ordzhonikidze's tirade when his investment budget was cut:

"Comrade Sergo [Ordzhonikidze] unexpectedly resurrected the issue in a confrontational manner. I'll not relate the full discussion, but he said: 'You want to play the role of government bureaucrat, but when these factories fall apart, I will have to answer, not those of you who are conducting here such serious discussions.' Why must Sergo create such an atmosphere when he knows we cannot satisfy all requests, that we must be objective? It is difficult for us without you [Comrade Stalin] because we must restrain ourselves. He [Ordzhonikidze] even made the amusing accusation that I shouted at him and that he would not tolerate this.... It is not even worthwhile to deny this ridiculous statement because he can out-shout anyone." [12]

Investment Maximization?

We posit a simple optimization rule: Subject to resource and technology constraints, the goal is to maximize real investment each year. Marx's expanded reproduction and Preobrazhensky's primitive accumulation

---
[12] Kaganovich to Stalin, August 20, 1931, in Khlevnyuk et al., *Stalin i Kaganovich. Perepiski,* 55.

support such a simple resource allocation strategy: Maximize investment in each year, leaving "enough" consumption as the residual.[13] The first mathematical growth model formulated by a Russian economist, P. A. Feldman, supported an investment-maximizing strategy: The more plowed into the investment goods sector, the higher the growth rate.[14] The only clear constraint on the investment-at-any-cost strategy is that if not enough is left over for consumption, a weak or unmotivated labor force could depress growth. Indeed, the doubling of the investment rate between 1928 and 1937 (from 13 to 26 percent)[15] seems to confirm the pursuit of a singular "investment first" strategy.[16]

Surprisingly, the expectation of a pattern of steady growth of investment accompanied by fluctuations in the buffer-sector consumption is not supported by the empirical evidence: The most noted Soviet scholar on Soviet growth, A. L. Vainshtein, found that investment fluctuations were four times as large as fluctuations in consumption,[17] a finding confirmed by others.[18] Moreover, consumption did not appear to act as a buffer for investment.[19] Investment cycles, beginning in the early 1930s, provide the most significant contradiction of the expectation of steady and rapid growth of investment.[20] This contradictory evidence calls for a reasonable explanation of why a leadership, bent on massive capital accumulation, appeared to waiver, at times preferring consumption over investment.

Investment, Consumption, and Effort: A Model. Why would a Politburo – dedicated to industrial capital accumulation, convinced that economic limits did not apply to them, and with coercive power – trade off investment for consumption in the very process of building the industrial

[13] Erlich, *The Soviet Industrialization Debate,* 147–8.
[14] Evsey Domar, "A Soviet Model of Growth," in *Essays in the Theory of Economic Growth* (New York: Oxford University Press, 1957), 223–61.
[15] Bergson, *The Real National Income,* 217, 237.
[16] Paul Gregory and Robert Stuart, *Soviet Economic Structure and Performance,* 4th ed. (New York: Harper & Row, 1990), chapter 7.
[17] A. L. Vainshtein, "Dinamika Narodnogo Dokhoda i Ego Osnovnykh Komponentov," *Ekonomicheskie i Matematicheskie Metody* 3, no. 1 (January–February 1967), 21.
[18] Volkhart Vincentz, "Wachstumsschwankungen der Sowjetischen Wirtschaft: Ausmass, Auswirkungen, and Urasachen," *Bericht des Bundesinstututs fuer Ostwissenschaftliche und Internationale Studien,* no. 15 (March 1979), 9.
[19] Wolfram Schrettl, "On the Volume of Soviet Investment and Some Implications," *Forschungsbericht* (1974).
[20] Mark Harrison, "National Income," in *The Economic Transformation of the Soviet Union, 1913–1945,* eds. R. W. Davies, Mark Harrison, and S. G. Wheatcroft (Cambridge: Cambridge University Press, 1994), 48–53.

capital stock that would guarantee its future? Surely, any reduction of capital investment must have been a bitter pill to swallow. Construction would have to be cancelled and factory completions delayed. Regional and industrial leaders would be outraged. There was no pressure from an organized consumer lobby to raise living standards. Labor unions were unofficial arms of the state. Stalin lacked any instincts for compassion and concern for the working class. If investments were to be sacrificed for consumption, the Politburo had to have a strong justification.

Worker living standards clearly affect production. If they are below subsistence, the labor force shrinks due to excess mortality. There is also a breaking-point wage, although above subsistence, at which workers strike. A rational Politburo would, therefore, have maximized investment subject to avoidance of these two extreme cases. But the Politburo had to contend with another issue: work effort. Upon reflection, it is clear that worker effort would be a linchpin in the administrative-command economy. Coercive work requirements and severe punishment for parasitism could ensure that virtually all able-bodied adults had jobs in the labor force. Hence, the supply of labor would be basically fixed, as remaining outside the labor force ceased to be an option. With guaranteed job rights, shirkers and lazy workers could not even be fired,[21] and early hopes of a new Socialist man were rather quickly dashed. In such a setting, output growth would depend primarily on labor effort. In the long run, economic growth would depend on physical and human capital accumulation, but if the Politburo wanted more output right away, it could only be brought about by more effort.

The standard managerial, psychological, economic, and sociological literatures teach that work effort depends on workers feeling they are receiving a fair wage.[22] If they receive less, they reduce their effort. If they receive too small a fraction of the fair wage, they strike. The positive link between effort and the fairness of wages appears to be fairly universal, and it would apply to the administrative-command economy, except in

[21] David Granick, *Job Rights in the Soviet Union: Their Consequences* (Cambridge: Cambridge University Press, 1987): 300–9.

[22] This literature is summarized in George Akerlof and Janet Yellen, "The Fair Wage–Effort Hypothesis and Unemployment," *Quarterly Journal of Economics* 105, no. 2 (May 1990), 256–68; George Akerlof, "Gift Exchange and Efficiency Wages: Four Views," *American Economic Review* 74, no. 2 (May 1984), 78–83; Lawrence Katz, "Efficiency Wages Theories: A Partial Evolution," in *NBER Macroeconomics Annual 1986*, ed. Stanley Fisher (Cambridge, Mass.: MIT Press, 1986), 235–75. Peter Howitt, "Looking Inside the Labor Market: A Review Article," *Journal of Economic Literature* 40, no. 1 (March 2002), 125–38.

the unlikely case of the emergence of a new "socialist" way of thinking about work.

We apply fair-wage theory to the administrative-command economy using a simple model that requires some notation and graphs. We attempt to keep our explanation as simple as possible for nontechnical readers. The fair wage–effort model was first formulated by Nobel laureate, George Akerloff, who asserts that the principle "if people do not get what they deserve, they get even" has been universally demonstrated in experiments, social exchange theory, and the personnel management literature. In the Akerloff model, workers supply their "full" labor effort at the fair wage. If they receive less than the fair wage, they reduce their effort. Below a critical minimum, they supply no effort. Effort (e) is, therefore, a positive function of the ratio of the actual wage (w) to the fair wage (a):

$$e = f(w/a)$$

If w is less than the fair wage, effort will be less than full. If $w = a$, workers receive the fair wage, and they supply full effort. If w exceeds a (if workers are overpaid), they may or may not increase their effort above their full effort.[23] If workers receive w' (the "strike" wage), they supply no effort.

The fair-wage model has been applied to enterprises or to single industries in market economies. We apply it here to the entire administrative-command economy, where the physical supply of labor is administratively fixed and effort determines the volume of output.[24] This application allows us to relate the real output of the economy to the volume of effort and ultimately to the volume of consumption. The ideas behind this model are not complex and could easily have been understood by an average member of the Politburo and by Stalin himself.

Our Soviet fair-wage–effort model considers an administrative-command economy, with a fixed quantitative supply of labor that produces one good (Q) that can be used either for investment (I) or consumption (C). C is what is left over after I ($C = Q - I$). Because the

---

[23] Akerloff and Yellen relate studies that show that overpayment does not bring about an increase in effort; see Akerloff and Yellen, "The Fair Wage–Effort Hypothesis," 258.

[24] These matters were first explored in a model of Wolfram Schrettl, which is integrated in this context with the fair-wage–effort model. See Wolfram Schrettl, "Anspruchsdenken, Leistungsbereitschaft, and Wirtschaftzyklen," in *Wachstumsverlangsamung und Konjunkturzyklen in Underschiedlichen Wirtschaftssystemen*, ed. Armin Bohnert et al., (Berlin: Duncker & Humblot: 1984), 153–1; Wolfram Schrettl, "Konsum und Arbeitsproduktivitat," *Beck'sche Schwarze Reihe, Band 271* (Munich: C. H. Beck, 1984), 42–65.

supply of labor is fixed, Q, I, and C also approximate per-worker output (labor productivity), per-worker investment, and per-worker consumption.[25] Per-worker consumption is nothing more than the average real wage. The dictator can either choose C and then accept the resulting I or, alternatively, choose I and accept the resulting C. Once he has chosen one, he has chosen the other.

Figure 4.1 shows how the model works. Panel A shows that, with a fixed supply of labor, output (Q) depends on effort (e). Panel B shows that e depends on the "wage bill" – the production of consumer goods (c). As more consumer goods are produced, e increases up to the fair-wage point a ($w = a$), where workers are receiving enough c to earn the fair wage. Increases in consumption beyond this point do not call forth more effort and production in this variant.[26] Panel C combines the first two figures to relate Q to c. Up to the fair-wage point (a), more consumption will call forth more output. Beyond a, further increases in consumption will not call forth more output. The 45-degree reference line in Panel C reveals the amount of investment at each level of production and consumption. Where the output line and reference line intersect (x), all output is devoted to consumption. To the left of this intersection, (positive) investment is the *horizontal* distance between the reference line and the output line. At a, investment equals x-a. The maximum investment is located to the left of the fair wage, at c^*, where investment is the horizontal distance b-c^*. At the strike wage (w'), there is no output, consumption, or investment. Panel D plots these vertical distances: the I curve. It shows an inverted U-shaped curve, with investment reaching a maximum, I^*, at c^*. At other consumption levels, such as a, I is not maximized.

A dictator bent on maximizing I would, therefore, choose the "optimal" level of consumption (c^*), which yields I^* but is below the fair wage, a. This choice is optimal because it yields the maximum investment possible in that period. Note that the dictator is sacrificing current output in making this choice. If he had chosen a, more Q would have been produced ($Q(a) > Q^*$). Nevertheless, the dictator's goal is to achieve the maximum investment in each period. According to the dictator's objective function, the greater investment compensates for the current sacrifice of consumption, effort, and output.

---

[25] This is a useful simplifying assumption. It applies less well to per-capita values than to per-worker values because of the rise in the labor force participation rate in the 1930s.

[26] Hence, we draw the production curves as horizontal after the fair wage, but this result is not essential to our basic findings.

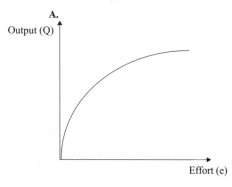

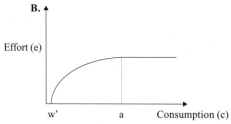

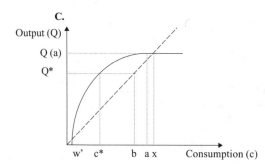

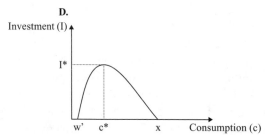

FIGURE 4.1. Choice of maximum investment.

A.

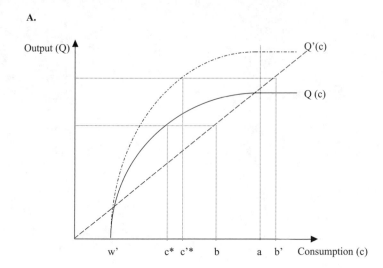

B.

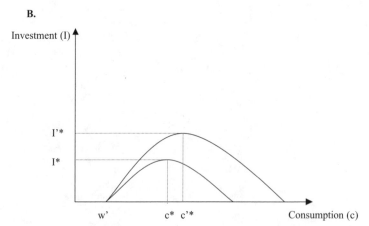

FIGURE 4.2. Dynamics of an increase in capital through investment.

The dictator must make this choice in every period. Thus, the model has two dynamic features: The amount of *I* chosen today affects tomorrow's capital stock. *Ceteris paribus* more *I* today means more capital stock tomorrow.[27] Figure 4.2, Panel A, shows the effect of more investment today as an upward shift of the production curve *Q* tomorrow. Panel B shows the corresponding shift upward and to the right of the U-shaped *I* curve. The higher today's *I*, the higher tomorrow's capital stock, which is the

---

[27] Tomorrow's *K* equals today's *K*, plus *I*, minus depreciation.

basic justification for investment maximization. If the capital-formation effect were the only dynamic feature of the model, everyone eventually wins from investment maximization. In the next period, the investment-maximizing dictator gets a higher investment and simultaneously gives workers more consumption! Panels A and B show that both optimal consumption and optimal investment increase as a consequence of capital formation (from c^* to c'^* and from I^* to I'^*). In fact, the Politburo was expecting enormous increases in productive capacity as modern technology was installed in the backward Soviet Union in the early 1930s.

The second dynamic feature is the fair wage itself. *If workers decide to supply less effort at the initial fair wage, they have raised their perception of the fair wage.* An increase in the fair wage occurs whenever workers demand more consumption to produce the same volume of output as before. Figure 4.3, Panel A, shows an increase in the fair wage (from *a* to *a'*) and the rightward shift in the output curve resulting from the associated reduction in effort. Panel B shows the downward shift (and to the right) of the inverted U-shaped investment curve. In effect, workers have become more dissatisfied and punish the dictator by reducing effort. Hence, any increase in the fair wage should alarm the dictator. A higher fair wage forces the investment-maximizing dictator to increase c and reduce I *ceteris paribus* because of the loss of output and effort. In Panels A and B of Figure 4.3, consumption rises from c^* to c'^* and maximum investment falls as a consequence of the increase in the fair wage. This reduction in investment does not mean that the dictator has become soft on workers or has changed priorities. The dictator remains consistent in his goal of maximizing investment in each period. The loss of effort and output, however, have left him with no choice but to reduce investment and to increase consumption.

The more complete dynamics of this model have been worked out elsewhere and are beyond the scope of this book.[28] What they suggest, intuitively, is that a dictator, bent on maximizing investment in each period, exhibits unexpected behavior. Depending on the effects of investment and changes in the fair wage, a dictator maximizing investment in each period could increase investment and reduce consumption, increase both investment and consumption, increase consumption and reduce investment, or even reduce both consumption and investment. Declining investment would result when workers demand a higher fair wage. Although the model and its dynamics may appear complicated, its

[28] Wolfram Schrettl and Paul Gregory, "Fair Wages and Unfair Dictators," German Institute for Economic Research (DIW), working manuscript, Summer 2002.

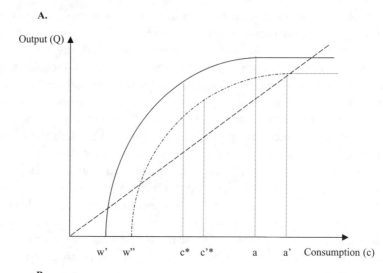

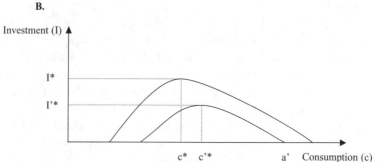

FIGURE 4.3. Dynamics of an increase in the fair wage.

intuition would have been apparent, particularly to Politburo leaders who worried constantly about peasant and worker sentiment and unrest.

The most appealing feature of the model is that it argues that a dictator with stable planners' preferences would modulate between optimistic increases in investment and relative neglect of consumption and cutbacks of investment at the expense of consumption. The model answers the puzzled R. W. Davies' query about "major shifts in [investment] policy which do not appear to be imposed by objective constraints or some kind of systematic necessity.... The evidence from policy makes this appear as *a voluntary decision* [author's italics] by the leadership – indeed, by Stalin himself."[29] At a minimum, it shows that the Politburo faced

[29] R. W. Davies, "Why Was There a Soviet Investment Cycle in 1933–37?" (Paper presented at summer Workshop–Information and Decision Making in the Soviet Economic

rather complicated choices that would not automatically yield the expected investment-at-any cost strategy.

The model provides an alternative interpretation of cutbacks in investment to a change in dictatorial preferences, where the dictator chooses to give workers more consumption at the expense of investment (a "voluntary" movement from c^* to a in Figure 4.1). In the fair-wage model, the dictator, confronted with a higher fair wage, must maximize investment at a lower investment and an increased consumption (the movements from c^* to c'^* and from I^* to I'^* in Figure 4.3, Panels A and B).

To make the correct dynamic choices, the dictator must be able to anticipate the effects of investment on economywide productivity and on worker morale. Substantial increases in investment would be called for when the productivity effect would be substantial. Reduced investment would be called for when the productivity effect is small but worker dissatisfaction would be increased.

Stylized Facts: The Investment Cycle. Although planners initially attempted to compile physical investment balances, the planning of investment in "completely disgraceful"[30] rubles was an established feature by the summer of 1931. Investment limits in rubles were more important than any physical balance.[31] Politburo discussions of investment were in rubles, although there was endless discussion of specific projects. Nominal investment figures were linked with cost-reduction targets in investment planning; so, in a sense, the Politburo pretended to plan real investment, but cost-reduction targets were largely ignored. Five-year investment plans were stated in constant prices, such as those of 1926/1927 or of 1932, but the operational annual investment plans were in nominal rubles. The archives do not yield official estimates of investment in constant prices; the figures we cite, therefore, are Western recalculations. It is likely that planners themselves had only a vague idea of real investment. The amount of investment finance could differ from the investment plan because the plan was in constant prices whereas investment finance was in current prices.

Bureaucracy, University of Warwick, July 16, 1999). Also available as PERSA Working Paper no. 16 (December 2001) at www.Soviet–archives–research.co.uk., Warwick, England.

[30] Davies, *Crisis and Progress*, 66.

[31] Physical equipment balances were indeed prepared; in 1934, Gosplan drew up 111 balances and 156 in 1938, but there were virtually no balances prepared for the operational quarterly plans. Eugene Zaleski, *Stalinist Planning for Economic Growth 1933–1952*, (Chapel Hill: University of North Caroline Press, 1980), 98.

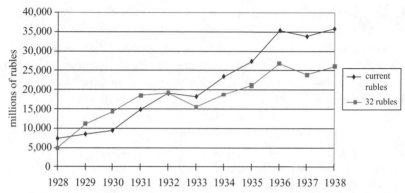

FIGURE 4.4. Nominal and real (1932 prices) investment, USSR, 1928–1938.
Source: R. W. Davies, "Why Was There an Investment Cycle in 1933–37?"; price
deflators are from Eugene Zaleski, *Stalinist Planning for Economic Growth 1933–
1952,* 660–2; H. Hunter and J. Szyrmer, *Faulty Foundations: Soviet Economic
Policies, 1928–1940,* 48.

Figure 4.4 shows nominal and recalculated real investment for the period 1928 to 1938. Contrary to the expected rapid and steady growth of
investment, both the nominal and real figures show investment cycles –
periods of rapid growth in investment followed by retreats to slower growing or even declining investment.[32] There were even two years of declining
real and nominal investment (1933 and 1937). In the first investment cycle, nominal investment increased rapidly from 1928 to 1932, followed
by an absolute decline in 1933. Investment remained cautious from 1934
to the beginning of 1935, when a second upswing began. Investment rose
rapidly in 1935 and 1936 but then declined again in 1937.[33] These stylized facts do not fit the image of a Politburo dedicated to investment at
any cost, using consumption as a buffer for bad times.

The Dictator and the Fair-Wage Model

The fair wage is psychologically determined and nonquantifiable; hence,
we cannot produce a time series chart of fair wages for the period 1929
to 1938. Rather, we have the stylized facts of the investment cycles of the
1930s. The archives, however, allow us to examine Politburo decisions

---

[32] Davies cites work by Zaleski, *Stalinist Planning* 506–7, that shows investment cycles in
the Soviet Union during this early period.
[33] We use official Soviet estimates for real investment in 1932 prices cited in Zaleski, *Stalinist
Planning,* 258, extrapolated to 1940 using data provided by Hunter and Szyrmer, *Faulty
Foundations,* 41.

to see if they are those expected from an investment-maximizing dictator, concerned about balancing investment and worker morale. The fair-wage model predicts that the dictator should try to gauge worker sentiment to detect changes in the fair wage, take whatever steps possible to restrain increases in fair wages, and base investment plans on the real investment capacity of the economy, which changed according to past investment and fair wages.

The pace of capital accumulation was a key point of contention during the party debate in the mid-1920s. When Stalin and his allies gained control of the Politburo in 1929, they justified their massive investment program on the grounds that they had inherited an economy that had been underinvesting (an "investment hunger") and overconsuming.[34] In particular, the peasant population had been overconsuming given changes in land ownership and the reduction in the tax burden. Thus, the literature has already established that Stalin and his crew felt that they had inherited an economy located near the fair wage in Figure 4.1, Panels C and D. In effect, the economy was consuming too much and investing too little. After gaining control of decision making in mid-1929, they were free to move from point a to c^*. As workers saw themselves receiving less than the fair wage, they could punish the dictator by withholding effort, unless the dictator could convince them to accept a lower fair wage.

Our first step is to test whether the dictator had an intuitive understanding of the fair-wage model. Did the Politburo and Stalin use the link between effort and wages as an integral part of their decision making? The archives provide numerous expressions of Stalin's and the Politburo's belief in a strong link between consumption and work effort. Consider Stalin's rhetorical question to Molotov (in a letter dated September 1930) on the decline in production and the high turnover of industrial workers: "Could it be that this is because of poor consumption supplies? Is it true that they were better provisioned last year?"[35] When oil production was threatened, the Politburo dispatched the following telegram to Baku (August 26, 1933):

In order to improve the supply conditions of your workers, consistent with your request, we are sending for this quarter: 764 tons of meat, 56 tons of vegetable oil [follows a long list of products]. We have satisfied your request to bring the provisioning of oil workers to the level of Moscow and Leningrad.[36]

---

[34] Erlich, *The Soviet Industrialization Debate*, 56–8.
[35] Cited in Osokina, *Za Fasadom*, 71.
[36] Khlevnyuk et al., *Stalin i Kaganovich. Perepiski*, 312.

When Stalin decided to stimulate grain, cotton, and sugar production, he issued the following instructions to the Politburo Commission of Manufactured Consumer Goods (June 12, 1932):

Your main task is to send the maximum quantities of manufactured consumer goods to the wheat, sugar, and cotton regions in May, June, and July reckoning that they will be in place already for July and August. If this is not done the commission deserves to be buried alive.[37]

These examples show a dictator actively directing consumer goods to elicit more effort and output, sometimes even finely calibrating shipments to achieve a very specific result.

Stalin's and the Politburo's conclusion of the close link between pay and effort in the late 1920s and early 1930s was actually nothing new. V. I. Lenin came to the same conclusion in 1921 when he argued in favor of foreign concessions to improve worker living standards. In excerpts from his report, he argued the following:

We must consider the fact that labour productivity will not rise until the workers' condition improves.... We must put at the heart of our concessions policy the task of improving the condition of the workers at the enterprises of the first category, and then at the rest.... They are very well aware that if we fail to improve the condition of our workers and peasants because of our prejudices, we shall multiply our difficulties and altogether undermine the prestige of the Soviet power.... You know that we must have that improvement at all costs. We shall not grudge the foreign capitalist even a 2,000 percent profit, provided we improve the condition of the workers and peasants. It is imperative that we do it.[38]

If the Politburo regarded consumption as a residual, buffer sector, it would have accorded it precious little attention. Consumption, however, was one of the most frequent items on the Politburo's agenda, and in Stalin's own words, the "provisioning of workers" had become one of "the most contested issues" confronting the Politburo. He called the Ministry of Trade "the most complicated ministry."[39] The Politburo named itself as the highest trading organization, deciding not only general trade policy but also trade plans, prices, assortment, and even openings of new stores.[40] More Politburo time was probably spent on consumption (especially emergency sessions) than on any other issue.

---

[37] Ibid., 162.
[38] V. I. Lenin, "Report on Concessions at a Meeting of the Communist Group of the All-Russia Central Council of Trade Unions, April 11, 1921," in *Collected Works*, 4th English ed., vol. 32 (Moscow: Progress Publishers, 1965), 300–15.
[39] Ibid., 71.
[40] Ibid., 28.

Tracking Worker Sentiment. Western scholars had long wondered whether the Soviet leadership kept two sets of books: one of official statistics based on ministry and enterprise reporting; the other, the secret books of the OGPU/NKVD or of the Politburo itself. Indeed, later chapters show how the center battled ministries and enterprises for more information and could have used a second channel of economic information. Most information gathered by the vast network of OGPU/NKVD and its informants during the 1930s, however, focused on political threats and notably on worker and peasant unrest. Moreover, this secret-police information (as was shown in Chapter 2) was largely fashioned to suit the current interests of the Politburo, and it was designed to uncover plots and reveal dangers rather than to point out positive events.

The fair-wage model predicts that the dictator must monitor worker sentiment for increasing dissatisfaction with living standards, which, in the model's language, translates into increases in fair wages. The Politburo used three measures of worker sentiment; namely, statistics on labor productivity and labor turnover, and regular secret-police reports on the countryside and city. Declines in labor productivity, increases in labor turnover, and increased strike activity and demonstrations were signs of growing labor unrest. Labor productivity was a constant disappointment. With the massive capital investments of the First Five-Year Plan (1928–1932), labor productivity was expected to soar, causing costs of industrial goods to plummet. Figure 4.5 shows that the opposite happened. In 1931, nominal investment grew a phenomenal 60 percent, but labor productivity fell at an annual rate of 10 percent. In 1932, nominal investment grew at an exceptional 28 percent rate, but labor productivity continued to fall at the same rate as before. When the leadership reversed itself and reduced nominal investment in 1933, labor productivity growth became positive and investment costs started to fall.[41]

The OGPU/NKVD reports suggested that falling labor productivity was linked with depressed real wages. The head of the Ukrainian executive committee (Petrovsky) on a visit to Dnepropetrovsk could not organize even small meetings without being challenged on "supply difficulties." At one such meeting, he was told: "Comrade Petrovsky is respected by us. If another leader had come to us, he would have had even more unpleasantness because the workers are now furious. Even those who favor

---

[41] The data in this figure are not very reliable. Cost figures were reported cleansed of the effect of wage increases; suppliers and builders were violating pricing decrees and charging more than official prices, but these are probably the figures the leadership itself used.

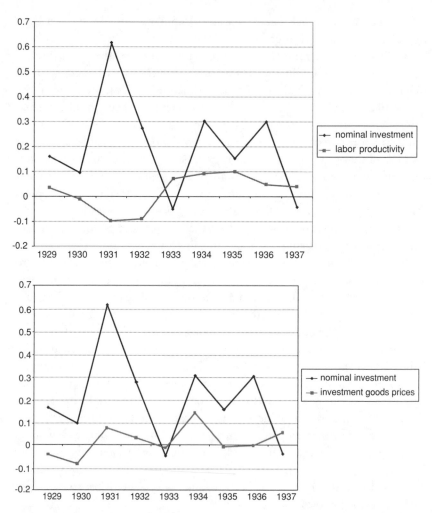

FIGURE 4.5. Annual growth rates, 1929–1937, nominal investment and labor pro-
ductivity.
Source: E. Zaleskii, *Stalinist Planning for Economic Growth 1933–1952*, 662;
R. W. Davies, *The Soviet Economy in Turmoil, 1929–1930* (Cambridge, Mass.:
Harvard University Press, 1989), 540.

Soviet power are now incensed."[42] In the first quarter of 1930, ninety-two
strikes were recorded; the largest was one in which six hundred workers
took part. Factory workers refused to take part in obligatory demonstrations, and changed jobs at rapid rates for jobs with better rations. During

[42] Osokina, *Za Fasadom*, 80.

harvests, they streamed out of factories in search of agricultural goods.[43]
Women in factories complained: "We must work but there is no bread."
Factory walls were covered with graffiti: "Life has become worse than
before the revolution,"[44] or "They demand labor productivity but they
do not see how things are going for workers. Mornings we come to work
without eating; for lunch they give us a piece of bread without meat.
100 gr. of meat for a whole family."[45]

The combination of declining labor productivity and direct reports of
growing worker unrest would have been convincing evidence that workers were demanding a higher fair wage. The fair-wage model predicts that
as effort falls, the economy's capacity to produce output, either consumption or investment, falls, and an investment-maximizing dictator must
cut investment and raise consumption, an action that was taken by the
Politburo in 1933.

Restraining the Fair Wage. The fair-wage model also predicts that an
investment-maximizing dictator would attempt to convince workers that
their actual wage, no matter how low, is the fair wage. In fact, the first
two five-year plans, described as "visions of the future" (see Chapter 5)
delivered a clear message to workers: "Accept sacrifice now for the sake
of a brighter future." The first five-year plan heralded a remarkable "revolution from above" that would overcome backwardness. Sacrifices must
be made to build new plants, dams, and electricity networks. People must
work harder; enterprise managers must find ways of producing more from
the same capacity. Stalin, in a November 1929 article, declared the USSR
"a country of metal, a country of the automobile, a country of the tractor"[46] that would exceed the United States in output by 1941. Workers
in effect should accept a lower fair wage in return for this bright future.
Although the second five-year plan's industrial targets were more modest,
it promised that consumer goods would at least double or perhaps even
triple by 1937.[47]

A second message of Soviet propaganda was that consumption shortfalls were due to deliberate sabotage by enemies. In a typical maneuver,
Stalin postured himself as an advocate of the working class. In a Central

[43] Ibid., 80–2.
[44] Ibid., 81.
[45] Ibid., 82.
[46] These and other quotes from Stalin are from R. W. Davies, *The Soviet Economy in
Turmoil, 1929–1930* (Cambridge, Mass.: Harvard University Press, 1989), 95–6.
[47] Davies, *Crisis and Progress*, 137–8.

Committee Plenum of November 25–28, 1934, consumer advocate Stalin urged: "We must stand strongly with both feet on the ground, considering the requirements of real people, getting near to the consumer." Trading organizations must be compelled "to respect the consumer and treat him as a human being."[48] In response to OGPU/NKVD reports on poor living conditions,[49] Stalin even ordered the execution of forty-eight supply officials and published their "confessions" in the press.[50]

Paying Only Priority Workers a Fair Wage: Rationing. Consumer goods were required to motivate the work force, but more consumer goods meant fewer investment goods. Stalin's initial attempt to defy the forces of this gravity was a targeted rationing system. The rationing program, which Stalin personally wrote, was put in place on December 15, 1930, by a Politburo decree, "About Worker Supplies."[51] Stalin's goal was to limit overall consumption without lowering labor productivity in priority sectors.[52] If consumption could be shifted from nonpriority workers to investment, the dictator could have both investment and high work effort of priority workers. A slogan that circulated in the early 1930s summarized this strategy: "He who does not work *on industrialization* [author's italics] will not eat." Those who contribute less should consume less. It was hoped that nonpriority workers, primarily in agriculture, could be forced, by threat of severe punishment or imprisonment, to produce even if paid less than their fair wage. The output of nonpriority workers was, therefore, considered set administratively (Qa), and they would receive only subsistence consumption (Cs). The investment "surplus" of nonpriority workers would, therefore, be $Qa - Cs$. Priority workers would be paid a fair wage (a) to produce the fair-wage output (Qf). The investment surplus of priority workers, therefore, would be $Qf - a$. Investment (I), therefore, is:

$$Qa - Cs + Qf - a = I$$

With Qa administratively determined and Cs at subsistence, priority workers could be paid their fair wage (a) and produce the fair-wage output (Qf) without reducing investment. Stalin was wagering that he could

[48] O. V. Khlevnyuk and R. Davies, "The End of Rationing in the Soviet Union 1934–1935," *Europe-Asia Studies* 51, no. 4 (1999), 575.

[49] Osokina, *Za Fasadom*, 28–33.

[50] Ibid., 84.

[51] Ibid., 85.

[52] The description of Stalin's rationing program is based primarily on Khlevnyuk and Davies, "The End of Rationing," 557–609.

limit the consumption of nonpriority workers and raise investment, without harming the productivity of priority workers.

Rations were to be sharply differentiated according to location and place of work. Workers from key industrial centers (Moscow, Leningrad, Donbass, or Baku) or from priority factories and institutions were to receive more. There was even supposed to be differentiation within a plant, with "shock" workers receiving more. The army and secret police were allotted generous ration norms, and the elite (the apex of which received the famed "Kremlin ration") were treated best of all. The rationing system was even applied to penal workers in the gulag, who received rations 20 percent lower than free labor with norms tied to work effort. The rationing system applied only to nonagricultural workers and employees, except for some producers of agricultural raw materials. Those workers outside the rationing system were to fend for themselves, by either producing their own goods (peasants) or buying them at the much higher commercial prices. In some cases, peasant households were not even permitted to buy in commercial stores.[53]

Stalin's rationing system was in effect during the crucial period December 1930 to late 1934. Its logic fits the fair-wage–effort model perfectly as an attempt to have one's cake (investment) and eat it too (low consumption without destroying incentives). Its replacement by a "market" distribution system in late 1934 and early 1935 was heralded as a victory for socialism – a sign of abundance. Stalin's new slogan was, "Things are getting better, life is becoming happier."[54]

Rationing was abandoned for a number of reasons: First, the bureaucracy could not manage a highly differentiated distribution system. In factory cafeterias, where shock workers were supposed to receive more, those seated at tables were surrounded by hungry workers who immediately took their place.[55] In the gulags, the differentiation between prisoners and free laborers disappeared under the crush of the administrative burden. The supply administration was only able to handle the distribution of special rations to the elite, numbering fewer than five thousand.[56] Stalin referred to this inability to differentiate as "mechanical distribution" that

[53] The rationing system required a massive bureaucracy of more than twenty thousand workers, under the direction of the Ministry of Trade/Supply. Most of the administrative distribution of consumer goods took place outside of the trade network. Stores (*magaziny*) were renamed as "closed distribution points" and the like. The state trade network received what was left over after goods had been shipped to the state's own distribution network.

[54] This section is based on Khlevnyuk and Davies, "The End of Rationing," 557–609.

[55] Osokina, *Za Fasadom*, 121–2.

[56] Ibid., 134.

ran counter to consumer incentives.[57] Second, the rationing system encouraged speculation and crime. Ration cards were bought and sold; speculators diverted rationed goods to the commercial market and pocketed the profits (rather than the state budget). The OGPU/NKVD reported a "flood of speculation." In the beginning of 1934, the OGPU/NKVD handled ten thousand cases of speculation per month. In 1935, one lack persons were punished for speculation. The rise in both petty and large-scale theft was astronomical. Workers stole from the shop floor, taking even priority items such as cars. Theft became a routine part of Soviet daily life. Illegal private trade thrived, despite severe penalties including execution.[58] Third, the level of consumption, even of privileged industrial workers, was apparently too low to provide work incentives as noted by the quotations from disgruntled shock workers cited earlier. Fourth, the rationing system, with its low prices for rationed goods, deprived the state of needed turnover tax revenues. Sales at commercial prices were too low to compensate the budget for low ration prices. Fifth, to encourage technical crops, such as cotton or flax, peasants had to be included in the rationing system and manufactured consumer goods had to be sent to the countryside (thereby violating the initiative to limit rural consumption).[59]

Gauging Investment Capacity. The fair-wage model suggests that reductions in investment are not voluntary; they are forced by the reduced investment capacity of the economy. The archives do tend to confirm that cutbacks in the investment budget were ordered when the leadership concluded that physical investment capacity was lacking. The Politburo, which constantly monitored major projects, was well aware in the early 1930s that too many projects had been approved, that investment resources (primarily construction materials) were lacking, and too few factories were being completed. The Politburo commission, which proposed the first reduction in investment in July 1932, did so "with the aim of bringing the amount of finance into conformity with the *physical volume of work in the plan and to concentrate material resources on crucial sites* [author's italics]."[60] Molotov silenced the shrill protests of industrial ministers against these cuts by declaring that they originated with Stalin himself. A contemporaneous letter from Kaganovich to Stalin dated July 24,

---

[57] Khlevnyuk and Davies, "The End of Rationing," 564.
[58] Osokina, *Za Fasadom*, chapter 3.
[59] Khlevnyuk, *Stalin i Kaganovich. Perepiski*, 131.
[60] Davies, *Crises and Progress*, 230.

1932, also concluded that the economy lacked the physical ability to continue investment at the earlier pace:

At the evening Politburo meeting, we decreed to reduce the financing of capital investment to 700 million rubles in accordance with your letter. At the same time, we tied this question with the issue of lowering construction costs. We heard reports [from the various ministries]. The picture is an unhappy one. Instead of reductions, costs are rising. The main thing is that construction materials are expensive because of transport issues. The labor force is gathered without consideration of demand and the presence of construction materials. The result is huge delays and low productivity.... The fulfillment of the plan is measured by the expenditure of money, not by the physical volume of work. We set up a commission to work out concrete measures for the battle for real lower costs. As far as cuts are concerned, we are carrying them out at the expense of construction sites without cost estimates and *sites not covered by construction materials* [author's italics].[61]

In other words, with construction projects encountering bottlenecks, particularly of construction materials, labor was being wasted, and it was better simply to cut back on the volume of investment. If more investment funds were allocated, they would simply bid up prices.

After the 1933 cutback in investment, battles continued to be fought between the industrial ministers and regional authorities demanding more investment and those who worried about the capacity of the economy (Molotov, the finance minister, and at times the head of Gosplan). Stalin decided the outcome each time. The 1936 investment plan, discussed between July 21 and 28, 1935, illustrates the process. With Molotov away, Stalin headed the discussions. On July 21, he wrote Molotov that the Chairman of Gosplan (Mezhlauk, who replaced Kuibyshev upon his death) had proposed an investment budget of 19 billion rubles, and added "I proposed a figure of 22 billion."[62] Four days later, Molotov replied "I consider it extremely undesirable to increase the construction program above 22 billion rubles. I am guided in this by the desire to *strengthen the ruble* and also to *reduce the cost of construction* [author's italics]."[63] A few days later, Stalin wrote Molotov that the plan had been increased to 27 billion rubles:

22 billion was not enough, and, as can be seen, could not be enough. The increase in school building (+760 mln), light industry, timber, food industry and local industry (+900 mln rubles and more), in defense (+1 billion 100 mln), in health,

---

[61] Khlevnyuk, *Stalin i Kaganovich. Perepiski*, 243.
[62] Cited in Davies, "Why Was There a Soviet Investment Cycle in 1933–37?," 7.
[63] Ibid., 7.

on the Moscow canal project and other items (over 400 mln rubles) determined the physiognomy and size of the control figures for 1936.[64]

In the final letter in this sequence, dated August 2, Molotov grudgingly accepted: "I would have preferred a smaller amount of capital construction, but I think that we shall cope if we put our shoulders to the wheel even with the approved plan of 25 billion rubles."[65]

In this budget cycle, advocates of investment expansion won the day. Nominal investment grew by 30 percent in 1936. A year later, however, the investment budget was cut by 4 percent. Thus, from one year to the next, the economy had gone from rapid growth of investment (1936) to negative growth (1937). We have less information on this second cut in investment. What we do know is that actual investment began to lag behind planned investment. Thus, it is not even clear that there was a high-level intent to reduce investment. It may have just happened. In a memorandum dated May 16, 1936, Gosplan Chairman Mezhlauk reported that April capital investment was lower than required by the plan. The gap between planned and actual investment increased throughout the year. In a further report, dated October 15, 1936, investment – measured in 1935 prices – was only 47 percent of the annual plan instead of the expected 70 percent. The Ministry of Heavy Industry reported its investment for 1936 at 92 percent of the planned amount.[66] We have some anecdotal information (cited in Chapters 7 and 8) that suppliers of equipment and construction were refusing to enter into contracts. Although the investment finance was there, the supply of real investment was not. If this story is correct, the 1937 reduction in investment, like that of 1933, was also due to the reduced capacity of the economy to produce investment goods.

Stakhanovism and its Hidden Dangers. The end of rationing by early 1935 meant that the Politburo could no longer hope to channel consumer goods selectively to priority workers while depriving others.[67] The Politburo, therefore, turned to Stakhanovism to raise labor effort exogenously through a combination of incentives and patriotic appeals. In the

---

[64] Lih et al., *Stalin's Letters to Molotov*, 251.

[65] Cited in Davies, "Why Was There a Soviet Investment Cycle in 1933–37?," 8.

[66] These results are reported in Davies, "Why Was There a Soviet Investment Cycle in 1933–37?," 9.

[67] This section is based primarily on R. W. Davies and Oleg Khlevnyuk, "Stakhanovism, the Politburo and the Soviet Economy" (paper for presentation at a conference on "Stalin's Politburo, 1928–1953," European University Institute, Florence, March 30–31, 2000).

mid-1930s, workers received base pay plus piece rates based on fulfilling output norms. Output norms, which determined worker compensation, specified how much workers were expected to produce per unit of time.[68] Output norms were supposed to reflect "best practice," but they were usually based on past results. An increase in norms meant to workers a *ceteris paribus* reduction in real wages. The leadership, on the other hand, wished to use increased norms to raise worker productivity.

Stalin's famous speech to Red Army graduates on May 4, 1935, declaring that "cadres decide everything," was a call for higher labor productivity: He declared that the mastery of the new technology could "bring about miracles."[69] The Minister of Heavy Industry, Ordzhonikidze, at the Seventeenth Party Congress in January 1934, called for higher co-efficients for blast furnaces, a call repeated in September 1934, and at the Seventh Congress of Soviets in January 1935. On May 12, 1935, eight days after Stalin's speech on cadres, Ordzhonikidze declared existing norms those of "yesterday." Kaganovich, the newly appointed Minister of Transportation, criticized his engineers for setting maximum daily loading only at fifty-five thousand to fifty-eight thousand freight wagons. The campaign to raise labor productivity that emerged from these declarations was named after A. G. Stakhanov, a coal miner who, on August 30, 1935, cut 102 tons of coal in 5¾ hours versus the quota of 7 tons. Although Stakhanov's feat was inspired by the general atmosphere, it was probably not directly organized by the Politburo, or by Stalin himself, but they embraced it after seeing its possibilities.[70] Encouraged by Stakhanovism, plans grew more ambitious. In September 1935, Gosplan raised the fourth-quarter production targets for 1935 for pig iron by 1 million tons and steel ingots by 700,000 tons. The revised version of the

---

[68] The number of norms and norm-setters was very large; 210,000 norms were in use in the Gorky Automobile Works alone. In the machine-building industry, there were 12,000 norm-setters.

[69] Quoted in Davies and Khlevnyuk, "Stakhanovism, the Politburo and the Soviet Economy," 13.

[70] Stalin was on vacation, and there was nothing about Stakhanov in the telegrams exchanged between Kaganovich and Stalin. Stakhanov's record was carefully organized, with the support of the supervisor of the mine section and the party organizer. Ordzhonikidze promptly phoned Moscow, and within a few days an enthusiastic campaign was organized in the central newspapers. On September 6, Ordzhonikidze wrote: "You can't get away from the fact that there are hundreds and thousands of real heroes among the rank and file, who demonstrate brilliant models of how to work." The Stakhanovite campaign spread in the next few weeks to the automobile and engineering industries, and then to the textile and footwear industries.

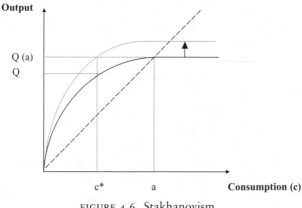

FIGURE 4.6. Stakhanovism.

1936 plan called for a substantial increase in production, but far short of the huge increase expected by Stakhanovism's most ardent supporters.[71]

Figure 4.6 shows some of the possible results of Stakhanovism using the fair-wage model of an economy initially operating below the fair wage, producing investment-maximizing consumption (c^*) at less than fair-wage consumption (a). The economy initially is producing an output Q, which is less than the fair-wage output Q (a). The optimal, but least likely, outcome of Stakhanovism – the new Socialist man variant – would be a *spontaneous* upward shift in the production curve so that Q (a) is produced without any increase in consumption (c^*). The entire increase in output goes to investment. This unlikely result requires a spontaneous increase in output with workers accepting norms that increase along with production to prevent their wages from rising. Workers work harder for the same wages simply for the good of society. A second result, by declining order of preference of the Politburo, would be the combination of a spontaneous increase in output with norms holding constant or increasing slower than the output increase – the movement from Q to some $Q' < Q(a)$. Workers work harder and get more pay. More output is produced, but investment *could be reduced* as a larger portion of output goes to consumption. Whether investment falls or rises depends on the pace of increase of norms. The worst outcome for the Politburo would be the movement from c^* to a. There is no spontaneous increase in output from the campaign, norms are held constant, the entire increase in output goes to harder-working workers, and investment drops.

---

[71] Quoted in Davies and Khlevnyuk, "Stakhanovism," 19.

These scenarios show that Stakhanovism carried with it serious risks to the leadership's investment program. By encouraging Stakhanovism in an industrial system based on progressive piece rates, workers could, of their own volition, raise consumption and depress investment. If workers increased their productivity and received the resulting increase in production, investment could decline precipitously.

Khlevnyuk and Davies conclude that Stakhanovism had, at best, only an ephemeral effect on productivity and output with an initial surge in productivity in late 1935. The average quarterly rise in productivity was lower in the fifteen months following Stakhanov's feat than in the six months preceding it. Figure 4.5 shows no perceptible advance in labor productivity during or after the Stakhanovite movement, despite the fact that some Stakhanovites raised their productivity substantially. Stakhanovism clearly did not achieve its desired result of raising labor productivity, but did it have some of the other negative effects described?

In the first months of the Stakhanovite campaign, the press reported huge wage increases for Stakhanovites, but attempts to increase output norms generally were rebuffed. As the number of Stakhanovites grew, the threatening upsurge in wages led factory directors to call for increases in norms, but Ordzhonikidze's first deputy resisted, remarking: "If you want to wreck the Stakhanov movement, revise the norms." From the perspective of the Ministry of Heavy Industry, Stakhanovism was yielding output increases and enabling them to meet the plan. The larger consequences of Stakhanovism were not their concern. Between August and December 1935, the average daily wage of industrial workers increased by 16 percent versus 5 percent for the same period of 1934. At the conference of Stakhanovites in November, a number of speakers criticized the old norms as out of date, but it fell to Stalin to order an increase in norms.

Stakhanovism also carried with it the risk of increased worker resentment. Ordinary workers interpreted the Stakhanovite movement as a plot to extract more work for the same wage. Hostility to Stakhanovism was captured in NKVD and party reports in the autumn of 1935. Many senior managers, factory directors, and engineers regarded Stakhanovite record-breaking as disruptive. Foremen and engineers were harassed by managers and higher officials to increase the number of Stakhanovites, and by Stakhanovites for failing to supply extra tools and materials. Ordinary worker resistance to Stakhanovism met with increasingly repressive responses. Authorities began to link even mild resistance with counter-revolutionary activity and sabotage. On November 28, 1935, the Central

Committee approved a decree "On the Struggle against Crimes Intended to Disorganize the Stakhanov Movement," and in December 1935, the USSR Procurator issued a circular treating anti-Stakhanovite action as terrorism. The Central Committee Plenum of December 21–25, 1935, reviewed NKVD material, which documented hundreds of cases of sabotage against Stakhanovites. Accidents, damage of machinery, and poor-quality materials were treated as crimes.[72]

We do not have a solid explanation for the second investment cutback of 1937. It followed a massive increase in investment in 1936, but the fair-wage analysis of Stakhanovism suggests that it could have, at least in theory, promoted a cutback in investment in its aftermath by promoting the idea that harder work deserves a bigger share of the pie and that the higher wages of Stakhanovites should be passed on to ordinary workers as increases in fair wages.

Forced Labor. A dictator could, in theory, "tame" the fair-wage–effort model by imposing pure force. Workers could be so closely monitored, punished, and controlled that they no longer decide how much effort to supply. Force began to be supplied in the early 1930s with the first large-scale use of gulag labor; however, the gulag labor force accounted for no more than 10 percent of the industrial labor force. The application of force to the entire labor force dates formally to December 20, 1938, when the Council of People's Commissars adopted the decree: "About the Obligatory Introduction of Work Books in All Enterprises and Organizations of the USSR."[73] In this legislation, the worker's contract with the enterprises was extended to five years. The work book had to list all compensation, punishments, rebukes, and reasons for firings. From January 1939 through June 1940, additional laws were passed that punished twenty-minute tardiness and levied criminal punishments for lateness, low-quality production, and drunkenness. Although these

---

[72] A report dated October 11 claimed that the collapse of the mine roof and the consequent death of nine of the fourteen members of a Stakhanovite brigade at Mine No. 204 in the Chelyabinsk Coal Trust was "a result of obvious wrecking methods"; six engineers were found guilty of wrecking. On January 23, 1936, Kaganovich, visiting the Tomsk railway, reported to Stalin that the administration of the line included "a group of counter-revolutionary and sabotaging elements" and proposed that they should be sent to trial.

[73] This section is based on A. K. Sokolov, "Period Prinuzhdeniia k Trudu v Sovetskoi Promyshlennosti i Ego Krizis," working paper, Institute of Russian History, Russian Academy of Sciences, August 2002.

measures were later interpreted as necessitated by the impending war, they were not motivated by the wartime emergency. Workers were obliged to work a seven-day week and were not allowed to leave an enterprise on their own volition. These criminal laws were not a mere formality; in 1940, 3.3 million workers were accused of violations. Of these, 1.8 million were sentenced to six months of corrective labor without interruption of their normal work, and 322,000 were sentenced to prison terms of two to four months. The application of force to the labor force was continued until the mid-1950s.

Concluding Comments

The Soviet investment cycle of the 1930s appears to be a puzzle at first glance. Soviet leaders, caught up in the fervor of creating an industrialized economy in the shortest time possible, actually cut investment two times (in 1933 and 1937). These investment cuts, moreover, were made by leaders who had earlier contended that there were no limits on investment or growth. The most direct explanation – that Stalin and the Politburo wavered in their dedication to accumulation – is unappealing. Their devotion to capital accumulation was so firm that we elevated it to a fourth core value of the Soviet system. Stalin's representations of himself as an advocate of the downtrodden consumer challenge credulity. A power-maximizing dictator, convinced that concessions to workers were required to remain in power, clearly would have cut investment for political gain. We cannot judge how seriously the Politburo took the threat of worker revolt in 1933 and 1937, but it did not appear that Soviet power was seriously threatened. Vested industrial and regional interests, to which a selfish dictator would pay more heed, were vocally arguing for more investment and were appalled by investment cuts.

The fair-wage model offers an appealing alternative. It allows for investment cycles by a stationary bandit who does not waver from the goal of investment maximization. The dictator continues to maximize investment each year; however, the capacity of the economy to produce investment varies with worker effort. Workers reduce their work effort when they conclude that they should be offered a higher fair wage; the economy simply has less for investment. The fair-wage model should apply to other times, places, and circumstances, not just to the Soviet Union of the 1930s. Indeed, socialist investment cycles were a feature of Soviet life, and they spread to the administrative-command economies of Eastern Europe as well in the postwar period.[74]

The fair-wage–effort model is a general model. It would be foolish to argue that it fully explains reality, but it might be reasonable to expect it to capture enough of reality to explain some basic tendencies, such as the investment cycle. The archives reveal that Stalin and his team believed in a tradeoff between effort and worker living standards, and many of their actions, such as rationing, Stakhonovism, and the introduction of force into the labor market, were designed to maintain investment without losing effort. The belief that reduced consumption harms effort could have been mistaken. The collapse of labor productivity that accompanied the first industrialization wave could have been the consequence of the influx of inexperienced workers from the countryside and not a collapse of effort, as the leaders believed. The growth of labor productivity that accompanied the first cutback in investment could have been a fluke. We must not assume that those who devise economic policy in any country, capitalist or socialist, understand "truth." Their assumptions could be completely wrong, and they could be applying the wrong model.

Modelers have always wondered whether the subjects they are modeling actually behave according to the model. We have here a rare case where we can read the thoughts of the agents being modeled – Stalin and the Politburo – and we find remarkable agreement between their interpretation of reality and the model's interpretation. The fact that the Soviet leadership felt compelled to cut investment during its initial industrialization drive again shows its inability to negate laws of economic behavior. The long-run lesson from the introduction of force into the countryside was that peasants react to reduced incentives by producing less. The strategy to extract surpluses for primitive accumulation from agriculture exacted a high long-run price in the form of a noncompetitive agriculture. Similarly, the investment-first strategy, which left workers with consumption levels that they regarded as unfair, exacted the price of an unproductive workforce. The long-run equilibrium is captured by the Soviet slogan: "They pretend to pay us and we pretend to work."

[74] Alexander Bajt, "Investment Cycles in European Socialist Economies: A Review Article," *Journal of Economic Literature* 9, no. 1 (March 1971), 53–63; Michael Bleaney, "Investment Cycles in Socialist Economies: A Reconsideration," *Oxford Economic Papers* 43, no. 3 (1991), 515–27; Peter Mihalyi, *Socialist Investment Cycles Analysis in Retrospect* (Amsterdam: Kluwer Academic Publishers, 1992).

Throughout the 1930s, the Soviet leadership vainly sought ways to maintain investment without the loss of work effort. Rationing's goal was to reduce the consumption of low-priority workers only, but ultimately the rationing system could not distinguish between high- and low-priority workers. Stakhanovism attempted to raise work effort through appeals to socialist heroism, but drove up wages faster than labor productivity. Stakhanovism evenly temporarily placed control of the distribution of resources between consumption and investment in the hands of workers. Ultimately, the leadership applied force and coercion to the industrial workplace. Impractical punitive measures for tardiness, laziness, and shoddy work replaced economic incentives. Although these measures remained formally in force for more than a decade, they also had to be abandoned. If enforced, massive numbers of workers had to be arrested. If not enforced, they were ignored.

5

Visions and Control Figures

"We are becoming a country of metal, a country of the automobile, a country of the tractor."

[Stalin, November 7, 1929]

"Not everyone has the nerves, strength, character, and understanding to appreciate the tremendous breakup of the old and the feverish construction of the new . . . we are bound to have those who are exhausted, distraught, worn-out, despondent, and lagging behind – and those who go over to the enemy camp. These are the inevitable costs of revolution."

[Stalin in a private letter to Maxim Gorky, January 17, 1929.][1]

The previous chapter explained how the Soviet leadership chose optimal investment by weighing investment against the loss of worker effort. This chapter is about the output plans – five-year plans and annual plans – that gave the Soviet economy its name as a "planned economy." The investment and output plans were linked at least in theory: Output plans specified the increases in production, but, in order to produce more, producers needed more capital. The investment plan was supposed to provide enough new capacity so that the planned output increases could be achieved.

The linkage between investment and planned output increases existed in practice. When managers were able to convince their superiors that their output targets could not be achieved, they were often offered more investment. On November 3, 1935, a meeting of the "Commission on Procurement of Timber in Gorky Region" was called to discuss the Gorky

[1] Both quotes are from Davies, *The Soviet Economy in Turmoil*, 96.

region's request to cut its timber production target by 8 percent. The request was denied but Gorky was given an additional fifty tractors to allow it to meet its production target.[2] On October 1, 1935, the government refused the Ministry of Heavy Industry's request to reduce its output growth figures but gave it an additional 700 million rubles of investment to meet its production target.[3]

The standard textbook interpretation is that planners' preferences were expressed through output plans and that the investment plan was derived from the output plan. In effect, the output plan was supposed to be the cornerstone of the planning system.[4] The previous chapter showed that planners' preferences were really expressed through the investment plan. That the investment plan was the cornerstone of resource allocation should come as no surprise. The dictator's clear goal was to create capital and new technology. Additional output would come as an automatic by-product of this capital accumulation.

At first glance, it would appear that the leadership's objectives could be seen concretely in the output plans. The Politburo's choices of the most ambitious variant of the first five-year plan and of forced collectivization in 1929 were indeed stark expressions of planners' preferences. However, in the era of five-year plans that followed, plans reveal surprisingly little about planners' preferences for the following reasons: Five-year plans were not converted into operational plans. The administrative-command economy was run by an indecipherable mix of preliminary monthly, quarterly, and annual plans that were often revised, and in some cases there were no operational plans at all. The complexity of this mix makes it nearly impossible to divine the leadership's goals by examining output plans.

Control Figures

Control figures refer to output targets, such as steel, coal, or freight-car loadings, to be produced in some future year or quarter. Textbooks on the Soviet economy suggest that the Soviet dictator optimized by ordering the

[2] E. A. Rees, "The People's Commissariat of the Timber Industry," in *Decision Making in the Stalinist Command Economy, 1932–37*, ed. E. A. Rees (London: MacMillan, 1997), 133–4.

[3] Khlevnyuk, "The People's Commissariat," 121.

[4] Paul Gregory and Robert Stuart, *Soviet and Post-Soviet Economic Structure and Performance*, 5th ed. (New York: Harper Collins, 1994), 155–8.

"maximum" quantities of control figures.[5] Clearly, no central planning agency could set output targets for hundreds of thousands of products, but Lenin had argued during the early years of Bolshevik rule that the economy could be controlled through its "commanding heights" of heavy industry, transportation, and defense. Not all aspects of economic life need be controlled, only the most important. In theory, the control of a few key control figures such as pig iron, chemicals, ores, grain, or freight-car movements could mean the control of the entire economy.

What is clear is that the party leadership could control only a few aspects of economic life, due to its extremely small staff. In January 1930, the Central Committee employed only 375 persons.[6] The ten-person Politburo, backed by a minuscule staff, could keep track of only a few commodities. The ruling elite were overworked and harried, deluged with paperwork, petitions, and inspections. Each full and candidate member of the Politburo had to become an expert on some economic matter. In March 1934, for example, the Politburo assigned member L. Kaganovich to head the transport commission, N. I. Ezhov to head the industry commission, and A. A. Zhdanov responsibility for agriculture.[7] These sector heads controlled their sectors, sometimes exerting more influence than the minister.[8] Selection to head a Politburo sector committee meant rapid advancement. Zhdanov was appointed full member of the Politburo in February 1935, and Ezhov was appointed Minister of Interior in 1936 and full Politburo member in October 1937 – in time to spearhead the Great Terror. Politburo members made factory inspections or ventured into the countryside to view collectivization and grain harvests, and to run collection campaigns.[9] Among themselves, they talked endlessly about steel, construction projects, processing equipment, and freight: "In the import commission we concluded to raise imports of nonferrous metals; we went far above the agreed-upon limit, instead of 67 million to 71 million. . . . Freight transport now is worse than last year. We are transporting little, 45–47 thousand cars per day."[10] "We are

[5] P. Gregory and R. Stuart, *Russian and Soviet Economic Structure and Performance*, 7th ed. (Boston: Addison-Wesley, 2001), chapter 6.

[6] Khlevnyuk et al., *Stalinskoe Politburo*, 14–15.

[7] Rees and Watson, "Politburo and Sovnarkom," 14.

[8] E. A. Rees, "The People's Commissariat of Transport (Railroad)," *Decision Making in the Stalinist Command Economy, 1932–37*, ed. E. A. Rees (London: MacMillan, 1997), 219.

[9] See, for example, Khlevnyuk et al., *Stalinskoe Politburo*, 114–15.

[10] Kaganovich to Ordzhonikidze, August 2, 1932, ibid., 125–7.

recovering peat 30 to 40 versts from the place of use and delivery is only possible with mechanized transport for which we need 4,000 tons of rail."[11] One Politburo meeting spent most of its agenda on automotive engineering details. These snippets show the fine line between knowing too much and knowing too little: Politburo members in their quest for information ran the risk of not seeing the forest for the trees.

The Politburo considered a wide variety of issues ranging from the momentous to the trivial – personnel appointments, firings, executions, foreign policy, the distribution of cars, critiques of newspaper articles, setting up commissions, machinery exports, property transfers, and prices of bread and metro tickets in Moscow. If the Politburo dictated planners' preferences by setting control figures, as the textbooks suggest, presumably the approval of annual and quarterly plans of control figures would have commanded most of its attention, requiring lengthy deliberations and evoking heated debate. The issues Kaganovich chose to pass on to Stalin during his absences from Moscow, among the thousands of tidbits, show that relatively little attention was devoted to production control figures.[12]

The operational plans of the Soviet economy were prepared by Gosplan and the ministries based on general directives of the top leadership. Instructions for preparation of annual and quarterly plans were issued by the Council of People's Commissars and the Politburo; if Stalin were absent, approval would be delayed until Stalin could sign off. A letter from Molotov to Kuibyshev (Chairman of Gosplan) dated September 12, 1933, illustrates Stalin's role:

Hello Valerian: I won't write much. We'll see each other soon.... I consider your comments on the control figures for 1934 correct. Using your range (21 billion + 15%), I wrote Stalin not long ago asking his opinion. I won't go into this matter in more detail. I am very happy about the perspectives for beets (Can we count on 130 million centners?). I doubt that it is wise to raise the cotton target to 26 million pods.

In a follow-up letter four days later (September 16, 1933), Molotov wrote: "Hello Valerian: Stalin communicated to me that he is agreed to [19]34

---

[11] Kirov to Ordzhonikidze, July 25, 1933, ibid., 130–1.

[12] In 1931, Stalin vacationed in the South from early August to early October. In 1932, Stalin was absent from Moscow for three months. In 1933, he was absent much of August, September, and October. In 1934, he was absent from June 30 to October 31. In 1935, he was gone only from August 1 to November 2. In 1936, most of his correspondence with Kaganovich was for the period August through October. Khlevnyuk et al., *Stalin i Kaganovich. Perepiski*, 129, 300, 409.

with the comment that capital investment will not be more than 21 million rubles. . . . Stalin said that he is agreed to the grain target of 698 million centners. You need to go on the basis of this figure."[13]

Stalin's vacations usually took place during the period June through October; therefore, Kaganovich's written reports relate primarily to the third- and fourth-quarter plans. We relate four letters describing Politburo deliberations on quarterly plans: Kaganovich to Stalin about the Politburo meeting of September 21, 1931, on the fourth-quarter plan:

The Politburo proposes to write in the protocol the following: a) the financing of investment in the main branches of the economy should be set to fulfill the annual plan of capital construction, b) the output plans of the main branches should not be lower than the third quarter. Thus, the transport plan should be set at 88.2 million tons, c) costs of production should be set to fall 9.5% for large-scale industry and 11% for the supply ministry. Both should achieve decisive improvements in cost reductions in the fourth quarter, d) budget reserves should be set at 800 million rubles, e) a commission [headed by Molotov with seven other members] should make the necessary calculations on the basis of these decisions.[14]

On September 26, 1931, Kaganovich communicated to Stalin the Politburo's final decisions: "For the fourth quarter plan, we decided to lower the state reserve from 800 million to 585 million. We added 70 million to the ministry of agriculture, to heavy industry 50 million and so forth."[15]

On June 7, 1932, Kaganovich reported to Stalin the Politburo's discussion of the third-quarter control figures:

Today we decided on the following directives for preparing the control figures of the third quarter plan: a) to direct Gosplan to stay within the limits of the third quarter investment plan (6800 thousand rubles), b) to pre-approve some preferences for the transport ministry for capital investment relative to the second quarter, c) to propose to [listed ministries] to work out measures for the lowering of construction costs and to call meetings of specialists and to hear their reports within a month, d) to propose to all ministries, within the limits of those assigned, to distribute special resources for the production of manufactured consumer goods (*shirpotreb*) and to report to the Commission on Manufactured Consumer Goods, e) Gosplan should additionally examine the development of manufactured consumer goods on the lines of industrial cooperation, f) to use no less that 70 thousand tons from the general metal fund in the third quarter for the production of manufactured consumer goods. I ask you to give your opinion. These decrees will not be prepared until receipt of your answer.[16]

[13] Khlevnyak et al., *Stalinskoe Politburo*, 134–5.
[14] Khlevnyak et al., *Stalin i Kaganovich. Perepiski*, 111–2.
[15] Ibid., 119.
[16] Ibid., 146–7.

On September 3, 1934, Kaganovich wrote Stalin about the fourth-quarter plan:

Before our departure, we worked out a series of positions on which we ask you to communicate your opinion: 1) We examined with the ministers the limits of the plan for the fourth quarter of 1934. We set the volume of gross production of union ministries at 11,170 million rubles that is 28.9% of the annual plan. We set the volume of capital work for the entire economy at 5,116.2 million. We expect an excess of expenditures over revenues by 1500 million rubles in the general government budget. I am sending you a draft of the decree. 2) After several variants we finally settled on the grain purchase figures which I am sending to you.[17]

On September 2, 1936, Kaganovich reported:

We [the Politburo] discussed with the ministers the fourth quarter plan. The volume of production of union and local industry was set at 19.7 billion rubles, which gives a 17.3 percent increase relative to the third quarter. The ministries proposed to establish tasks for each main administration, trust and enterprise for the production of completed production and a detailed assortment of production with high quality parts and corresponding to established standards. The Council of Labor and Defense is charged with approving this more detailed plan. We set the average daily loading of the rail system at 91,000 cars, the transport of commercial freight at 131 million tons, and the volume of passenger transport at 12 billion passenger kilometers. The volume of water transport is set at 12 billion tons and of sea transport at 7.8 billion tons. We set the volume of capital work at 7909 million rubles and financing at 7048 million rubles, taking into account the lowering of construction costs. Retail trade of state and cooperative stores is set at 28 million rubles. The market fund for grain is set at 3100 thousand tons, for grits at 230 thousand tons and for sugar at 360 thousand tons, for vodka at 20,300 thousand deciliters. We ask you to send your opinion.[18]

These control figures create an underwhelming impression. They are general and provide little real guidance. The 1936 fourth-quarter plan provides the most specific control figures, but sets only highly aggregated figures for industry. The 1931 fourth-quarter plan deals only in generalities. The 1932 third-quarter plan contained the most specific instructions, even micromanaging the distribution of metals, because it pushed a personal initiative of Stalin – the delivery of manufactured consumer goods to the countryside. All set investment limits, consistent with the previous chapter's thesis that the Politburo was primarily interested in the investment figures.

[17] Ibid., 473.
[18] Ibid., 658–9.

The immediate response of those required to carry out these instructions was also underwhelming. Kaganovich ended his letter on the 1931 fourth-quarter plan on the following sour note: "Gosplan is giving us useless information about the grain-fodder balance."[19] After the Politburo's discussion of the 1932 third-quarter plan, the Politburo met with the industrial ministers, who shrugged off the cost-reduction targets: "The most important and dangerous point is that the managers of production do not worry about the ruble [about the cost of production]."[20] The transfer of manufactured consumer goods to the countryside had been a persistent demand of Stalin in the summer of 1932: "The main task is to send the maximum amounts of manufactured consumer goods to the grain-, sugar-, and cotton-producing regions in June and July so that these goods will be available in July and August." Stalin warned Kaganovich: "The Politburo Commission on Manufactured Consumer Goods was formed so that this would be managed by you and Postyshev. From this day on, any weakness will be regarded as a weakness of Kaganovich and Postyshev."[21] Despite Stalin's intense interest, Kaganovich reported that the program was faltering:

Despite the fact that the ministers are beginning to understand the seriousness of the situation and are trying to fulfill the decision, we are helpless in practice. They still don't have information on fulfillment by quarters.... Fulfillment of the Politburo decree concerning the increase of manufactured consumer goods in the villages by 604 million rubles is going particularly badly. Unfortunately, we still don't have figures for June because goods going through supply bases do not count whether they go to the city or countryside.[22]

The Politburo's five-year plan directives create a similarly weak impression. The Second Five-Year Plan (1933–37) directives approved by the Seventeenth Party Congress in 1932 had eleven targets in physical units and five targets in value units.[23] The Politburo itself set only a few control figures, usually twenty or so key output targets. Table 5.1 shows the Politburo's 1951 control-figure directives for 1955 as proposed by

[19] Ibid., 119.
[20] Ibid., 154.
[21] Ibid., 162.
[22] Ibid., 174.
[23] Zaleski, *Stalinist Planning*, 117. The targets in physical units were coal, crude oil, coke, electric power, pig iron, mineral fertilizer, tractors, sown area, grain harvest, average grain yield, and industrial population. The value indicators (expressed as indexes) were national income in current and fixed prices, industrial production, machine building, per-capita consumption, and investment.

TABLE 5.1. *Targets for the Fifth Five-Year Plan*

Category	Growth	Factor
	Politburo/Malenkov proposals, 1951	Stalin (margin comments), 1951
National income	70%	
Investment	105%	
Consumption	50%	
Freight turnover	44%	
Trade turnover	74%	
Costs in industry	−20%	
Industrial labor productivity	52%	
Construction labor productivity	47%	
Wage fund	30%	
Industrial output	80%	70%
Group A (intermediate goods)	90%	80%
Group B (consumer goods)	70%	65%
Agricultural Output		
Grain	35–40	40–50%
Wheat	n.a.	55–65%
Cotton	55–65	
Flax	35–40	40–50%
Sugar beet	60–65	65–70%
Sunflower seeds	40–45	50–60%
Feed grains	2.5–3	

Source: RGASPI. 592-1-6: 3,6 (XIX Party Congress file located in Hoover Institution archives, films 2.2590–2602).

Deputy Premier G. Malenkov, along with margin corrections made by Stalin himself.[24] After two decades of planning, less than twenty indicators were given and most were aggregated figures, such as investment, consumption, and heavy industry. As late as 1951, Gosplan's detailed version of the five-year plan was broken down only into 127 physical products.[25]

The perfunctory manner in which the Politburo set control figures belies the stereotype of scientific planning. Control figures were set haphazardly. Stalin, acting often as an oracle from Sochi, appeared to pull the "optimal" number out of the air. We suspect that Stalin's oracle figures

[24] These figures are from the XIX Party Congress Fund of the Hoover Institution archives (RGAE, Fund 592).
[25] A. Tikhonov and P. Gregory, "Stalin's Last Plan," in *Behind the Façade of Stalin's Command Economy,* ed. P. Gregory (Stanford, Calif.: Hoover Institution Press, 2001), 176.

were based only on experience, intuition, and bargaining. Those responsible for producing the control-figure target would usually object that it
was too high. Kaganovich to Stalin: "Mikoian [responsible for grain collections and exports] of course objected."[26] There was considerable open
and concealed bargaining. Stalin to Kaganovich: "Sheboldaev [a regional
party boss] is asking for loans of five million puds for his 28 regions.... I
think that we can satisfy this request."[27] What the archives fail to say is
more telling. Lacking is a sense that the Politburo was convinced that the
control figures were vital instruments of central power. In fact, by 1951
Stalin paid little attention to control figures, regarding them as technical
matters for planning agencies.[28] It must have been apparent that setting a
few numbers, largely aggregated into broad categories like heavy or light
industry or retail sales, was not going to determine the overall allocation
of resources.

Five-Year Plans: Why Did They Survive?

Five-year plans were among the easiest to construct. They had to be prepared only once every five years, they used high levels of aggregation, and
they set only general goals for the economy. Eugene Zaleski, in his comprehensive study of Soviet plans, decisively demonstrated that five-year
plans were not operational. They were not translated into operational
plans and their record of fulfillment was poor. The targets of the first
five-year plan (1928–1933) were fulfilled, on average, less than 60 percent. The second five-year plan of 1933–1937 set more modest industrial
goals, but was fulfilled slightly over 70 percent (Table 5.2).[29] The third
five-year plan was interrupted by World War II. The fourth five-year plan
(1945–1950) showed the same pattern of nontranslation into operational
plans. The defense plan of the fifth five-year plan fell way below targets.[30]

Societies discard institutions that "fail." The nonexecution of five-year
plans could be interpreted as an institutional failure; yet, five-year plans
remained a revered pillar of the system until the end of the Soviet Union.

---

[26] Khlevnyuk, *Stalin i Kaganovich. Perepiski*, 91.

[27] Ibid., 556.

[28] Tikhonov and Gregory, "Stalin's Last Plan," 174–5.

[29] The mean absolute deviation from 100 percent plan fulfillment was slightly less than one
third, about three times the cumulated mean absolute deviation of the five individual
annual plans of this period.

[30] Paul Gregory, "Why Soviet Defense Puzzles: Archieves, Strategy, and Underfulfillment,
Europe–Asia Students 55, no. 6 (September 2003).

TABLE 5.2. *Mean Absolute Deviation from 100% Plan Fulfillment (Annual Plan vs. Five-Year Plan)*

	1933	1934	1935	1936	1937	1938	Avg. 33–37	5YP 33–37
Industry	16.1	15.5	11.7	11.9	16.9	10.4	14.4	30.5
Agriculture	11.3	7.8	9.3	19.6	17.7	na	13.1	29.9
Transport	11.3	12.6	10.5	11.4	11.7	7.3	11.5	24.3
Employment	10.4	6.4	6.9	6.6	4.4	4.7	6.9	21.1
Wage	2.8	11.2	7.6	12.0	5.7	5.9	7.9	66.5
All	10.4	10.7	9.2	12.3	11.3	7.1	10.8	34.5

Source: Compiled from Eugene Zaleski, *Stalinist Planning for Economic Growth 1933–1952* (Chapel Hill: University of North Carolina Press, 1980), 279.

The five-year plan was dropped during World War II and could have remained buried, but it was revived at the war's end. Its persistence suggests that the five-year plan remained of value to the Soviet leadership. If, as Zaleski concludes, the five-year plan served as a "vision of growth" to inspire the population, Soviet leaders must have concluded that it made a positive net contribution. The fact of plan failure could either be neutralized by focusing attention on the next plan or through false claims of success – a form of the "big lie." Indeed, officially, all five-year plans were successful, even those that failed miserably. The first five-year plan, which met only slightly more than half of its goals, was declared by the Seventeenth Party Conference of January/February 1932 as "assuring the completion of the construction of the foundations of socialism."[31]

That the secretive Soviet leadership published five-year plans with fanfare – usually as the culmination of a Party Congress – supports the Zaleski view that they were important public rituals. Virtually all five-year plans were approved well after they began, so there was little pretext that they were actually guiding resources. The First Five-Year Plan (for 1928 to 1933) was approved in the spring of 1929; the Fifth Five-Year Plan (1950 to 1955) was approved in August 1952.[32] By the time these five-year plans were finally approved, the leadership surely would have been aware that they could not be fulfilled. Each five-year plan, however, delivered a message. The First Five-Year Plan told of a Great Break-Through that would overcome Russia's backwardness in a remarkable short period of time

[31] Davies, *Crisis and Progress*, 134.
[32] Davies, *The Soviet Economy in Turmoil*, 67; Tikhonov and Gregory, "Stalin's Last Plan," 173.

if everyone pitched in and sacrificed. "Enemies" did not want the program to succeed; hence, everyone must be on guard against wreckers and other saboteurs. The First Five-Year Plan was released with breathtaking promises. Stalin, in a November 1929 article, triumphantly described the "unleashing of the creative initiatives and creative elan of the masses.... We are going full steam ahead to socialism along the road of industrialization, leaving behind our traditional 'Russian backwardness.'"[33] Wildly optimistic claims were made that Soviet industrial production, which then stood at 5 percent of the United States, would exceed the United States by the early 1940s.[34] Gosplan's initial April 1929 target for pig-iron production from new factories was set at 1.3 million tons. The optimal variant actually approved was for 2.6 million tons, but was raised to 6.1 million tons in December 1929.[35] Within an eight-month period, the target was raised by a factor of five!

That the first five-year plan was a political document is seen in the fact that revisions were directed by the party (through its Worker-Peasant Inspection). The state's planning agency, Gosplan, was relegated to the sidelines, forced to root for its fulfillment. An earlier skeptical Gosplan official (Strumilin) was forced to enthuse in September 1929, "our industrialization program is not only not exaggerated; on the contrary, it is too cautious."[36] Planners and plant managers, who pleaded for some semblance of realism, were labeled as class enemies and wreckers.[37] Enterprises were told not to prove that they could not produce their plans "but to present to the appropriate higher authorities the conditions under which these targets will be fulfilled."[38]

The message of the second five-year plan (1933–37) was that the great successes of the first five-year plan allowed for moderation but that benefits for ordinary people were not far off. The few targets for 1937 presented at the Seventeenth Party Conference of January 30 to February 4, 1932, were substantially lower than those proposed by Gosplan a half year earlier. Notably, the proposed increases in consumption of the second five-year plan were as fantastic as the industrial targets of the first five-year plan. By 1937, the production of consumer goods was at least to

---

[33] These and other quotes from Stalin are from Davies, *The Soviet Economy in Turmoil*, 95–6.
[34] Ibid., 68.
[35] Davies, *The Soviet Economy in Turmoil*, 498.
[36] Ibid., 92–3.
[37] Ibid., 67–70, chapter 6.
[38] Quote of Kuibyshev, in ibid., 185.

double or perhaps even triple – a goal cynically announced by the head of Gosplan and Politburo member, Kuibyshev. As remarked by R. W. Davies: "At a time when hunger was haunting the USSR, he [Kuibyshev] brazenly assured the conference...the Soviet Union will be the most advanced country in the world in its level, showing all working people what the working class can attain by creating socialism.'"[39] Although the fulfillment of the second five-year plan was considerably better than the first, the outlandish growth targets for the consumer sector meant that retail trade targets were met only 50 percent.[40]

Subsequent five-year plans did not carry as important messages as the first two. The drafting of the third five-year plan (1938–1942) was carried out as the Great Purges tore Gosplan and the country apart.[41] The purge of Gosplan began in March 1937, culminating in accusations that wreckers within Gosplan were disrupting the economy and undermining the defense of the country. Two chairmen of Gosplan (Mezhlauk and his successor Smirnov) were arrested and then executed, as was the chairman of the statistics committee.[42] The execution of the third five-year plan was interrupted by World War II, during which conventional planning was dropped in favor of specific mobilization plans. The fourth five-year plan (1945–1950) was a plan of reconstruction with rather simple priorities: to restore those branches destroyed by war to their prewar levels.[43] Stalin paid little attention to the fifth five-year plan, suggesting either that he had become convinced that five-year plans were unimportant or that his waning health prevented him from active participation.[44] The fifth five-year plan was the result of jockeying among planning agencies (Gosplan, the new State Supply Committee, and the Ministry of Finance) rather than the outcome of debate within the Politburo.

---

[39] Davies, *Crisis and Progress*, 137–8.

[40] Zaleski, *Stalinist Planning*, 157.

[41] Preparation of the third five-year plan began in February 1936 amid awards and praise for Gosplan on its fifteenth anniversary, with the instruction to complete the work within six months. In 1936, Stalin gave only very general instructions on harvests and electric power production. In 1928 and 1932, he issued much more specific targets. Although Gosplan's work on the third five-year plan was nearing completion in 1936, work was halted and then resumed in April 1937 mainly due to the growing threat of war. A number of articles appeared in 1937 that gave detailed figures on plan goals. In February 1938, Gosplan began work all over again, the result of which was the text presented by Molotov to the eighteenth Party Congress on March 14–17, 1939. Zaleski, *Stalinist Planning*, 161–212.

[42] This description is from ibid., chapter 8.

[43] Ibid., 503.

[44] Tikhonov and Gregory, "Stalin's Last Plan," 174–5.

Stalin attached importance to positive "visions of the future." Stalin to Kaganovich and Molotov (June 9, 1932):

It is necessary immediately to initiate a campaign in the press about the extremely rich perspectives of [our] oil reserves. It is necessary in a series of Izvestia articles to 'scream out' about the unbelievably rich reserves in these regions.... It is necessary to arrange a series of interviews with geologists, particularly Gubkin...with declarations about the unique reserves of oil in the eastern regions."

Stalin wished this optimistic information to be broadcast not only to lift spirits, but also because "It is fully possible that such a campaign will interest English–American companies to take up negotiations with us again and to offer compromises."[45]

Operational Plans

If the Soviet administrative-command economy was run by plans, it was not the five-year plans. Rather, it would be run according to shorter-term plans that provided more detail and issued actual instructions. Chapter 8 discusses operational planning and shows that virtually all "operational" plans were simply tentative agreements between producers and their superiors on what to produce and to whom to deliver the production. Most operational planning was done not by the Council of People's Commissars or by its official planner, Gosplan, but by the producers themselves. Operational plans often did not even exist (e.g., annual plans that were received only half way through the year or not at all), or they could be changed by interventions of a wide array of state and party officials. Insofar as operational plans did not serve as "visions of growth," they were compiled out of sight; changes in them were not noticed by the public.

Why the Stalinist Pattern of Growth?

Five-year plans were not translated into operational plans. Virtually all operational plans were preliminary and could be changed at will. According to Zaleski, resources were allocated by resource management, not by plans. Yet, comparative appraisals reveal that the command economies produced economic outcomes quite different from market economies. The USSR and Eastern Europe consistently produced more heavy industry and defense goods, fewer services, less foreign trade, higher investment rates, and lower urbanization than market economies at a similar level of

[45] Khlevnyuk, *Stalin i Kaganovich Perepiski, 151.*

economic development. These well-established empirical results demonstrate that planners' preferences not only differed, but also that these differences mattered. [46] The distinctive "Stalinist" pattern of growth indicates that, even if resources were not directed by plans, resource managers themselves operated according to implicit rules and practices that were transmitted from the Soviet Union to other planned economies.

These rules and practices were not related through high-level priority statements, which were either too general or too specific. Consider the Politburo's toothless decree of July 19, 1936:

> The Council of People's Commissars and the Central Committee consider the main objective of the industrial ministries for 1937 to be the decisive improvement in the quality of production, the guaranteeing of the completeness of production, and the consistency of delivered production with the assortment approved by the government according to state standards and technical conditions.[47]

The Politburo's priority statement of September 1932 was specific but related only to vehicles:

> Preserve the position of current users of vehicles with a slight increase to light industry producing items of manufactured consumer goods, continue the policy of mechanization of agriculture, and give preference to union over regional organizations.[48]

Stalin's cuts issued in July 1935 were even more specific:

> There are some things which must not be reduced: defense, locomotives under the ministry of transportation allocation, the building of schools – under the ministry of education, re-equipment under light industry, paper and cellulose factories – under the heading "Timber," some very necessary enterprises [enumerated] under heavy industry.[49]

Priorities do not have to be spelled out if they are understood by all. Heavy industry and defense mattered most. As Zaleski writes:

> The upshot...is that economic policy, as expressed in plans, is not implemented. The five-year plans are not actually put into operation and the annual and quarterly plan – poorly coordinated, late, and put into operation piecemeal – represent

[46] Gur Ofer, *The Service Sector in Soviet Economic Growth* (Cambridge, Mass.: Harvard University Press, 1973); Simon Kuznets, "A Comparative Appraisal," in *Economic Trends in the Soviet Union*, eds. Abram Bergson and Simon Kuznets (Cambridge, Mass.: Harvard University Press, 1963), 333–82; Paul Gregory, *Socialist and Nonsocialist Industrialization Patterns* (New York: Praeger, 1970).
[47] Khlevnyuk et al., *Stalinskoe Politburo*, 150.
[48] Valery Lazarev and Paul Gregory, "The Wheels of a Command Economy," *Economic History Review* 60 (May 2002): 324–48.
[49] R. W. Davies and O. Khlevnyuk, "Gosplan," in *Decision Making in the Stalinist Command Economy, 1932–37*, ed. E. A Rees (London: MacMillan, 1997), 55.

only one of the elements of a whole network of decisions.... To the extent that planned goals as a whole became impossible, the government is forced to make choices that it thought it could avoid thanks to plans.... The choices by government follow a pattern. Producer goods and freight traffic are regularly favored at the expense of agricultural production and consumer goods.... The results show a real Stalinist "model of growth."[50]

Thus, resource managers from the highest to the lowest levels clearly understood the tradeoff rules, which remained remarkably constant over time and space. Heavy industry is more important than light industry. Defense orders are more important than civilian orders. Orders should be filled from domestic production, not imports. Services are unimportant and can be neglected. These are rather simple rules, and they were apparently deeply embedded in the thinking of resource managers.

The Politburo could make only a few decisions itself. Most had to be delegated to agents who dealt directly with the managers of production in the industrial ministries. The next chapter turns to the hierarchical organization of the administrative-command economy, from the dictator at the apex to the enterprise at the lowest level.

Concluding Comments

The Soviet dictator retained the façade of five-year plans, despite the opportunity to ditch them after World War II. Five-year plans were proudly exported to satellite countries in Eastern Europe and in China. Soviet advisors in India assisted with the formulation of five-year plans in the 1950s and 1960s. The five-year plan was accepted as a key propaganda instrument to explain to the public at large the promises of communism. Five-year plans were announced with great fanfare followed by silence as major targets were abandoned as unrealistic. The astonishing success of the previous five-year plan would then be extolled as the next five-year plan was prepared. In the 1930s, the five-year plan explained why sacrifices were necessary by focusing on the brighter future. The principal message of all five-year plans was that "things are getting better; life is becoming happier," to use Stalin's expression.

The Soviet leadership kept the institution of the five-year plan because they concluded that it yielded benefits in excess of its costs. No harm could be done by focusing the population on the image of a brighter future. We should ask, however, whether unfulfilled promises imposed costs, not only in the postwar period, but also even in the 1930s when the sacrifices

---

[50] Zaleski, *Stalinist Planning*, 503–4.

were the greatest. The fair-wage model of the previous chapter suggested that worker effort depends on notions of fairness and equity. Indeed, workers in 1930 might have been persuaded to work hard for paltry wages if they were convinced that the sacrifices were necessary. They might also be convinced to sacrifice if they were told that "things were not going well" because of foreign enemies, drought, or other catastrophes. However, the drumbeat of Soviet propaganda was on the successes achieved despite great odds. The factories were spewing out cars, trucks, torpedoes, textiles, and manufactured consumer goods, they were told. Workers, whose real wages have not risen and living under trying conditions, at some point would ask: When do we get our share? If they conclude they are not, their response would be to demand a higher fair wage.

One small example typifies the possible consequences: On June 12, 1932, Stalin personally ordered "*Pravda* to publish the daily production of automobiles at the AMO and Gorky factories."[51] Shortly thereafter, the Council of People's Commissars received a request for automobiles from the Karagan Party Committee with the attached note: "Earlier we did not insist. Now with Gorky works in operation, I demand that you supply us." [52] If ordinary workers responded to the promises and claims of success as did this single party committee from a remote part of Kazakhstan, increased allocations of resources to consumption and away from investment would be required just to keep the current level of effort constant. If the claimed successes were not validated by real increases in living standards, workers indeed would become (as in Stalin's words at the beginning of this chapter) "exhausted, distraught, worn-out, despondent, and lagging behind."

[51] Khlevnyuk et al., *Stalin i Kaganovich. Perepiski*, 161.
[52] Karaganda Oblast Administration, Kazakhstan, to Sovnarkom. GARF 5446.14.2029v. 219-220.

6

Planners Versus Producers

The Planner vs. the Producer

Pencil sketch by Chairman of Gosplan, V. I. Mezhlauk, drawn at the March Plenum of the Central Committee of 1937 shows Politburo candidate member (Kosior) admonishing Deputy Minister of Heavy Industry (Piatakov): "I can't shut up this red-haired devil!" (RGASPI, f. 74, op. 2, d.170, l.30). Sketch from http://www.idf.ru

The first five chapters of this book describe how Stalin and his Politburo allies (Berliner's jockey) created the administrative-command system (Berliner's horse). These jockeys were few in number; they had to delegate to others to translate their instructions into concrete tasks. Most important, production was carried out by enterprises that were controlled not by the jockeys themselves, but by intermediate industrial and regional bodies that were held responsible for the results of the enterprises subordinated to them. The administrators of the administrative-command system, therefore, can be split into two rough groups: the "planners" and the "producers." The planners were the jockeys themselves, assisted by numerous experts. The producers were those who either produced the output or were held responsible for the production of the output. In the terms of Chapter 3, the planners issued the "general line" of the party with respect to its economic goals in the form of plans, instructions, and interventions, whereas the producers executed this general line.

During the NEP period, producers largely made their own decisions. They combined into trusts and marketed their output through syndicates, only loosely controlled by planners. As the Great Break-Through proceeded, ministerial and regional authorities replaced the trusts and syndicates. Enterprises that had earlier been free to decide what to produce and to whom to sell were now ordered what to produce, to whom to deliver, and at what prices. Just as the peasant opposed the imposition of force on the countryside, the producers opposed the imposition of force on them. Producers, unlike peasants, did not react with armed revolt. Rather, they reacted in more subtle ways with the aim of preserving as much authority as possible and protecting themselves against unreasonable orders. This chapter describes this battle between planners and producers.

The Delegation Dilemma

A democratic legislature or a dictator, be it a Stalin or a small group (a Politburo), can make relatively few decisions itself due to limits of time and space. The Politburo's decision-making capacity can be gleaned from its records. In the 1930s, between 2,300 and 3,500 decisions were registered annually in Politburo decrees.[1] In the early 1930s, the Politburo dealt with as many as fifty issues per meeting. At Stalin's request, the number of issues per meeting was temporarily limited to fifteen in

---

[1] Khlevnyuk et al., *Stalinskoe Politburo*, 15.

1932,[2] but by the mid-1930s, it was dealing with between one hundred and one thousand points per meeting.[3] Although the number of Politburo decisions appears large, it represented a miniscule portion of all the decisions required to run an economy composed of thousands of enterprises, spread out over the world's largest country. In January 1930, the entire staff of the Central Committee equaled 375 persons with the two largest departments being the Secret Department (103 persons) and the Chancellery Department (123). Other departments, such as the Organizational, Instructional, and Cultural departments, employed fewer than fifty persons each.[4] The Secret Department's 1932 wage bill was only 20,000 rubles per month.[5] Thus, the central party apparatus had fewer than four hundred persons to assist with the formulation, transmission, and monitoring of directives and orders. The largest central state agency – Gosplan, then including the Central Statistical Administration – employed only nine hundred persons in the early 1930s – too few, it felt, to get the job done. Gosplan's Department of Energy and Electrification (one of its most important departments) was staffed by only thirty persons. A Gosplan department head (chemicals section) complained that "we cannot present and decide even one issue because of the complete lack of workers."[6] In 1935–36, Gosplan's employment had grown to eight hundred, not including the Central Statistical Administration.[7]

That the dictator cannot make all decisions requires that some must be delegated. Logic suggests that the dictator would reserve the "important" decisions for himself while delegating the technical details to experts. Hayek wrote of the problems of delegation of a democratic legislature, but his insights apply equally to a dictator:

The objectionable feature is that delegation is so often resorted to because the matter in hand cannot be regulated by general rules but only by the exercise of

---

[2] Ibid., 25.

[3] Ibid., 196–250.

[4] Ibid., 14–15.

[5] The Secret Department's budget provides considerable detail, such as the number of cigarettes allocated to Stalin's office (5,000 to 6,000 per month), monthly food expenditures of Stalin's office (24,000 rubles), and the number of special ration categories provided to each office, which included all those who worked after 11 P.M. Ibid., 28–9.

[6] For examples of the serious complaints from Gosplan departments concerning the lack of personnel, see memos from Vagransky (energy and electrification) and Blinov (chemical section) to Gosplan director Kuibyshev. (State Archive of the Economy, Gosudarstvenny Arkhiv Ekonomiki, hereafter referred to as RGAE. This statement is from RGAE.4372.39.34.85, RGAE.4372.39.34, 9-93).

[7] GARF.9372.39.85-86.

discretion in the decision of particular cases. In these instances delegation means that some authority is given power to rule with force of law what to all intents and purposes are arbitrary decisions. ... The delegation of particular technical tasks to separate bodies, while a regular feature, is yet only the first step in a process whereby a democracy [read in this case: dictatorship] which embarks on planning progressively *relinquishes its power*. [Author's italics].[8]

In the Soviet case, the inevitable delegation of power posed a number of threats. First, Stalin and his allies, as specialists in totalitarian power, would clearly understand Hayek's insight about the potential loss of power through delegation; accordingly, they would be inclined to underdelegate to guard their political power. Second, there were only a limited number of "Old Bolsheviks" who were also technical experts. The more abundant nonparty specialists were of questionable loyalty. Many had belonged to the Menshevik Party and others had occupied technical positions, such as in banking or finance. How could power be turned over to such people? Third, it is inherently difficult to distinguish substantive decisions from technical ones. Is the decision to increase the production of ammonia sulfate by 10 percent a technical or substantive decision? Is the decision to locate a new plant in Stalingrad or Leningrad to be made by the dictator or by experts?

Whom Can You Trust?

The Soviet administrative-command economy was organized as a three-tiered system (Figure 6.1). The top tier consisted of the dictator. The second tier was made up of the bureaucratic agents, such as Gosplan (as the most important), the finance ministry, the labor department, and so on, that translated the dictator's directives into concrete tasks. We label these two tiers generically as planners. The third tier consisted of industrial ministries and enterprises responsible for fulfilling concrete tasks, called – in the difficult-to-translate Soviet parlance – "managers of production" (*khoziaistvenniki*). We label this third tier generically as producers.

The "dictator" consisted of the interlocking directorate of the Politburo and its state arm, the Council of Peoples' Commissars, hereafter denoted by its acronym SNK (*Sovet narodnykh kommissarov*). The directorate was interlocking because the key positions in SNK were occupied by Politburo members and by those being groomed for Politburo

---

[8] Hayek, *The Road to Serfdom*, 74.

Schematic version

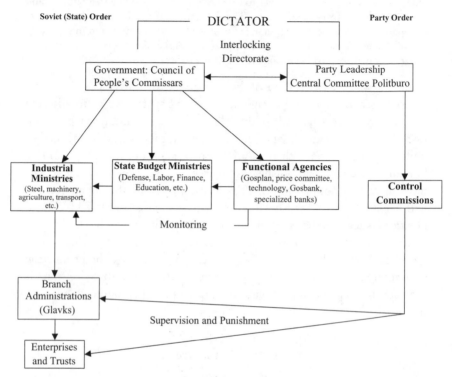

FIGURE 6.1. Central Soviet administration.

membership. The administrative-command system was divided into a party and state (Soviet) order. The state order, headed by SNK, was supposed to run the country on a day-to-day basis. The party order was to set basic policy through its "leading role." In practice, the party was heavily involved in the routine running of the economy.

SNK was organized into branch and functional organizations managed by a central administration headed by its long-serving chairman, V. Molotov – in effect, the "prime minister" of the USSR. Although the Soviet state was nominally under the control of a Central Executive Committee, its highest governing body was SNK, whose main task was the management of the economy. There was a "small Gosplan" within SNK, whose branch staffs were spread very thin. For example, all automobile and aviation business was handled by one person and two secretaries.[9]

---

[9] Lazarev and Gregory, "The Wheels of a Command Economy," 328–32.

SNK was made up of industrial ministries (ranging from three in 1930 to twenty three in 1939), of ministries funded directly from the state budget such as education, labor, and defense; and of state committees, such as Gosplan or the finance ministry, state control commissions (such as the Committee for Soviet Control), standing commissions, such as the Council for Labor and Defense, and assorted special commissions (such as the Price Committee, the Agricultural Procurement Committee, the Transport Committee, and the Fuel Committee). As a functional committee, Gosplan did not manage any specific sector of the economy, but it was responsible for preparing national economic plans. Its status was advisory rather than executive, and it reported directly to the highest political officials in the party and state.[10]

SNK had a number of consultative members including the Ministry of Interior (called OGPU, then NKVD, then MVD) and members from the various republican SNKs.[11] More than fourty thousand Ministry of Interior personnel were charged with guarding military factories in the early 1930s, a number that suggests they did more than physically guard facilities.[12] The interior ministry supplied "special communications" such as reports on working conditions, factory unrest, demonstrations, strikes, accounting violations, and construction defects in military aircraft. A "military acceptance" agency that was a part of the Ministry of Defense was present in enterprises producing for the military. The number of military inspectors in enterprises reached twenty thousand by 1940.[13]

Both the state and party had control commissions headed by the most "loyal" Politburo members that had the power to investigate wrongdoers up to the level of minister. The main control commission of the party, first named the Worker-Peasant Inspection and then the Party Control Commission, was among the most feared. The state's control commission, the Committee for Soviet Control, was also a powerful investigative organization. These control commissions often worked hand-in-hand with the Ministry of Justice and the procuracy, to which wrongdoers were referred after investigations. Wrongdoing by the highest-ranking officials was punished directly by the Politburo, which had the power to levy

---

[10] Davies and Khlevnyuk, "Gosplan," 32.
[11] On these matters, see Rees and Watson, "Politburo and Sovnarkom," 9–32.
[12] N. Simonov, *Voenno-Promyshlenny Kompleks v 1920-1950-e gody* (Moscow: Rosspen, 1995), 106–7.
[13] M. Harrison and N. Simonov, "Voenpriemka: Prices, Costs, and Quality Assessment in Defense Industries," in *The Soviet Defense-Industry Complex from Stalin to Khrushchev,* eds. J. Barber and M. Harrison (London: MacMillan, 1998), 326–47.

extreme penalties, even the death sentence. Notably, Gosplan was not an enforcer; it lacked punitive power. It could only threaten or ask punitive agencies to back it up. Gosplan routinely called on others to enforce its directives. In 1933, Gosplan requested that the Committee for Soviet Control investigate "the crude mistakes and noneconomic use of resources of pipe factories in Leningrad" and "in the shortest possible time to find the guilty and turn them over to the courts." It requested that the same commission investigate why the Ministry of Forestry Products did not build an electrical station in Arkhangelsk.[14] In 1934, Gosplan even asked the state procurator "to establish criminal responsibility for exaggerated orders, incorrect information about supplies, and receipt of funded materials and equipment without funds."[15]

The industrial ministries, called People's Commissariats (*narodnye kommissariaty*), constituted SNK's *branch* departments and were responsible for specific branches of the economy. They will be discussed in the next chapter. For now, they will be seen primarily in their role of protagonists to SNK, Gosplan, and the finance ministry. Industrial interests and regional authorities formed the lobbies that pleaded special interests.[16] The industrial ministries were more generously staffed than central institutions. The Ministry of Transportation had a central staff of 7,600 and a total employment of 62,000 in 1932 before being cut to 39,000 in 1933. In 1938, employment in the Ministry of Heavy Industry was 7,375, and in 1933 the Ministry of Light Industry employed between 2,547 and 3,989 persons, depending on how ministry boundaries are drawn.[17]

The party's and state's lack of expert staff dictated that most of the actual work of planning and running the economy be carried out by the better staffed functional committees, such as Gosplan and the finance ministry, but, most important, by the industrial ministries themselves. The Politburo and SNK were highly dependent on state committees, control commissions, and secret police to prepare and monitor plans, but they had to rely on industrial ministries for most of their economic information and for detailed planning work. Clearly, the all-powerful Politburo could have created a large internal staff. Perhaps those at the top did not

---

[14] RGAE 4372.31.35, 172, 204.

[15] RGAE 4372.32.27, 215.

[16] P. Rutland, *The Myth of the Plan* 237–57; P. J. Boettke and G. Anderson, "Soviet Venality: A Rent-Seeking Model of the Communist State," *Public Choice* 93, (1997), 37–53; and D. Treisman, *After the Deluge: Regional Crises and Political Consolidation in Russia* (Ann Arbor: University of Michigan Press, 1999), 30–2.

[17] These figures are from chapter 7, this volume.

want large staffs that might temper their power to decide. Or they felt that there were simply too few reliable staffers who could be trusted.

The central government of the USSR employed approximately one lakh persons in the mid-1930s. The breakdown of employment by state agencies is provided in Appendix B.

Vertical Versus Horizontal Relations. Early writers on the administrative-command economy, ranging from Hayek and Mises to contemporary writers such as Mancur Olson (see Chapter 1), paid little attention to the manner in which the dictatorship would organize its bureaucratic staff to manage producers. Mises and Hayek spoke vaguely of a central planning board that would deal directly with enterprises. Students of dictatorships also simplified it by assuming "costless coercion"; namely, that the dictator could costlessly persuade subordinates to do his bidding.[18]

Figure 6.1 describes the vertical hierarchy of an administrative-command economy. It does not explicitly show horizontal structures, which are nevertheless present. There are a number of ministries, a larger number of ministry main administrations, and thousands of enterprises, all of which can have horizontal relationships with others at the same level. The vertical structure has clear lines of authority: the Politburo/SNK is superior to the industrial ministry, which is superior to the enterprises. The vertical structure operates on the basis of "vertical trust." For the dictator's orders to be executed, vertical orders passed down through the formal hierarchy must be obeyed. Subordinates, such as ministries or enterprises, may also engage in informal horizontal relations that unleash conflicts between the formal "vertical" and the informal "horizontal" structures.[19] Instead of obeying the planner's instruction to deliver hundred units of output to B, A might deliver instead to C based on an informal agreement. The dictator must oppose horizontal relations among industrial ministries, or among factories, because they weaken control, particularly when they form into organized interest groups.

Figure 6.2 shows the source of conflict between vertical and horizontal structures. The right-hand diagram depicts the production and allocation of a particular industrial commodity such as pig iron, denoted by X in an administrative-command system. The demand curve D shows the quantity of X demanded by the various potential users at different prices. The price could be the official price or some more comprehensive price, which

---

[18] Wintrobe, *The Political Economy of Dictatorship*, 208–12.
[19] Ibid.

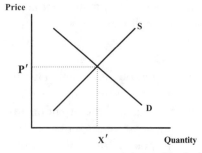
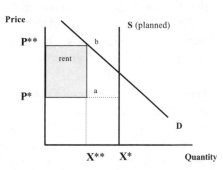

FIGURE 6.2. Vertical vs. horizontal structures.

captures the resources costs of potential users to acquire X. The supply
curve S shows the production of X ordered by the planner (which we
assume will actually be produced in this case).

If this were a market economy (see left-hand diagram, Figure 6.2), the
market would determine how much of X is produced, and all those willing
to pay the market price (P′) would get X′. In the administrative-command
economy, the dictator decides both how much X is produced and who
gets X. The dictator uses his "visible hand" of allocative power to reward
and punish either for economic or political ends. The dictator sets the
production of X at X* and its price at P*. At this price, the producer is
supposed to sell the entire output (X*) to authorized buyers at the official
price P*. In a pure vertical system, the dictator decides who gets X* among
all those willing to pay the official price, P*. If there is perfect vertical trust,
subordinates will obey orders, and only those designated to receive X will
actually get it.

Horizontal structures inevitably compete with vertical structures. The
producer of X realizes that it is producing a valuable commodity. In fact,
a number of buyers are prepared to pay well in excess of the official
price. Buyers are prepared to buy X** at P**. If the producer sells X**
to unauthorized buyers at P**, the producer gains a "rent" denoted by
the shaded area of the rectangle P*abP**. Those who are prepared to
pay more may also be those who supply the producer of X with another
valuable commodity, Y. The producer of Y also realizes that it is producing
a valuable commodity for which a number of buyers are prepared to pay
more than the official price. If producers of X and Y follow vertical orders,
they receive the official price P*, they have not violated any orders, and
they will receive rewards from the planner. On the other hand, both have

passed up the opportunity to sell above the official price. They could obtain, in addition to the official price, monetary bribes, maintain good relations with their own best customers, or receive preferential treatment if the buyer happens to be a supplier.

If the reward from the horizontal transaction (the rent) exceeds the reward for vertical loyalty, the producer will engage in illegal or unplanned horizontal transactions. In extreme cases, horizontal transactions dominate vertical transactions. The planner loses effective control of transactions and serves instead as a kind of referee, who must organize and control the rents of various competing interest groups.[20] The effective loss of control leads to "red sclerosis,"[21] of an economy dominated by interest groups.

The dictator (SNK/Politburo) does not have the time, resources, and information to set the production and distribution of the thousands or millions of Xs in an actual economy. A Gosplan must draw up plans for output (the Xs in the diagram) and its distribution among users consistent with the dictator's preferences. Gosplan, other functional agencies, and control commissions may also obstruct horizontal transactions, which threaten the vertical distribution plan. To perform these tasks, planners require accurate and timely information and would have to decide at what level of detail to plan. With 20 million distinct products, Gosplan could plan only aggregated products. Even if Gosplan planned only a few specific products, its less than one thousand specialists would be overwhelmed if it planned actual transactions, with instructions on dates, times, and terms of delivery. Planners would have to pick and choose their tasks.

Encompassing Versus Narrow Interests. Neither Stalin nor Hayek and Mises anticipated that the dictatorial interlocking directorate itself would inevitably be split into "them" (those representing narrow interests) and "us" (the relatively few representing "encompassing" interests). The number of top party officials who could occupy encompassing positions, independent of branch or regional interests, was limited. Of the ten Politburo members, only three to five could represent encompassing interests. In the early 1930s, they included Stalin, his deputy (Kaganovich), and Molotov, his prime minister. One or two other Politburo members could chair encompassing institutions like control commissions, Gosplan, or SNK's central executive committee. Other Politburo members represented

---

[20] Boettke, *Calculation and Coordination,* 145–52.
[21] Olson, "The Devolution of Power, 9–42.

narrow – military, industrial, or regional – organizations that had to fulfill export plans, military budgets, or meet industrial production targets.
Sergo Ordzhonikidze, one of the most influential Politburo members,
headed the heavy industry ministry. A. Mikoian (at the time, candidate
member of the Politburo) headed the embattled trade/supply ministry.
Politburo member A. A. Andreev headed the transport ministry before
being replaced by Kaganovich. Once Politburo members were assigned
jobs as managers of production, they began to represent narrow interests.

The conversion of trusted associates from us to them appears to have
caught Stalin off guard, who expressed dismay (particularly with his old
colleague, Ordzhonikidze) to Kaganovich:

> I do not understand how the Politburo was able to agree with the proposal of
> [Ordzhonikidze] concerning the import of more axles and wheels and quality
> steels. Both proposals represent direct violations of the July decision of the Central
> Committee concerning metal imports for 1931. As far as I understand it, they have
> simply hoodwinked you. *It is bad and disgusting if we begin to deceive each other.*
> [author's italics].[22]

Stalin's correspondence differentiates between us and them in his rejection of Mikoian's proposal to establish a grain reserve in his own
ministry. Stalin to Kaganovich on September 4, 1931: "How could you
[Kaganovich] allow such a betrayal? We should place this grain in the
reserves of the state so that it can be distributed only with the permission
of the Politburo or SNK."[23] Again, Stalin to Kaganovich (September 6,
1931): "We are against the anarchistic-syndicalist view that profits go to
the ministry and losses to the state. We regard the state higher than the
ministry."[24] When heavy industry minister Ordzhonikidze took advantage of his Politburo status to protect his enterprises from criticism (by A.
Vyshinksy, then deputy procurator), Stalin wrote Kaganovich two angry
letters on the same day, August 29, 1933:

> I learned that you [the Politburo] disputed the point in Vyshinsky's speech where
> he calls for ministerial responsibility in the matter of producing incomplete equip-
> ment. I consider such a decision wrong and harmful. It is a crude violation of the
> decision of the Central Committee. It is sad that Kaganovich and Molotov could
> not stand up to the bureaucratic pressure of the minister of heavy industry. . . . If
> you educate cadres in such a manner, we will not have one faithful party member
> left. A disgrace![25]

---

[22] Khlevnyuk et. al., *Stalin i Kaganovich. Perepiski*, 80.
[23] Ibid., 80.
[24] Ibid., 88.
[25] Ibid., 318–19.

Faced with the need to delegate and the surfeit of Politburo members loyal to encompassing interests, Stalin needed Gosplan and other functional agencies to serve as 100 percent loyal agents. The appointment of reliable persons could not alone ensure loyalty, even after the 1929 to 1930 purge of Gosplan removed "unreliable specialists." Stalin had to tolerate questionable experts, some attracting Stalin's personal wrath, until the Great Purges of 1937 to 1938. In effect, Gosplan and other functional agencies were offered an implicit contract: "If you serve as my loyal agent, you will not be held responsible for concrete economic results."[26]

The archives show that Gosplan understood this implicit contract only too well. There are virtually no documented cases of Gosplan departing from encompassing goals in the 1930s, with the exception of 1929 to 1930, when its leadership was purged for advocacy of moderate growth rates.[27] This first purge made Gosplan wary of any hint of disloyalty as is seen in Gosplan Chairman Kuibyshev's alarmed defense, when *Pravda* charged it with "skepticism" about plan fulfillment in July 1931. Kuibyshev had to lobby his Politburo colleagues for almost one month before Gosplan was absolved and *Pravda* reprimanded.[28] Gosplan cleared any substantive changes in policy with the Politburo (and Stalin personally) and obediently implemented arbitrary changes from above. The rare lapses of Gosplan disloyalty in the 1930s were isolated concessions at relatively low levels to make plans more realistic or to show understanding for failure to meet production targets. In a little-known case, a Gosplan official was rebuked for approving lower production targets, and the Politburo issued stern reprimands to the director of the trust and the plant manager – the usual penalty for plan failure; the guilty Gosplan official was issued an ordinary reprimand.[29]

Although Gosplan was divided into branch departments, the archives do not provide concrete evidence of lobbying for their branches, at least in this early period. Perhaps Stalin's open dislike of branch specialists served as a rein. Stalin to Molotov about the undue influence of Gosplan specialists: "It is sometimes even worse than that: not Gosplan but Gosplan 'sections' and their specialists are in charge."[30] The feared

[26] Gregory, *Restructuring the Soviet Economic Bureaucracy,* 23.
[27] Davies, *Soviet Economy in Turmoil,* 118–19.
[28] Khlevnyuk et al., *Stalin i Kaganovich. Perepiski,* 34.
[29] Khlevnyuk et al., *Stalinskoe Politbüro,* 86.
[30] Lih et al., *Stalin's Letters to Molotov,* 174–6.

tendency of branch departments to lobby for lower production targets may have materialized later, prompting another purge of Gosplan and the execution of its chairman.[31]

Most of Gosplan's official dealings were with the highest executive body of the state, SNK, its immediate superior, although it had considerable dealings with the Politburo as well. Judging from its actions, SNK considered Gosplan an honest broker: SNK used Gosplan as an internal staff department to prepare plans and state decrees but did not give Gosplan authority to issue its own operational state decrees. With a few exceptions, Gosplan's decrees had to be approved by SNK, although approval was usually a formality. SNK also relied on Gosplan to evaluate the flood of requests and petitions it received. When the industrial ministries tried to circumvent Gosplan, SNK sent their petitions back to Gosplan, as another sign of confidence. In its zeal to make its decisions on the side of SNK, Gosplan routinely complained that ministry plans did not prove that they complied with government programs. In this early period, ministries could request inputs without providing justification for their requests,[32] leaving Gosplan with the impossible (and unwelcome) task of checking consistency with state directives.

In keeping with its implicit contract, Gosplan actively avoided responsibility for concrete results. Throughout the 1930s, Gosplan asked to limit its role to generalized planning and avoid the setting of concrete tasks, such as delivery plans, for which it could be held responsible. Gosplan consistently tried to dodge SNK requests for expertise on material requests with protests that "we are simply not equipped to deal with such matters."[33] Gosplan sought, on numerous occasions, to be relieved of what it called "syndicate work," ostensibly because it lacked personnel. Nevertheless, Gosplan found itself drawn inadvertently into operational work.

A concrete example shows the fine line between planning and operations (syndicate work) that Gosplan had to navigate: In April 1933, Gosplan was freed at its own request from operational planning of printing, which was transferred to the Ministry of Forestry Products. A prescient internal memo warned that the "planning of paper means the

---

[31] Alexei Tikhonov and Paul Gregory, "Stalin's Last Plan," in *Behind the Facade of Stalin's Command Economy*, ed. P. Gregory (Palo Alto, Calif.: Hoover Institution Press, 2001), 165–6.

[32] Lazarev and Gregory, "The Wheels of a Command Economy," 329–30.

[33] RGAE, 4372.30.25, 186.

planning of printing for which the Ministry of Forestry Products is not suited,"[34] and reminded Gosplan of the national importance of printing. The memo correctly predicted that complaints against the Ministry of Forestry Products would be turned over to Gosplan. Indeed, Gosplan's freedom from planning paper was shortlived. Complaints mounted because paper planning meant the planning of printing. Gosplan reluctantly resumed the planning of both paper and printing, under the condition that publishers prepare their own plans, still leaving it with the substantial tasks of planning capital investment and distribution of printing.[35]

Gosplan consistently planned at a level of aggregation well above actual transactions to avoid blame for plan failure and routinely ceded resource-allocation authority to the industrial ministries. In a telling quote, Gosplan declared: "Gosplan is not a supply organization and cannot take responsibility either for the centralized specification of orders by product type or customer or the regional distribution of products."[36] Any power grab would have been unwelcome anyway by an agency that employed nonparty technicians, who in Stalin's words should be "hounded out of Moscow"[37] and who are turning the Politburo "into a court of appeals or a council of elders."[38]

It appears that no planner could distinguish between important and routine matters. Much Politburo time was devoted to trivial matters, such as travel requests or which particular enterprise should get more steel or an imported car. Kaganovich's account to the absent Ordzhonikidze of Politburo discussion of arcane engineering issues shows the bogging down in details:

Yesterday was a Politburo meeting, the second after the departure of the "master" [Stalin]. The "master" had asked to clarify whether parts in the M.1 are taken from the Buick? Indeed some of the parts ... are from the Buick and are different from the Ford. It is difficult for us to figure this out, and we asked the Ministry of Heavy Industry to report. Some think that this is OK; others think that this will negatively affect the quality of production.[39]

If the Politburo considered such trivia, any Gosplan decision could be interpreted as an incursion on its territory.

---

[34] RGAE, 4372.31.36, 33–4, 57.
[35] RGAE, 4372.31.39, 5.
[36] RGAE, 4372.32.28, 144–7.
[37] Lih et al., *Stalin's Letters to Molotov*, 174–6.
[38] Ibid., 174–6.
[39] Khlevnyuk et al., *Stalinskoe Politburo*, 150.

The Economics of Illusion

One constant of the Soviet administrative-command system is that information was almost exclusively generated by the producers themselves.[40] Peter Boettke wrote of the "economics of illusion" that apply in this situation; namely, the proclivity of producers to conceal or to distort information to pull the wool over the eyes of superiors.[41] The ministries were required to submit a voluminous amount of reporting (*otchetnosti*):[42] all reporting forms were confirmed by Gosplan's statistics office with agreement by the affected ministries, the Ministry of Finance, and Gosbank.[43] These formal reports were also supplemented by numerous ad hoc requests for information and for special reports. "They" (the industrial ministries) controlled the flow of information. "We" (the Politburo/SNK/Gosplan) did not gather its own independent information, although it did receive ad hoc information from its control commissions, the interior ministry, and military inspectors. The ministries had a strong *information advantage* relative to their superiors. Clearly, the administrative-command system could not be effectively administered with incorrect information. Thus, Gosplan and industrial ministries clashed regularly over information.

Producer Opportunism. The dictator had a simple goal for the managers of production: They should faithfully produce the goods ordered with a minimum expenditure of resources. The industrial ministry's and the enterprise's goal was "to fulfill the plan,"[44] the meaning of which was far from obvious. According to the principle of one-man management

---

[40] Gregory, *Restructuring the Soviet Economic Bureaucracy*, 16–17.

[41] P. J. Boettke, *Why Perestroika Failed: The Politics and Economics of Socialist Transformation* (New York: Routledge, 1993); for information distortions by managers, see Berliner, *Factory and Manager*, 160–81.

[42] Annual reports and balances broken down by main administrations to the Ministry of Finance (GARF, 5446.16?.1365,18); monthly and quarterly balances to State Bank (Gosbank) branch banks and to the finance ministry; monthly and quarterly balances to State Bank (Gosbank) branch banks and to the finance ministry; annual and monthly balances to Gosbank in cases where the enterprises have credits from Gosbank. On these rules, see *Sobranie Zakonov SSSR 1931*, no. 14, article 138, Decree of February 26, 1931, about the order of consideration and approval of reports and statements by economic organizations that are functioning on a self-financing basis, see *Sobranie Zakonov SSSR 1932*, no. 19, article 108/b of March 10, 1932; Decree of SNK, no. 1568 of July 3, 1934, about accounting reduction presenting by departments and economic organizations to the State Bank.

[43] GARF, 5446.16a.1365, 18.

[44] Belova, "Economic Crime and Punishment," 131–58.

(*edinonachalie*), the minister was responsible for the ministry plan, the enterprise manager for the enterprise plan. Managers, therefore, could use their information advantage to extract easy plans and excessive materials. The plan represented a multidimensional contract constructed on the basis of imperfect information. It was this contract/plan that Stalin feared would be fulfilled only on paper. Hence, one-man managers fought for plans/contracts that suited their "narrow" interests.[45] A benign interpretation of managerial opportunism was their desire for a quiet life.[46] A more sinister interpretation was rent-seeking to enhance political and financial clout.[47] The planner's task, however, was to give producers a tough life and to prevent rent-seeking. Stalin's complaint to Kaganovich (August 30, 1931) about Ordzhonikidze sums up this conflict:

Instead of pressing on his own people to produce more iron, [Ordzhonikidze] is pressing on the state's funds; that is, on the working class, forcing the working class to pay with its currency resources for incompetence, intrigue, and bureaucratism.... That is why I think we cannot make any concessions to people and organizations trying to use the working class's currency resources for the convenience (*spokoistvie*) of its apparatus.[48]

This struggle constituted the basic principal/agent conflict of the administrative-command economy, and Gosplan served on the front lines of this battleground.[49]

Information Asymmetry. The archives provide abundant evidence that the industrial ministries withheld information: In May 1933, two months after SNK's approval of the directives for preparing the second five-year plan, Ordzhonikidze's Ministry of Heavy Industry (hereafter referred to by its acronym, NKTP[50]) proposed that it, along with other ministries and republics, submit their control figures three months *after* the deadline *without* figures for enterprises: "The approved dates, if we

---

45 Khlevnyuk, *Politburo*, 17–40: Ordzhonikidze was converted from an avid advocate of unrealistic growth rates as head of the control commission to more realistic rates as the head of NKTP. Kaganovich (Stalin's first deputy) underwent a similar conversion when he was appointed Minister of Transportation.

46 Berliner, *Factory and Manager*, D. Granick, *Management of Industrial Firms in the USSR* (New York: Columbia University Press, 1954).

47 Lazarev and Gregory, "Commissars and Cars: A Case Study in the Political Economy of Dictatorship," *Journal of Comparative Economics*, in press.

48 Khlevnyuk et al., *Stalin i Kaganovich. Perepiski*, 72.

49 Gregory, *Restructuring the Soviet Economic Bureaucracy*, 15–17.

50 NKTP stands for Narodny Kommissariat Tiazheloi Promyshlennosti.

hold to the order of processing of control figures, will lead to rushed results and will lower the quality of planning at the most important stages
of work."[51] NKTP further complained about "repeated planning work
for the ministry, its trusts and enterprises." Gosplan opposed the proposal for delay: "Such a procedure [that excludes enterprise plans] will
contain mistakes and distortions and will require changes and corrections."[52] As would prove to be typical, NKTP lost the battle but won
the war. By the time SNK ruled against NKTP in June, NKTP had already won its delay. In another typical case of January 13, 1934, Gosplan
complained that NKTP had yet to submit its equipment balances despite Gosplan's deadline to complete the balance three days later.[53] On
January 1, 1935, the deputy minister of NKTP (Piatakov, of the cartoon
at the chapter opening) requested an amendment of SNK's own decree to
allow NKTP to report freight shipments quarterly rather than monthly,[54]
ostensibly to prevent excessive work and duplication. Gosplan argued
categorically against NKTP's initiative,[55] stating that, if granted, freight
reports would lose all operational meaning. Gosplan's struggle to extract information is also illustrated by its inability to fulfill a seemingly
simple decree to raise wages by 20 percent in the Buryat-Mongolian
Republic because of excessive wage fund requests by regional opera-
tors and the failure of the regions to deliver the information, despite its
urgency.[56]

Industrial ministries, for their part, felt entirely justified in delaying information: plans were constantly revised, wasting the time of ministerial
specialists. Superior instructions were viewed as ill-conceived and irritating. Ordzhonikidze wrote: "I am obligated to tell you that all is not well.
They give us every day decree upon decree, each successive one is stronger
and without foundation."[57]

Level of Aggregation. When Mises and Hayek first raised the problem
of highly aggregated plans, they did not anticipate that producers would
actually lobby for generalized plans. As early as 1925, when an industry

---

[51] This statement is from GARF, 5446.14.3, 34–7.
[52] GARF, 5446.14.3, 32.
[53] RGAE, 4372.32.34, 64a.
[54] GARF, 5446.16.239, 2. No. 2078 from September 8, 1934, about the order of making
   and approval of annual and quarterly balances and delivery plans.
[55] GARF, 5446.16.239, 16.
[56] RGAE, 4372.32.28, 266.
[57] Khlevnyuk, *Stalin i Ordzhonikidze*, 32.

official complained that Gosplan's plans did not specify concrete tasks, Gosplan responded:

> Of course, for many organizations it would be a considerable relief to receive without any of its own efforts a fully prepared plan with detailed tasks. But consider what kind of a super-bureaucratic result would be achieved if Gosplan, sitting in Moscow, took upon itself the role of some kind of a all-union nanny.[58]

This quote suggests considerable naivety on Gosplan's part; namely, the conviction that it could prepare a detailed operational plan that is good for everyone. By the time Gosplan began the real work of planning, such illusions had disappeared. Instead of planning a relatively small state sector, Gosplan was now being asked to plan the entire economy. The dictator had no other planner to turn to other than Gosplan. The industrial ministries had begun their fight for generalized (aggregated) plans as ferociously as for more resources. In April 1933, Gosplan complained that the documents submitted by the ministries "lacked details, economic justification, and suffered from such incompleteness that it was impossible to use them."[59] Ministries gave little detail particularly for construction projects. In both 1932 and 1933, Gosplan complained that NKTP's construction plan lacked a regional breakdown and did not even provide any information on "how the most important industrial locations are being satisfied in their need for new construction."[60]

Gosplan must have been torn between its desire to have more information and its real ability to process it. Even in the case of a relatively homogeneous commodity – cars and trucks – which was allocated at the highest levels, Gosplan could not plan at the level of supply plans and made numerous attempts to transfer operational planning to ministry supply organizations. Just as the dictator had to walk a fine line between its "leading role" and direct interventions, so did Gosplan have difficulty in determining the appropriate level of detail.

Dual Planning and Nonplanning. Ministries and enterprises were obligated by law to fulfill their plans, an arrangement that assumes that there is one plan. According to a Gosplan complaint, NKTP, in February 1934, gave its enterprises one plan to produce in excess of the state plan,

---

[58] S. G. Strumilin, *Ocherki Sovetskoi Ekonomiki. Resursy i Perspektivy* (Moscow: Nauka, 1928), 312.
[59] RGAE, 4372.31.36.
[60] RGAE, 4372.31.25: 89, 385.

while simultaneously submitting to Gosplan a second plan, corresponding to the lower targets approved by the state. The deputy director of Gosplan warned against such dual planning: "The system of two plans breaks plan discipline and introduces elements of disorganization into the economy."[61] The archives disclose an even more extreme ministerial practice, which we term "nonplanning." In January 1934, Gosplan reported that the Ministry of Light Industry did not even prepare a plan below the level of its main administrations. Only quarterly plans were prepared for the enterprises and trusts; there were no annual plans. Cotton textile trusts prepared their 1933 annual plans in 1934, for reporting purposes only. To quote the Gosplan report: "Until that time, no one was even interested in the 1933 plan.... Enterprises declared to our representatives that they had not seen annual plans for a period of years."[62] The factories without plans were among the most significant, with their industries located in the vicinity of Moscow.

Nonplanning allowed ministries to reserve for themselves maximum flexibility to squeeze more output from their enterprises, to accumulate hidden reserves, and generally to deal with enterprises out of sight of central authorities.

Abuse of Discretion. In 1932, Gosplan, no longer wishing to approve minor plan changes, authorized ministries to redistribute financing among construction projects within a 10 percent limit.[63] NKTP responded to its newfound freedom by redistributing capital investment in 465 of its 650 construction projects,[64] applying the 10 percent rule on multiple occasions to the same projects. In August 1935, Gosplan complained of the widespread abuse of this minor rule change:

The capital investment plan for GlavUgol [the coal administration of NKTP] was revised twice in this year.... While executing the plan, NKTP cut GlavUgol's account, citing its right to redistribute 10% of its subordinates' investment. These cuts have led to the reduction of planned investments by 8.5 million rubles.

Through an accounting sleight, NKTP reduced coal investment by another 24.5 million rubles. Gosplan concluded as follows: "Thus, the actual amount of investment in the coal industry was reduced by 33 million

---

[61] RGAE, 4372.32.34, 9–10.
[62] RGAE, 4372.32.53a, 136–40.
[63] *Sobranie Zakonov SSSR*, no. 33 (196), April 27, 1932.
[64] RGAE, 4372.33.85, 244.

rubles."[65] According to a Gosplan study, NKTP's redistributions of investment in 1935 alone were enough to build eight large production facilities.[66] The abuse of the 10 percent rule was so widespread that Gosplan concluded that NKTP's 1935 investment plan was fulfilled only in a "ritual" fashion.

"Deception of the State." The early studies of the Soviet enterprise uncovered a rich slang vocabulary – "pulling the wool over the eyes" (*ochkovtiratel'stvo*) or "misdirection" (*lipa*) – for the multitude of deceptions practiced by enterprises on their superiors in the ministries.[67] That enterprises cheated is well established. The archives, however, reveal that ministers and high-ranking party officials engaged in or tolerated high-level deception of the state, as the following three examples show: in September 1933, Kaganovich described the low quality of textiles as follows to Ordzhonikidze:

They are producing scandalously low quality, and the party must get involved. In order to fulfill the plan in meters, they are artificially stretching the cotton cloth and someone buying five meters, after washing a shirt for adults gets one that fits a child.[68]

Upon being informed of this practice, Stalin instructed Kaganovich (September 24, 1933):

On the textile industry, you must press on all including the secretary of the Moscow committee and the secretary of the central committee. The guilty must be punished obligatorily, not considering who they are or their "communist" rank.[69]

Kaganovich could complain to Ordzhonikidze about ministers, but was less diligent when Ordzhonikidze himself tolerated acts of deception. At the end of July 1932, Ordzhonikidze's Kommunar Factory was accused of delivering combines to agriculture lacking essential parts. On the basis of these complaints, SNK requested the justice ministry to investigate.

[65] RGAE, 4372.33.85, 244.
[66] A Central Statistical Bureau's survey of capital investment shows that NKTP's total investment in 1935 was 9,042 million rubles; thus, the "reported" internal reallocations constituted about 5 percent of the total (RGAE, 1562.10.468, 1–5); 322 million rubles would cover the cost of constructing eight average metal-working plants like the Gorky Plant with the planned capacity of five thousand milling cutter machines per year (RGAE, 1562.10.531, 41).
[67] Berliner, *Factory and Manager.*
[68] Khlevnyuk et al., *Stalinskoe Politburo*, 137.
[69] Khlevnyuk et al., *Stalin i Kaganovich. Perepiski*, 359.

In August 1933, the justice ministry issued a report authored by its deputy minister, A. Vyshinsky, which concluded that "the process gives us a basis for posing general questions concerning the work of Soviet economic institutions. I refer to the ministry of agriculture, and I refer to NKTP." The incensed Ordzhonikidze mounted a vigorous defense claiming that the missing parts had been sent separately to avoid theft. He organized, in Stalin's absence, a Politburo rebuke, signed by Kaganovich and Molotov, accusing Vyshinsky of levying "incorrect accusations against the ministry of agriculture and NKTP."[70] Upon hearing of this action, Stalin dispatched an angry letter to Kaganovich, Molotov, and Ordzhonikidze (August 29, 1933) declaring that the failure was NKTP's and that "for such a matter the minister must be held responsible."[71] The chastised Kaganovich wrote to Stalin two days later that "Our decree truly was a mistake. The procuracy had just started to turn things around and we give it one of the nose. This is why you correctly criticize us."[72]

After Kaganovich was appointed to head the transport commission, he reported to Stalin (October 13, 1933):

We uncovered the old transport ministry instruction on accounting of freight transport, according to which re-addressed wagons are included in the count, such as for example if a freight car arriving in Moscow is re-addressed to Ivanovno, it is counted [in Moscow shipments]. This scandalous practice has been legalized, that is, the deception of the state was made law. This instruction was issued years ago so it is even difficult to find the guilty parties, but that it was allowed is a scandal.[73]

Deception of the state was, therefore, practiced and tolerated by the three largest ministries of the 1930s – NKTP, the Ministry of Light Industry, and the transport ministry. Note that Stalin did not distinguish between those who actually carried out the deception, such as the Kommunar Factory, or the cotton textiles trusts, or the minister. As Stalin declared: "For such a matter, the minister must be held responsible."[74]

Horizontal Dealings: Cars and Trucks Horizontal transactions were, by definition, illegal because they were outside of the plan/law. To prevent such abuses, particularly valuable products were planned down to actual

---

[70] Ibid., 320–3. (Contains this quotation and previous quotation.)
[71] Ibid., 318.
[72] Ibid., 325.
[73] Ibid., 387.
[74] Ibid., 318.

deliveries to end users. A three-person commission composed of Molotov, Kaganovich, and another Politburo member planned the distribution of cars and trucks to final users between 1932 and 1937. This "Molotov Commission" was assisted by Gosplan in gathering and processing orders for vehicles.[75] In rare cases, Stalin intervened to change the commission's decisions, such as Stalin's command to double the allotment to agriculture (September 30, 1933):

> From the 9,600 trucks you give only 2,000 for the agriculture ministry and the state farms. What kind of nonsense is this? Now that we have created through the political departments some solid bases in agriculture – and agricultural problems are far from being liquidated – you, for some unknown reason, shift attention from agriculture to "other users." The bird has sung too early (*Rano ptashka zapela*).[76]

That the Molotov Commission approved vehicle-distribution plans down to the last digit (9,378) gives the impression of a tightly controlled allocation that would leave no room for horizontal vehicle transactions. The fact, however, was that horizontal transactions could not be suppressed even by the Politburo.

The Molotov Commission's final vehicle distribution plan was turned over to the tractor and vehicle supply department of NKTP to prepare actual deliveries. Only in the highest priority cases would the Molotov Commission order specific deliveries. Surprisingly, there was virtually no follow-up on actual deliveries outside of agriculture, and Gosplan never knew the vehicle inventories of various agencies. Table 6.1 provides extremely rare information for the first quarter of 1932 on the final automobile-delivery plan and actual deliveries. It shows that not only did actual car deliveries not equal the number ordered by the Molotov Commission, but also that the producer amended the final distribution in the "planning aftermarket," especially the regional distribution. There was also an active secondary market in which decommissioned or lost vehicles were sold. Stalingrad had two thousand registered cars and trucks at the beginning of 1933. During the year, five hundred were reported unrepairable and 220 were lost. Thus, almost 40 percent of all vehicles disappeared into a black hole of unofficial transactions in one year alone! Organizations, not officially allowed to own vehicles, bought used cars and reassembled them, or purchased documents of decommissioned

---

[75] This section is based on material in Lazarev and Gregory, "The Wheels of Command," 324–48.

[76] Khlevnyuk et al., *Stalin i Kaganovich. Perepiski*, 365, 367–8, 379.

TABLE 6.1. *First Quarter 1932 Plans, Cars*

	Molotov Commission: Delivery Plan	Supplier: Actual Deliveries
Army	48	48
Agriculture	27	27
Reserve	29	31
Large-scale industry	50	50
Police	21	21
Miscellaneous[a]	20	8
Other ministries	14	14
Russian Republic	8	5
Moscow	22	9
Leningrad	30	6
Ukraine	2	8
Road Transport Commission	13	13
Other republics	17	2
Total	301	242

[a] Various governmental organizations
Source: Valery Lazarev and Paul Gregory, "The Wheels of Command," *Economic History Review* 55, 2 (May 2002), 335.

vehicles and assembled new ones from spare parts. Or they simply stole the cars, an expression that could have encompassed illegal purchasing. Automobiles destined for one user were redirected by "mistakes" of railroad officials. Automobiles turned over to hard currency stores for sales to foreigners were sold to OGPU officers or to swindlers at low ruble prices. A capital stock census revealed that the union of small-scale establishments acquired 87 vehicles in 1935, whereas according to quarterly plans, it had received only 30 vehicles.[77]

The vehicle archives do not reveal the terms of these unofficial exchanges of vehicles, but it is doubtful that the producer, allocating vehicles to unauthorized users, or organizations, reporting their vehicles as lost, were transferring them to others on a charitable basis. What is remarkable about these unplanned exchanges is that they were of a commodity that was among the most tightly controlled – a product whose allocation the Politburo decided itself. If we can detect unofficial exchanges of such highly centralized commodities, they must have been rampant for other products.

[77] RGAE, 1562.11.106,16-22.

On Whose Side Was the Dictator?

The dictator's support of loyal agents in disputes with industrial ministries was by no means automatic, even when Gosplan sincerely attempted to represent its interests, as the following examples show: Gosplan's protracted battle with NKTP against staffing and wage increases became public with NKTP's attack on "unnecessary labor accounting" in its newspaper, *For Industrialization.* NKTP unilaterally imposed an abbreviated labor accounting form. To counter NKTP's "illegal" move, Gosplan cited SNK's own decree of May 9, 1931, which forbad agencies to "introduce changes to the reporting forms without the approval of Gosplan [and of other affected committees]."[78] Gosplan also showed that the abbreviated form contradicted SNK's own April 6, 1932, decree "On the Planning and Accounting of Wages." Despite NKTP's obvious violations of two state decrees, SNK accepted NKTP's argument that it was following SNK's own campaign to reduce "nonproductive" personnel – simpler forms meant more workers in the factories and fewer accountants. The deflated Gosplan was left with empty threats of "selective surveys."[79]

SNK reacted to conflicts between Gosplan or the finance ministry and the industrial ministries by forming "compromise" commissions of high-level officials from the conflicting agencies. In a high-stakes 1933 dispute, the finance ministry charged NKTP with avoiding profit taxes by violating standard accounting rules.[80] SNK assigned Gosplan to find a compromise, but its proposal was rejected by NKTP and, in September, a second commission was formed; however, its further concessions did not satisfy NKTP, and a new commission was formed on November 11. NKTP gained a final victory with a February 4, 1935, memo from SNK stating, "the question about the disagreement between NKTP and the finance ministry has been removed from discussion."[81] In 1935, NKTP failed to report its 1934 profits, while claiming an additional 330 million rubles for 1935 investment from these profits, while asserting that the finance ministry had incorrectly calculated its 1934 profits.[82] The finance ministry rejected the 330 million on the grounds that it could not evaluate NKTP's claim

---

[78] The quotes in this paragraph are from *Za Industrializatsiu*, no. 22, 1933.

[79] RGAE, 4372.31.34, 3, 54; and RGAE, 4372.32.53a, 136.

[80] GARF, 5446.16.269, 2–24.

[81] NKTP achieved a similar victory in 1934 by drawing out a dispute on the reported balances of enterprises for 1934 until October 1935, when the issue was dropped (GARF, 5446.16.108).

[82] GARF, 5446.16.210.

without the 1934 figures. SNK again sided with NKTP, despite the obvious rule violation, because NKTP needed supplemental financing to complete key construction projects.

Construction was also a constant thorn of contention between the ministries, which wanted automatic construction credits, and the finance ministry and the state bank (Gosbank), which fought to limit construction expenditures. SNK had itself issued directives forbidding banks to finance construction projects without construction budgets.[83] Nevertheless, ministries routinely delayed submission of construction budgets; yet, few banks officials had the courage to stop priority construction projects, fearing charges of disruption of "important government projects." In January 1935, SNK itself demanded construction budgets from NKTP.[84] NKTP's military shipbuilder, Kharkov Shipbuilding, was warned in the summer of 1935 that its financing would be cut off if it did not finally submit its construction budget. The factory dispatched a telegram to Molotov and the Defense Council on August 3, 1935, asserting its right to build its new plant and stating that the withdrawal of financing threatened an important government objective. The issue went to the top of SNK, which demanded an explanation from the bank, which was only enforcing state decrees. NKTP's requests for delaying submission of construction budgets were commonplace and prompted conflicts too numerous to mention.[85]

The dictator's siding with industrial ministries against its loyal agents is explained by the effective games that producers could play. Ministries could cite conflicting rules, use their personal influence, or employ delaying tactics. Their most potent argument, however, was the threat to production or to the completion of a vital construction project. In such

---

[83] RGAE, 4086.2.230, 233.

[84] GARF, 5446.16.306.

[85] In 1934, NKTP's first deputy minister, Piatakov, petitioned to delay cost estimates for the series of construction projects of the chemical and nitrogen industries (GARF, 5446.15a.88). On August 2, 1935, he petitioned to delay budgets for eleven defense plants and continue their financing (GARF, 5446.16a.49). Also in 1935, Piatakov asked for delays in budgets for factories in the aviation industry (GARF, 5446.16a.44). The ministry of finance normally would agree to the first delay. For example, it agreed to NKTP's requests for the military-chemical and nitrogen plants described previously, except for plant #98, which already had one delay. As a result, the director of the Chemical Industry Main Administration, to whom the chemical plant #98 was subordinated, appealed directly to the chairman of Gosplan and the Deputy Chairman of SNK with a request to intervene personally and order financing continued. The finance ministry did not grant delays for the aviation plants because these plants had already received delays. Besides, the finance ministry noted that these plants were relatively small and it was easy to prepare cost estimates.

cases, the dictator had to decide whether the general rule that Gosplan was trying to enforce was more important than the resulting loss that the producer was threatening. Thus, the dictator was forced into constant choices between his own rules and "what was best," enforcing Hayek's conclusion (see Chapter 2) that dictators will not allow themselves to be bound by general rules. In making such decisions, the dictator also had to take into account that a number of ministers were also Politburo members and thus part of the decision-making process. The dictator did not always side with producers; in fact, producers thought that the dictator sided more often with its loyal agents. Rather, what these examples show is that the dictator was prepared to throw its loyal agents overboard when deemed necessary for production.

Concluding Thoughts

Planners and producers were not fond of each other. Producers felt bombarded with arbitrary instructions that changed from one minute to the next and wondered out loud, "Why do they need us?" Planners viewed producers as unreliable, distorters of information, and doing their own thing irrespective of the enlightened orders from above. Producers concluded that the less their superiors knew the better. The dictator's main planning organization, Gosplan, was caught in the middle. It was obliged to make decisions on the side of the dictator as a loyal agent, but the more meaningful its decisions, the greater the risk that it would be held responsible for bad results. Hence, Gosplan issued general, nonoperational plans and avoided the planning of actual transactions. Contrary to its stereotype as a power-hungry organization, the Gosplan of the 1930s actually attempted to minimize its power. Gosplan could not count on the dictator, who ignored its own rules when they harmed production.

According to scientific planning, the dictator sets general rules and guidelines but turns the actual allocation of resources over to expert planners. Gosplan was anything but a scientific planner, despite the fact that it operated at the very center of power in the 1930s. Its chairman from 1930 to 1934, Kuibyshev, was a member of the Politburo and a deputy prime minister. Gosplan constructed generalized plans. Most transactions were determined in contract negotiations between buyers and sellers. Although its opinions were sought by the highest political authorities, Gosplan sought to be freed of such obligations. Gosplan had no power, it had to plead with others to compel compliance. This image of Gosplan is consistent with Eugene Zaleski's depiction of Soviet resource allocation as centralized management rather than centralized planning.[86] It also jibes with Raymond Powell's description of resource allocation as ad hoc responses by a large number of state and party officials to nonprice signals.[87]

What would have happened had planning really been turned over to professionals to prepare operational scientific plans for the entire economy? Trotsky favored an all-powerful Gosplan, staffed by planning specialists rather than by "a regime of party secretaries."[88] This was the Gosplan that its first leaders anticipated. Gosplan's pioneers, G. M. Krzhizhanovsky and S. G. Strumilin, worked on administrative planning methods. "Materials for a Balance of the Soviet National Economy, for 1928–1930," released in 1932, represented the most sophisticated attempt to create a national economic plan.[89] The 1929 purge of Gosplan, however, demonstrated that Stalin and his associates were not prepared to turn the allocation of resources over to nonparty "skeptics" who were not trustworthy and did not understand the true needs of society. Gosplan's pioneers removed themselves into academic positions, a wise move that spared both Krzhizhanovsky and Strumilin from the Great Purges. The nonparty specialists who remained behind proved less fortunate. With rare exceptions, they were executed during the purges, much to Stalin's personal satisfaction.

Gosplan's planning methods, such as the national balances, being developed in the late 1920s were primitive. If the dictator had turned resource allocation over to a Gosplan headed by Strumilin or Krzhizhanovsky, the result would have been chaotic. The 1928–1930 balances, for example, were for highly aggregated products, such as building materials and industrial, agricultural, and consumer products. In all, only some sixty balances could be prepared for an economy that produced millions of distinct commodities.[90] Any scientific plan that Gosplan would have prepared at this time would not have given meaningful instructions to enterprises and would have still required an enormous amount of political intervention. Given the principal agent problems between the center and producer, there would have been the added problem of producer opportunism. We, therefore, reject the possibility of pure scientific planning by a counter-factual Gosplan of the 1930s.

[86] Zaleski, *Stalinist Planning*, 482–572.
[87] Powell, "Plan Execution," 51–76.
[88] Getty and Naumov, *The Road to Terror*, 38.
[89] S. G. Wheatcroft and R. W. Davies (eds.), *Materials for a Balance of the Soviet National Economy 1928–1930* (Cambridge: Cambridge University Press, 1985).
[90] Ibid., Appendices A–C.

7

Creating Soviet Industry

"As long as a pack of narcissistic and self-satisfied bureaucrats like Rukhimovich sit in the ministry of transport and are avoiding fulfilling the decrees of the Central Committee and are sowing seeds of skepticism, the decrees of the Central Committee will put off until doomsday. It is necessary to drive out this pack, to save the railroads."

Stalin to Kaganovich on his opinion of the soon-to-be fired minister of transport, September 19, 1931.[1]

"From the decrees that are being received I guess the impression is that we are idiots. Generally speaking, I am obliged to tell you that things are not well. They give us every day decree upon decree, each successive one is stronger than the previous and without foundation."

Complaint of Minister S. Ordzhonikidze about bureaucratic interference.[2]

Despite an extensive literature,[3] we still know relatively little about how the industrial ministry, or the People's Commissariat as it was called in the 1930s, really operated. Industrial ministries were the highest managers of

---

[1] Khlevnyuk et al., *Stalin i Kaganovich. Perepiski*, 109.

[2] Khlevnyuk, *Stalin i Ordzhonikidze*, 32.

[3] Industrial ministries have been discussed in the following theoretical and applied literatures: Gregory, *Restructuring the Soviet Economic Bureaucracy*; William J. Conyngham, *The Modernization of Soviet Industrial Management* (Cambridge, Mass.: Cambridge University Press, 1982); David Dyker, *The Future of Soviet Economic Planning* (Beckenham, Kent: Croon Helm, 1985); Alice C. Gorlin, "The Power of Industrial Ministries," *Soviet Studies* 37, no. 3 (1985); Stephen Fortescue, "The Technical Administration of Industrial Ministries," Soviet Industry Science and Technology Work Group, Centre for Soviet and East European Studies, University of Birmingham, England, February 1986; David Granick, "The Ministry as the Maximizing Unit in Soviet Industry," *Journal of Comparative Economics* 4, no. 3 (1980); Michael Keren, "The Ministry, Plan Changes,

production (*khoziaistvenniki*). They, not Gosplan, carried out most operational planning. Insofar as ministers were responsible for final results, they took selfish actions to protect themselves (see Chapter 6). The struggle over control of resources was an even more basic source of conflict. The dictator desired to own and control resources, but producers had operational control of capital assets and, at least initially, physical control over output. Whoever controlled capital and output exercised power. This nexus was not overlooked by Stalin's chief rival, L. Trotsky, who, in the mid-1920s, argued that an authoritative Gosplan, rather than the party, should control resources – an organization that he intended to head.[4] It was recognized again with the 1932 breakup of the super ministry, the Supreme Council of the National Economy. Any organization, separate from the party that controlled virtually all of industry, constituted a threat to the "leading role of the party."

Whereas the previous chapter looked at the industrial ministry's dealings with planners, this chapter examines the inner workings of the ministry. We study the two dominant industrial ministries of the 1930s, the People's Commissariat of Heavy Industry (NKTP) and the People's Commissariat of Light Industry (NKLP). Henceforth, we use their respective acronyms, NKTP and NKLP.[5] Both were founded in 1932. From its founding in 1932 until his death in 1937, NKTP was headed by Sergo Ordzhonikidze, Politburo member and early Stalin loyalist.[6] The second minister of NKTP was the former director of Gosplan, V. I. Mezhlauk, who perished in the Great Purges in 1938. L. M. Kaganovich, a master bureaucrat, Politburo member, and Stalin deputy, served as minister in the post-purge period until NKTP's final breakup in 1939. NKLP was headed from 1932 to 1937 by I. E. Liubimov, a less well-known figure, who also perished in the purges. NKTP was in charge of virtually all heavy industrial goods – metals, mining, machinery, and defense goods. NKLP

---

and the Ratchet Effect in Planning," *Journal of Comparative Economics* 6, no. 4 (1982); V. G. Vyshniakov, *Struktura i Shtaty Sovetshogo Gosudarstva i Upravleniia*, chapter 3 (Moscow: Nauka, 1972); and D. V. Averianov, *Funktsii i Organizatsionnaia*.

[4] E. H. Carr, *The Bolshevik Revolution 1917–1923*, vol. 2 (New York: MacMillan, 1951).
[5] NK stands for People's Ministry (Narodny Kommissariat). TP stands for Heavy Industry (Tiazhelaia promyshlennost). LP stands for Light Industry (Legkaia promyshlennost).
[6] The histories of the People's Ministry are covered in Khlevnyuk, "The People's Commissariat of Heavy Industry," 94–123; E. A. Rees, "The People's Commissariat of Timber Industry," 124–49; Rees, "The People's Commissariat of Transport," 203–34; and Voncent Barnett, "The People's Commissariat of Supply and the People's Commissariat of Internal Trade," in *Decision Making in the Stalinist Command Economy, 1932–37*, ed. E. A. Rees (London: MacMillan, 1997), 176–202.

covered cotton, linen, wool textiles, and leather goods.[7] Each production branch was managed by a Main Administration, or *glavk*, which directly supervised enterprises and trusts in that branch.[8]

The story of the "managers of production" is clearly that of the most significant *khoziaistvennik* of the 1930s – Sergo Ordzhonikidze. Unlike other party leaders who were addressed as Comrade Molotov or Comrade Stalin, Ordzhonikidze was known to colleagues and subordinates alike as "Sergo" or "Comrade Sergo." He guided the Caucas Party through the civil war. He accepted Stalin's call to Moscow, where he occupied a number of central-party positions, including the chairmanship of the Worker-Peasant Inspection. He became a Politburo member in 1930. With his appointment to head the Supreme Council of the National Economy, he was placed in charge of virtually all industrial production. With the breakup of the Supreme Council in 1932, Ordzhonikidze became the Minister of NKTP. As a key Politburo member and close associate of Stalin, Ordzhonikidze wielded enormous influence. He was crude, short-tempered, impatient, outspoken, and did not shy away from conflicts with other top leaders. Stalin complained bitterly of Ordzhonikidze's fierce independence, which created "the danger of the destruction of the leading group."[9] Stalin tried unsuccessfully to reason with Ordzhonikidze.

It is clear that we, members of the Central Committee, should not and cannot put pressure on one another.... Bolsheviks cannot take such a path, if they wish to avoid turning our Bolshevik party into a conglomerate of departmental interests.

Stalin's irritation grew as Ordzhonikidze continued to defend ferociously NKTP's interests. By September 1936, Ordzhonikidze had to accept the arrest of his first deputy (Yu. L. Piatakov), who was executed in 1937. Stalin to Kaganovich (September 11, 1936): "Better to fire Piatakov immediately not waiting the results of any investigation."[10] As the Great

---

[7] In December 1936, NKTP's defense industries were spun off to become the Ministry of Defense Industry. In August 1937, an independent Machine Building Ministry was established. On January 24, 1939, NKTP was divided into several independent ministries.

[8] We study a representative NKTP glavk, its Main Administration for Metals Industry, Gump, which directed metallurgical production, metal pipes, refractory materials, coke-chemical products, and metals-ore mining. Gump was one of thirty-four glavks of NKTP and was the second largest in terms of employment in 1937. We study several glavks of the light industry ministry, as will be explained.

[9] Khlevnyuk et al., *Stalin i Kaganovich. Perepiski*, 51.

[10] Ibid., 673.

Purges loomed, Ordzhonikidze saw more of his key personnel fired and arrested and his authority crumbling. He committed suicide immediately before the plenum of the Central Committee scheduled for February 19, 1937, an embarrassing fact covered up as heart failure. Ordzhonikidze's suicide was his last act of defiance, for Stalin had characterized suicide as a last opportunity "to spit on the party, betray the party."[11] Just as it is difficult to separate the creation of the system from Stalin, so is it difficult to separate the creation of Soviet industry from Ordzhonikidze.

The Soviet command economy was organized as a "nested dictatorship," meaning that each organization duplicated the administrative and control structures of its superior in the vertical chain of command.[12] The Council of People's Commissars (SNK) was the industrial ministry's dictator, the industrial ministry was the main administration's (glavk's) dictator, the glavk was the enterprise's dictator. The industrial ministry was structured like SNK, the glavks were structured like the industrial ministry, and the enterprise was structured like glavks. Each unit had a small central staff, branch departments, and functional departments, such as planning and finance, to deal with issues that transcended branch boundaries. The organization of NKTP and NKLP is explained in Appendix B. The sheer organizational complexity of NKTP provoked the following outburst from Ordzhonikidze: "No matter how often we reorganize the structure of our apparatus, when you take it and picture it on paper, you can't find anything of such a formless character anywhere."[13] Appendix B shows that the glavks carried out the real business of the ministry. Whereas the ministry was responsible for overall production, the glavk had to produce and distribute output. In the metals glavk, over half of its employees worked at times in supply. An even higher percentage of light-industry glavk personnel worked in supply and distribution.

Material Balances and Industrial Organization

The Soviet contribution to the theory of planning is the material balance.[14] Material balances are administrative tallies of the supplies of and

[11] Getty and Naumov, *The Road to Terror*, 218.
[12] Paul Gregory and Andrei Markevich, "Creating Soviet Industry: The House That Stalin Built," *Slavic Review*, 61, 4 (Winter 2002), 801–9.
[13] RGAE, 7297.38.104, 2.
[14] For a discussion of material balances and their development, see Gregory and Stuart, *Russian and Soviet Economic Structure and Performance*, 6th ed., 104–8.

TABLE 7.1. *Simplified Material Balance*

Production (Supply)	Uses (Demand)
Steel =	Steel used by steel producers + Steel used by machinery producers + Steel used by others
Machinery =	Machinery used by steel producers + Machinery used by machinery producers + Machinery used by others

demands for resources, such as steel, cement, grain, vehicles, and machinery. Current production, imports, and draw-downs of inventories make up the supply. Demand equals the approved input requests of all users.[15] The balance between supplies and uses is achieved by administrative orders, not by adjustments of prices. If the demand exceeds the supply, an administrative decision is made to cut back on usage or to increase supply. Table 7.1 provides a conceptual material balance of two products, steel and machinery.[16] Planned production makes up the available supplies of steel and machinery. The demand for steel equals the steel industry's demand for its own steel, the machinery industry's demand for steel, and the demand for steel by other users. The demand for machinery likewise equals the steel industry's demand, the machinery industry's demand, and the demand of other industries for machinery. The material balance plan, therefore, consists not only of production, but also of deliveries. An *ex ante* balance can fail for a number of reasons. If machinery producers do not get steel, they cannot produce their output target. If steel producers do not produce their control figure, they cannot supply machinery producers. Ordzhonikidze summed up the material balance when he reminded metal producers (June 1932):

No matter how much you complain, no matter what demands you place on machine building for deliveries or whomever else, all your demands can be sent back with complete justification because you gave no metals. ... All your demands must be backed by your giving enough metals for their work.[17]

If all industry were combined (internalized) under a single administration, all production and deliveries would be within one organization, whose performance is judged on the basis of the organization as a whole, not of a

[15] Requests for materials and supplies were called *zaiavki*. Approved requests, basically approvals to buy, were called *nariady*.
[16] Table 7.1 is conceptual because it ignores inventories, imports, and exports to focus attention on the basic allocation problem.
[17] RGAE, 7297.38.10, 4, 15.

particular division.[18] If industry were subdivided into separate units (ministries or glavks), the steel glavk is responsible for steel, and the machinery glavk for machinery. These glavks may preferentially supply their own enterprises, although they are part of the same ministry. From the vantage point of the minister who is responsible for both steel and machinery, both machinery and steel should be treated equally, whereas other users of steel and machinery in foreign ministries may be neglected.[19] These alternative organizational arrangements suggest a general rule: The more integrated the production structure, the greater the likelihood that resources will flow to their highest and best use. The more production is broken into smaller units, the greater the tendency to favor one's over foreign enterprises. A highly integrated Supreme Council of the National Economy (prior to its breakup in 1932) thus might be more evenhanded than an NKTP in dealing with its customers.

Preferential treatment might be avoided if balances were compiled and executed by encompassing organizations such as SNK or Gosplan, at least in theory, but most balances were prepared not by Gosplan, but by the ministry or glavk supply department, such as Steel Supply (see Chapter 6). For Steel Supply, machinery producers belonged to a foreign glavk and vice versa. Customers from NKLP were even more remote, falling under a foreign minister. In a market economy, profit-maximizing firms obtain supplies through the market rather than self-supply if costs can be reduced.

Ministry Rules of the Game

Economic institutions can operate on the basis of formal or informal rules. European labor markets and the U.S. civil service use written rules, whereas U.S. private labor markets use unwritten rules, called implicit contracts. The Soviet dictator preferred to operate without constraining rules and disregarded rules in conflicts between producers and planners (see Chapter 6). Although institutions in a hierarchical economy might be expected to rely on written rules, both NKTP and NKLP operated for

---

[18] Let W_{ss} be the marginal product of steel used by the steel industry. Let W_{sm} equal the marginal product of steel used in the machinery industry. The single manager of the combined steel and machinery industry would be inclined to allocate steel so that marginal products are equal in the two branches, $W_{ss} = W_{sm}$. This is the defintion of "evenhanded" as used herein.

[19] The minister would aim for $W_{ss} = W_{sm}$, but the director of the steel glavk would favor his own enterprises so that $W_{ss} < W_{sm}$, and the director of the machinery industry would favor his own enterprises so that $W_{mm} < W_{ms}$.

years without formal charters, and their ultimate charters said little about operating rules. The thousands of pages of official documents in the NKTP and NKLP archives do not yield one clear statement of formal rules and procedures.

Both NKTP and NKLP were formed on January 5, 1932, with the splitting up of the Supreme Council of the National Economy into three industrial ministries – heavy industry, light industry, and forestry products.[20] Their founding charters distributed enterprises among the three ministries, with most going to NKTP, and said little about governance. NKTP's charter was not approved until November 11, 1937; it decreed only that NKTP should

manage the fulfillment of approved government plans of production, finance, and capital construction, and, to this end, it should organize the work of subordinated enterprises, accord them technical assistance, organize supply and distribution of production, and direct the selection of personnel.[21]

NKLP's charter, approved in 1938, establishing it as a Union-Republican Ministry with offices in Moscow and in the republics, also provided no clear operating instructions.[22] NKTP's Main Administration of Metals Industry (Gump) was formed in 1931 "for the strengthening of economic and technical management of the metallurgical industry."[23] Gump's formal charter of June 1933 simply declared it responsible for plan fulfillment and technical management ("extracting optimal indicators") of enterprises producing ferrous metals, iron ore, coke-chemical and fired bricks.[24]

Fulfill the Plan! What Plan? The charters of the industrial ministries and glavks were explicit on two points: They clearly delineated the industrial activities of each agency by assigning specific enterprises to them, and they unambiguously stated that each agency is responsible for fulfilling the *plan*. For the ministry, the plan was the aggregated total of all its glavks. The glavk plan was the aggregated plan of its enterprises. The legal

[20] Decree Number 8 of the Central Executive Committee and the SNK in GARF, 5446.1.65, 13.
[21] Charter for NKTP approved by SNK 10.11.1937 (*Svod Zakonov i Postanovleniy Raboche-Krest'ianskogo Pravitel'stva.* 1937), 375.
[22] Charter for NKTP approved by the SNK 21.07.1938 (*Svod Zakonov i Postanovleniy Raboche-Krest'ianskogo Pravitel'stva.* 1938), 207.
[23] Decree No. 640 of SNK of September 11, 1931, in RGAE, 3429.1.146, 809–10.
[24] RGAE, 4086.2.272, 6.

obligation to fulfill the plan raised massive ambiguities:[25] plans included nonoperational five-year plans, annual plans (typically referred to as industrial-financial plans), quarterly, monthly, and even ten-day (decadal) plans. In some cases, there was no annual plan at all or it was prepared retrospectively.[26] Plans also included supply plans. Moreover, both output and supply plans were frequently changed, and they were multidimensional with production targets, both in physical and value terms, production assortments, labor productivity targets, cost reductions, capital construction completion dates, and so on. Which of these plans was the ministry or glavk to fulfill?

The most important plan was the production, or *val*, plan.[27] As an official of NKTP, Comrade Zolotorev, declared at a ministry meeting of 1934: "Fulfillment of the plan is fulfillment of the production plan."[28] Enterprises admitted that they fought most "for fulfillment of quantitative indicators" and often in this battle "experienced very many losses which were reflected in quality."[29] Earning enough revenues for financial self-sufficiency (called then and later full economic accounting) was not important. Production of the most important products and deliveries to the most important branches – defense, military orders, or whatever else was considered priority – had to be fulfilled first at the sacrifice of other plans. Defense production occupied a special position, as this directive of Ordzhonikidze indicates: "All orders for the Ministry of Defense must be fulfilled exactly according to the schedule not allowing any delays."[30] Orders for defense were declared "the main task of glavks and sectors of heavy industry" according to an NKTP decree of February 1932.[31] Priority plans were examined in special meetings, which issued special directives, such as NKTP's June 8, 1937, meeting on special steel targets for defense.[32] Heavy industry occupied a lofty position. As Ordzhonikidze said, "I am prepared to give ferrous metallurgy whatever it needs, take

---

[25] Belova, "Economic Crime and Punishment," 131–58.
[26] Eugenia Belova and Paul Gregory, "Dictators, Loyal and Opportunistic Agents: The Soviet Archives on Creating the Soviet Economic System," *Public Choice*, 113, 3–4 (December 2002), 274–5.
[27] "Val" denotes *valovaia produktsiia*, or gross production. It was commonly denominated in ruble terms in the constant rubles of a base year, such as 1926/27 prices.
[28] RGAE, 7297.28.335, 5.
[29] RGAE, 7297.38.177, 10.
[30] RGAE, 7297.38.304, 22.
[31] NKTP No. 24ss (ss = absolutely secret) from February 7, 1932, in RGAE, 7297.38.5, 11.
[32] RGAE, 7297.38.304, 81.

all, just do what you are required to do,"[33] or the Gump Directive (No. 219) of October 1933 to allocate additional materials "in order to guarantee the uninterrupted work of the factories of the trust Eastern Steel (Vostokstal)."[34] Whole enterprises were transferred to ensure supplies to priority branches, such as NKTP's Order (No. 51) of March 1932, which assigned five factories "to satisfy in necessary quantities the demands of these enterprises without any delay."[35] Major construction projects were also privileged. SNK Decree No. 1794 from August 21, 1933, "About Automobile Factories,"[36] gave special resources for completion of the Stalin and Gorky plants.

Insofar as ministries and glavks did much of their own planning, they prepared their own plan-decrees, which they lobbied their superiors to sign. NKTP in 1932 ordered its mining glavk to prepare a draft decree within five days for the development of the sulfur industry to submit to SNK for signature.[37] At a June 8, 1937, meeting, Mezhlauk ordered the Defense Mobilization Department (GVMU) and two steel glavks to jointly prepare a decree for SNK on special steels for defense.[38] The superior would send such "bottom-up" draft decrees out for evaluation. For example, in February 1932, the Administration for Nonferrous Metals and Gold Processing (*Glavtsvetmetzoloto*) draft decree for an additional 13,800 tons of metal was cut in half by Ordzhonikidze after receiving the evaluation of his construction department.[39]

Responsibility: One-Man Management. Rules are less important if responsible people are in charge. Kaganovich, to Stalin (September 21, 1931): "The repeated experience of my work . . . has demonstrated that the main thing of course is the people in charge of ministries."[40] Indeed, more Politburo attention was devoted to personnel matters – Stalin's forte – than to any other subject.[41] Cadre policies were spelled out beginning in the

[33] RGAE, 7297.38.10, 10.

[34] RGAE, 4086.2.276, 28–9.

[35] RGAE, 7297.38.5, 27.

[36] RGAE, 7297.1.25, 17.

[37] Decree No. 59 from March 16, 1932, "On the question of insuring the production program and capital construction of Trust Soiuzsevera for 1932," in RGAE, 7297.38.5, 38–40.

[38] RGAE, 7297.38.304, 81.

[39] NKTP issued Decree No. 70 of February 14, 1932. RGAE, 7297.1.1, 263.

[40] Khlevnyuk et al., *Stalin i Kaganovich. Perepiska*, 114.

[41] E. A. Rees and D. H. Watson, "Politburo and Sovnarkom," in Rees (ed.), *Decision Making*, 9–31.

1920s, when the Politburo itself filled 647 *nomenklatura* positions. Party documents from the 1930s spell out appointments procedures in some detail.[42] Stalin's decision to fire the Minister of Transport, M. L. Rukhimovich, went to Kaganovich on September 19, 1931. The Politburo then submitted three potential candidates six days later. Stalin's selection (A. A. Andreev) was unanimously supported by the Politburo on September 26.[43] Rukhimovich was formally fired on October 1. Stalin then objected to Andreev's proposed list of deputies (too many came from the Northern Caucasus) and proposed his own candidates. The Politburo approved the new management team on October 5, 1931. Thus, the appointment of a new Minister of Transport was the main focus of the Politburo for a three-week period, underscoring the extreme importance of high-level appointments.

Once appointed to head a ministry, glavk, or enterprise, one became personally responsible for its results according to the Soviet principle of one-man management, called *edinonachalie*.[44] Unlike other operating procedures that were left vague, edinonachalie was enshrined in internal NKTP and NKLP decrees.[45] The founding document of NKLP's cotton procurement and processing glavk of February 2, 1935, reads: "The glavk director, acting on the basis of edinonachalie, bears full responsibility to the minister for the technical and economic condition of trusts, enterprises, and organizations subordinated to the glavk for the fulfillment of their plans, directives of the government and of the minister."[46] Clearly, the one-man manager had to delegate in a complex organization. Ordzhonikidze delegated considerable authority to his first deputy, Yu. L. Piatakov, who was particularly reviled by Stalin for his questionable loyalty.[47] Another deputy, I. P. Pavlunovsky (1932–33), and then the former Minister of Transport, M. L. Rukhimovich (1933–36), were successively responsible for the massive "special" (military) department. NKTP's 1937 charter stated that "the minister issues directives within the limits of his

[42] Khlevnyuk et al., *Stalinskoe Politburo*, 15–16.
[43] Khlevnyuk et al., *Stalin i Kaganovich. Perepiski*, 111–27.
[44] Gregory, *Restructuring the Soviet Economic Bureaucracy*, 57–9.
[45] Decree No. 330 of April 15, 1934, "For the Purpose of Strengthening One-Man Management in the System of Management of NKLP and the Placing of More Responsibility on the Directors of Institutions," in RGAE 7604.1.362, 1.
[46] RGAE, 7604.1.564, 1, 4–9.
[47] At one time, Piatakov was considered as a potential head of government. Likely Stalin's hate was associated with his fear of Piatakov.

responsibility to execute the laws and decrees of SNK,"[48] but in practice more than half were signed by deputies.[49] The proliferation of signing authority provoked Ordzhonikidze in June 1934 to complain: "The ministry is issuing an unbelievable number of decrees. Virtually anyone can sign these documents. If, in one glavk, forty people can sign, where can this eventually lead?"[50] Although responsibility was delegated, it was clear that the minister had the final authority. NKTP's last minister, Kaganovich, allowed different points of view to be expressed, but he was rarely contradicted. His suggestions became final decisions. He exercised power on the spot, such as in a meeting of July 17, 1937, in which he heaped abuse on those involved in an accident at a copper plant, and summarily fired the director.[51]

Personal responsibility applied from the highest to the lowest levels. When the ill-fated transport minister (Rukhimovich) blamed deteriorating equipment for poor performance, Stalin dispatched an angry letter complaining to Kaganovich: "Decrees of the Central Committee cannot save the day although they have great significance" in the face of such bureaucratic opposition. Kaganovich to Stalin (September 6, 1931) on Rukhimovich's request to delay construction projects due to the lack of rails: "It seems to me that Rukhomovich is trying to relieve himself of responsibility in advance for the nonfulfillment of the construction plan."[52] When candidate Politburo member, G. I. Petrovsky, confronted with desperate famine in Ukraine, tried to lower the grain-collection targets for which he was personally responsible, Kaganovich gleefully tattled to Stalin (letter of June 12, 1932):

From the very first line, he [Petrovsky] tried to place blame on the Central Committee.... He polemizes against those who speak the truth, that they were far removed from the village and did not know the circumstances, but if so then he must admit that he hid the truth from the Central Committee and only then began

[48] RGAE, 7297.28.35, 2–14.
[49] The distribution of the workload can be seen from the distribution of decree signing. The minister signed fewer than half of the decrees. First Deputy Piatakov signed the most decrees and clearly directed the daily activities of the ministry. Pavlunovsky and then Rukhimovich signed directives classified as secret and related to defense production. The same regime applied to the glavks where the deputy director or chief engineer could also sign directives. The director of the glavk, however, signed a higher proportion of glavk decrees than the minister did for the ministry.
[50] RGAE, 7297.38.106, 1.
[51] RGAE, 7297.28.4, 22.
[52] Ibid., 84.

to speak when they uncovered his misconduct. Practically his letter prepares the ground for a denial of grain collections for this year, something that cannot be allowed.[53]

If the highest party officials were held responsible, one-man managers in the ministries and glavks could scarcely avoid responsibility. They could not plead that supplies had not been delivered or that accidents had occurred. As stated by Ordzhonikidze in a speech on June 16, 1934: "That director, that engineer, that shop boss, that technical director who does not ensure that the directives of the ministry, the government, or the Central Committee are fulfilled exactly is not a director."[54] Ordzhonikidze derided managers who felt that their responsibilities to the state could be avoided: "There are wise men (*umniki*) who think that decrees of the ministry and of glavks can be fulfilled or not fulfilled as they wish."[55] Ordzhonikidze made an example of one such wise man by firing on January 8, 1934, the director of the Iaroslavl' Rubber Factory, a Comrade Mikhailov, for telling a trust conference that it was impossible to fulfill his plan: "The plan, approved by the government, is the law. Any argument against an approved plan is a violation of party and Soviet discipline. Any director who speaks against an approved plan cannot remain a director."[56] Ordzhonikidze showed no tolerance for the excuse of lack of supplies (June 6, 1932): "You get up and you cry that you don't have this or that but you never say what is necessary to correct the situation. You are placing the blame on others when you yourself are to blame."[57] Again, Ordzhonikidze on September 20, 1934: "We will not listen to those people who say our materials have not been delivered, but we say that a good manager, a good shop director, a good master technician knows how to organize things and produce the required results."

The clear message is that a good manager resorts to any and all means to get the job done at any price (*liuboi tsenoi*). A manager who attempted to use official channels was usually told to solve the problem himself.[58] Thus, superiors, ranging from SNK to the glavk director, implicitly condoned informal activities. Almost by definition, good managers were those who turned to unofficial channels to get things done – no questions asked by

[53] Ibid., 164.
[54] RGAE, 7297.38.106, 12.
[55] RGAE, 7297.38.106, 3.
[56] NKTP Decree NKTP No. 32, January 8, 1934, in RGAE, 7297.1.25, 192.
[57] RGAE, 7297.38.10, 4.
[58] Belova, "Economic Crime and Punishment," 139–40.

their superiors. *The system itself condoned and encouraged the horizontal dealings that ultimately threatened the dictator's hold on power.*

Edinonachalie did not mean that subordinates automatically obeyed orders. From the highest to the lowest levels, orders were not fulfilled or, worse, were ignored. In a letter of September 22, 1930, to Molotov, Stalin proposed to establish "a standing commission for the sole purpose of systematically checking on the fulfillment of the center's decisions," noting that "without such reforms the center's directives will remain completely on paper."[59] In an earlier letter of August 21, 1929, he confided to Molotov: "I am afraid that the local OGPU will not learn about the Politburo's decision, and it will get bogged down in the bowels of the OGPU."[60] Ordzhonikidze recorded similar complaints for his own ministry: "I see, I curse, I act like an animal, but in order to deal with an issue, in order to ensure that it will be done, the leadership itself must go into hysterics for three to four hours and to drive to hysterics the ones who have to fulfill the task."[61] Ordzhonikidze, in a speech on the tenth anniversary of NKTP's newspaper, *For Industrialization,* declared:

Often, practically every day, we make beautiful decisions – it would be impossible for them to be better. If you take all our decisions, decrees, and orders – just fulfill them, nothing more is being asked. But fulfillment doesn't go well. The newspaper must follow every day that our decisions are fulfilled.[62]

Ordzhonikidze's haughty reaction to orders from Gosplan is instructive:

Today they gave me your order, addressed directly to the chemical department . . . I regard such a directive through the director . . . [not through me] as incorrect. Therefore, I request that all directives be sent in the usual order. They think that they can give the factories orders bypassing us, but why the devil do we exist and why should I sit here."[63]

Thus, Stalin could feel that his orders were enlightened and should be obeyed, while his subordinate, Ordzhonikidze, could conclude that orders from above were "without foundation"[64] while praising his own orders as "beautiful."

[59] Khlevnyuk et al., *Stalinskoe Politburo*, 96.
[60] Lih et al., *Stalin's Letters to Molotov*, 168.
[61] RGAE, 7297.38.104, 2.
[62] RGAE, 7297.38.252, 2.
[63] Khlevnyuk, *Stalin i Ordzhonikidze*, 32.
[64] Ibid., 32.

Scapegoating and Punishment. The Soviet *edinonachal'nik* (one-man manager) had to fulfill contradictory and changing plans. He could not object because plans were issued unanimously by the highest party officials. Candidate member of the Politburo, Petrovsky, could not argue that his grain-collection targets were impossible because they had been issued by the omniscient Central Committee! Lacking official assistance, the one-man manager had to turn to unplanned channels. The only allowable explanation for failure was human failure, which could be interpreted as deliberate sabotage (wrecking). Under these circumstances, no edinonachal'nik could have a clean record, which could withstand careful examination. Yet, the supply of talented edinonachal'niki was limited. Institutional arrangements, therefore, had to resolve a dilemma: Plans failed regularly, and plan failure was officially due to human failure; yet, the sacrifice of the limited supply of managerial talent had to be limited to symbolic numbers.[65]

To resolve this dilemma, the Soviet system created an elaborate ritual of blame and punishment. The various players in this ritual usually understood their roles well. The manager shifted blame to subordinates, who tried to blame their subordinates, until blame finally settled on someone down the hierarchy. Experienced managers positioned themselves to blame scapegoats for plan failures – one of the most durable features of the Soviet system.[66] Ordzhonikidze's first deputy (Piatakov) served as a lightning rod for most ministry miscues. Deputy directors or chief engineers were more likely to pay the price of plan failure than the enterprise director. The lower the level of an acceptable scapegoat the better. NKTP minister Kaganovich had his deputies propose major programs, while he pointed out what could go wrong and disassociated himself from potential failures.[67] Stalin, the most experienced scapegoater of all, let others introduce plans and initiatives, while sitting on the sidelines as a critic and blaming others when things went wrong. Stalin turned down the chairmanship of SNK in 1930 perhaps to divorce himself from responsibility for concrete results.

At the ministerial level, plan failures set into motion a ritual of investigation, blame, and punishment. A blame commission would be established to identify the reason for nonfulfillment, to punish the guilty, and to offer corrections. Punishments ranged from rebukes (*vygovory*),

---

[65] These matters are discussed in Getty and Naumov, *The Road to Terror*, chapters 4–5.
[66] Gregory, *Restructuring the Soviet Economic Bureaucracy*, 129.
[67] RGAE, 7297.28.4, 15; RGAE, 7297.28.5, 11–17; RGAE, 7297.28.6, 117.

to firings, to criminal trials and even execution. Gump's July 1933 investigation of an accident at the Makeevsky Plant, which destroyed one of its blast furnaces, is a typical example.[68] The Commission found the chief of the blast furnace department and the blast furnace engineer responsible. The chief was dismissed and sent to a smaller plant, but he was promised reinstatement if the plant fulfilled its six-month plan. The blast furnace engineer, as relative newcomer, was demoted to acting engineer, his wage was reduced by 20 percent, but he was also promised reinstatement if he could repair the blast furnace within one month. Other guilty parties received severe rebukes. Note that the Makeevsky Plant manager successfully shifted the blame to lower-level scapegoats. Rebukes were entered into the official's party record, but they could later be removed. Purging the record clean was common, especially when the defendant had the support of a high-level patron.[69]

Scapegoats who refused to accept blame and to admit their mistakes were regarded as not being team players. Stalin's longtime colleague and fellow Georgian, A. S. Yenukidze, refused to accept blame in the summer of 1935 when he, as head of Kremlin security, was accused of security lapses and improper associations. Yenukidze made the mistake of defending his record, although the party line was that the Kremlin had been infiltrated by terrorists. Kaganovich to Yenukidze at the Central Committee Plenum of June 6, 1935:

If you are sincere, Comrade Yenukidze, about your readiness to accept punishment so that others draw lessons from it, then you ought to have analyzed your situation more honestly, you ought to have told us how enemies had wormed their way into your organization, how you gave cover to good-for-nothing scoundrels. Instead, you slurred over the matter and tried to prove that nothing out of the ordinary had taken place.[70]

Yenukidze was demoted to a provincial job and was executed in 1938, another victim of the Great Purges. The unfortunate Yenukidze should have followed the example of the sycophant Kaganovich when reprimanded by Stalin for his failure to condemn NKTP's poor-quality tractors. Kaganovich to Stalin (September 7, 1933):

On the matter of tractors I am in agreement with your conclusions. I regard it necessary to tell you that the management of this process was incorrect and, for that

---

[68] Gump's Decree No. 138 from July 7, 1933, in RGAE, 4086.2.275, 46–8.
[69] Belova, "Economic Crime and Punishment," 153–6.
[70] Getty and Naumov, *The Road to Terror*, 174.

reason, I was partially uninformed. We have a tradition, introduced by you, that if even a small issue arises, you gather us together and raise this issue to a principally higher level and then the unclear becomes clear and the incomprehensible becomes comprehensible. Comrade Molotov was really in charge of this process and didn't communicate with anyone. This explains to a large degree why instead of a direct and simple statement that the minister bears responsibility for this matter, we ended up with subtle hints ... *I accept your reprimand that I made a mistake and I did not understand the importance of this matter*" [author's italics].[71]

Punishment took on an ominous tone during the Great Purges of 1937 to 1938. Imprisonment and executions replaced the milder slaps on the wrist of earlier periods. On an inspection trip of August to October 1938 to investigate plan failures in coal mining, NKTP's deputy director, Comrade Makarov, inspected various coal mines and heard reports from the field director and from directors of different mines. After evaluating these reports, he declared as "disgraceful work" mines with 35 percent fulfillment, "definitely bad work" those with 40–60 percent fulfillment, and "unsatisfactory work" those with 85 percent fulfillment. Makarov identified the reasons for failure, placed blame on specific individuals, suggested remedies, and levied punishment. He turned some mine directors over to the courts, fired others, but kept on other managers who gave assurances that the situation would be immediately corrected.[72] Fortunately for most mine directors, Makarev refrained from charges of wrecking, which would have spelled inevitable execution.

Whereas the glavk was more likely to punish managers, the minister was more likely to reward them, at least within NKTP. In the 1930s, NKTP rewarded directors and deputy directors with cars and motorcycles, shop directors and chief engineers with bicycles and watches, as well as monetary awards.[73] Ministries controlled such rewards because they feared that glavks were too ready to reward their personnel.[74]

The Battle for the Plan

The expression "the battle (*bor'ba*) for the plan" recurs regularly in the archives. This term was later used by economic administrators in the

---

[71] Khlevnyuk et al., *Stalin i Kaganovich. Perepiski*, 333.

[72] RGAE, 7297.28, 58.

[73] NKTP Directive No. 12 of January 5, 1934, "About the Rewarding of Technical Workers and Leading Workers in Factory No. 8." In RGAE, 7297.1.25, 41.

[74] NKTP Directive No. 76, 1935, "About Forbidding Glavks and Trusts to Reward Managerial Personnel of Factories and Trusts without the Approval of the Ministry." In RGAE, 7297.44.9, 16.

1970s and 1980s, suggesting that each successive generation engaged in a battle for the plan.[75] Battling for the plan refers to the minister's or enterprise manager's struggle to obtain inputs and meet output targets and to extract good results from subordinates. It refers to the swirl of negotiation, bullying, petitions, excuses, and pleadings that surrounded all plan negotiation and execution. The terms of the battle were simple: The subordinate wished to maximize its well being, defined broadly to include salary, bonuses, perks, career advancement, and – importantly in the context of the late 1930s – to avoid repression. The superior wished to extract the maximum production with a minimum of scarce resources without placing the subordinate in a situation where plan fulfillment was impossible.[76]

In the Soviet nested dictatorship, each level waged the same battle. Just as ministries did not share information with the center, the glavks did not share information with one another or with the minister, prompting the following outburst from Ordzhonikidze:

Who is going to believe our figures if someone detects that we are giving false figures on tractor production? Comrade Afanas'ev should punish that person who deceived him with the harshest possible measures, should take him out and thrash him and throw him out. We don't need such liars.[77]

Glavks, like the ministry (see Chapter 6), obfuscated by issuing two plans. In a collegium meeting of March 5, 1933, Ordzhonikidze complained:

We must liquidate the practice of our glavks issuing to their enterprises plans in excess of those approved by the ministry. This may have been allowed last year, but if it continues it will cause an over-expenditure of funds and create a difficult financial situation. We must insist that the glavks issue plans that correspond with those approved by the collegium.[78]

The battle for the plan was about production and materials. Ministers, glavk directors, and enterprise managers lobbied fiercely for lower production and higher inputs. Ordzhonikidze lobbied for lower steel targets and resisted a lower investment budget, during negotiations over the second five-year plan.[79] Mikoian, the minister of trade, constantly lobbied for lower export targets, much to the chagrin of Stalin, who referred

[75] Gregory, *Restructuring the Soviet Economic Bureaucracy*, chapter 5.
[76] Belova and Gregory, "Dictators, Loyal and Opportunistic Agents," 273–4.
[77] RGAE, 7297.38.9, 4.
[78] RGAE, 7604.1.137, 9.
[79] Davies, *Crisis and Progress*, 292–301.

to him as "a self-satisfied bureaucrat."[80] Kaganovich to Stalin (August 31, 1931):

There was an intense debate [within the Politburo] about the volume of grain exports in the September export plan. Mikoian demanded a lower plan; we gave a plan of 1.34 tons as proposed by the trade ministry. Last year we had the same situation, and I remember how we had to put on pressure to get plan fulfillment for September. Of course, last year was a different situation, but this year's plan is lower, and it must be fulfilled.[81]

Optimal Tautness. The superior's job was to apply pressure on outputs and inputs, the master of which was Stalin. Stalin and Defense Minister Voroshilov to Kaganovich, Molotov, and Kuibyshev (September 14, 1933):

In connection with the huge under-fulfillments of military orders for aviation, tanks, artillery, munitions, we ask you to examine this question in the military commission, calling in people from the factories and decisively force fulfillment and punish the guilty.[82]

In this case, "punish the guilty" probably meant that a few token victims should be shot. Again, Stalin to Kaganovich:

The situation with artillery is very bad. Mirzanov [an Ordzhonikidze deputy] has ruined a perfectly good factory. ... Pavlunovsky [Ordzhonikidze's deputy for military production] has confused things and is ruining artillery production. Sergo [Ordzhonikidze] must be pressured that he, entrusting this great business to two or three of his favorites-idiots, is prepared to sacrifice the interests of the state to these idiots. It is necessary to drive out and lower in rank all the Mirzanovs and Pavlunovskys. Baku oil is also going poorly. This year we'll get 15 million tons of oil. Next year we must have 21–22 million tons. Despite all this, the oil glavk is sleeping and Sergo gives us only optimistic promises. This will be a disaster for us if we are not able to force NKTP to immediately deal with these issues, and at every meeting of the Polituro he must give us answers on what measures he has taken.[83]

Stalin also forced grain regions to fulfill their procurement targets by pressuring his own Politburo colleagues and by threatening to fire regional leaders.

From the minister's point of view, the glavks were too easy on their enterprises. Ordzhonikidze complained at an NKTP meeting of September 1934 that his glavks were allies of enterprises rather than taskmasters:

---

[80] Khlevnyuk et al., *Stalin i Kaganovich. Perepiski,* 52.
[81] Ibid., 74.
[82] Ibid., 343–4.
[83] Ibid., 395.

Our glavks are managing their enterprises, in my opinion, as if they have only recently separated. What does this mean? It means that they gather as poor beggars here in Moscow; they act as petitioners for their enterprises, in order to get as much as possible and to give their enterprises as small a production program as possible. This isn't any good; there is no kind of administration in this. We are not people with such weak nerves that we could not put our shoulders to the wheel. The glavk should lead. When factories demand from the glavk, it should examine to the last point, should give a factory a taut production program, and force it to fulfill it.[84]

Ordzhonikdze's plea to subordinates to be tough taskmasters illustrates Holland Hunter's and J. Szyrmer's optimal tautness[85] – the notion that an administrator can extract optimal indicators by imposing tough plans. If the plan is too easy, less output will be produced. If it is too tough, output can even fall. An optimally taut plan is one that extracts the maximum output from producers. The search for tautness was based on pure intuition, as the director of an NKTP supply organization reported in 1930:

We often allocate our funds in part and look how much we gave yesterday, in the last quarter to determine the needs of the glavk.... We'll give 100 units to one glavk, 90 to another; in the next quarter, we'll do the reverse and we see what happens. You see, we do it on the basis of "feel," there is no explanation.[86]

Such experimentation took place under the drumbeat of constant pressure from below. Gump complained (August 20, 1937) that "factories are saturating us with telegraphic demands for the release of supplementary fuels without any justification." Gump ordered that it would not even consider fuel requests unless "all orders for supplementary fuel include detailed justifications starting with proof of full use of internal resources, their need for production programs, and the use of specific expenditures."[87]

An amusing exchange between Ordzhonikidze and a deputy illustrates the difficulty of finding optimal tautness. Ordzhonikidze to a deputy (Muklevich):

Tell us please how it happened that they received 50 percent of supplies and fulfilled the production program 100%?"

[84] RGAE, 7297.28.334, 42.
[85] Hunter's original article is Holland Hunter, "Optimal Tautness in Developmental Planning," *Economic Development and Cultural Change*, 9, no. 4, part I (July 1961), 561–72. It can also be found in Hunter and Szyrmer, *Faulty Foundations*, 57–63.
[86] RGAE, 7297.5.2, 12–14.
[87] RGAE, 4086.2.3415, 32.

Subordinate (Muklevich):

In July, I told my people to prepare a report about the fulfillment of plans for individual branches. I then began to edit these reports and saw that the production program had been fulfilled 102% but only 40 percent of supplies had been received. I believed there was something left over from the previous year. I looked into the report for the previous year – again 103% and supplies only 40%. I couldn't look at the year previous to that because I could not find it.[88]

The head of NKTP's supply department provides a frank account of the problem of "defeating the greedy opportunists" and "making the process of supply healthy" (in a meeting of December 12, 1937):

Our problem is that we can't really check orders and are not able to check them.... We operate partially on the basis of historical material – we are supposed to give you so and so much in this quarter, and at the same time you are supposed to give us this much. We are supposed to go to SNK and assure them with full responsibility that we are demanding the minimum from the general balance of materials to ensure the provisioning of this or that enterprise. When we receive our materials, we distribute them and then we send letters to SNK saying "you insult us, you gave us too little; you must give us more."[89]

Superiors, bombarded with requests to lower the plan, rarely granted relief. NKTP received a rare concession from SNK in April 1935 to reduce its targets for civilian ships after Ordzhonikidze informed Molotov that he could not meet his 550 million ruble production target.[90] Ordzhonikidze proposed to move a substantial portion of civilian orders to 1936 so that he could fulfill military orders and attached a corresponding draft decree for SNK to sign.[91] Gosplan, which evaluated the request, reluctantly agreed, "although these obligations were placed on NKTP by special decrees of the government."[92] In this case, the minister protected his shipbuilding glavk, which likely had to prove its case to a reluctant Ordzhonikidze. More often, the minister rebuffed glavk attempts to reduce production plans. When NKTP's Defense Mobilization glavk (GVMU) unilaterally lowered its production targets without approval of the ministry, its management was severely punished. Despite Ordzhonikidze's fears that glavks were too sympathetic to their enterprises, they usually denied requests for lower production targets. Kosogorsky Metal Combinat's request for lower production targets to

[88] RGAE, 7297.28.335, 32.
[89] RGAE, 7297.5.2, 12–14.
[90] GARF, 5446.16a.84, 6–8.
[91] GARF, 5446.16a.84, 9.
[92] GARF, 5446.16a.84, 3.

allow necessary repairs was denied three times by Gump. When the Petrovsky Factory requested Gump (August 8, 1937) to lower its targets, the reply was: "The third quarter plan was approved by the government. I don't have the authority to change it. Considering the tight situation with pig iron balances, I request you take measures for the unconditional fulfillment of the third quarter plan."[93] The deputy director of the Kramotorsky Factory was reprimanded in October 1932 for shutting down a blast furnace without permission.[94]

Us Versus Them. The superior (the minister in dealing with glavks, or the glavk director in dealing with enterprises) took a more encompassing view than subordinates in matters of supply. Indeed, Ordzhonikidze had to remind subordinates in June 1932 of their interdependence: "No one is demanding that you promise [other glavks] mountains of gold. You just tell them what you can do and what is necessary. Let us then do honest battle and correct this situation."[95] NKLP minister, Liubimov, urged his troops to present a unified front (November 1, 1933):

You must carefully consider what kind of material you use, what kind of paint and create a fuss (*skandalit'*) about everything. We must create a fuss together ... not going separately to the inspection commissions or elsewhere, but going through the minister and together with the minister.[96]

The minister or glavk director engaged in regular redistributions of tasks and materials among subordinates. Reluctant glavks or enterprises were ordered to compensate for shortfalls elsewhere in the organization. NKTP ordered "donors" to increase their supplies to the Lugansk Locomotive factory for its on-time commissioning,[97] and to the Mariupol' Steel factory to increase its deliveries to Kharkov Shipbuilding.[98]

The minister's pitch that "we are in the same boat and must help each other" met stiff resistance in the glavks. Both Gump and Glavspetsstal (Main Administration of Specialty Steels) produced steel ingots, and they supplied each other with metal products. Gump, as the largest producer of steel ingots, was appointed the "planner" of steel ingots. Gump and Glavspetsstal's dispute over the 1937 second-quarter output and delivery plan was only one of many. Glavspetsstal informed Gump that its

[93] RGAE, 7297.44.1, 310.
[94] Directive No. 734 of October 26, 1932, in RGAE, 7297.44.1, 310.
[95] RGAE, 7297.38.10, 4, 15.
[96] RGAE, 7604.1.169, 4.
[97] Directive No. 96 of February 22, 1932.
[98] NKTP Directive No. 267s in RGAE, 7297.38.5, 310.

Zaporozhstal factory was unable to supply Gump's enterprises with steel
ingots according to plan because "Zaporozhstal's metal balance is extremely unfavorable" and its ingot production was necessary to fulfill
Zaporozhstal's own plan.[99] Gump protested to NKTP that Glavspetsstal
regularly did not meet its plan obligations and that it "engaged in out-
rages in the question of metal supply" allocating ingots preferentially to
its own enterprises. Moreover, Gump reminded NKTP of Glavspetsstal's
habit of fighting for low plan figures for its own enterprises at the expense
of higher production targets for Gump.[100] Gump concluded (October 31,
1937) that it could plan only its own production:

When Gump encompassed all factories of ferrous metallurgy, it took on the responsibility for planning all metallurgical shops of machine building enterprises.
Now factories of ferrous metallurgy have been removed from Gump and have
been assigned to other Glavks (Glavspetsstal, Glavtrubostal) and almost all factories of "small" metallurgy have been allotted to other ministries. Gump will now
plan only the production of enterprises subordinated directly to it.[101]

Gump's outrage against other glavks notwithstanding, Gump was
also guilty of failing to meet its supply obligations to other glavks
within NKTP. Ordzhonikidze singled out a Gump official (Comrade
Dukarevich): "Dukarevich is an entirely rotten and shady person. When
people go to him for supplies, he only answers – we don't have anything.
We can't give anything."[102]

Horizontal Dealings

Horizontal dealings offer a way out of the misallocations caused by supplier preferences for those within the same unit. If a foreign unit (machinery) has a higher and better use of steel than a steel manufacturer, it
can make an informal deal with steel producers that could improve the
efficiency of resource allocation. The machinery producer, for example,
could offer the steel supplier better machinery or more timely deliveries
in return for more steel. If supply reliability improves, both the steel and
the machinery producer can specialize and the overdemanding of inputs
could be reduced.[103]

[99] RGAE, 4086.2.3566, 11.
[100] RGAE, 4086.2.3566, 9–10.
[101] RGAE, 4086.2.3561, 30.
[102] RGAE, 7297.38.106, 1.
[103] Susan Linz and Robert Martin, "Soviet Enterprise Behavior Under Uncertainty," *Journal of Comparative Economics* 6, no. 1 (1982), 24–36.

Gigantic nonindustrial ministries such as the Ministry of Transportation, the NKVD's Gulag Administration (the largest construction organization), and the Ministry of Trade, which managed the production of manufactured consumer goods, competed with NKTP and NKLP for resources. Supplies and deliveries had to be balanced not only within industry, but also among transport, trade, and construction. Horizontal dealings among these agencies would normally go unrecorded, but we do have information on NKTP's disputes with other ministries and two months of the NKLP minister's correspondence with NKTP (from May and June 1934). The small number of letters between NKLP and NKTP (less than ten in two months) suggests that interministerial complaints were limited, probably for good reason. Ministries were headed by national leaders (e.g., Ordzhonikidze, Mikoian, and Kaganovich) and unresolved disputes had to be submitted directly to the Politburo or SNK. All wanted to avoid the label of troublemaker, except Ordzhonikidze. Disputants could not know in advance who would win, and Politburo patience was limited. Accordingly, our hunch is that administrative resolution was a last act; informal resolution was preferred.[104] When NKLP could not reach a compromise with NKTP on equipment deliveries, NKLP Minister Liubimov wrote to Stalin and Molotov complaining: "Despite all my pressure on NKTP, I was not able to obtain the equipment that is required to complete this construction on time."[105] The archives do not contain Stalin's or Molotov's answer to Liubimov, but this letter at least shows the format for high-level complaints. The complaining party had to demonstrate that all possible measures had been taken before submitting the matter to the highest authority.

Informal agreements were more common: an informal quid pro quo conflict resolution is revealed in NKLP Minister Liubimov's letter of June 1934 to Ordzhonikidze. One of NKTP's factories was supposed to supply two vacuum pumps to a trust of NKLP by the first quarter, but NKTP asked for a delay until September. Liubimov requested Ordzhonikidze to order his factory to deliver on time, arguing that the pumps were needed to complete the Balakhinsky Factory, which produced cellulose sulfate used

---

[104] Belova and Gregory have described a number of high-level disputes resolved by administrative means, where the disputing parties were an industrial ministry and Gosplan or the finance ministry. The procedure was to form a compromise commission, in which each party was represented, to hammer out a resolution acceptable to all parties. The industrial ministry was frequently the de facto winner in such disputes. Belova and Gregory, "Dictator, Loyal, and Opportunistic Agents," 275–6.

[105] RGAE, 7604.1.291, 4.

by both NKLP and NKTP. NKLP had not been able to meet NKTP's last order for cellulose sulfate, but if the pumps were delivered, NKTP would surely receive its orders.[106] Another deal between NKTP and NKLP took on a more subtle form that required considerable trust. In May 1934, NKLP requested additional materials from NKTP for the reconstruction of its Baturin Chemical Factory, which NKLP needed to meet its textile production targets. NKLP asked for NKTP's help, offering to stop bothering NKTP for future deliveries of chemicals once this factory was finished.[107] Thus, NKLP was proposing a deal that would be implemented over a long time.

A conflict between NKTP and the Ministry of Transport shows another reason for private agreements: lack of confidence that even the highest political authority could resolve the matter. In 1934, the transport ministry requested 46,600 tons of metals for bridges; NKTP offered half the requested amount. SNK supported NKTP by substantially reducing the transport ministry's request.[108] When NKTP failed to deliver even this smaller amount, SNK denied its request (November 21, 1934) to delay delivery and demanded punishment, bluntly stating:[109] "Request of Comrade Piatakov [first deputy minister of NKTP] for delay rejected. Order the control commission to bring the guilty to their responsibility for the violation of the SNK decree."[110] Despite SNK's stern ruling, and after further negotiation, NKTP won its delay.[111] Perhaps NKTP had no metals to deliver, but it is remarkable that SNK was unable to force its most powerful ministry to carry out an explicit order.

A 1935 NKTP–NKVD (People's Commissariat for Internal Affairs) dispute over a housing settlement was also resolved by the parties themselves. The settlement had been built by NKTP in the course of construction of the Iaroslavl' hydropower station, after which the project was transferred to the NKVD.[112] All project material, equipment, transport, and other technical equipment was to be transferred to NKVD, but NKTP

[106] Disputes within a glavk were assigned to the glavk director. Such conflicts were to be resolved internally and not passed on to arbitration organs. Glavk dirty linen was not supposed to be washed in public.
[107] RGAE, 7604.1.453, 12.
[108] GARF, 5446.27.92, 24.
[109] GARF, 5446.16a.689, 20.
[110] GARF, 5446.16a.689, 20.
[111] GARF, 5446.16a.689, 1–3.
[112] Joint decree of SNK and Central Committee, No. 2074 of September 14, 1935, in GARF, 5446.16.433, 6–8.

requested, among other things, that "the constructed settlement be given to NKTP's Iaroslavl' Rubber Combinat because a large number of the workers of this settlement actually work there and are very much in need of housing."[113] By the time, the control commission appointed to look into this matter began its work, NKTP and NKVD had already reached a compromise, and the matter was dropped.

There is even more evidence of informal dealings at the glavk level. In the report of its metals supply organization, Gump concluded that "for all practical purposes, the enterprises with their large staffs of supply agents [called pushers, or *tolkachi*, in Russian] in reality determine the allocation of resources."[114] Gump had to resist fiercely the acquisition of unplanned materials by their subordinated trusts and enterprises. On August 27, 1937, Gump reported "instances when Steel Supply (Stal'sbyt) organizations distributed metals at their own discretion without permission despite limitations in their order documents," and that "Steel Supply was not reporting receipt of materials although they were ordered to report without delay."[115] Because these informal dealings were under the table, we lack good documentation. What we do know is that tolkachi were a significant expense for supply organizations and enterprises – an expense that had to be hidden under other cost categories. Bonuses were paid to tolkachi even for planned deliveries, suggesting that their efforts were required just to get suppliers to send contracted materials.[116]

Breaking Up Ministries and Glavks

The administrative-command economy can be organized, as historical experience has shown, either by industrial branch or by region. Throughout most of Soviet history, the industrial-branch principle prevailed. Such an administrative organization meant that orders for the production and delivery of output originated in industrial ministries and in their branch main administrations. The 1930s began with one industrial ministry, the Supreme Council of the National Economy, and ended with twenty-two

[113] GARF, 5446.16.433, 3–5.
[114] RGAE, 4086.2.3568, 336–45.
[115] RGAE, 4086.2.3415, 76.
[116] The Rostow supply agency, for example, paid its tolkachi an extra 6 rubles for every delivery of metal if it was 80 percent of the approved amount, an extra 12 rubles for every shipment of low-quality metals, and also an expense account equal to the average wage. On this, see Belova, "Economic Crime and Punishment," 140.

industrial ministries in 1941.[117] NKTP started with thirteen glavks in 1932 and had thirty-four glavks in 1938. In a rare display of consistency, the dictator repeatedly supported the splitting up of organizations, called *droblenie*, and opposed ministerial empire building from 1930 to the end of the Soviet period.

Ordzhonikidze threatened to resign over the breakup of the Supreme Council, but it proceeded anyway. SNK rebuffed NKTP's 1935 request to create its own independent supply department on the grounds that it would create "uncontrollable" organs.[118] SNK turned down NKTP's demand for its own locomotives.[119] The 1934 Seventeenth Party Congress transferred enterprises from national ministries to republican and local ministries despite widespread opposition.[120] SNK even opposed NKTP's June 2, 1935, request that it be reassigned factories producing "List 68" orders for the military, which had been placed under the Ministry of Local Industry of the Russian Republic.[121] Even in minor disputes, the government consistently acted to prevent the strengthening of one organization at the expense of another, such as its return of a student dormitory that had been taken over by NKTP to the weaker NKLP, evoking a defiant response from NKTP.[122]

The splitting up of ministries and glavks intensified the them-versus-us supply problem. The chances of receiving materials and other inputs on a timely basis through official supply channels were favorable only if the product were produced within your own organization, such as within your own glavk. The more remote the supplier, such as in another glavk or even in another ministry, the lower your chances unless a higher authority intervened on your account. The supply problems intensified by

---

[117] Rees and Watson, "Politburo and Sovnarkom," 24.

[118] GARF, 5446.16.99.

[119] GARF, 5446.15a.66.

[120] GARF, 7604.1.402, 4, 39 (the appellation of the Ministry of Light Industry), 11–13 (the appellation of the SNK of Ukraine Republic), 24–25 (the appellation of the Ministry of wood industry), 30 (the appellation of the executive committee of Leningrad region). National ministries such as NKTP and NKLP were to retain major enterprises, on which they should focus their full attention. Republican governments, such as Ukraine, made claims for enterprises that were opposed by the "donor" ministries. The eventual list of enterprises to be transferred evoked vocal protests from ministries, in particular from NKLP and the forestry ministry. NKLP appealed the loss of its Polygraph Institute to the Russian Republic, arguing that it served national interests. The forestry ministry argued that some of the enterprises to be transferred were quite large and prepared cadres and produced for exports.

[121] GARF, 5446.16a.20.

[122] GARF, 5446.16.100.

splitting up could be addressed in three ways: first, producers could invest in patrons who could order foreign units to supply, as is evidenced in the number of supply interventions cited earlier in this chapter. Patrons in the state and party apparatus were, therefore, doomed to a life of reviewing petitions, claims, and complaints (see Chapter 3). Horizontal or unplanned transactions represented a second approach to the failure of foreign units to deliver supplies. Although unsanctioned by superiors, horizontal deals could correct the misallocation of resources and, as noted, managers were implicitly instructed to take this route, no questions asked. The third approach is self-supply or autarkic production; namely, the creation of integrated production structures that allow, say, a manufacturer to produce its own raw materials, manufacture its own products, and deliver them with its own railroad cars. David Granick demonstrated the highly autarkic nature of Soviet industry.[123] Unlike market economies in which firms specialize, Soviet enterprises were highly unspecialized. Machinery manufacturers produced their own metals and metal producers produced their own machinery. When producers discriminate in their deliveries against foreign producers, agents supply themselves. If machinery producers cannot count on metal producers to deliver steel, they must produce their own steel. In so doing, they increase the security of supply but lose the advantages of specialization and economies of scale, the very process that Adam Smith concluded creates "the wealth of nations."

In a market economy, the degree of specialization is determined by comparative advantage and by transactions costs. If the costs of arranging market transactions are low, enterprises will specialize and acquire materials, spare parts, and transportation from other suppliers and will reap the benefits of specialization. In some cases, such as suppliers that must produce a product suited only to one type of buyer, there may be a reluctance to specialize; however, in most cases, concern about the reliability of suppliers does not prompt autarkic supply chains.[124] In the Soviet administrative-command economy, concerns over the reliability of the supply chain were so great that enterprises became autarkic and sacrificed the benefits of specialization. The autarkic tendencies of producers in the administrative-command economy were a major source of inefficiency.

---

[123] David Granick, *Soviet Metal Fabricating and Economic Development* (Madison: University of Wisconsin Press, 1967).

[124] See, for example, Paul Joskow, "Contract Duration in Long Term Contracts: Empirical Evidence from Coal Markets," in *Case Studies in Contracting and Organization*, ed. Scott Masten (New York: Oxford University Press, 1967), 104–29.

Concluding Thoughts

Enterprises, supervised by their ministerial glavk and by their ministry, produced the output of the Soviet administrative-command economy. All three organizations were held responsible for final results; hence, we classify them generically as producers, or as "managers of production," to use the Russian term. The archives' description of the workings of the ministry clearly dispels any myth of harmony between planners and producers, even though certain producers were among the most influential members of the Politburo. Although ministries and glavks largely operated without rules, all unit heads were responsible for final results. Even though one-man managers could shift blame to others by scapegoating, ultimate responsibility could not be avoided. The need to fulfill the plan confronted the ministry and the dictator with a hard choice. Managers could fulfill their plan obligations only by engaging in the informal horizontal relations that undermined dictatorial power. When confronted with this choice, the ministry instructed subordinates to get things done "by any means and at any price." Those who ignored this advice were poor managers.

If institutional efficiency were measured by the degree of obedience to central orders, the ministry and glavk failed miserably. The principal/agent conflicts between dictator and ministry were persistent and acute. Capacity was concealed, inputs were overdemanded, and information was hidden, even though three ministries were headed by Politburo members. The "battle for the plan" reveals Zaleski's resource management in operation – the shuffling of resources in response to petitions, complaints, and arbitrary changes. The weakest point of the system was supply. Most of the struggle related to supply, not to production. The ministry and its supply departments were saddled with the task of finding administrative balances, and as many or more ministerial personnel were engaged in supply and deliveries as in production. In effect, the touted material balances were executed within the ministry, not by Gosplan or other national agencies. Agents supplied themselves first and foreign firms later, if at all. As ministries were split into smaller units, the supply problem of them versus us intensified, and agents defended themselves by creating autarkic production structures.

Our description of administrative balances puts another nail in the coffin of scientific planning. Supply officers worked on intuition, in full knowledge that enterprises were overdemanding inputs. The absurdity of the situation is brought home by the fact that enterprises were meeting their output targets with only 50 percent of their necessary inputs. Some degree of order was imposed by angry orders from superiors to supply priority factories in heavy industry, defense, and key construction sites. Even the ruling elite, however, could not ensure that a material would be delivered in the quantity and timeframe that it had ordered (recall the dispute between NKTP and the transport ministry in this chapter). The ministry and its enterprises performed a delicate balancing act in their own dealings. The ministry's job was to impose optimal tautness to extract as much as possible without assigning impossible tasks. Plan failures, if widespread, meant ministry plan failure.

Three explanations can be offered for the consistent policy of breaking up production organizations. A scientific planning dictator or a stationary bandit would be motivated by considerations of technical efficiency. As technology and the mix of output change, technologically different products should be managed separately. The technology of aluminum is quite different from steel. When aluminum becomes important, it must be directed by a separate organization. Indeed, the new glavks that were spun off from Gump (which was initially the sole producer of metallurgical products) were those that employed different technologies, such as the Nonferrous Metal, Gold, Platinum, and Rare Elements Glavk in 1932 and the Special Steels and Ferrous Alloys Glavk in 1937. We cannot judge the extent to which technological factors caused ministries to spin off new glavks, but the archives give a sense that certain product types matured into independent units in their own right, just as certain product groups (e.g., textiles) matured into independent ministries.

A power-maximizing dictator would fear concentrations of alternate power. A Supreme Council of the National Economy that controlled virtually all industrial enterprises would inevitably become as powerful as the Politburo and could not be tolerated, even if it were headed by a party loyalist. The fact that the Ministry of Heavy Industry alone dominated industrial production was enough of a danger. The power-maximizing dictator's fear of concentration of economic power explains the stubborn and persistent opposition to all empire-building efforts, even relatively trivial ones.

A power-maximizing dictator might have yet another reason for splitting up units. A "selfish" dictator consolidates power by buying the loyalty of activists with the offer of benefits, such as rapid advancement.[125] But if the number of high-level positions is fixed (and retirements do not take

[125] Lazarev, "Evolution of the Soviet Elite," 3–17.

place), promises of advancement cannot be honored, and loyalty falters. The creation of new ministries and glavks expands the numbers of high-level positions. The rank of minister carried with it a number of perks, which were the same for newly created ministries. Moreover, the new minister could now act independently and create an independent power base. Kaganovich's former deputies rarely contradicted him as minister, but when they were appointed ministers, they immediately began to quarrel with him. NKTP, which contained the prizes of industry, was split up at a faster pace than NKLP. *Presumably "gifts" of positions in heavy industry were more valuable; therefore, NKTP was split up more quickly.* That agents opposed the splitting of their own units suggests that they had something of value to lose. The NKLP archives document one such power struggle over rents: on June 23, 1932, the trust Union-Kino (Soiuzkino) protested directly to Stalin and Kaganovich that NKLP was trying to replace them with a ministry administration for the purpose of expropriating their considerable movie box-office earnings.[126] NKLP labeled the complaint absurd, denied that it was only interested in the money, and argued that Soiuzkino was simply opposed to any kind of external control.[127] We do not know the resolution of this dispute, but Chapter 9 will show the high value of cash in the administrative-command system.

During the 1930s, NKTP was run by three quite different ministries, or "jockeys," to use Berliner's term: Ordzhonikidze was a key member of the ruling elite with a fierce streak of independence. The shortlived Mezhlauk was a professional planner and technocrat. Kaganovich was also a major political figure who had risen to the top as a Stalin lackey. Despite their differences, they all appeared to follow the same procedures in running the ministry, although the ministry functioned largely according to informal rules. Thus, the jockey did not appear to matter. More than this, jockeys basically duplicated the behavior of their superiors, and each unit was organized and operated like its superior. Stalin's Great Terror of 1937 to 1938 wiped out virtually all of the jockeys, and they were replaced with young, upwardly mobile leaders without any apparent change in the way the system operated. These are rather compelling facts, suggesting that the choice of jockey was not a significant matter.

---

[126] Soiuzkino was a powerful independent organization, responsible for Soviet filmmaking and important to the dictator as a source of propaganda.

[127] RGAE, 7604.1.129, 15, Correspondence with the Central Committee, Politburo, and Central Executive Committee of the Russian Republic on the production activities of light industry.

8

Operational Planning

"At the meeting of the Politburo's transport commission it came out that the ministry of transportation does not know its plan at all, although even in current circumstances, it must know its plan."

Kaganovich to Stalin, August 30, 1933[1]

"We protest the excessively frequent changes in the plan for the third quarter for the production of rails, which, in the period June–July, has been changed six times. Such orders completely disorient the factory and lead to breakdowns in plan fulfillment."

Director of Makeevsky Metallurgical Combine to Ministry
of Heavy Industry, July 22, 1937[2]

Our placement of operational planning near the end is remarkable, considering that planning was one of the three core principles of the administrative-command system. Selected aspects of planning have been mentioned. We showed that long-term planning served primarily motivational rather than resource-allocation functions (see Chapter 5). Chapter 3 explained that Stalin was highly distrustful of planning experts whom he accused of turning the Politburo into a "council of elders" making only general decisions, and that his principal rival, Trotsky, favored consolidation of resource-allocation power in the hands of specialists, not party loyalists. Earlier chapters confirmed Zaleski's dismissal of scientific planning: Chapter 6 showed the tensions between Gosplan and the industrial ministries over information needed for planning, the arbitrary ad hoc interventions in plans, the fight for generalized plans, the ministry

---

[1] Khlevnyuk et al., *Stalin i Kaganovich. Perepiski*, 321.
[2] RGAE, 4086.2.3567, 5–7.

practice of dual planning and nonplanning, and the outright deception of planners. Scientific planning was also unwelcome from a political point of view. Those who favored balances over heroic effort were punished, as the 1929 purge of Gosplan taught.[3] Chapter 7 studied the "opportunism" of producers as they attempted to extract easy plans from the center and the chaotic system of supply planning.

In the early 1930s, the structure of the Soviet economy was relatively simple. There were three industrial ministries (heavy, light, and forestry products) and three large nonindustrial ministries (transportation, gulag construction, and trade). Various republican and regional authorities managed enterprises of regional or local significance. The multiplication of ministries, regional authorities, and main administrations throughout the 1930s required the planning of an increasingly complex administrative structure. By the early 1950s, plans were drawn up for fifty-two different agencies,[4] and the number of centrally set planned indexes was slightly under ten thousand.[5] If we take these fifty-two "planned" agencies, 260 annual and quarterly plans had to be produced per year, placing planners on a veritable treadmill of perpetual planning.

Any economic system that allocates resources by administrative orders, rather than the market, must solve the material-balance planning problem discussed in Chapter 7. Irrespective of the planning model chosen, outputs cannot be produced without inputs. To produce machinery, steel is required; factories cannot be built without construction materials; steel cannot be produced without ore and coke. A plan, therefore, must be a plan of outputs *and* their use as inputs by others. A plan cannot simply set outputs and hope that there will be enough inputs. Rather, the plan must be a consistent balance. In a market economy, consistency is ensured by the price system: only those willing to pay the going price will receive the goods. If a construction company does not have the resources to buy enough construction materials, it will not build the plant. The quantity supplied will equal the quantity demanded. In a planned economy, this consistency must be achieved by administrative orders.

The Two Faces of Planners

Whereas the story of the dictator is Stalin's and of the ministry is Ordzhonikidze's, there are two stories of Gosplan. One is of its

[3] Davies, *The Soviet Economy in Turmoil*, 118–20.
[4] The investment plan was allocated to fifty-two distinct agencies. Tikhonov and Gregory, "Stalin's Last Plan," 183.
[5] Zaleski, *Stalinist Planning*, 486.

professional party leaders, the other is of its technical experts. V. V. Kuibyshev, Gosplan's chairman from 1930 to 1934, represents the first face. He joined the party in 1904; he was as an old Bolshevik, who held an impressive array of jobs until his death in 1935: full member of the Politburo from 1927, chair of Central Control Commission from 1923 to 1927, chair of the Supreme Economic Council from 1927 until being named to head Gosplan in 1930. From 1934 to his death in 1935, he chaired the Committee of Soviet Control. Kuibyshev was less impressive than his resume. He was an alcoholic who poorly withstood pressure; he was severely browbeaten by other Politburo members; and on more than one occasion, he sought to retire from public life. His superior (Molotov) wanted to fire him. References to Kuibyshev are less than flattering. Stalin warned Molotov (September 12, 1933) not to leave him in charge because "Kuibyshev might drink."[6] Kuibyshev's nerves were easily rattled by conflict. Kaganovich quoting Kuibyshev to Stalin (August 12, 1931): "If we don't normalize relations, it cannot work out for me because these conflicts end with victory by Sergo and he doesn't take his words back."[7] Kuibyshev organized the technical commissions that prepared the five-year, annual, and quarterly plans. He was the link between Gosplan and the Politburo, whose meetings called to discuss plans were put off when Kuibyshev was not present.[8] Kuibyshev converted Gosplan from a think tank of leading planning specialists to one staffed by party appointees. Gosplan became a cheerleader for ambitious plans, evoking from one of Gosplan's founders the famous quip: "It is better to stand for higher plans than to 'sit' [meaning to sit in jail] for realistic ones."[9]

V. I. Mezhlauk, Kuibyshev's deputy chairman of Gosplan from 1931 to 1934 and then chairman of Gosplan from 1934 to 1937, represents the professional-planner side of Gosplan. It was Mezhlauk who organized the system of planning and distribution and authored the text, *About Planning Work and Measures for its Improvement*. He is credited with being the "main theoretician of administrative planning methods."[10] Mezhlauk was the editor of the newspaper *For Industrialization*. Plans for the period 1931 to 1937 were signed by Mezhlauk, who wrote the commentaries. His highest party position was as a member of the Central Committee.

---

[6] Khlevnyuk et al., *Stalin i Kaganovich. Perepiski*, 40.
[7] Khlevnyuk et al., *Stalinskoe Politburo*, 133.
[8] Khlevnyuk et al., *Stalin i Kaganovich. Perepiski*, 40.
[9] Remark by S. G. Strumilin, *Ocherki Sovetskoi Ekonomiki*, quoted in Carr and Davies, *Foundations of a Planned Economy*, 886.
[10] K. A. Zaleskii, *Imperiia Stalina. Biograpficheckii Entsiklopedicechekii Slovar'* (Moscow: Beche, 2000), *entry.* "Mezhlauk."

Mezhlauk received his law degree from Kharkov University in 1917, the same year he joined the party. He spoke several European languages and knew Latin and Greek. He had a distinguished military record in the civil war and was credited with transporting the assets of the state bank of Ukraine to Moscow as the Red Army withdrew. From the civil war through the early 1920s, he served as deputy commissar of the railroads. He then served as deputy minister of the Supreme Council of the National Economy, heading its metallurgy division. The Politburo dispatched him twice to the United States and Europe for study, and he served on the board of the Soviet–American Council for Exchange of Economic Research.[11] He served as Minister of Heavy Industry for slightly more than a half year in 1937. He was arrested in January 1937 and executed in 1938.

The striking contrast between the poorly educated, party bureaucrat Kuibyshev and the formidable Mezhlauk symbolized the polarity of Gosplan itself. Was Gosplan to be an organization that compiled plans according to established principles or an organization that blindly carried out party directives even if they defied economic logic?

Planning and Models of Dictatorship

The four models of dictatorship described in Chapter 1 call for alternate approaches to planning. A scientific-planning dictator would be content to set general guidelines and turn the task of finding a material balance over to a Gosplan. Gosplan would use scientific coefficients to estimate the material requirements of producers (e.g., how much steel is needed to produce efficiently one unit of machinery). Gosplan would balance production with its uses for each planned commodity to create a supply plan. It would adjust inputs and outputs until it had a material balance before issuing binding output and delivery instructions. The dictator would maintain a hands-off approach, interfering as little as possible. The empirical result would be one in which plan outcomes would be close to *ex ante* plans. Perhaps, in the early years, planners would not plan well as they learned their skills, and errors might be significant. But as time passed, planning experts would become better at their jobs and *ex ante* plans would be more closely fulfilled.

A stationary bandit would act as a development planner, actively choosing the best strategies for economic development and growth. The

---

[11] *Mezhdunarodny Fond Demokratii Aleksandra Iakovleva*, available at http://www.idf.ru/

stationary bandit would set investment rates and distribute investment among branches, set the terms of trade of agriculture and industry, and change decisions of scientific planners if they conflicted with development objectives. All decisions would be made with the goal of rapid economic growth and development. Under this model, political intervention would be more intrusive. The planner, however, would be the right hand of the stationary bandit and, as such, *ex ante* plans would be largely realized.

A selfish dictator would be loathe to turn resource allocation over to planning experts. Instead, the dictator would set as many output and input targets as allowed by information constraints (or let Gosplan do so only as a first variant) without concern about the existence of a material balance. As producers are confronted with massive imbalances, they must appeal to the dictator for lower output targets or for more inputs, and the dictator makes thousands of ad hoc adjustments based largely on political considerations. This selfish dictator resembles Raymond Powell's dictator (see Chapter 1), responding to a barrage of nonprice signals such as telephone calls, personal appeals, and petitions from producers. The selfish dictator would carefully monitor any plans prepared by experts and would intervene whenever such plans did not yield the desired political results. Empirically, this model would yield plan outcomes that diverge significantly from (or are not at all related to) *ex ante* plans. In fact, one might question whether this is really a planned economy. The parts of the plan that might be relevant are those that have little political significance and, hence, escape the dictator's attention.

The vested-interest or corporate-state model of planning would be a bottom-up planning in which corporate interests impose plans on the planning authority. Producers would set their own output plans and would be in charge of distributing those outputs among their own and foreign producers. There would be little overall coordination; hence, this multitude of separate plans would be inconsistent and the actual allocation of resources would be settled by battles among interest groups. Unlike the power-maximizing dictator, inconsistencies would not be solved by petitions to a powerful dictator. Rather, they would be decided horizontally on the basis of the comparative power of the combatants. Only in the case of severe impasses would the dictator be called on to play the role of arbiter. Like the previous model, *ex ante* plans would not be fulfilled, largely due to coordination problems.

These four planning models differ with respect to consistency and degree of delegation. The scientific planner and the stationary bandit would aim for consistent plans, whereas the power-maximizing dictator would welcome inconsistent plans and corporate planning would be incapable of producing balanced plans.

Chapter 3 demonstrated the limited decision-making capacity of any dictator. Hence, the dictator must delegate either to scientific planners, such as Gosplan, or to corporate interests, such as industrial ministries. Delegation is unavoidable in all four cases, and it could proceed by frequency (the dictator taking annual planning while delegating quarterly planning), by aggregation (the dictator planning broad product categories and delegating the details), or by plan penetration (the dictator planning only the immediately subordinate organization and delegating the planning of enterprises to subordinates). Irrespective of the planning model, the dictator requires the assistance of experts to create a consistent plan. On the degree of delegation, Zaleskii writes: "it is sufficient to compare the number of centrally established indexes (9,490 in 1953) with the list of industrial products (more than 20 million) to realize the extent of jurisdiction of intermediary agencies and enterprises."[12] Planning experts would be in a better position to know all the facts. The industrial ministries would have even more detailed information due to their information advantage, but they too would lack an overview of plan consistency. If planning power were delegated to Gosplan, it could strive to create a consistent plan for the entire economy. If planning power were delegated to ministries, separate plans would be created that would not constitute a unified whole. The dictator's planning dilemma, therefore, is that planning decisions must be delegated out of either sheer necessity or the desire for a consistent plan. Yet, any delegation of planning power is a first step whereby the dictator "progressively relinquishes its power."[13] If Gosplan or ministries decide who gets steel or machinery, they, not the dictator, exercise power. As a specialist in the exercise of power, the Soviet dictator would be reluctant to delegate his main source of power – the power over resources.

Presumably, the dictator would try to make only the most important decisions, but earlier chapters showed the difficulty of distinguishing trivia from substance. High party officials were drawn constantly into petty disputes and petty issues. Gosplan also could not pull itself out of the mire of tedious details, despite numerous attempts. Although Gosplan did not particularly seek power in the 1930s, the industrial ministries did not shirk power. In the early 1930s, the Ministry of Heavy Industry produced most heavy industrial production and was headed by a powerful

---

[12] Zaleskii, *Stalinist Planning*, 486.
[13] Hayek, *The Road to Serfdom*, 71–5.

Politburo member, S. Ordzhonikidze. Delegation of heavy-industry planning to him would have markedly simplified planning, but it would have been tantamount to handing Ordzhonikidze virtually unlimited economic power. The dictator's dilemma was palpable: planning must be delegated, but every delegation reduces the dictator's power. Delegating planning to a single agent (Gosplan) meant empowering experts of questionable loyalty who would consider only the economic implications, not the political factors, which only the dictator would understand.

The official Soviet claim of scientific planning (the first planning model) has been long dismissed,[14] starting with the early works on the Soviet enterprise by Berliner and Granick.[15] The *coup de grâce* to the myth of scientific planning was delivered by Zaleskii's exhaustive study of Soviet planning for the period 1933 through the early 1950s. Zaleskii showed that outcomes bore little resemblance to *ex ante* plans and that resource management rather than plans allocated resources.[16] Plans were never meant to be operational; they were instead a "vision of growth, itself at the service of a development strategy,"[17] based on overly optimistic assumptions that imploded when confronted with hard reality. Balanced plans were impossible: the overly ambitious plans authorized enterprises to claim huge volumes of resources, and no experienced manager would voluntarily limit claims to resources. Whereas output plans were based on wildly optimistic assumptions, the claims on these outputs were virtually unlimited. Hence, *ex ante* "material balances" that were the supposed basis of planning could only be achieved *ex post* by resource managers. Complicating matters was the fact that plans were uncoordinated. The five-year plans, the annual plans, and the quarterly plans were compiled independently and were changed frequently. According to Zaleskii, the institutions of centralized resource management, as practiced by the Politburo and SNK, were the one constant of the system. Other institutions, such as industrial ministries and main administrations, were constantly reorganized, but SNK and the Politburo were not.

Reality is complicated. There was probably some use of all four planning models. Scientific planning may have been the dictator's intent, but proved unworkable due to the information and management problems emphasized by Hayek and Mises. Soviet practice did not use a pure model;

[14] *Gosplan USSR, Metodicheskie Ukazaniia.*
[15] J. Berliner, *Factory and Manager*; D. Granick, *Management of Industrial Firms.*
[16] Zaleskii, *Stalinist Planning*, 484–90.
[17] Ibid., 483.

the issue is which model dominated? The fact that Soviet planning practice was removed from scientific planning does not establish which alternate model – the stationary-bandit, the selfish-dictator, or the vested-interest model – was in actual use.

Although Soviet specialists initially focused on scientific planning and development planning,[18] more recent writers have focused on the last two models. Peter Rutland supports the selfish-dictator model, arguing that plans were designed to further the political aims of the party, whose "first priority ... is to effect structural change in the economic system to bring economic power securely into their hands,"[19] and that "It is difficult to see how the Bolshevik Party would have maintained itself as a coherent political force over the decades if it had not taken on this major role of close supervision of and involvement in daily economic life."[20] Five-year and annual plans only served as symbolic rituals, similar to the May Day Parade on Red Square, to legitimize the system.

Peter Boettke and G. Anderson support the vested-interest model, claiming that the Soviet economy was actually a quasi-mercantilist economy in which the party "grants" monopolies to powerful political figures. These monopolies form distributional coalitions, which contend with one another for economic rents in the form of investment resources or other material and political rewards. The distribution of resources is more the outcome of horizontal dealings among coalitions than of bottom-down management by a powerful centralized party. The dictator's role is to referee the distribution of economic rents among interest groups.[21] Mancur Olson agrees that planned economies, after an initial period of firm central control, fall prey to distributional coalitions, which capture resources for narrow interest groups.[22]

Operational Planning

We use the archives of the Ministry of Heavy Industry (NKTP) and the Ministry of Light Industry (NKLP) to examine Soviet operational

---

[18] Michael Montias, "Planning with Material Balances in Soviet-Type Economies," *American Economic Review,* 49, no. 5 (December 1959), 963–85; Herbert Levine, "The Centralized Planning of Supply in Soviet Industry," in *Comparisons of the United States and Soviet Economies* (Washington, D.C.: U.S. Government Printing Office, 1959).

[19] Rutland, *The Myth of the Plan,* 104, 259.

[20] Ibid., 241.

[21] Boettke and Anderson, "Soviet Venality," 37–53.

[22] Olson, "The Devolution of Power," 9–42.

planning in practice. Earlier studies of Soviet planning, most notably Zaleskii's, relied on published sources. We go behind the scenes to examine the annual and quarterly plans actually used by producers to determine whether resources were allocated *ex ante* or *ex post* and the degree to which plans were prepared by representatives of the dictator or by the producers themselves. If resources were allocated *ad hoc*, were they allocated by a representative of the dictator, such as SNK or the Politburo, or by the producers themselves? Were plans sufficiently stable to serve as fixed points for producers? Or is it a misnomer to refer to the Soviet economy of the 1930s as planned?

Five-year plans were discussed at the highest levels. As "visions of growth," they were published in the press and discussed in party congresses. Operational planning, to the contrary, took place out of sight in Gosplan's branch departments, ministerial planning departments, glavks, and enterprises. Yet, these operational plans, battled out in the trenches, constituted the supposed core of the planning system. If plans actually guided resource allocation, it was these annual, quarterly, and monthly plans put together out of sight of the public. From Zaleskii's limited account of quarterly planning, we understand that operational planning was messy, irregular, improvisational, and complex. The annual, quarterly, and monthly plans were poorly coordinated, deadlines were rarely met, and information was provided late.[23] The story we tell based on ministry archives is similarly complicated, confusing, and messy, largely because the process itself was not transparent.

We analyze here the plans and plan correspondence found in the various ministry and glavk archives. We use the exchanges of paperwork between Gosplan, SNK, and the ministry, between the ministry and the glavk, and between the glavk and the enterprise. These archives were reasonably well maintained, and the plan as the "law" would be among the most important of documents. Therefore, we must presume that we are working with a relatively complete collection of planning documents. The analysis of planning material is complicated by inconsistent terminology.[24] The annual plan is usually referred to as the "technical industrial–financial plan" (*tekhpromfinplan*) but, in some cases, the same terminology applies to the quarterly plan. Industrial–financial plans (*promfinplan*) usually refer to

---

[23] Zaleskii, *Stalinist Planning*, 500–3.

[24] Outputs and input assignments are referred to as plans, projects of plans, control figures, programs, or limits. "Val" (gross production, or *valovaia produktsia*) can refer to both value and physical units.

TABLE 8.1. *Stages of Annual Planning: Government and Ministries*

Stage	Date	Action
First	June–July	SNK and Gosplan prepare general targets
Second	August–October	Gosplan, ministries, and republics prepare detailed targets
Third	October–December	Gosplan and finance ministry bargain with ministries
Fourth	December–January	Plan "approval"

Source: Andrei Markevich and Paul Gregory, "Was the Soviet Economy a Planned Economy? Answer of the Soviet Archives of the 1930s," Zvenigorod International Conference, Zvenigorod, Russia, June 2001.

enterprise plans composed of many planning indicators, not to the shorter summary version. The glavks, like the ministry, assigned enterprises operational plans higher than the confirmed plan or its draft variant. "Steel Trust," for example, reported to Gump that its production program for the first five months of 1937 was fulfilled "79.8% according to operational tasks but 87.6% according to Gosplan's targets."[25]

What follows are largely case studies of the planning of metals within NKTP by its Main Administration for Metals (Gump) and of different light industry products within the NKLP. We focus on metals because they were approved at the highest levels; their production was managed first by one (Gump) and then by three glavks, all under the supervision of the NKTP minister. We would expect metal production (pig iron, rolled steel, special steels) to be among the best planned of sectors given their high priority and attention from the center. Light-industry products were planned by various glavks and regional authorities of NKLP. Although their priority was lower, they had the advantage of less scrutiny. Due to the better organization of NKLP archives, we have somewhat more information on its planning methods than on those of NKTP.

The Planning Process. Chapter 6 showed that planning deadlines were not observed. Ministries sought to submit data to Gosplan as late as possible, and one of Gosplan's most common complaints was that ministries were delaying the preparation of plans. It therefore comes as no surprise that operational plans were released with considerable delays. The annual plan for the national economy (with a January 1 starting date) was formulated in four general stages according to the following timetable (see Table 8.1). Once "approved," the ministries had to transmit it down

[25] RGAE, 4086.2.3548, 51–4.

TABLE 8.2. *Stages of Enterprise Plans*

Stage	Date	Action
First	October–December	Enterprises submit information to glavks
Second	January–March	Glavks meet with enterprises to approve major indexes
Third	March–later	"Final" plans approved by glavks

Source: Andrei Markevich and Paul Gregory, "Was the Soviet Economy a Planned Economy? Answer of the Soviet Archives of the 1930s," Zvenigorod International Conference, Zvenigorod, Russia, June 2001.

to the enterprises in the form of their "final" industrial–financial plans (*promfinplan*). Table 8.2 shows the three stages of planning of enterprise plans.

The planning phases given in Table 8.1 reveal that the first phase of annual planning officially excluded the ministries. It was conducted by the Politburo, SNK, and Gosplan. However, the ministries were not excluded entirely. Kaganovich's correspondence with Stalin refers to meetings with ministers on the same day that the Politburo considered annual or quarterly plans.[26] Kaganovich's descriptions of Politburo meetings to decide national control figures show that it dealt only with highly aggregated figures, such as the gross output of heavy and light industry, grain collections, or freight transport. The Politburo did not set the control figures for specific products in its annual plan directives (see Chapter 5). In any case, the first phase designated the major control figures and limits (e.g., investment limits) that set the general tone of plan discussion and negotiation between ministries and Gosplan and then between ministries and glavks. After the first phase, planning became a process of information exchange and negotiation (*torg*), which reached their peak in the fourth stage. Gosplan played a key role throughout the process. SNK and the Politburo approved the plans proposed by Gosplan, with their added "corrections."[27] SNK did not approve individual ministry plans; rather, the annual ministry plan broken down by enterprises was approved as a package in the 1930s. SNK also approved the ministries' investment plans, broken down by glavks, as well as some title lists of specific investment projects. Gosplan was also supposed to prepare major balances, such as for metals,

[26] Khlevnyuk et al., *Stalin i Kaganovich. Perepiski.* 658–9.
[27] Andrei Markevich [in Russian], "Was the Soviet Economy Planned? Planning in the People's Commissariats in the 1930s," PERSA Working Paper No. 25 (Version 23, January 2003), University of Warwick, England, Department of Economics.

TABLE 8.3. *Planning Phases for the 1934 Annual Plan, Ministry of Heavy Industry, for 1933*

Date	Action
September 20	Glavks submit control figure material to NKTP planning department
September 20	Glavks develop production limits and capital investments by enterprises
September 23	Glavks submit to NKTP's labor department their limits for labor and rationalization of labor for all enterprises and trusts, obtaining preliminary agreement with the planning department
September 25	NKTP planning department issues to the glavks their limits on costs
September 27	Glavks formulate their limits of costs by enterprises
October 1	Give enterprise and trusts directives and limits for the form and instructions of control figures
October 5	Through republican authorities, issue directives and limits to enterprises subordinated to republican and local authorities
October 5	According to the limited form, issue certain glavks their control figures not waiting the receipt of control figures from enterprises
November 1	Issue control figures to all enterprises
November 20	All enterprises submit their control figures to trusts on the basis of enterprise control figures and send to glavks
November 20	Republican authorities prepare their control figures on basis of control figures of enterprises and submit to glavks
December 1	Glavks submit their summary control figures

Source: NKTP Directive No. 645 from September 16, 1932, "About the Order and Deadlines for Preparing the Control Figures for Heavy Industry for 1933." RGAE, 7297.1.1.1, 269; RGAE, 7297.28.5.1, 100.

but these were approved after the annual plan had been prepared. In addition to the annual plan, special plans, such as "About Ferrous Metals," could be prepared separately.

As part of the first phase of planning, SNK would issue instructions on planning schedules to each of the ministries under titles such as "About the Order and Deadlines for Preparing the Control Figures for Heavy Industry for 1933." Table 8.3 shows the instructions for NKTP's 1934 plans, broken down into twelve separate phases to be carried out in 1933. The 1939 plan was divided into nineteen separate phases to be carried out in 1938. A number of phases were to be completed on the same day, such as five phases to be completed on September 25 and six phases on October 1 for the 1934 plan. Each phase required ministry glavks, functional departments, or enterprises to supply information, such as cost estimates, output figures, or enterprise targets. The planning process required complicated exchanges of information between glavks and enterprises, enterprises and glavks, glavks and ministry departments, and with the ministry planning sector. The 1934 process, for example, was to end with the glavks giving summary figures to the ministry planning department.

Rather than using general instructions that were valid for each year, SNK issued new instructions each year. As was demonstrated in earlier chapters, the dictator avoided general rulemaking, although it would have been relatively easy to work with fixed schedules that carried over from plan to plan. As noted in Chapter 6, the ministries fought not only the plan targets, but also the schedule itself. NKTP in particular engaged in numerous battles to bend reporting deadlines.

Structure of Plans. Ministry plans consisted of three obligatory parts: the text described the main tasks and priorities of the plan, the summary tables gave the ministry's main targets, and the detailed tables contained the actual plan directives of the glavks and sometimes of large enterprises. The ministry did not approve enterprise plans; rather, this was the task of the glavk. Each plan was broken down into constituent parts. The most important was the plan of production and assortment and the capital investment plan. Secondary plans were the labor plan, the cost plan, and sometimes the plan for the social sphere, such as the operation of kindergartens and clinics. The financial plan was kept separate and was approved by the finance ministry, not Gosplan. Distribution or supply plans were handled separately and were usually compiled last. The two most important plans were the production plan and the capital construction plan.[28] If changes were introduced into the ministry's capital investment plan, the finance plan had to be changed as well; changes to the finance plan were relatively automatic, as is shown by NKLP's matter-of-fact communication to the finance ministry:

As a consequence of corrections to the title list for housing construction for 1933, NKLP's finance sector is introducing the following changes in the annual financial plan for housing construction from the account of special capital and the budget of the central construction bank.[29]

[28] RGAE, 4086.2.3452, 3453, 3454.
[29] RGAE, 7604.2.740, e.6.

Although the production and capital investment plans dominated other plans, SNK or Gosplan would conduct periodic campaigns for the fulfilment of other indicators. For example, the collegium of NKLP in 1933 adopted the directive: "About Measures to Insure the Fulfillment of the Labour Productivity Plan for 1933," directing

attention of directors of glavks and republican ministries of light industry (and a list of other executors) that the major indicator for judging the work of enterprises in the current economic year is the degree of fulfilment of the labour productivity plan and the wage plan.[30]

In 1937, SNK adopted a directive stating that "plan fulfilment must be evaluated not on the basis of gross production but on the production of finished and completed production according to standards of quality and assortment."[31] That such special instructions were required at all suggests the dominant role of gross production in the assessment of plan fulfilment. When plan failures in other areas became acute, it was necessary for central authorities to focus attention on secondary indicators, like quality or labor productivity.

Actual planning within the ministry was done by the ministry's planning economic administration, which we call its planning department. The planning departments of both NKTP and NKLP varied between 50 and 100 employees each in the 1930s, but their ranks were supplemented by temporary workers during peak planning periods. For example, in the fall of 1938, NKTP's planning department was supplemented by an additional 100 economists and technologists from other departments to handle the peak-load work.[32] Other departments of the ministry were responsible for parts of the plan, with the planning department maintaining the books on the overall plan. The glavks were responsible for branch plans (e.g., Gump for metals, Glavsherst for wool products) and the functional departments, such as labor and finance, were responsible for labor and financial plans, respectively. The supply department was responsible for the planning of distribution.

The planning department of the ministry occupied a key position in operational planning. It served as the ministry's main contact with Gosplan and with the glavks and large enterprises. There were even occasions when the minister would organize a shadow planning department to check the

[30] RGAE, 7604.1.119, 125–6.
[31] *Sobranie Zakonov*, 1937, no. 24, 98.
[32] RGAE, 7297.28.5, 1, 77–90.

work of the official planning sector. For example, in 1938 as the ministry was preparing its annual plan for 1939, NKTP Minister Kaganovich organized an alternative group of planning specialists to "free them from their work for 15–20 days to study the materials along with the planning sector and to present to the collegium their results for the discussion of the 1939 plan."[33]

Although, theoretically, all major decisions concerning the plan were to go to the minister and to the collegium of the ministry, the collegium rarely discussed more than the first draft of the plan. Complete collegium agendas of NKTP (1938) and NKLP (1933) show that the collegium did not discuss plan changes, but accepted carte blanche the planning department's proposals (Table 8.4).

Planning Delays: Preliminary Plans. Although the official timetable called for annual plan approval by late December or early January, NKTP's annual metals plan was usually confirmed by SNK after more than half of the plan year had run its course. The metals glavks received their annual plans even later, but on different dates depending upon their priority. Annual glavk plans were regularly "corrected," and the sum of the quarterly plans did not add up to the annual plan. The lack of an annual plan at the beginning of the year dictated that quarterly planning be based on preliminary limits and drafts of preliminary annual indicators. The ministry and glavks processed preliminary annual indicators in two planning phases – the first in October to December of the preceding year, and the second in January of the plan year.[34] Enterprises negotiated protocols of advance loadings (*avansovaia zagruzka*) with the glavk using these preliminary drafts of annual indicators. In the case of Gump, commissions consisting of four representatives from Gump and three enterprise representatives negotiated the advance loading plan,[35] which set the projected annual volume of output (val) and its assortment. Other plan indicators, such as labor, costs, productivity, and new products, were not even considered at this point. The glavk was placed in the uncomfortable position of negotiating with enterprises prior to having its own plan in place.

The advance-loadings protocols constituted a key step in enterprise operations. Enterprises refused to enter into supply contracts until the

[33] Protokol Zasedaniia Kollegii NKTP, September 7, 1938, RGAE, 7604.3.136, 1.81.

[34] RGAE, 4086.2.3452, 3453, 3454.

[35] RGAE, 4086.2.3452, 3453, 3454.

TABLE 8.4. *Meetings of Ministry Collegiums of NKTP and NKLP to Discuss the Annual Plan*

NKLP, 1933 Meetings on 1934 Plan

Date	Action
September 22	Discussion of production program and plan of capital investment
October 25	Refining of the deadlines for working out the plan, directives for the financial plan, and the plan of supply
October 27	Approval of the plan of capital investment by glavks
October 29	Approval of the capital investment plan as a whole
November 1	Approval of the production plan by glavks
November 2	Approval of the production plan for selected glavks

NKTP Meetings on the 1939 Plan

Date	Action
September 7	Begin work on the formulation of the plan. Establish the first deadlines and directives for the capital investment plan and the supply plan
September 13	Approval of the NKTP plan guidelines as a whole, refinement of deadlines for the Glavk plans
September 16	Discussion of the plan, refinement of deadlines for preparing the plan
September 26	Directives to the planning department
October 25	Directives to the deputy ministers for preparing the title list of investment
October 29	Discussion of plans of specific glavks, directives to specific glavks about plan preparation and to the planning department for the aggregated plan
November 3	Approval of production program of specific glavks, directives to specific glavks and to the planning department for the aggregated plan
November 5	Approval of the production program and plan of capital investment for specific glavks
November 14	Approval of production program and plan of capital investment for specific glavks, directives for labor and costs
November 16–17	Approval of production program and plan of capital investment for specific glavks, refinement of deadlines for presenting the summary plan of production and capital investment for NKTP, and directive for the financial plan
November 19	Approval of directives on costs and labor, directives for the financial plan
November 23	Approval of plan of capital investment, directives for labor and costs
November 25	Approval of plan of capital investment for specific glavks
December 13	Approval of the deadline and order of preparation of the "PR" plan of the ministry
December 14	Approval of the financial plan

Source: RGAE, 7604.1.133; RGAE, 7604.1.176; RGAE, 7298.28.4-8.

approval of its assortment by the glavk in the advance-loadings protocols. For example, "Steel Trust" wrote to Gump:

We didn't receive protocols of advance loadings with orders for rolling mills for the fourth quarter. Funds, orders and supplementary orders for our production are coming. We ask you to send the protocol of advance loadings for the fourth quarter. Before its approval, we will refrain from concluding contracts.[36]

Besides approving the advance-loading protocols, the glavk also had to rush to approve the enterprise's preliminary labor limits. For example, Gump issued preliminary 1937 labor limits to its Trust Nerudostal only on December 21, 1936, which were declared "valid until government approval."[37] Thus, enterprises and glavks began the plan year only with preliminary and tenuous agreements on output and labor inputs. Neither glavk nor enterprise had anything approaching an approved plan.

Hence, the ministry planning department, glavks, and enterprises dealt with delays of confirmed plans by using preliminary operational plans, the most important of which was the advance-loading plan. Through custom and practice, glavks and enterprises learned to operate without confirmed plans. Receipt of the annual plan after the year was half over does not constitute proof that this was not a planned economy. What it does mean is that the economy's operational units produced and delivered outputs on the basis of fragile preliminary agreements that could be changed at any time.

The quarterly plan was prepared according to the same basic scheme as the annual plan. About a month to a month and a half prior to the beginning of the quarter, the ministry's planning department, based on directives received from Gosplan, gave the glavk its draft production limits for the upcoming quarter. The ministry simultaneously sent a copy of those limits to the labor department, the financial department, and the cost sector of the ministry. For example, Gump received its preliminary quarterly limits for 1937 from NKTP's planning department from one week to one month before the start of the quarter.[38] The first-quarter limits often were received by the glavk simultaneously with its preliminary annual production limits in the summer of the previous year – sometimes much earlier than for subsequent quarters.[39]

[36] RGAE, 4086.2.3562, 14.
[37] RGAE, 4086.2.3431, 56.
[38] RGAE, 4086.2.3450, 9, 31, 41.
[39] For example, NKTP's planning department sent Gump its preliminary limits (authorized by SNK) for the first quarter of 1937 already on July 25, 1936. RGAE, 4086.2.3450, 48–52.

The number (and detail) of limits depended on the importance of the branch, who headed the branch, and priorities. Gump, having the highest of priorities as the key producer of metal products, received limits for pig iron, steel, rolled steel pipes, coke ammonia, ammonia sulfate, and cement, released as generalized figures for the entire glavk.[40] Gump then had to distribute production tasks among its enterprises through its branch departments. On December 12, 1932, Gump's planning department sent preliminary limits for the first quarter of 1933 to its coke-chemistry department, based on limits it received from NKTP. Upon receipt of their production limits, the enterprises then negotiated with the glavk, and the negotiated production limits were then sent back to the ministry planning department for approval.[41] During the course of negotiations, the glavk could challenge production limits handed down by the ministry, but every reduction required approval from the ministry. For example, one month into the third quarter, the deputy head of Gump's planning department informed NKTP's planning department of its proposed changes stating that these changes had been coordinated already with NKTP's planning department and requesting confirmation.[42]

The ministry planning department sent these bottom-up figures to Gosplan and SNK; after approval, they became the "final" quarterly plans submitted back to the glavk and then to the enterprises. In Gump's case, the "final" plan figures for the quarter were sent by NKTP according to their order of approval. The first production figures, approved early in the first month of the quarter, were for pig iron, steel, iron ore, coke, ammonia products, refractory materials, and cement. Gump received its fourth quarter of 1937 figures for these products three days after the start of the quarter[43] and its breakdowns by trusts and enterprises in both natural and value terms later.[44] Gump received its rolled steel assortment last, from two weeks to one month into the plan.[45] At times, the breakdown of

[40] RGAE, 4086.2.3450, 41, 31, 9.
[41] RGAE, 4086.2.65, 19.
[42] "Gump's preliminary limits of gross production for the third quarter of 1937 differ from the plan authorized by NKTP as follows: in the metals industry 50.9 million rubles instead of 51.5 and in fireclay industry 53.8 instead of 52.5 million rubles." RGAE, 4086.2.3450, 22.
[43] RGAE, 4086.2.3450, 5–7.
[44] Sometimes the breakdown was approved by the government simultaneously with the aggregate figures for the glavk. In such cases, NKTP was able to transmit these breakdowns simultaneously with the aggregate figures. Such a case occurred, for example, in the second quarter of 1937 in a letter of the planning department of NKTP to the deputy director of Gump, Kanner, on March 3. RGAE, 4086.2.3450, 34–40.
[45] RGAE, 4086.2.3450, 11–14, 2–4.

rolled-steel products by factories was issued simultaneously with Gump's overall figures.[46] The rolled-steel figures were delayed by the fact that steel-supply organizations had to gather orders that had to be reported to the ministry. Gump, together with steel-supply organizations, determined which enterprises would actually produce this assortment. Before issuing "final" quarterly figures, the planning department of NKTP required a complete glavk plan with all indicators for the current quarter along with a complete accounting for the previous quarter. For example, NKTP's planning department informed Gump of its fourth-quarter breakdown of pig iron, steel, and rolled steels by factories and its assortment of rolled steels ten days into the quarter and ordered:

According to the authorized industrial program for the fourth quarter 1937, you must present to the planning department your detailed plan for the fourth quarter with actual performance for the third quarter in natural and value terms no later than the fifteenth of the month [five days later].[47]

The ministry approved the volume of production first as it constituted the main interest of the ministry. Other indicators, such as costs and productivity, were approved later, if at all.

Trusts and enterprises received their preliminary production limits for the upcoming quarter from Gump several days before the start of the quarter, except for the assortment of rolled steels.[48] The enterprise assortments of rolled steels for the third quarter 1937 were received more than two weeks into the quarter.[49] The limits for some products could be delayed even more. Gump sent to Kuznetsk Metallurgical Combine its limit on producing spikes for the second quarter of 1937 three weeks after the quarter began.[50] Thus, enterprises began every quarter with targets that glavks distributed prior to the approval of glavk limits by higher organizations. Gump gave its enterprises their limits for the fourth quarter on June 28, 1937; Gump itself received its own authorized plan broken down by enterprises from NKTP only on July 5, 1937. Gump gave its enterprises their production and assortment plans for rolled steels on July 17,

---

[46] Such a case occurred, for example, in the fourth quarter 1937 in a letter of the planning department of NKTP to the chief of Gump, Ryazanov, on October 10. RGAE, 4086.2.3450, 2–4.

[47] RGAE, 4086.2.3450, 4.

[48] For example, Gump sent the production limits for the second quarter 1937 to enterprises on March 16, fifteen days prior to the beginning of the quarter; and limits for the third quarter on June 27, three days before the beginning of the quarter. RGAE, 4086.2.3566, 3492.

[49] RGAE, 4086.2.3566, 3492.

[50] RGAE, 4086.2.3566, 101.

1937; Gump received its own targets from NKTP only on August 8, 1937.[51]

The complicated story told so far is only of the top-down flow of orders to glavks and then to enterprises. Annual-plan targets arrived with serious delays. Quarterly targets had shorter delays but the period of implementation was shorter and the delays varied by product type. Once targets were received by enterprises, the bottom-up flow of information began.

Within two weeks of receipt of production limits from the glavk, enterprises were supposed to return their proposed breakdowns of production between gross and net (*tovarnaia*) production for the quarter and by months and the production of each major production facility (e.g., steel mills).[52] The glavk would then inform the enterprise whether its proposals had been approved. For example, the deputy director of Gump informed Kosogorsky Metal Plant six weeks into the quarter that its plan for the third quarter of 1937 had been accepted without changes.[53] Other plan indicators, not associated with the volume of output, were submitted to enterprises still later, if they received them at all during the quarter. For example, Gump transmitted limits on costs of production, approved by Gump but not the ministry, for the second quarter of 1937 on May 3, 1937, more than one month into the quarter.[54]

Enterprises negotiated constantly with the glavk over output targets throughout the planning process. They pointed to technological difficulties, poor condition of equipment and plants, and possible interruptions and repairs to justify lower plan targets. Gump typically tried to delay capital repairs. The director of the Komintern Plant requested on February 15, 1937, that Gump consider the need for capital renovations in setting plan targets.[55] The director of the Odzhonikidze Factory, in a letter to Gump on April 3, 1937, used an accident at one blast furnace and the reduced productivity in another to request a 90-ton reduction in the pig-iron target.[56] Gump denied the Petrovsky Factory request on August 8, 1937, to reduce production from one furnace because of delayed repairs,

[51] RGAE, 4086.2.3492 and 3450, 23–6; RGAE, 4086.2.3492 and 3450, 11–14.
[52] See, for example, the letters from Gump to its enterprises from August 27, 1937, and from July 17, 1937 (RGAE, 4086.2.3492) requesting characteristics of aggregates, such as rolling mills and so on. RGAE, 4086.2.3566.
[53] RGAE, 4086.2.3566, 88.
[54] RGAE, 4086.2.3566, 21, 66, 71.
[55] RGAE, 4086.2.3566, 135–36.
[56] RGAE, 4086.2.3566, 8.

ordering it to put off the repair and to raise its production of sheet iron, stating, "in accordance with the protocol of the meeting organized by the deputy minister of heavy industry, your factory must in full guarantee the white tin plan for the third quarter."[57] Gump also denied the Kosogorsky Metallurgical Combinat's repeated requests for lower production plans to allow them to shut down a furnace and clean a gas line.[58] Gump ordered the Petrovsky Factory to delay a capital repair of its pipe shop. Gump did not deny all requests. On July 20, 1937, Gump requested of the ministry planning department "in relation to the change in deadlines for repairs and in the assortment for pig iron for the third quarter of 1937 to change the pig-iron plan for three (enumerated) factories without changing the overall pig-iron plan."[59] In two letters to Sulinsky Factory, Gump under-scored the firmness of the deadline, ordering the factory to "undertake all measures to complete reconstruction before 1937 September 1," and to report "every 10 days on the course of reconstruction work."[60] Gump's interest was so great that it asked the factory to request "whatever assis-tance is required from Gump."[61]

Although secondary plan targets were of lesser importance than output and assortment, they were nevertheless negotiated. An illustration of the negotiation (*torg*) of planned-cost targets was Svobodny Sokol Factory's debate with Gump concerning its cost-reduction target. Initially, on May 3, 1937, Gump set the figure at 18.6 percent.[62] The factory director ar-gued for a 14.5 percent figure in a letter of May 13, a figure that – by his calculation – corresponded with the approved wage fund and expendi-ture norms. The director asked Gump "to avoid and not allow galloping changes of limits," which in the second quarter were "raised for unknown reasons three times in designating limits for lowering costs."[63] As a con-sequence of the protest, the glavk proposed a compromise figure of 16 percent, basically splitting the difference.[64]

Supply organizations, such as Steel Supply (*Stal'sbyt*), Coke-Chemicals Supply (*Kokskhimsbyt*), and Refractory Materials Supply (*Ogneupors-byt*), gathered orders for production. Supply organizations dictated the

[57] RGAE, 4086.2.3567, 156–61.
[58] RGAE, 4086.2.3567, 89, 91, 94.
[59] RGAE, 4086.2.3450, 21.
[60] RGAE, 4086.2.3450, 110.
[61] Ibid.
[62] RGAE, 4086.2.3566, 37.
[63] RGAE, 4086.2.3566, 35.
[64] RGAE, 4086.2.3566, 22.

assortment of rolled steel based on orders, and they concluded general supply contracts with enterprises. At the beginning of each quarter, after the receipt of limits for production, enterprises concluded a plan with supply organizations that determined how much of their production would remain at the factory for further processing, such as pig iron into steel, how much would be distributed within the glavk, and how much would be delivered to others "on the side" (*na storonu*). In this fashion, supply organizations played a key role in metal balances. Preliminary supply agreements could be changed in the course of plan fulfillment either by a supply organization (in the case of changes in orders) or by the enterprise (in the case of a supply interruption). However, enterprises often did not produce in accordance with orders of supply organizations, a problem that glavks together with supply organizations tried to overcome. Supply organizations also received approval of annual plans for their activities.[65] As with production-enterprise plans, supply-organization plans passed through several stages, which strung them out over an entire year. For example, the annual supply plan for the coke-chemical supply department for 1937 was approved in May 1937, and even this was not the final stage of approval.[66]

The timetable of operational planning was similar in NKTP and NKLP, but light-industry enterprises (e.g., wool producers) received their quarterly plans on a more timely basis because, as nonpriority products, fewer high-level approvals were required. For example, both the Main Administration for Wool Products and its enterprises received their approved plans prior to the start of the quarter.[67]

In sum, the annual and quarterly operational plans that were supposed to run the Soviet planned economy were received after the plan had started, and most work was based on projections of what the final figures would be. Moreover, the *promfinplan*, which the enterprise was supposed to fulfill as a matter of law, was really only an output and an assortment plan. Although the *promfinplan* included many other financial and technical indicators, nonproduction plans were simply reconstructed *ex post* to serve as a benchmark for future plans. The enterprise's job was to meet its production and assortment targets, none of which were

[65] Prior to 1936, the mentioned supply organizations were independent. In 1936, they became departments of Gump.

[66] RGAE, 4086.2.3429, 1–2.

[67] Andrei Markevich and Paul Gregory, "Was the Soviet Economy a Planned Economy? Answer of the Soviet Archives of the 1930s," Zvenigorod International Conference, Zvenigorod, Russia, June 2001.

final at the moment production took place. Thus, actual production was carried out on the basis of preliminary agreements that were not binding on superior organizations. Preliminary plans drove the economy.

Changes and Interventions. The delay of approved plans was not the ministry's, glavk's, or enterprise's major problem. Earlier chapters showed the propensities of superior organizations to intervene, to make changes in plans, to gain "resource mobility." In fact, the political leadership viewed its ability to intervene at will a great strength of the system. Stalin wrote:

It is possible to say that the Central Committee is destroying the principle of planning and reduces the authority of the five year plan when its changes the five year plan. But only impossible bureaucrats can speak in this manner. For us, for Bolsheviks, the five year plan is not something that is a law that is forever given. For us the five year plan, *like any plan*, is only a plan approved *as a first approximation* [author's italics] which must be made more precise, to change and improve on the basis of experience, on the basis of executing the plan. No five year plan can consider all the possibilities, which are hidden in the foundation of our movement and which are uncovered only in the process of work, in the process of carrying out the plan in factories, plants, and collective farms, in the regions, and so forth. Only bureaucrats can think that planning work ends with the creation of the plan. *The creation of the plan is only the beginning* [author's italics]. The real direction of the plan develops only after the putting together of the plan.[68]

Earlier chapters also described how the industrial ministries protected themselves from changes from the center: they delayed submitting information, they argued for last-minute submission of plans, and they prepared their own (dual) plans that were independent of the state plan. The ministries fought with Gosplan for more materials, for more capital – battles that Gosplan had to wage without reliable information.

The schedule of annual and quarterly planning required that each player submit information on a timely basis. Yet, both the superior and the subordinate stood to benefit by delaying information. Hence, information transmitted from both above and below was chronically delayed. In one collegium meeting (April 6, 1933), NKLP's planning department complained about the lack of information from below as follows:

We must say that the control figures [for the cotton industry] that we are reporting are, to our great regret, exclusively the work of the planning department itself.

---

[68] I. V. Stalin, *Voprosy Leninizma*, 10th ed. (Moscow, 1937), 413.

Despite the many demands from the planning department and from the ministry, the cotton industry has still not given any indicators of the plan, with the exception of capital investment, which it returned exactly in the same form as was received from the planning sector. We do not have material ready on costs of production not because of our fault but because several glavks to this day have not given us the materials.[69]

Not surprisingly, the planning department used the same pressuring tactics that Gosplan applied to the ministry. In a collegium meeting of NKLP, the planning department complained of extreme pressure from Gosplan to deliver input requests, which were being delayed by glavks. The minister (Liubimov) issued the following threat:

If the glavks by tomorrow are not able to provide all elements of the plan, then we will do it for the glavks themselves. We'll do it in a very simple manner: We will give those glavks that can prove their orders, and we'll give to those who can't what is left over from those submitting their orders. I want to receive all elements of the plan by one o'clock.[70]

Gump failed to issue the first limits for the quarterly plan of rolled steel to one of its trusts in the fourth quarter of 1937, while at the same time bitterly complaining that the trust had delayed submissions of its own materials.[71] Such delaying stratagems created a vicious cycle. The glavk could not plan because the enterprise gave it no information; the enterprise could not supply information because it had no plan! Enterprises drew out the submission of their own plan materials; the later the plan, the more likely it was to correspond to the final version. Eastern Steel (*Vostokstal*), for example, submitted to Gump its plan for gross and net production only in the beginning of the second month of the second quarter 1937.[72] Such delays from below occasioned rebukes from Gump, which ordered its enterprises to submit their material on time.[73] Gump demanded that Eastern Steel representatives come immediately to Moscow to agree on the quarterly assortment of rolled steels.[74] The glavks did not hurry to provide enterprises with plan tasks, which called forth protests. The trust, Pipe-steel (*Trubostal*), complained in a letter of January 10, 1937, to Gump that "monthly operational production targets were received from you

[69] RGAE, 7604.1.152.16, 118.
[70] RGAE, 7604.1.815, 9–11.
[71] RGAE, 4086.2.3455, 3.
[72] RGAE, 4086.2.3455, 22.
[73] For example, see letters and telegrams from Gump to its enterprises and trusts. (RGAE, 4086.2.3567).
[74] RGAE, 4086.2.3561, 145–8.

not earlier than the last two to three days of the month and our factories, receiving their limits on the last day, are not able to distribute them among their shops on time." The letter demanded that Gump submit production figures by the 23rd–24th of the preceding month;[75] otherwise, the trust and the production units would have to work them out independently.[76]

Enterprises had no choice but to work on the basis of preliminary limits received from the glavk, but final quarterly plans were required for comparisons of reporting for the quarter. Although enterprises worked largely without final plans, they nevertheless had to submit reports on plan fulfillment at the end of each planning period. These final reports had to include not only the production and assortment figures, which comprised the centerpiece of the system, but also other lower-priority figures such as costs and profits. Delays were such that enterprises had to rely on their own calculations, which they submitted to the glavk for final approval. The Dzherzhinsky Steel Plant still lacked approval of its 1937 third quarter financial results, required for its final quarterly report, and it had to demand of Gump (in a letter dated August 29) that it give it its quarterly plan in final confirmed form.[77] If we consider the confirmed plan as "the plan," this large enterprise had already operated two of the three months of the quarter without a plan.

Ministry, glavk, and enterprise plans could be changed at any time. Although NKLP's annual plan was usually approved on time prior to the beginning of the plan year, approval meant little. For example, changes in NKLP's 1936 plan continued through December.[78] Enterprise plans could be changed by virtually any superior organization – SNK, Gosplan, the ministry, or the glavk. The majority of changes were made according to the normal order of correcting and finalizing plans. As described, the planning process proceeded through a number of phases from preliminary to final, and at each stage superiors could change plan tasks. Interventions were considered a perfectly normal part of the process. The glavk had little choice but to implement directives of the ministry and of the government concerning changes in quarterly plans of enterprises. For example, Gump was forced to change the 1937 second-quarter plan for Krasnoe Sormovo Factory in the first month of the quarter "in connection

[75] RGAE, 4086.2.3561, 161.
[76] Such a situation occurred with the planning of the assortment of rolling stead for the trust Vostokstal for the fourth quarter 1937 (RGAE, 4086.2.3455, 3–11).
[77] RGAE, 4086.2.3567, 2.
[78] Markevich and Gregory, "Was the Soviet Economy a Planned Economy?"

with the directive of the deputy minister of heavy industry to raise production designated for the Main Administration for Transport Machinery
(*Glavtransmash*)."[79] Although almost all interventions called for higher
targets, the ministry occasionally would lower quarterly plans, such as
NKTP's lowering of Gump's 1937 second-quarter coke-ammonia target
by 500 tons.[80] Some changes were tied to administrative reorganizations
as factories were transferred from one glavk to another.[81] Glavk reac-
tions to changes in quarterly plans were pained and the response slow.
The glavk was more inclined to challenge decisions of the ministry than of
SNK. According to the initial 1937 fourth-quarter plan, Gump was supposed to produce 101,000 tons of the 160,000-ton plan of rolled steel. On
October 10, 1937, the ministry decided on its own to raise Gump by 500
tons to compensate for a decrease in the production plans of another
glavk (*Glavspetsstal*) – a case noted in the previous chapter. In its immediate protest (November 19, 1937), Gump reminded the ministry that it
was responsible for rolled-steel targets and that any changes should have
gone through Gump.[82] On June 9, 1937 (near the end of the quarter),
Gump raised KMK Factory's target for ammonia sulfate from 6,080 to
6,290 tons.[83] In May 1937, Gump raised the Dzherzhinsky Factory's plan
for marketed output from 6.5 to 8.4 percent.[84]

Enterprises registered protests with their glavk against frequent plan
changes. On July 23, 1937, the frustrated director of the Makeevsky Metallurgical Factory protested to Gump against "changes in the assortment
of rolled steel not at all associated with the metals balance" and requested
"to leave the assortment of rails in correspondence with the metals balances and stop the undue pressure on the factory."[85]

Producers, from the ministry to the enterprise, occupied a weak position when resisting plan increases because the limits that were being increased were preliminary. The production figure that was being changed
constituted an *informal agreement* with superiors. Even preliminary

---

[79] RGAE, 4086.2.3566, 2.
[80] RGAE, 4086.2.3450, 32.
[81] Administrative changes were agreed to at the level of the government or the ministry
and had to be carried out by the glavks. The planning department of NKTP on May 31,
1937, informed Gump and Glavmetiz that their quarterly and annual plans had to be
amended because of the transfer of the Lsvensky Factory from Glavmetiz to Gump in
accordance with a decree of the government dated May 26, 1937.
[82] RGAE, 4086.2.3450, 1.
[83] RGAE, 4086.2.3566, 100.
[84] RGAE, 4086.2.3566, 50.
[85] RGAE, 4086.2.3567, 5–7.

agreements between the ministry and Gosplan provided little protection from changes. The Minister of Light Industry, Liubimov, tried to head off changes in a meeting of the ministry on November 12, 1936, declaring that the ministry should "insist on its position and disprove the projections of Gosplan, which do not take into consideration the lack of raw materials at our factories and trusts because this result will predetermine the nonfulfillment of our production program."[86] Despite NKLP's insistence on its earlier targets, Gosplan imposed plan increases in December.

Enterprises reacted most sharply and rapidly to large and repeated increases in plan targets. The director of Novomoskosvsky Tin Factory requested that Gump reexamine its plan targets after two successive increases in its 1937 third-quarter plan (first to 3,000 tons and then to 3,800 tons). The director argued that the higher targets could not be fulfilled and violated "earlier agreements" with the planning department of Gump.[87]

Concluding Comments: Was This a Planned Economy?

The planning process was chaotic and opaque. If the description of operational planning is difficult for outsiders to comprehend, it must have been equally so for its participants. Despite the muddle of the planning process, two major points stand out: The vaunted *promfinplans* of enterprises, the end product of planning, were constructed only retrospectively. The multitudes of targets in the *promfinplan* – outputs, assortments, quality, costs, productivity, new technologies, and so forth – had little meaning. In the 1930s, the enterprise was planned, in reality, according to two indicators – output and the assortment of output. These were the only two indicators that planners even pretended to set *ex ante* and thus to guide enterprise operations. The second point is that the system itself shied away from final plans. All plans, down to the final moments of the quarter or the year, were labeled as drafts or preliminary. A search of the records of both NKTP and NKLP uncovered only one ministry plan signed by the minister and with the complete set of planned indicators – the NKLP plan for 1939.[88] In fact, the official keeper of the ministry plan was its planning department, which prepared preliminary plans and kept track of planned changes. The fact that there were no final plans gave free rein to interventions, and it also created enormous uncertainties for the enterprise

---

[86] RGAE, 7604, 1, 815, 9–11.
[87] RGAE, 4086.2.3567, 135.
[88] Markevich and Gregory, "Was the Soviet Economy a Planned Economy?"

and the glavk, which operated on the basis of tenuous preliminary agreements that provided no protection against arbitrary plan changes. There was no firm anchor for operations.

Our confusing description of operational planning sheds light on conflicting versions of Soviet planning. One version claims that the Soviet economy was not planned at all and cites two types of evidence: first, enterprise plans were changed too frequently and, second, plans were not realized.[89] The other version cites evidence that although enterprise plans were not fixed, ministry plans were. Basically, the changes of enterprise plans were simply a reshuffling among enterprises of a fixed ministry plan.[90] Our evidence looks directly at the ministry and glavk plans and shows that plans at that level were subject to intense negotiation and that plans approved at the highest level (SNK) were more firm than others. However, the Politburo and SNK regarded their ability to change plans as a basic strength of the system. Ministry plans were by no means immune to arbitrary interventions. Moreover, the plan was really the output plan and its assortment; there were no true operational *promfinplans* that covered items other than output. The fact that plans ranging from five-year plans to quarterly plans came closer to being fulfilled in the late thirties than in the early thirties is explained not by better planning, but by "planning from the achieved level"; namely, that next year's plan was simply this year's plan plus a growth adjustment. Our description of planning also supports the Powell model of resource management (see Chapter 1), in which higher authorities – the highest being SNK, the Politburo, and Stalin – served as the "court of appeals." Plans morphed into something that bore little resemblance to the original plan as higher-ups responded both collectively and individually to thousands of appeals. Although early Soviet planners anticipated that some corrections would be needed for planning errors,[91] in reality, there were avalanches of corrections.

The political elite spent much of its time responding to thousands of requests and petitions for plan alterations. Some examples from the thousands of cases in the archives: on September 12, 1933, Molotov wrote the chairman of Gosplan: "The Crimeans were in my office. They wanted me

[89] Keren, "The Ministry," 327–42.
[90] David Granick, "The Ministry as the Maximizing Unit," 255–73; Alice Gorlin and D. P. Doane, "Plan Fulfillment and Growth in Soviet Ministries," *Journal of Comparative Economics* 4, no. 3 (1983), 415–31. Also see J. Wilhelm, "Does the Soviet Union Have a Planned Economy?," *Soviet Studies* 21 (April 1979), 268–73.
[91] S. G. Strumilin, *Na Planovom Fronte 1920–1930 gg* (Moscow: Gospolizdat, 1958), 133–65.

to reduce the harvesting targets for the second region. . . . We must check and decide."[92] Stalin's correspondence speaks of hundreds of visits by officials to his Sochi dacha asking for plan corrections and favors. Stalin approved the requests of two Caucas party leaders for loans of grain on September 6, 1935, after gaining their support for the firing of an official who had fallen out of favor. [93] The demands for more resources of some industrial ministers (e.g., the persistent Ordzhonikidze) were so fierce that Stalin openly wondered whether Gosplan could resist the relentless pressure.[94] As the Politburo responded to all these petitions and requests, plans were changed, adjustments were made here and there, sometimes disrupting the entire plan. Although the first quarter 1933 vehicle-distribution plan had already been approved, the Politburo tripled the Kazak Party Committee's allocation of vehicles (to collect emergency grain supplies)[95] and ordered a radical change in car distribution, allocating 90 percent to "organs of control over agricultural producers."[96] These two Politburo interventions alone rendered the original plan inoperable.

We posed four models of operational planning at the beginning of this chapter – scientific planning, stationary-bandit planning, planning to maximize political power, and planning by vested interests. We can rule out scientific planning as infeasible, for the reasons cited long ago by Hayek and Mises. Resources were being allocated, at best, by feel and intuition and planning experts had little or no idea about the relationships between inputs and outputs. This leaves three potential planning models. Although the industrial ministers and regional authorities did attempt to determine their own plans, they did not dictate plans. Their influence was felt more in the resource-management phase, when they – as the ad hoc controllers of their own production – decided to whom to deliver. This book is full of instances where the producing ministry or glavk decides on the distribution of its output, irrespective of state directives. Penalties for disobedience were not severe, and the producer could also argue that it

[92] Khlevnyuk et al., *Stalinskoe Politburo*, 134.
[93] Khlevnyuk et al., *Stalin i Kaganovich. Perepiski*, 224, 556–7.
[94] Khlevnyuk et al., *Stalinskoe Politburo*, 134.
[95] This statement is from GARF, 5446.14a.628, 143–4; Russian Center for the Preservation and Study of Documents of Contemporary History (*Rosiiskii Tsentr Khraneniia i Izucheniia Dokumentov Noveiishei Istorii*), whose title was recently changed to Russian State Archive for Social and Political History, or RGASPI. Hereafter, we refer to documents from this archive as RGASPI, referred to as RtsKhINDI. This document is from RGASPI, 17.3.914, 10–11.
[96] RGASPI, 17.3.915, 8.

was acting in the interests of production. It does appear from the actions of ministers that the higher the level of plan approval, the more seriously the plan target was taken. Politburo or SNK approval meant more than ministerial approval.

We cannot conclusively answer whether resource management was conducted for economic or political gain. The operational planning system, however, could not have been constructed better for the exercise of political influence. There were no final plans. Everything was tentative. Everything was subject to arbitrary change by someone higher up in the chain of command. Even if every political intervention were made with the intention of economic efficiency, the overall result would have produced the opposite effect given the impossibility of coordination. What we have documented is that a multitude of petitioners approached SNK, the Politburo, Stalin, the minister, or the glavk director and that some requests were granted and others denied, all presumably in the public interest. We cannot guess what went on behind the scenes, but we do know that savvy politicians, such as Stalin, would weigh the political implications of rejecting an influential regional or industrial leader. We have one empirical study of the allocation of vehicles by the Politburo, which strongly concludes that political factors determined the allocation of one of society's scarcest resources and that economic factors were ignored.[97] One of the most important conclusions that can be drawn from this massive evidence is that what constituted the "economic good" was almost impossible to see. The Politburo could not distinguish trivia from substantive matters. There was no way to achieve *ex ante* material balances. Perhaps the best evidence of all for the power-maximizing model is the noneconomic actions of the Soviet dictator – the Great Purges, the purge of specialists, and so on.

---

[97] Lazarev and Gregory, "Commissars and Cars."

9

Ruble Control: Money, Prices, and Budgets

Money, prices, and finance were not supposed to matter in the administrative-command economy. What counted were the administrative decisions that allocated bricks, machines, wheat, garments, manufactured consumer goods, and labor. This chapter examines a number of issues concerning financial transactions and their components – money, credit, prices, and the state budget. Were money and credit passive instruments of physical planning or "did money matter?" Were money, credit, and prices simply used to track physical transactions and, if so, how well? Or were physical resources allocated based on bidding processes based on financial clout? Given that investment was planned in rubles (see Chapter 4) financed from the state budget, to what extent did the state budget itself determine the physical volume of investment?

This chapter explains why the Soviet financial system did not operate according to this original intent. As financial arrangements evolved, Soviet leaders experienced two money shocks. First, money continued to matter. Enterprise managers sought to accumulate money, especially cash through any means possible, be it unauthorized price increases or nefarious under-the-table transactions. Second, the supply of money and credit could not be kept in line with the supply of real goods, even with a single financial accounting center. Enterprises issued each other illegal credits and used money surrogates when cash was particularly short. The central bank, as the lender of last resort in an economy of soft budgets, was forced to issue credits against its will.

The story of the Soviet financial system is the story of the long-serving minister of finance, G. F. Grin'ko, who served from 1930 to 1936. Grin'ko was born in the Ukraine in 1890, the son of a government official. He attended Moscow University but was expelled in 1913 for revolutionary activity as a member of the Socialist Revolutionary Party and was drafted into the army. He joined the Bolshevik Party relatively late (in 1919). After holding a number of positions in the Ukraine, he came to Moscow in 1926 as a deputy chairman of Gosplan and was named Minister of Finance in 1930. Grin'ko never held a high party post, rising only to membership status in the Central Committee. He was fired from his post as finance minister in 1937 and was executed in 1938. Grin'ko had no practical experience in banking and continued to rely on financial specialists who had been trained in the prerevolutionary period.[1]

Despite his relatively low political status, Grin'ko played a significant role in high-level decision making that belies the proposition that money was passive. In the Stalin–Kaganovich correspondence, Grin'ko is accorded great respect as someone "who knows the numbers" and whose advice is to be taken seriously. For example, when Grin'ko proposed a bitter reduction of investment spending in July 1932, Stalin replied: "I read Grin'ko's memo. He engaged in some exaggerations and in administrative one-sidedness and so forth. But in general Grin'ko and his associates are correct and it is necessary to support them."[2] Although Grin'ko was often the bearer of bad news, his views were respected as a technical expert and, in this fashion, he had a substantial impact on policy.

Ruble Control

The financial expression of physical transactions – ruble expenditures or revenues, credit, cash, and prices – was supposed to be important only in that they provided authorities with a convenient summary of physical transactions. "Ruble control" was the Soviet term describing the tracking of physical transactions with financial transactions. If X is ordered to deliver to Y 100 units of steel at a price of 5 rubles, then Y must pay X 500 rubles as a financial expression of the physical transaction. X's

---

[1] *Bolshaia Sovetsaia Entsiklopedia*, vol. 7 (Moscow: Sovetskaia Entsiklopedia, 1975), 337; *Who Was Who in the USSR* (Metuchen, N.J.: Scarecrow Press, 1972), 217. One such prominent expert was V. K. Sitnin, who graduated from the Moscow Institute of Economics and worked as a consultant for Gosbank from 1931 to 1941, was a staff member of the Ministry of Finance, and served in the army from 1941 to 1950. He worked in the Ministry of Finance 1950–1960, was deputy minister and 1st deputy minister of finance from 1960 to 1965, and was chairman of State Committee on Pricing, USSR Council of Minister from 1970 to 1974.

[2] Khlevnyuk et al., *Stalin i Kaganovich. Perepiski*, 245.

accounts should show the receipt of 500 rubles and Y's account should show the expenditure of 500 rubles. The 100 units of steel are transferred not because of the 500 rubles, but because of the administrative order. If Y does not have 500 rubles, it will receive it from some other source, such as the ministry or the state budget. Thus, Y has a soft-budget constraint,[3] unlike a market-economy enterprise, which could buy the steel only if it had the 500 rubles.

For ruble control to work, someone must keep track of all transactions, comparing payments and receipts with physical directives. As in any other economy, cash transactions would be harder to track than bank transactions; therefore, all transactions among enterprises should be in the form of bank transfers. A single monopoly bank should serve as a huge accounting center to make sure that "money follows the plan." Financial authorities should ensure that enterprises have the necessary cash or credit to fulfill the plan and expend them appropriately.

Figure 9.1 shows ruble control as the monitoring of vertical transactions (see Chapter 6). It shows two ministries issuing vertical physical production orders, each to two of their subordinated enterprises. The double lines show the ministry's output orders; the bold lines show the officially ordered deliveries; and the regular lines shows official payments to be made in terms of official bank transactions, in "bank money." The dotted lines show unofficial horizontal transactions. The dotted bold lines show the physical flows of unofficial deliveries; the regular dotted lines show the resulting financial flows. Payment options for horizontal transactions are more varied than the official transactions that must be conducted in bank money. Unofficial deliveries can be paid in cash, in barter, and in unofficial credits from the selling enterprise to the buying enterprise. Note that all dotted-line transactions escape the official scrutiny of ruble control. Figure 9.1 shows that financial authorities must wage the same battle against cash, barter transactions, and unofficial credits as planning authorities do in their struggles against unplanned physical transactions (by strictly limiting enterprise cash holdings) and against granting unofficial interenterprise credits.

At first glance, this socialist theory of "passive" money, credit, and prices appears workable. Money, unlike steel, garments, and machinery, is homogeneous. A monopoly bank could keep better track of financial transactions than a Gosplan that must track thousands of physical

---

[3] Janos Kornai, *Economics of Shortage* (Amsterdam, New York, Oxford: North-Holland Publishing Company, 1980).

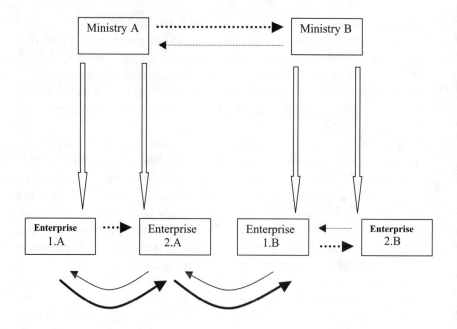

Explanation: <u>Physical Flows</u>

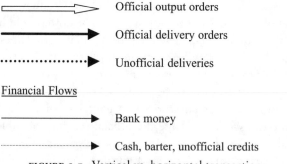

                                    Official output orders

                                    Official delivery orders

                                    Unofficial deliveries

<u>Financial Flows</u>

                                    Bank money

                                    Cash, barter, unofficial credits

FIGURE 9.1. Vertical vs. horizontal transactions.

goods. Neither battle was waged successfully insofar as enterprises came up with innovative ways to defeat ruble control. One device should be clear from earlier chapters: financial flows from one enterprise to another reflect the financial side of microtransactions. Yet, physical planning and directives took place above the level of transactions in terms of aggregated quantities. This fact tells us that ruble control could not be used to check the conformity of physical flows to plans, because there were no plans that went into that much detail. To check for correspondence with physical plans, the financial transactions would have to be aggregated themselves. Therefore, at best, ruble control would consist of checking aggregated physical targets, like tons of aggregated metals, with value figures, such as millions of rubles of aggregated metals sales. Financial planning could check the fulfillment of physical plans only at the same level of aggregation.

The passive nature of money – the notion that the physical plan dictates financial transactions rather than money and credit determining physical transactions – lies at the heart of a workable planning system. If enterprises were able to bid for resources outside the chain of planned transactions, then which enterprise got what would be determined by their financial bargaining power: by how much cash they had, what goods they had to barter, and whether they could attract unofficial credits. Any extra liquidity outside the official sphere of liquidity represented a source of unofficial transactions. The battle against unofficial transactions would, therefore, be fought on the financial side as a battle against extra cash holdings and against unofficial credits. Indeed, the history of Soviet financial planning is a struggle against unauthorized cash holdings and against unofficial credits.

The Socialist Theory of Banking

Market economies have a two-tiered banking system to control the money supply and issue credit. A central bank occupies the upper tier and determines the quantity of money. Banks that accept deposits and make loans, according to the central bank's general rules of behavior, occupy the second tier. Most credit is distributed by commercial banks, but some are granted outside of the banking system, such as commercial credits offered by businesses. From the beginning, the founders of the Soviet financial system assumed that money and credit would work differently in an administrative-command economy.[4] There could be only one bank;

---

[4] V. K. Sitnin, *Vospominaniia Finansista* (Moscow: Luch, 1993); V. K. Sitnin, *Kontrol Rublem v Sotsialisticheskom Obshchestve* (Moscow: Gosfinizdat, 1956); I. N. Tsipkin, *Sovetskiy Kredit*, part 1 (Moscow: n.p., 1933); V. M. Batyrev and V. K. Sitnin, *Planovaia Kreditnaia Sistema SSSR* (Moscow: Ogiz, 1945); M. N. Bogolepov, *Sovetskaia Finasovaia Sistema* (Moscow: Gosfinizdat, 1947); M. N. Bogolepov, *Finansovy Plan piatiletia* (Moscow: n.p., 1929); and M. S. Atlas, *Razvitie Gosudarsvennogo Banka SSSR* (Moscow: Gosfinizdat, 1958). This literature is surveyed in R. W. Davies, "A Short-Term Credit in the USSR: Some Post-War Problems," *Soviet Studies* 5, no. 1 (1953/54). For additional references, see R. W. Davies, *The Development of the Soviet Budgetary System* (Cambridge: Cambridge University Press, 1958); F. Holzman, "Financing Soviet Economic Development," in *Capital Formation and*

credits granted by others would be illegal. Production and distribution would be directed by administrative orders. Such socialist financial arrangements have broad implications for prices and the demand for money: If the monopoly bank is always ready to supply enterprises credit for planned transactions, there should be no incentive to raise prices. If the state sets the price of steel at 5 rubles, there would be no particular advantage to X to sell at 8 rubles. The extra revenues in X's bank account could be used only for planned activities anyway. The extra earnings could not be translated into discretionary unplanned purchases.

Specialists who had worked in finance before the revolution were openly skeptical that this socialist financial system could work. They could not believe that "money does not matter" at all. If the quantities of money and credit exceed the supply of goods at established prices, prices must rise. If state spending exceeds revenues, money must be issued. If enterprises do not pay each other on time, credit is issued whether the central bank wishes it or not. Enterprises will raise their prices when they have buyers competing for their product, and money will continue to be demanded for its own sake.

A simple set of figures shows that the primary intent of the Soviet financial system was not realized. Under the principle that finance serves as a passive handmaiden of physical planning – "money follows the plan" – money and real output should have grown at the same rate. Between 1932 and 1936, real gross domestic product (GDP) expanded by 50 percent at most; the supply of consumer goods scarcely increased, if at all; but the money supply at least doubled and maybe *tripled*. Money was not following the plan; other factors were determining the supply of money and credit.

Money Matters

The first surprise for Soviet financial authorities was that money matters, contrary to the stereotype that bricks, steel, and tractors, not money, are what count. The Soviet financial system used two types of money – cash and bank money. Cash was used to pay workers and to buy consumer goods. Enterprises maintained two current accounts with Gosbank: one

Economic Growth, ed. Moses Abramovitz (Princeton, N.J.: Princeton University Press, 1955); Holzman, "Soviet Inflationary Pressures, 1928–1957, Causes and Cures," *Quarterly Journal of Economics* 74, no. 2 (1960), 167–88; and A. Arnold, *Banks, Credit, and Money in Soviet Russia* (New York: Columbia University Press, 1937).

from which they could draw cash to pay workers and "bank money" accounts, which they used to pay for materials, taxes, and other transactions. Both accounts were to be strictly controlled and segregated by the branch bank of Gosbank. Bank money supposedly could not be converted into cash. In theory, funds could be expended only with bank permission and only for designated (*tselevye*) tasks. If enterprises did not have sufficient funds for planned tasks, they received subsidies arranged either by the ministry or through the state budget.

An evening meeting of NKTP in November 1935 shows that financial self-sufficiency (called then and now "full economic accounting") was not a priority. Comrade Tal' reported on a survey asking ministry officials if they could get by without subsidies. Tal' reports,

The first to receive this survey, Comrade Birman, passed it to his neighbor not filling it out [laughter in the hall]. It then went to Comrade Makarov. I don't know whether he had agreed with Birman beforehand, but he did the same – he passed it on without filling it out ... When the survey got to Comrade Puchkov, he wrote that he could manage in two half years. Comrade Zolotorev answered simply: '1936.' Comrade Fishman responded: 'The enterprises of [my] glavk can make do with considerably less subsidies than planned and will be able to get by without subsidies from the first quarter of 1936. The survey is small but as you see it teaches an interesting lesson. *Ordzhonikidze*: It is a shame you did not continue it. *Tal*: We will continue it. *Ordzhonikidze*: Now they won't fill it out, they fear we will use it against them and publish the results.[5]

These considerations suggest that producers should have had little interest in prices. Higher prices bring in more bank money, which could not be converted into cash for workers or for purchases of consumer goods. The seller, therefore, should be content with the official price set by a number of organizations ranging from the Politburo (Stalin set prices of wholesale agricultural goods in some cases), the ministry of trade, and ministry and glavk pricing departments. It was these state prices that were supposed to be used in general and local contracts negotiated during the "contract campaigns" (see Chapter 7), which set prices, delivery dates, assortment, and quality. Official prices were supposed to be published in price handbooks, but they were often missing, or they had never been set. The massive Main Administration for Metals (Gump) employed only three persons in its pricing department (see Table 6.3). Hence, producers had considerable leeway in setting prices, particularly in the seller's market of the 1930s. Steel, for example, was distributed by

[5] RGAE, 7297.38.177, 181.

NKTP's Stal'sbyt (Steel Supply), which negotiated general contracts and attached consumers to specific metals plants for local contracts. Steel-Supply had a virtual monopoly over metals distributions,[6] as did other ministry supply departments, such as Chemical Supply or Wool Supply.

That the lack of interest in money would keep even monopolists from exercising their market power is not supported by the facts. A note from a chemical manufacturer–buyer of specialized machinery (presented with an invoice 50 percent above the contract price) to its bank urging payment clearly summarizes the buyer's dilemma: "If we don't pay, the seller will tell us: 'If you don't want to pay, we'll keep that in mind when we consider your next order.'"[7] The State Arbitration Commission, which handled complaints of illegal price increases, reprimanded Moscow-Stamp in its 1935 report for raising prices despite receiving price increases in 1934 and Artel'-Kim for raising its prices by 15 to 45 percent. Both cases were turned over to Central Union and the price inspectorate of the Ministry of Trade.[8] The Arbitration Commission deemed Union Wool's unauthorized price increase of sufficient importance to notify the deputy prime minister (April 15, 1935): "The Chief Arbitrator of Leningrad province has informed me that Union Wool gave the order to increase prices on average by 60 percent contrary to SNK Decree No. 45 of April 10, 1935, no. 45 and without approval of the Ministry of Light Industry."[9] Even the Ministry of Defense faced illegal price increases, although military procurements were supposed to be in fixed prices. Insofar as defense worked on the basis of budgets in rubles, an increase in the price of, say, tanks meant fewer tanks. Military buyers complained of cost-plus pricing based on "how much it costs – independently of whether the resulting cost is the result of correct work or poor management."[10] As late as 1937, the Ministry of Defense lacked, the authority to audit enterprise production costs.

Why did sellers demand unauthorized price increases when their losses were subsidized and payments were in strictly controlled bank money that supposedly could not be converted into cash? The archives show that, virtually throughout the Soviet period, producers were able to siphon bank money into cash. In fact, siphoning was so widespread that it represented

---

[6] GARF, 8424. 1.1, 8.
[7] Stenographic report from a meeting of the Construction Bank, May 1933, in RGAE, 1880.1.28, 92.
[8] "First Results of Contract Completions in 1935," *Biulletin Gosarbitrazha No. 4*, 8–9.
[9] GARF, 5446.16.4308, 19.
[10] Simonov, *Voenno-Promyshlenny*, 93.

an unanticipated source of inflationary pressures.[11] Siphoning is also seen in the fact that increases in bank money and credit led to increases in cash money, as will be shown later in this chapter.[12] What benefits could enterprise managers expect from this extra money? Managers lacked property rights (they owned no shares or stock options), and their perks (company car or company apartment) were tied to their official positions. Their only recourse was to siphon money from the enterprise's accounts for their own or the enterprise's use.[13] Figure 9.1 stresses that cash represented one way to pay for horizontal transactions.

In theory, producers who wished to maximize their informal rents through "hidden" horizontal transactions (see Chapter 3) should favor *lower* official prices. The greater the gap between the price that eager customers are willing to pay and the official price, the higher the producer's rent from bribes.[14] Thus, in demanding higher prices, producers would pass up the chance for bribes and other under-the-table payments. Yet, the archives provide absolutely no evidence of producers lobbying for lower prices: "Even a single example of a producer seeking lower official prices has yet to be found."[15]

The archives leave little doubt as to the value of cash. Party members took great risks to accumulate it. The Party Control Commission files, covering more than three thousand cases of crimes ranging from misdemeanors to embezzlement,[16] show regional party officials extorting cash from local enterprises,[17] party officials ordering local banks to transfer large sums into their personal accounts, and even the selling of party memberships. In one of the most spectacular cases of the 1930s, the managers of Ukraine's social insurance fund embezzled an astronomical 5 million rubles between 1932 and 1935 using shady accounting practices, even selling vacations in the fund's resort facilities.[18] Officials of a fur trust established a national bribery scheme that led to the execution of several

[11] M. Harrison and B. Y Kim, "Plan, Siphoning, and Corruption in the Soviet Command Economy," *Warwick Economic Research Papers*, no. 606, 2001, 4.

[12] A. Tikhonov and P. Gregory, "Central Planning and Unintended Consequences: Creating the Soviet Financial System, 1930–1939," *Journal of Economic History 60*, no. 4. (2000).

[13] Boettke and Anderson, "Soviet Venality," 37–53.

[14] Andrei Shleifer and Robert Vishny, "Pervasive Shortages Under Socialism," *Rand Journal of Economics 23*, no. 2 (Summer 1993): 237–46.

[15] Mark Harrison and B. Y. Kim, "Plan, Siphoning," 4.

[16] Belova, "Economic Crime and Punishment," 131–58.

[17] KPK, 6.1.56, 64–5. Party Control Commission (Kommissia Partiinogo Kontrolia), hereafter referred to as KPK.

[18] KPK, 6.1.38, 20–30; 6.1.68, 80.

of its officials. A remarkable quarter million party members were expelled between 1939 and 1952 for embezzlement.[19]

Loss of Control of Money and Credit

The second money surprise was the inability to control the supply of money and credit, a problem already apparent during the NEP (1921–28). The NEP economy was supposed to be regulated by a "dictatorship of finance," whereby the finance ministry set credit limits supposedly equal to the value of production at established prices. The NEP's distinguishing feature was the merging of enterprises into integrated trusts, whose products were sold by syndicates, which became "centers of credits and accounts, which took on planning, supply, distribution, and even construction."[20] During the NEP, state credit limits were circumvented by unofficial credits in the form of promissory notes (*veksel'*), which syndicates arranged. The holders of these promissory notes exchanged them for money (at a discount) at the state bank (Gosbank) or at other banks. Syndicates even assumed responsibility for the IOUs of their less-than-creditworthy enterprises and bailed out insolvent enterprises.[21] Currency and short-term credit both increased by nearly identical factors of 1.6 to 1.7 between late 1925 and late 1928 alone, despite efforts by financial authorities to apply the brakes. As syndicates, trusts, and enterprises issued one another credits, Gosbank was forced to monetize them, and thereby expand the money supply willy-nilly; if it refused, other banks would step in. Without the threat of insolvency, credit expansion was automatically converted into monetary growth. The combination of soft budget constraints, commercial credits, and commercial banks competing for deposits caused the state bank to lose control of the money supply already during the NEP.[22]

Just as Stalin replaced a private agriculture he could not control with collectivized agriculture, the NEP experience convinced financial

---

[19] KPK, 6.6.1; 6.6.3.

[20] I. N. Tsipkin, *Sovetskiy Kredit*, 56.

[21] We know little about the working relationships among syndicates and their member enterprises during the NEP period (see E. V. Bogomolova, *Upravlenie Sovetskoi Ekonomiki v 20-e gg: Opyt Regulirovaniia i Samoorganizatsii* [Moscow: INION RAN, 1993]; and V. I. Kantorovich, *Sovetskie Sindikaty* [Moscow: n.p., 1928]).

[22] Arthur Arnold, *Banks, Credit*, 279, shows that although Gosbank reduced its loans and discounts in 1926/27 and 1927/28 by 243 million and 817 million rubles, respectively, its note issue was 333 million and 337 million rubles. Even though Gosbank was refusing promissory notes, its competitors were not.

authorities of the need to create a "command" financial system that could strictly control cash and credit.

The Financial Debate. Two competing views of money and credit were placed before Soviet decision makers at the beginning of the Great Break-Through. The "leftist" utopian vision was that banks, money, and credit should not play an active role.[23] Budget grants and planned credits would replace bank and commercial credits. Money and credit would automatically follow materials, output, and labor as enterprises fulfilled their plans. According to Yu. L. Piatakov, the chairman of Gosbank in 1930 and an advocate of the leftist view: "Relationships will be so organized in the socialist sector that nonfulfillment of plan responsibilities would happen only in exceptional cases."[24] Thus, "the question of credit discipline is a question of plan discipline."[25]

Specialists with practical banking experience, on the other hand, argued that money and credit would continue to play their traditional roles of deciding who gets credits and in monitoring their use. It would be against human nature to assume that everyone will fulfill their plans exactly as ordered. These specialists characterized the utopian ideas of the Left as being born "in the minds of young people ... influenced by the cult of the plan [*kul't plana*]."[26] Banks would have to continue to grant credits on a discretionary basis, check whether goods had been delivered and accepted, and determine whether appropriate payments had been made.

The leftist credit reform of January 30, 1930, required that all enterprise transactions be cashless, made Gosbank the monopoly bank, banned commercial credits, and automatically credited the seller's account without the buyer's permission, whether or not the enterprise had funds – a utopian practice called "planned automatism." The reform assumed perfect plan discipline and that planned automatism would result in credit following goods without Gosbank monitoring.

To the utopian's chagrin, Gosbank's automatic crediting allowed enterprises to demand unlimited credit, as a report of the Worker–Peasant Inspection sardonically pointed out: "The first period of credit reform is a period of complete money saturation and satisfaction of

---

[23] Arnold, *Banks, Credit*, 358–63.
[24] *Vestnik Pravleniia Gosbanka* (VPG), 1930, no. 15–16, 11.
[25] *VPG*, 1930, no. 8, 8.
[26] Sitnin, *Vospominania Finansista*, 29.

clients."[27] Large abnormalities and direct distortions, such as shipments of out-of-season and unordered commodities, invoicing at inflated prices, shipments of unordered goods, submission to Gosbank of problem loans for payment, and invoices for future deliveries became commonplace.

Although the reform's intent was to place Gosbank in charge of all money and credit, Gosbank lost control. Gosbank was starved of information and overwhelmed. According to Gosbank's chairman, "relations of the industrial and sales enterprises with other enterprises has become so complicated that, in the end, no institution has a full picture of the financial situation of any enterprise."[28] A newly created centralized clearing system not only lost many payments, but also unprocessed accounts grew by a factor of ten in the first two months of the credit reform, reaching a total of forty thousand. No one could tell whether an enterprise's debt was rising or falling.[29]

Money and credit grew at astronomical rates: Gosbank's credits rose by 87 percent and banknote issues by 78 percent in the course of the 1929–30 economic year alone, repeating the NEP experience that credit growth leads automatically to monetary growth.[30] Planned automatism transmitted responsibility from uncreditworthy customers to creditworthy ones, and ultimately to Gosbank and the state budget, as the lenders of last resort.[31]

The 1931 Reforms: Installing a Command Financial System. The failure of the 1930 credit reform brought in a new Gosbank administration, which threw planned automatism out of the window, starting with reforms in January 1931. A new credit regime was announced in SNK decrees of January 24 and March 20, 1931. As in the 1930 decree, Gosbank remained the monopoly supplier of bank credit, commercial credits were not permitted, and financial transactions among enterprises were still to be cashless; however, new features were added that converted Gosbank into an administrative-command center for finance. Now Gosbank was to

---

[27] GARF, 374.7.943, 31–2.
[28] VPG, 1930, no. 8, 3.
[29] Davies, *The Soviet Economy in Turmoil*, 325.
[30] VPG, 1930, no. 30–1.
[31] The linkage to the budget was as follows: The state's prime revenue source in 1930 was the enterprise excise tax and similar taxes, which were paid into the state budget irrespective of the availability of funds in the enterprise's account. If enterprise funds were insufficient, excise taxes were paid by Gosbank credits, which translated directly into an increase in the money supply.

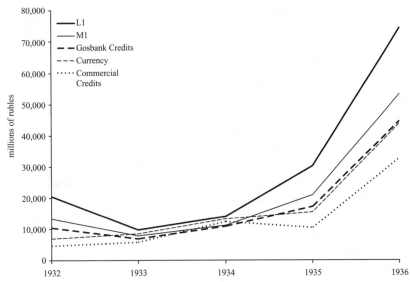

FIGURE 9.2. Monetary aggregates, 1932–1936 (on January 1 of each year).
Source: O. Khlevnyuk and R. Davies, "The End of Rationing in the Soviet Union 1934–1935," Table 1, A. Arnold, *Banks, Credit, and Money in Soviet Russia*, Table 62. M1 is the sum of currency in circulation plus Gosbank credits; L1 is M1 plus commercial credits.

actively monitor transactions, settling invoices only with the agreement of buyers. Gosbank was to issue credits primarily for trade rather than for production and grant enterprises their own working capital to make them self-financing. An additional SNK decree of July 1932 spelled out insolvency procedures to combat soft budget constraints. The intent of this second wave of reforms was to limit credit expansion. Bank credit was to go only to trading organizations. Production enterprises were to use their own working capital; bankruptcy provisions were to create a hard budget constraint.

Figure 9.2, plotting the various measures of money and liquidity between 1932 and 1936, shows the stark failure of the second waves of reforms: M1 (currency in circulation plus Gosbank deposit accounts) tripled and currency almost doubled. Between 1932 and 1936, M1 grew at an annual rate of 43 percent, Gosbank credits at 80 percent, and L1 at 38 percent, while real GDP grew at about 10 percent per annum in 1928 prices and at about 4 percent in 1937 prices. Commercial credits did not expand as rapidly, but they did not disappear. Clearly, these rapid expansions were not what the framers of the 1931–32 reforms had in mind. The monetary and liquidity aggregates were outgrowing the real economy.[32]

Figure 9.2 raises three key questions. First, why did commercial credits persist despite official opposition? Second, why did Gosbank credits rise so substantially despite official commitments to limit their growth? Third, why did currency in circulation grow so rapidly?

The Persistence of Commercial Credits. Although the credit reforms of 1930 to 1932 appeared to ban commercial credits, the legality of different types of enterprise-to-enterprise credits (promissory notes, bills of exchange, seller-to-buyer credits, buyer-to-seller credits) remained uncertain.[33] "Illegal" commercial credits remained a constant of Soviet economic life as is seen in a 1938 statement by Gosbank's director: "Although our laws forbid enterprises from crediting one another, in fact nothing has changed as a result of these laws."[34] One can understand Gosbank's frustration with commercial credits: as the designated sole source of credits in the economy, commercial credits of one enterprise to another represented the financial parallel to unplanned horizontal exchanges. Moreover, when enterprises failed to pay, Gosbank was left holding the bag as lender of last resort. Gosbank's frustration may have been tempered by the realization that commercial credits were unavoidable and often necessary. Unless all transactions are paid instantaneously, credits are automatic.[35] Moreover, enterprises, trusts, ministry main administrations, and the ministries had better information required for borrowing and

---

[32] Bergson, *The Real National Incomes*, 261, cites an average annual growth rate of 12 percent from 1928 to 1937. If we take this rate for 1932 to 1936, this suggests a growth factor of approximately 1.6, well below the growth rates of money and credit aggregates. If we take Bergson's estimates in "late" prices, the growth factor is only 1.3.

[33] Arnold, *Banks, Credit*, 349–51.

[34] RGAE, 2324.20.4489, 30.

[35] V. K. Sitnin, one of the intellectual framers of the financial system, used the hypothetical example of three firms "Ore," and "Coke," and "Machinery" to demonstrate that an administrative-command economy automatically generates commercial credits, whether the financial authorities like it or not. Each time a delivery of raw materials is made, a credit is created, whether advanced deliberately by Gosbank or spontaneously by the firms themselves. Clearing payments cannot be made with every movement of materials. Moreover, according to Sitnin, such credit operations redistribute resources. If Ore and Coke are paid expeditiously at prices that reflect their resource costs, no redistribution takes place; but if they are paid late, not at all, or at prices below their resource costs, resources are redistributed. In cases of nonpayment or delayed payment, "the party that suffers is not the party that receives resources, and is unable to pay for them, but the party that supplies those resources, *the creditor*." V. K. Sitnin, "Payments in Ferrous Metallurgy," *Ekonomicheskaya Zhizn'*, no. 69, 1933.

TABLE 9.1. *Distribution of Gosbank Credits, 1933–1936 (Percentages)*

Agency	1933	1934	1935	1936
Trade Organizations	23	29	34	28
NKPP (food industry)	17	16	17	20
Delivery Committee (Komzag)	16	15	12	11
NKTP (heavy industry)	9	9	11	11
Agriculture	8	6	5	5
NKLP (light industry)	7	6	6	10
NKPS (transport)	4	3	3	3
NKLes (forestry)	4	4	3	3
Prom Kooperatsia (cooperation)	4	2	2	1
Vneshtorg (foreign trade)	3	4	2	1

Source: RGAE, 1562.16.74.

lending decisions than Gosbank.[36] Commercial credits also could be tailored to unusual circumstances, such as nonstandardized production. Out of a hundred heavy-industrial enterprises producing nonstandardized linens in Leningrad, only five were credited by Gosbank. The others operated with commercial credits.[37]

Table 9.1 confirms that trade organizations, which accounted for just 10 percent of national income in 1930,[38] did receive more than half of Gosbank credits in the mid-1930s as the 1931 reforms advocated, with trade, food supply, and agricultural procurement as the prime recipients. Production enterprises were not cut off entirely. In both 1933 and 1936, the industrial ministries and transportation received one third of Gosbank credits. Table 9.2 shows that enterprises that lacked Gosbank credits were more inclined to use commercial credits. Trade ranked first in both Gosbank and commercial credits; heavy industry ranked second in commercial credits, but fourth in Gosbank credits; and transport ranked eighth in Gosbank credits, but fourth in commercial credits. These reversals were either a use of commercial credits to thwart central directives or essential "informal" credits, without which production enterprises could not have completed their plans.

Commercial credits also persisted because some enterprise managers actually preferred commercial credits to Gosbank credits. The newspaper,

[36] RGAE, 7733.14.900, 13.
[37] *Ekonomicheskaia Zhizn'*, no. 8. 1933. Hereafter referred to as *EZ*.
[38] Davies, *The Soviet Economy in Turmoil*, 489.

TABLE 9.2. *Enterprises Credits: Commercial vs. Gosbank (Rank Orderings)*

Sector	Commercial Debts	Commercial Credits	Gosbank Credits
Trade	1	1	1
Heavy Industry	2	2	4
Food Products	3	3	2
Transport	5	4	8
Supplies	4	5	3
Agriculture	6	6	6
Light Industry	9	7	5
Foreign Trade	10	8	9
Cooperation	7	9	10
Forestry	8	10	7

Source: RGAE, 7733.14.900.

Economic Life, cited the following case:

Moscow Bread Factory Number 4 was supposed to receive 800,000 rubles from Gosbank. Actually only 136,000 were provided. Instead of demanding additional funds, the bread factory chose to negotiate with Union-Flour (Souzmuka) that it delay posting its bills. The commercial credit received by Moscow Bread Factory in 1931 and 1932 from its suppliers [such as Union-Flour] reached 1.7 million rubles.

Enterprises preferred commercial credits because "It is safer. You can spit on all the bank's demands for balance of the enterprise budget, for improvement of responsibility."[39] Enterprises avoided turnover taxes by being paid in IOUs: two enterprises in the Leningrad Combinat Trekhugol'nik, for example, concealed their revenues for nine months and thereby saved more than a million rubles in taxes.[40] Union-Flour hid profits of 71 million rubles, while applying for government grants "to cover losses" in the amount of 54 million rubles.[41] A 1936 internal report concluded that enterprises used (unplanned) commercial credits "to hoard inputs and to create float (immobilize monetary funds), and to conceal their inability to properly organize their monetary funds."[42]

Gosbank as the Lender of Last Resort. Why did Gosbank continue to issue credits despite its charge to keep the growth of credit equal to the

---

[39] *EZ*, no. 8, 1933.
[40] Minister of Finance, Grin'ko, cited this example in his inaugural address. *EZ*, no. 24, 1933.
[41] *EZ*, no. 24, 1933.
[42] RGAE, 7733.14.900, 13.

real rate of growth of the economy? The most convincing answer is that Gosbank could not avoid being the lender of last resort in the face of soft budget constraints. A decree of January 20, 1932, "On the Order of Registration of Insolvent and Defective Enterprises and Farms," made an abortive effort to impose hard budget constraints by setting an insolvency procedure.[43] This decree created for a time an "unplanned" wholesale market as buyers refused goods, but the records from the 1930s reveal no bankruptcies.[44] According to a frustrated Gosbank chairman writing in 1938, "If one enterprise is sitting on an overdue payment, it can be complacent. It will receive money for wages and other needs."[45] Industrial ministries, their branch departments, and even central authorities argued that enterprise closures would cost them planned output. The state could not afford the loss of output of the insolvent plant, and the plant in turn could not produce without material deliveries, which had to be paid for. Hence, by everyone's calculation, the losses from closing a firm were too high; it was better to bail them out. Enterprises, obviously, were aware of this cost/benefit calculation, and acted opportunistically.

Both Gosbank credits and legal commercial credits arranged by ministries and enterprises kept insolvent enterprises in business. When credits were not repaid, arrears grew. Overdue credits called nonpayments or arrears were the growth industry of the 1930s, expanding at 27 percent per annum between 1934 and 1939. Arrears did not reach large proportions of GDP in the 1930s: at their peak (in 1937), they amounted to about 2 percent of GDP, unlike the massive arrears of the mid-1990s, which reached almost half of GDP.[46]

---

[43] According to this order, an enterprise could be put on notice if it failed to pay invoices on time or if it failed to repay bank loans. If it failed to pay for ten days after the notice, the enterprise could be declared to be in default, and in case of a second failure in the same quarter, also in ten days, the enterprise could be declared insolvent.

[44] Enterprises could avoid payment obligations if they refused delivery of goods. Refused goods ended up under the jurisdiction of local branches of Gosbank. Newspapers of the time often announced sales of manufactured commodities. An example: "The Chudov branch of Gosbank, because of the failure of due payments, is announcing the sale of insulators, owned by the Komintern factory. All questions should be directed to the Chudov branch of Gosbank." (*EZ*, no. 36, 1933.) In some instances, such sales were used to contravene higher orders. For example, the Middle Volga local Gosbank branch, under pressure from the local government, forced a chain of cooperatives to sell sugar that was intended for delivery to other regions. As a result, there was enough sugar for a year and a half in this area, while other regions were experiencing shortages.

[45] RGAE, 2324.20.4489, 54.

[46] C. Gaddy and B. Ickes, "Russia's Virtual Economy," *Foreign Affairs* (Sept.–Oct. 1998), 53–67. Also see Padma Desai and Todd Idson, *Work Without Wages: Russia's Nonpayment Crisis* (Cambridge, Mass.: MIT Press, 2000).

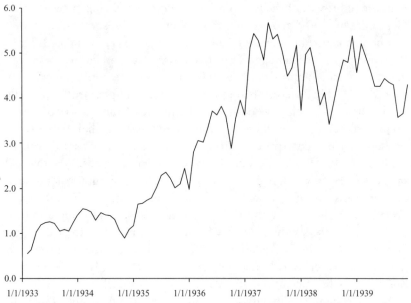

FIGURE 9.3. Interenterprise arrears, 1933–1939 (monthly, millions of rubles). *Source:* RGAE, 2324.20.637.

Figure 9.3 shows bursts of arrears, such as in 1935 and 1936 and in early 1937.[47] Arrears then stabilized as Gosbank, the lender of last resort, issued credits to cover nonpayments. Financial authorities were not pleased with the industrial ministries' tolerance of financial indiscipline. A 1938 report by Gosbank declared: "Nonpayments have become a systematic feature with which we have to come to terms,"[48] and that "there is a massive redistribution of resources from healthy to unhealthy organizations *by order of the ministry* [italics added]. When authorities wish to hold someone responsible, nothing happens."[49] Failures of payments raised alarm signals throughout the 1930s.[50] Financial authorities

---

[47] RGAE, 2374.20.637.

[48] RGAE, 2324.20.4489, 28.

[49] RGAE, 2324.20.4489, 30.

[50] According to a report prepared for the Ministry of Finance, slightly more than 50 percent of commercial credits and some 70 percent of enterprise debts were classified as illegal between 1932 and 1936. "Legality" was defined by payment status, with seriously overdue payments placed in special ledgers (called *kartoteka* 2 and 3 accounts), which the ministry could freeze at will. For example, on January 1, 1937, 525 million rubles of enterprise accounts were classified as frozen (*aresty*), out of total arrears of 3,625 million. (V. K. Sitnin, *Debitorsko-Kreditorskaia Zadolzhennost' v 1935 Gody,* RGAE, 7733.14.900.)

conceded that unpaid credits "directly violated the major rules of the credit reform."[51] Some arrears were offset by ministerial or regional authorities, or ministries would reshuffle financial resources from profitable to unprofitable enterprises, but most were left to Gosbank. A financial specialist wrote in his memoirs that "every year Gosbank issued credits to deal with nonpayments."[52] These settlements constituted only short-term palliatives, as a Gosbank report of 1933 attested: "The one-time program to eliminate mutual arrears in the Ministry of Heavy Industry was the main administrative measure last year. It had only a short-term effect, and after a short period of time the debtor–creditor relationship returned to its original condition."[53] Gosbank's clearing operations resulted in reductions in the volume of arrears in 1937, 1938, and 1939, but each time, Gosbank credits had only a temporary effect. According to a Gosbank report from 1937, "At the end of the year, Gosbank carried out an artificial amortization of overdue credits and unpaid bills of suppliers. This amortization is not reliable and will lead to the growth of credit arrears in the coming year."[54]

Clearing debts proved to be too difficult for Gosbank, which had to turn to deal makers with knowledge of local conditions. By the late 1930s, most clearing was accomplished via regional or ministerial settlement organizations. As of 1939, the 108 active Bureau for Mutual Settlements (*Biuro vzaimnykh raschetov*, or BVR) established by Gosbank were handling only 11 percent of clearing operations.[55] The reversion of clearing operations to local and industrial authorities was another serious loss of central control over transactions. Decentralized clearing operations did, however, offer the major advantage of reducing the amount of Gosbank refinancing.

Money Surrogates. Unlike modern market economies, where demand deposits and cash are interchangeable, the Soviet administrative-command economy attempted (remember siphoning) to draw a strict line between cash and bank money. In the 1930s and thereafter, financial authorities feared the inflationary effects of wage growth and, accordingly, fought to limit enterprise wage funds.[56] In fact, the Politburo itself had to approve

[51] RGAE, 7733.14.900, 4.
[52] Sitnin, "Payments in Ferrous Metallurgy," 40.
[53] RGAE, 7733.12.332, 50.
[54] RGAE, 7733.15.325, 56.
[55] Davies, "A Short-Term Credit," 23.
[56] Granick, *Job Rights in the Soviet Union,* 58–60.

monetary emissions, and a Gosbank chairman and finance ministers were fired or reprimanded for not being able to limit monetary emissions.[57]

The fact that currency in circulation almost doubled between 1932 and 1936 shows that Gosbank and Ministry of Finance officials could not restrain emissions. Clearly, cash demands were growing as industrial employment expanded and industrial wages were bid up.[58] Despite the doubling of currency, wage arrears grew in the mid-1930s. Unpaid salaries amounted to 359 million rubles on January 1, 1936, about one fifth the size of the commercial debt.[59]

Just as market economies respond to currency shortages by creating substitutes, Soviet enterprises and organizations produced money surrogates to soften wage arrears. Money substitutes were already sufficiently widespread during the NEP to require official action: on February 29, 1924, the Committee for Labor and Defense issued a special decree prohibiting "all government, cooperative and private organizations, and enterprises from producing any kind of monetary substitutes, without special permission of the Ministry of Finance."[60] Under this decree, the finance ministry could even liquidate organizations that illegally issued money substitutes. Centralization of financial administration in 1930 and 1931 was supposed to put a stop to money surrogates, but they did not disappear. On June 3, 1930, SNK issued a special decree, according to which "other forms of payment" were allowed only with agreement of the People's Commissariat of Finance.[61] Unlike the 1924 decree, no punishment for producing unauthorized money substitutes was specified.

The use of money surrogates peaked in 1934 and 1935. Investigations conducted in the summer of 1935 uncovered 1,340 cases of substitute monies.[62] A Ministry of Finance report showed that in July and August of 1935, monetary authorities devoted considerable resources to the fight against self-printed money.[63] The battle against money surrogates was intensified by a special decree of May 31, 1935, which provided criminal punishments for "unlawful making of securities and money substitutes." Managers of printing establishments that took orders for money

---

[57] Khlevnuk and Davies, "The End of Rationing," 586–90.
[58] Holzman, "Soviet Inflationary Pressures," 167–88.
[59] This calculation was made in a report prepared by V. K. Sitnin, in RGAE, 7733.14.900, 7.
[60] *Denezhnoe Obraschenie i Kredit v SSSR,* 1938, 112.
[61] Ibid., 241.
[62] RGAE, 7733.13.764, 39.
[63] RGAE, 7733.13.761, 22.

surrogates and managers of stores that accepted them were to be prose-
cuted as well.[64]

In the Urals, substitute money was widely used for payments to or-
phanages, which passed it on as salaries to their workers, who then spent
it in local stores. Workers became accustomed to vouchers (*talony*) as
a normal means of local exchange.[65] A local newspaper article entitled, "Who Outlawed Money in the Irtish Area?," a clipping of which
landed in the archives of financial authorities, explained that in Eastern
Kazakhstan salaries went unpaid for five to six months. As a result, village
governments and machine tractor stations printed vouchers for advance
wage payments. One worker was quoted as saying "We need money, but
instead we get vouchers. Whether you want to or not, you have to use the
vouchers to buy the garbage they call food."[66] Some vouchers circulated widely, and some even changed hands at a premium (e.g., those of
the Molokov Machine Tractor Station). In most cases, though, vouchers
exchanged below face value.[67]

The state's battle against money surrogates could paralyze public services because full compliance meant that all potential money surrogates,
including student lunches tickets, bus tickets, or movie tickets, had to be
approved by the Ministry of Finance. A high party official warned the
Minister of Finance in 1935 that "it is difficult to see the current tickets as money substitutes. On top of that, in many cities, such substantial
numbers of tickets are in circulation that their exchange would require a
couple of tons of paper."[68]

Despite administrative threats, local courts typically refused to take on
money substitute cases. Lacking the threat of punishment, on August 21,
1935, SNK amnestied issuers of unlawful money surrogates printed prior
to May 31 of that year. Ministry of Finance officials correctly viewed
money surrogates and arrears as two sides of the same coin. In both
cases, enterprises lacked the liquidity to pay. In the one case, they accumulated arrears vis-à-vis suppliers; in the other, they printed money
surrogates to pay workers. Their superiors were confronted with the
same choice: toleration or bankruptcy. When faced with such a choice,
they typically looked the other way. Under the circumstances of harsh

[64] *Denezhnoe Obraschenie i Kredit v SSSR*, 1938, 318.
[65] RGAE, 7733.13.764, 36.
[66] RGAE, 7733.13.764, 59.
[67] RGAE, 7733.13.764, 73.
[68] RGAE, 7733.13.764, 63.

limitations on credits, the enterprises preferred to lose creditworthiness rather than forego production.

State Budgets, Exports, and Investment Finance

Just as financial payments for goods, services, and wages were the financial counterparts of current physical transactions, payments into and expenditures from the state budget represented the financial side of physical investment transactions. Although enterprises accumulated depreciation and earned profits, virtually all investment finance was centralized in the state budget, being paid out of the "expenditures on the national economy" account. In theory, investment finance was to follow the physical investment plan. However, there were virtually no physical balances of equipment or construction (see Chapter 4). All planning was in rubles. Although the Politburo did carefully monitor major construction sites, the physical planning of investment was quite weak. SNK and Gosplan approved title lists of investment projects for funding, and each investment project was supposed to have an approved budget. But Chapter 6 showed that ministries and glavks were reluctant to submit cost estimates, and many investment projects were built without any cost figures. Chapter 4 discussed the investment plan, which was a plan (usually stated in constant rubles) broken down into state agencies, such as ministries and regional authorities, giving these agencies the authority to draw on investment finance from the state budget (as administered by various investment banks). Chapter 6 showed that these investment banks and the finance ministry were reluctant to exercise strict control over spending, fearing that they could be accused of sabotaging key state projects.

The link between the investment plan and the state budget was as follows: The investment plan (and title list) gave ministries, glavks, and enterprises the right to draw investment finance equal to the fixed-price figure in the investment plan, plus any cost increases or minus any cost reductions. According to the theory that "money follows plan," if the investment plan authorized a specified amount of investment spending for the entire economy, that amount of investment finance should automatically be available. Such was not the case.

Investment Finance Formulae. The physical side of investment – the plants, equipment, and inventories – can be thought of as capital goods imported from other countries (mainly equipment) and of plants and equipment produced domestically. In most market economies, the two can be combined because the value of imported capital can be converted into domestic currency by the market exchange rate. In the Soviet administrative-command economy, imports of capital goods, paid for in foreign exchange, were strictly segregated from domestically produced capital goods, paid for in domestic currency. Imported capital had to be paid out of export earnings, whereas domestically produced capital goods could be paid for out of the centralized investment fund in the state budget. Thus, there are two investment finance formulae: one for imported capital, the other for domestically produced capital.

IMPORTED CAPITAL. In the 1930s, the Soviet economy required imported equipment and technology to build its own industrial base. In the early 1930s, 89 percent of turbines, boilers, and generators and 66 percent of machine tools were imported.[69] Because the 1918 default deprived the Soviet Union of access to foreign credit, capital goods imports were limited by export earnings. Thus, *capital imports = export earnings – consumer goods imports.*

The Politburo devoted an enormous amount of time and debate to the export–import plan. Stalin headed the Politburo's foreign exchange commission, which he ran with an iron hand. It was one of the few cases where Stalin took formal control of a key allocative activity. Stalin's chief protagonists were the minister of trade, A. I. Mikoian (candidate member of the Politburo from 1925 and a full member from 1935 on and one of the few old Bolshevik survivors of the Great Purges), the industrial ministers who wanted capital imports, and the few officials pleading for imports of consumer goods. Under Stalin's guidance, the currency commission ensured that virtually all foreign exchange was used for capital goods, which it distributed itself. Much passion was generated by ministers (heavy industry, transportation, and others), arguing their desperate needs for imported capital. Stalin viewed himself as protecting the national interest against greedy ministers (e.g., the insistent Ordzhonikidze): "These funds must be used in the interests of the government, not the interests [of one ministry]."[70] He was particularly irate when Ordzhonikidze

[69] Franklyn Holzman, "Foreign Trade," in *Economic Trends in the Soviet Union*, eds. Abram Bergson and Simon Kuznets (Cambridge, Mass.: Harvard University Press, 1963), 297–8. Also see Anthony C. Sutton, *Western Technology and Soviet Economic Development, 1917–1930* (Stanford, Calif.: Hoover Institution Press, 1971).

[70] Khlevnyuk et al., *Stalin i Kaganovich. Perepiski*, 88.

strong-armed the Politburo in his absence to approve a large foreign order for heavy industry:

[Ordzhonikidze] is attempting to rob the state's currency reserves for the imports of metals, but this metal, for the Cheliabinsk Works, appears to be without an owner because it is virtually being sold in bazaars. Criminals and rascals![71]

Stalin rejected any number of requests for imports, stating that these goods should be produced at home. He forcefully rejected diversions of foreign exchange to consumer goods, issuing orders "not to import Rolls Royce automobiles."[72] Most important, Stalin held the line against demands to import wheat:

The import of grain now when foreigners are crying about grain shortage in the USSR would give only a political minus. I advise to hold back from importing. Barley and oats must be exported, because we very much need the foreign exchange.[73]

Mikoian, responsible for procurements of agricultural products and their export, raised Stalin's ire with his frequent requests to lower his collection and export targets. Kaganovich to Stalin (August 30, 1931): "There was a heated debate about the September grain export plan. Mikoian wanted a lower plan."[74] Such selfish actions prompted an outburst from Stalin: "From the third point of Mikoian's telegram, it is clear that there are not limits to [his] bureaucratic narcissism."[75] Clearly, Mikoian's job of forcing grain procurements was vital because grain was the main source of foreign exchange. The Politburo broke down grain-collection plans by regions and by calendar months and carefully monitored fulfillment, sometimes receiving reports every five days.[76] Oil exports also occupied many hours of Politburo discussion.[77] Alarm rose when Baku threatened underfulfillment.[78] Stalin's currency commission kept the export–import plan under tight control. Few imported consumer goods slipped through Stalin's net.

FINANCING DOMESTIC CAPITAL. Domestic capital goods had to be financed from state budget revenues (or from currency emissions) according to the formula: *domestically produced capital goods = state*

---

[71] Ibid., 101.
[72] Ibid., 350.
[73] Ibid., 462; August 30, 1934.
[74] Ibid., 74.
[75] Ibid.; August 19, 1931.
[76] Ibid., 509.
[77] Ibid., 309.
[78] Ibid., 312.

budget revenues – state budget noncapital expenditures + currency emission.[79]

Just as imports of capital equipment were reduced by the amount of imports of consumer goods, so was domestically produced capital limited by the amount of noncapital expenditures from the state budget. Investment was financed from state budget revenues not devoted to other uses, such as public consumption, defense, or administration, or, if approved by the Politburo, by currency emissions. Stalin clearly summarized this budget formula in a December 25, 1947, Politburo meeting [author's italics in the following]:

Comrade Stalin, upon hearing the deputy ministers of the Council of Ministers, said: "The plan is very swollen and is *not within our capacity.* . . . It is necessary to set the [investment] plan at 40 billion rubles instead of the mentioned 60 billion. We have to keep in mind that because of the lowering of [consumer] prices and the replacement of the rationing system *we have lost 50 billion rubles [from the budget].*"[80]

In this case, Stalin was being led by the availability of investment finance in setting the investment limit! He did not first set an investment limit and then find the necessary funds.

The budget battle involved a number of participants. The finance minister's job (no finance minister, including Grin'ko, in this period was a member of the Politburo) was to keep track of state revenues and currency emission, to focus on the need for maintaining the value of the ruble and to balance the state budget.[81] The consumption/investment tradeoff was reflected in several ways: First, low consumer goods prices reduced budget revenue through lower turnover tax collections, and subsidies of necessities such as bread constituted a noninvestment expenditure. Second, the more the state spent on public consumption (education and health), the less was available for investment. The budget battle between construction projects and equipment and physicians' wages, retail price subsidies, and education is captured in a Politburo exchange of April 29, 1934, between Stalin's deputy Zhdanov and Grin'ko. Zhdanov proposed to raise the salaries of medical personnel: "If we raise the salaries of doctors here and there, we'll not get results. Therefore, we should focus on the highest

---

[79] This formula omits forced bond purchases by the population – a device used in the 1930s and thereafter.

[80] These notes were made by a senior economic official, Malyshev, and are cited in Khlevnyuk, "Sovetskaia," 7–8.

[81] Gregory and Tikhonov, "Central Planning," 1017–38.

TABLE 9.3. State Budget, Second Five-Year Plan, 1933–1937 (Billion Rubles)

Income	1933[a]	1937[b]
Profit taxes	6.6	72.9
Turnover taxes	19.6	216.1
Miscellenous taxes	7.6	39.0
Depreciation	2.0	20.2
Resources from population	8.2	44.6
Other	0.6	17.7
Allowance for price reductions	0	−55.0
Total	44.6	355.5
Expenditure		
Financing of national economy	30.2	211.4
Social and cultural measures	9.5	75.4
Administration, defense	2.5	19.0
State loans	1.0	10.0
Other	1.4	15.7
State reserve	0	14.0
Total	44.6	355.5

[a] The year 1932 represents the actual budget.

[b] The year 1937 represents the projected budget.

Source: From Stalinist Planning for Economic Growth, 1933–1952 by Eugene Zaleski. Copyright © 1980 by the University of North Carolina Press. Used by permission of the publisher.

priority categories – rural doctors, directors of hospitals, epidemiologists, and doctors in 'deficit' professions and raise only their salaries." Grin'ko's unequivocal answer: "We must rule out any project that costs 345 million in this year. We cannot raise anyone's salary, but if we do so only on a very limited scale."[82]

Table 9.3 shows the state budget of the Second Five-Year Plan for 1933–1937. Turnover taxes, the difference between the prices at which the state trade network purchased goods and the prices that consumers paid, constituted the bulk of revenues. If retail prices fell, so did turonover taxes.[83] The profit tax was based on the difference between wholesale prices and the costs of production. Hence, any lowering of costs should be reflected in higher profits taxes. Table 9.3 shows that some two thirds of the state budget was used to finance the national economy (for investment and short-term credits).

[82] Khlevnyuk et al., Stalinskoe Politburo, 51.

[83] For example, Table 9.3 shows an allowance of 55 billion rubles to be subtracted from 1937 revenues for retail price reductions.

Stalin, his Minister of Finance, and the Chairman of Gosbank understood that state spending in excess of state revenue meant monetary emissions that threatened the "stability of the ruble" (domestic price stability).
This fact is reflected in a communication from Kaganovich to Stalin of
July 17, 1932:

> I sent you Grin'ko's letter about the financial situation. We must discuss this matter
> today. Our situation is somewhat difficult. The demand for currency is rising every
> day and reaching 150–160 per day, but we can satisfy this demand at most 30–40
> or a maximum of 50 million. We are already experiencing wage arrears. Grin'ko
> has raised the issue of lowering capital expenditure assignments by 1.5 trillion
> rubles. Comrade Molotov thinks 1 trillion is possible. I think that we should
> not make a mechanical reduction but go from trust to trust and compare their
> investment financing with their actual production of construction materials and
> thus limit the reduction to 500 million.[84]

Chapter 4 addressed the difficult choice of tradeoff between consumption and investment. More investment means a larger capital stock but
less consumption and, hence, less work effort. We considered this choice
in terms of labor effort, real wages, and investment. This chapter shows
that every physical tradeoff is also reflected in a financial tradeoff. The
battle between consumer subsidies, physicians' wages, and expenditures
on schools versus more expenditures on investment is the other side
of the coin of the tradeoff between physical consumption and physical
investment.

Chapter 4 also showed that investment surges were associated with
higher prices of investment goods and explained this phenomenon as the
result of a bidding war for investment goods. The budget formula es-
tablishes the financial link: increased revenues from profit taxes and from
turnover taxes depended on lowering costs of production, which required
higher labor productivity. If labor productivity declined (or failed to rise
according to plan), costs would rise and both profits tax and sales tax
revenue would fall, creating a potential closed circle. If higher investment
lowers labor productivity, state revenues fall and there is less investment
finance.

The budget formula also shows that if investment is financed by budget
deficits – monetary emission – the growth of the money supply could create
an excess demand for investment and bid up prices of investment goods.
As Stalin warned in 1947: "If we swell construction, then *extra money*

---

[84] Khlevnyuk et al., *Stalin i Kaganovich. Perepiski*, 230.

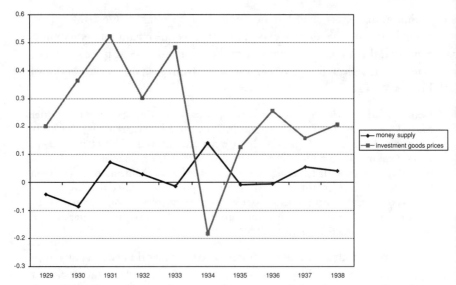

FIGURE 9.4. Annual growth rates of money and investment goods prices, 1929–1938.

will appear on the market and there will be devaluation [rise in prices]."[85] Figure 9.4 shows, indeed, that monetary growth was positively associated with investment-price inflation, at least up until the period of 1934 to 1935.

Closing Remarks

If "money is the root of all evil," the administrative-command economy appeared to offer the best opportunity to either eliminate it or harness it for the general good. Although Marxist utopians attempted to eliminate money entirely in the War Communism period (1918–early 1921), their efforts thereafter turned to using money in the interests of the plan. Money, instead of being evil, could be used to ensure – through the device of ruble control – that everyone was carrying out their planned tasks. Actually, such a system appeared workable. Money could be more easily measured than physical quantities of goods, and the dictator could legislate one center of accounts – a monopoly state bank to handle all transactions.

[85] These notes were made by a senior economic official, Malyshev, and are cited in Khlevnyuk, "Sovetskaia," 8.

A law of accounting is that for every physical transaction, there must be an equivalent financial transaction, either explicit or implicit, and the Soviet administrative-command economy was no exception. In fact, this accounting law was the basis for the notion of ruble control: by monitoring financial transactions, you were also monitoring physical transactions. What appeared simple in theory was difficult in practice. The physical plan was not finely broken down; therefore, financial authorities could not match each financial transaction with a planned task. The greatest danger of all, however, would be reversion to a system whereby a producer's liquidity (cash, bank money, or credit) determined its claim on resources, not the plan. It was for this reason that financial authorities battled so fiercely to limit the supply of currency and credit to the growth of the real economy. Throughout the entire period of the 1930s, Gosbank and the finance ministry failed miserably in this endeavor. Liquidity always outgrew real goods and services. During the NEP, the excess growth of liquidity was primarily due to unofficial credits. Much effort was devoted in the 1930s to banning unofficial credits, and these efforts were in part successful. Although enterprises continued to credit one another, at least unofficial credits did not grow. The major reason for the loss of control of money and credit was the soft budget constraint. Financial authorities, like physical planners, could not enforce hard budget constraints. A financially bankrupt enterprise that produced steel at an enormous loss was better than a shuttered enterprise that produced no steel. To keep such enterprises in business, there had to be a lender of last resort, and this role was played by Gosbank. Ultimately, Gosbank had to supply the credit to keep insolvent businesses open.

The story of investment finance also illustrates the fact that even administrative-command economies cannot escape accounting realities. In any economy, the amount of physical investment must equal the amount of society's savings. Insofar as the state accounted for virtually all savings, the amount of physical investment was, therefore, limited by the amount of state savings in the state budget. This accounting reality meant that if the dictator wanted physical investment to increase by 50 percent in one year, the amount of funds for investment in the state budget would have also to increase by 50 percent – at the sacrifice of military goods, consumer subsidies, and health and education.

This chapter reprised a recurrent theme: the inability of rules to withstand the real pressures of production. The dictator's idea was familiar: if all money and credit come from one source, Gosbank, the dictator can monitor all vertical transactions. Yet, to produce their production plans, producers needed more money and credit than Gosbank was willing to supply. Hence, they created their own money (surrogates) and credit (commercial credit). To some extent, financial authorities were more successful in controlling horizontal financial relations. Although they could not eliminate commercial credits, they prevented them from growing. Monetary surrogates, although annoying, did not constitute a significant portion of cash.

10

The Destruction of the Soviet
Administrative-Command Economy

The Soviet administrative-command economy continued to have positive economic growth until 1989. The negative growth thereafter is indicative of an economic system in collapse.[1] Although the USSR began the postwar era with high rates of growth (which were matched by much of Europe and exceeded by the economic miracles in Germany and Japan), its growth declined steadily after 1970. Figure 10.1 summarizes the deep dissatisfaction with growth performance after the 1960s. Whereas growth in Western industrialized economies turned down in response to energy crises in the mid-1970s and early 1980s, they bounced back so that no long-term declining trend was evident. More troubling was that growth was faltering despite continued rapid growth of the capital stock, whose rates were matched only by Japan, which was wringing out three times faster growth (Figure 10.2). Even more threatening was that reforms in China, begun in 1979, were producing rapid growth. Continuation of this trend meant a gradual decline in the share of world output and military power.

The fateful decision in favor of radical economic reform was not forced by outright collapse. The party elite were reasonably satisfied, and the Soviet population was not in open opposition. The administrative-command system, on the eve of its radical change, was "inefficient but stable."[2] Gosplan's projections called for an annual growth rate of some

[1] Directorate of Intelligence, *Handbook of Economic Statistics, 1991*, Washington, D.C., CPAS 91-10001 (September 1991), 37.
[2] Ellman and Kontorovich, *Destruction*, 13.

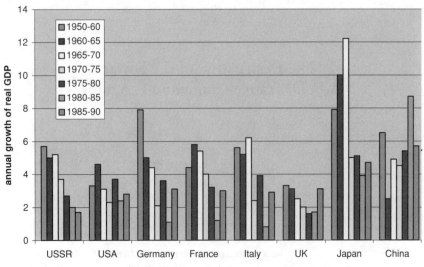

FIGURE 10.1. Soviet GDP growth in comparative perspective.

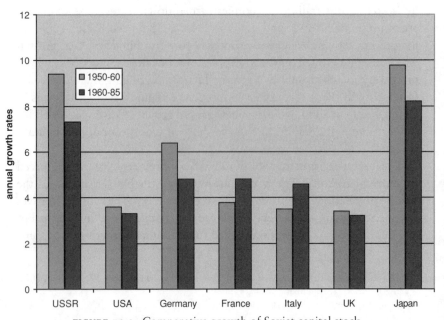

FIGURE 10.2. Comparative growth of Soviet capital stock.

3 percent through the year 2000.[3] Declining Soviet growth rate, coupled
with the acceleration of growth in China, Southeast Asia, and the marked
recovery of the U.S. economy, were troubling but do not fully explain the
fateful steps that eventually spelled the demise of the system.

Ironically, it was Stalin's legacy that made radical reform possible.
Mikhail Gorbachev, at age fifty-four, was the first young General Secretary of the Communist Party since Stalin, who had assumed the position
at the age of fifty. Khrushchev and Brezhnev became general secretaries
when they were nearly sixty years of age. Gorbachev was elected by the
Central Committee to the position in March 1985, touted as a leader
with fresh reform ideas. His academic reform advisors promised that the
administrative-command system could be saved with relatively minor adjustments, such as opening the economy to the West, giving more authority
to enterprises, and reducing the power of the bureaucracy. None recommended fundamental change. Gorbachev's reforms, which came to be
known as *perestroika*, were generally similar to the Chinese reform, but
they were being applied in an economy of gigantic industrial enterprises
and with a long tradition of communal agriculture. Although the aging
party leadership generally opposed radical reform (Gorbachev had only
three reformers on the Politburo), the power of the General Secretary was
still supreme. The skeptical party leadership accepted perestroika with
only muted protests. Many accepted forced retirement with scarcely a
whimper.[4] Gorbachev's subsequent actions would have horrified Stalin:
the dictator himself set in motion a process that would destroy not only
the administrative-command system, but also the party itself. The ultimate
enemy had come from within!

Despite its flaws that were obvious from the very beginning, the
administrative-command system had proven to be stable and immutable.
Transplants of new market elements into the administrative system were
stubbornly rejected. Each successive reform consisted of warmed-over
ideas of earlier eras. A long succession of administrative reshufflings
failed to yield improvements. Measures to make the planning system
more "scientific" through technical norms, computers, and mathematical economics also failed to bring improvements. The most promising
approach – to allow enterprises to make more of their own decisions –
had been proposed already in 1931 by the Minister of Heavy Industry,

[3] Ibid., 91.
[4] Ibid., chapter 2; Valery Boldin, *Ten Years That Shook the World: The Gorbachev Era as
     Witnessed by his Chief of Staff* (New York: Basic Books, 1994), chapters 2–3.

S. Ordzhonikidze.[5] These very same ideas resurfaced in 1961 as the Liberman reform proposals, and they were partially implemented with the Kosygin reform of 1965. These same reform principles formed the core of Gorbachev's own perestroika proposals after 1985.

Although his reform ideas were not new, Gorbachev differentiated himself from earlier reformers by his willingness to destroy the opposition to reform. Gorbachev believed that modest reforms could unleash the "hidden reserves" promised by his reform advisors if bureaucratic opposition could be stifled. Gorbachev undertook two changes that, in effect, destroyed the system. The landmark enterprise law of July 1987 freed enterprises from ministry tutelage, although some administrative controls remained. With the passage of the enterprise law, the industrial ministries and regional authorities no longer controlled enterprises. The end of the leading role of the party dates to the Politburo's September 1988 resolution eliminating the sectoral departments of the Central Committee and "divorcing the party from the economy."[6] The two pillars of administrative allocation – the tutelage of enterprises by ministries and interventions by party officials – were liquidated without creating an alternate allocation mechanism. Prices were still set by state agencies; property was still owned by the state. Gorbachev had created the worst of all worlds – a headless monster without direction – without the ministry or the market, left to stumble around on its own. The economy went into free fall, conservative forces unleashed an abortive coup, and the Soviet Union ended as a political entity to be replaced by fifteen newly independent states.

Declining Growth: Sources

Declining growth was indeed a bitter pill to swallow. A whole succession of Soviet leaders had based claims of superiority on more rapid growth that would eventually "bury the West." Economic growth represented the most favorable playing field. Operational plans called for the growth

[5] Ordzhonikidze's proposal went well beyond the discussion limits allowed by Stalin. After these notions were labeled "right opportunism," Ordzhonikidze fired the liberal editor of his NKTP paper. He continued experiments with metallurgy in 1934 and 1935, attempting to apply economic accounting to small production units, reducing subsidies, reducing the interference by glavks and ministries, and letting managers decide on labor staffing. For a discussion, see Khlevnyuk, "The People's Commissariat of Heavy Industry," 109–11.
[6] Y. Beliik, "Changes in the Central Committee Apparatus," in Ellman and Konotorovich (eds.), *The Destruction of the Soviet Economic System* (Armonk, N.Y.: Sharpe, 1998), 166–7.

of physical goods, rather than their efficient production or their quality (see Chapter 9). The most effective monitoring was of output, not their quality or their cost economies (see Chapter 7). Moreover, Soviet growth may have been overstated by conventional methods.[7]

This monograph begins with the 1930s and concludes with Stalin's "last plan" of 1952.[8] Hence, it might capture the system under its most favorable circumstances, as an underdeveloped country sought its well-defined goal of rapid industrialization. On the negative side, it was experimenting with new institutions and its planning and control procedures were more primitive than in later periods. However, the basic features of the system were put in place quickly, and they remained remarkably unchanged until the late 1980s. Hence, the early system may reveal the causes of the later decline in growth. The book describes a "nested dictatorship" headed by a dictator (Stalin or the Politburo), but composed of hundreds or thousands of minidictators. In a multilayered system, each superior was the subordinate's "dictator"; each subordinate emulated his "dictator."

Complexity. As market economies develop, there is no evidence that increasing complexity – as measured by number of products, firms, or technologies – makes them function less effectively. Mises and Hayek, however, contended that administrative systems suffer from computational problems that should become more acute with complexity. An administrative economy consisting of a few ministries producing few goods with first-generation technologies would be easier to manage than what comes after. Indeed, the Soviet economy was initially organized as three industrial ministries (that did their own construction) plus trade and transportation ministries. At the outbreak of World War II, there were some forty ministries, a slew of regional authorities, and each ministry had been split up into separate departments. In 1953, there were less than ten thousand centrally set indexes[9]; by the mid-1980s, there were fifty thousand.[10] The administrative-command economy of 1985 was more complex than that of 1930. Market economies allow markets to deal with growing

---

[7] Notably, as Russian economists received the freedom to reexamine official Soviet growth figures, they concluded that they were overstated primarily due to the failure to adjust for deteriorating quality. G. Khanin, *Sovetsky Ekonomichesky Rost: Analiz Zapadnykh Otsenok* (Novosibirsk: Eko, 1993).

[8] Tikhonov and Gregory, *Stalin's Last Plan*, 159–92.

[9] Zaleski, *Stalinist Planning*, 486.

[10] Ellman and Konotorovich, *Destruction*, 109.

complexity through their specialization in information on time and place. Democratic market economies tolerate giant national and international concerns that may internalize economic decision making and allow them to accumulate enormous economic power.

Our study showed that the dictator feared concentration of economic power and followed a consistent policy of splitting up economic units (see Chapter 7). With an incentive system that encouraged the supply of own units and the neglect of foreign units, resources could not flow to their highest and best use. Enterprises replaced the unreliable supply system with horizontal transactions and, more often, by self-supply. Modern economies grow through specialization and outsourcing as they mature. In the Soviet Union, the economy despecialized as it matured.

Market economies grow through "creative destruction."[11] As technology and tastes change, new industries are created and old industries are destroyed. In the United States, for example, the largest firms are replaced by a new list after a couple of decades. The Soviet industrial structure, to the contrary, remained frozen over long periods of time. The largest producers of vehicles in 1933 were still the largest producers of vehicles in 1998. The achievement of administrative "balances" was so difficult and time-consuming that planners could not depart from the existing equilibrium. When the USSR began to produce its own cars and trucks in the early 1930s, different agencies favored quite different distributions of vehicles. After the first distributions were made, largely based on ad hoc or political considerations, vehicles thereafter were allocated "from the achieved level," whereby each year's plan was basically last year's plus some minor adjustments (see Chapter 8). Planning from the achieved level froze the existing allocation of resources and remained a constant to Soviet economic life. Already in the 1930s, supply agencies distributed materials "based on historical experience" (see Chapter 8). In the 1980s, when a producer of welded materials wished to economize by using thinner metals, the official answer was: "I don't care about new technology. Just do it so that everything remains the same."[12]

Growing complexity is not a disadvantage in market economies. In fact, certain new theories of growth (endogenous growth theory) suggest that earlier innovations and changes make subsequent innovations and changes easier; hence, the growth rate should accelerate rather than

---

[11] Joseph Schumpter, *Capitalism, Socialism, and Democracy* (Cambridge, Mass.: Harvard University Press, 1934).

[12] Ellman and Kontorovich, *Destruction*, 49.

slow down. The administrative-command system apparently yielded the opposite result.

Investment Decision Making. The law of diminishing returns applies universally. If one factor of production, such as capital, expands relative to other factors, eventually returns to that factor decline *ceteris paribus*. Even if decision makers make correct investment choices, it is increasingly difficult to substitute capital for labor as the number of high-return projects diminishes.[13] The fourth pillar of the administrative-command economy was exceptionally rapid capital accumulation. Figure 10.2 confirms the relatively rapid expansion of the Soviet capital stock up to the end. We expect high rates of return and more straightforward investment choices in a relatively poor country such as the USSR in 1930. It is clear that an industrializing country must build plants to produce steel, concrete, tractors, or machinery. As the economy matures, choices among alternate technologies become more complex. Diminishing returns does not predestine an economy to declining growth. Japan experienced rapid capital accumulation for a half century before experiencing declining growth.

Investment was one of the few decisions that the dictator, either Stalin alone or with the Politburo, made personally. Planners' preferences were expressed in the program of capital investments, which consisted of the investment budget, its financing, and the list of investment projects in the title list. The decision of how much to invest was more reasoned than most other economic decisions and the dictator's objective was to maximize investment in each year – a more primitive goal than maximizing investment over a period of time (see Chapter 4). The dictator used data on worker discontent, available finance, and real investment resources to make this decision, and optimization is reflected in the investment during the very period of initial capital accumulation. Figure 10.3 shows that the growth rate of industrial capital was exceptionally rapid throughout the entire Soviet period, but grew most rapidly during the initial industrialization drive. The return to this initial investment, however, was relatively low given that capital grew at a rate 3 percent faster than output. Only during the "Golden Growth" period of the 1950s did industrial output grow at the rate of the industrial capital stock.

Industrializing market economies obtained higher rates of return (output growing as fast or faster than capital stock) than did the USSR at

[13] Martin Weitzman, "Soviet Postwar Growth and Capital-Labor Substitution," *American Economic Review* 60, no. 4 (September 1970): 676–92.

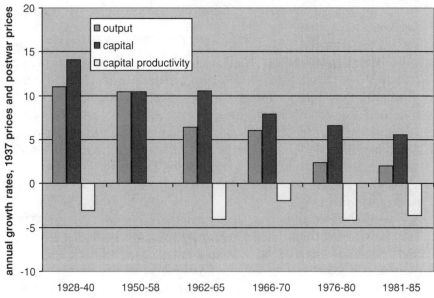

FIGURE 10.3. Industrial output, industrial capital, and capital productivity, USSR.

the start of their industrialization.[14] The likely explanation for relatively low initial Soviet returns was poor investment decisions. If so, the dictator would be culpable as the investment decision maker. The dictator, at times, did use economic considerations, such as basing the White Sea Canal's go-ahead on lowering its construction costs.[15] In 1925, Stalin had objected to the cost of the Dneprstroi metallurgy complex and favored alternate projects that cost one third as much,[16] despite the power lobbying for Dneprstroi. Stalin also applied economic logic to limit the destructive practice of approving more projects than could be built that created a lengthy queue of unfinished construction. Stalin agreed with Gosplan's opposition to investment fragmentation in 1932: "Is this excessive spreading of investment necessary? It is not!"[17] It was a theme Stalin continued at a 1947 Politburo meeting:

[14] Simon Kuznets, *Modern Economic Growth* (New Haven, Conn.: Yale University Press, 1966), 75–85; Arnold Harberger, "Evaluating Development Experiences in Latin America and East Asia," Third Senior Policy Forum, East West Center; Honolulu, Hawaii; May 1997.

[15] M. Y. Moryukov, "Penal Labor and the Economics of the White Sea Canal," in *The Economics of Forced Labor: The Soviet Gulag*, eds. P. Gregory and V. Lazarev (Stanford, Calif.: Hoover Institution Press, 2003).

[16] Lih et al., *Stalin's Letters to Molotov*, 87–91.

[17] Quoted in Davies and Khlevnyuk, "Gosplan," 41.

Comrade Stalin, upon hearing the deputy ministers of the Council of Ministers, said, "The plan is very swollen and is not within our capacity. We should give money only to projects that can be placed on line, and not spread it out among many projects. They are building all kinds of nonsense in new, unpopulated areas and they are spending a lot of money. It is necessary to expand old factories. Our dear projectors project only new factories and swell construction."[18]

These bursts of economic rationality did not prevent Stalin and the Politburo from making major investment blunders, such as the White Sea Canal whose depths were too shallow to support planned cargo transport and the Baikal Amur Mainline whose construction was stopped.[19] Stalin later became an ardent advocate of Dneprestroi, and his wholesale support for regional investment projects won him favor with regional Central Committee members during the conclusive battle with the right opposition in 1929. Throughout the period, there was intense political lobbying for investment projects, both by industrial ministers and by regions, which suggests that many investment choices were based on political considerations (see Chapters 4 and 5). Stalin offered the Ukraine major investments when he felt its political support shifting (see Chapter 3).

Politics aside, the rational choice of investment projects, even with the best of intentions, is not at all obvious in an administrative-command system, which cannot calculate rates of return.[20] Hence, Stalin's sense of economic rationality was often no better than anyone else's. If investment decisions were based primarily on political factors, the Soviet dictator would have been a power maximizer. If based primarily on economics (granted the lack of clarity on what was a good economic decision), the dictator was a stationary bandit. All investment decisions would be clothed in the garments of economic rationality. Few political leaders would admit that a major investment project was being funded purely for political reasons. In one specific investment case study (the distribution of vehicles), the dictator reveals himself clearly as a selfish dictator (see Chapter 8).

Although we cannot measure the extent of political investment decision making in the 1930s, it remained a constant feature of Soviet life. In 1982, when Gorbachev was the Politburo's representative of agriculture, he battled Gosplan over agriculture's investment allocation (his

---

[18] Notes from a Comrade Malyshev of a December 1947 Politburo meeting quoted in Khlevnyuk, "*Sovetskaia.*" 7.

[19] Khlevnyuk, "Economy of the Gulag," 123; Christopher Joyce, "The Karelian Gulag," in *The Economics of Forced Labor: The Soviet Gulag*, eds. P. Gregory and V. Lazarev (Stanford, Calif.: Hoover Institution Press, 2003).

[20] Grossman, "Scarce Capital," 311–43.

personal power base), prompting a former Gosplan official to remark, "His [Gorbachev's] mentality was typically Soviet – political will transcended common sense."[21]

Chapters 6 and 7 revealed the surprising lack of central control over investment decisions and the lack of information required to make rational investment decisions. Ministries refused to provide breakdowns of investment plans, they withheld investment cost budgets, and they bullied financial officials for attempting to enforce rules that were "threatening important government objectives" (see Chapter 6). Although the investment budget was centralized as was its distribution among agencies, the cumulated cost of approved projects did not correspond with the amount of investment finance, creating the peculiar Soviet phenomenon of "long construction" (*dolgostroi*), which turned the Soviet landscape into a graveyard of unfinished construction projects. Clearly, an unfinished project uses resources but makes no contribution to output. In the period 1955 to 1977, according to official Soviet statistics, the volume of unfinished construction varied from a low of 73 percent to 92 percent of total investment.[22] Chapters 6 and 7 also explain that the capital stock was poorly maintained. Enterprise pleas for capital repairs were routinely denied, creating a massive backlog of deferred maintenance.

Coercion: Can the System Work Without the Stick? The extreme concentration of power was not a historical accident. The Bolsheviks could attract only a small minority of votes under the most favorable of circumstances. Capital accumulation at the extreme rates and in the form desired by the dictatorship required extreme force in the countryside. The hundreds of thousands of producers (in ministries, branch administrations, and enterprises) had to be forced to obey administrative orders because exchanges were not founded on mutual agreement.

The major divide was between those who issued orders and those responsible for carrying them out – the "managers of production" in ministries and enterprises (see Chapter 6). For managers, failure meant reduced bonuses, public humiliation, firing, imprisonment, or even execution. Whereas the dictator or minidictator sought to impose optimally taut tasks on subordinates, managers wanted easy plans or a quiet life, the exact opposite of their superior. The tension between planner

---

[21] G. Zoteev, "The View from Gosplan," in Ellman and Kontorovich (eds.), *The Destruction of the Soviet Economic System* (Armonk, N.Y.: Sharpe, 1998), 88.

[22] *Ts.S.U. SSSR, Narodnoe Khoziaistvo SSSR v 1977 g.* (Moscow: Statistika, 1978), 362.

and producer constituted the basic principal–agent conflict described in Chapters 6 through 8. Producers lied, cheated, withheld information, demanded excessive materials from the "social fund," produced less than capacity, overcharged, and delivered to whomever they wished. As far as the dictator was concerned, the issue was not whether to use force, but how much force to apply to managers. The history of dictatorial coercion of producers is a pendulum swinging between too much and too little coercion. In 1929 and 1930, the first terror was imposed on managers and specialists as scapegoats for the disastrous results of the Great Break-Through. As experienced managers were fired and imprisoned, output collapsed; cooler heads prevailed in the Politburo (but not at the party grassroots), and a period of relaxation followed. The Great Purges of 1937 to 1938 again applied extreme coercion, wiping out a whole generation of managers. It is notable that the most rapid growth of the 1930s occurred between these two episodes of repression.

The amount of terror that the dictator could apply was limited. If too many were punished, too few would be left. If too few were punished, there would be no deterrence. Moreover, punishment is productive only if it improves performance. Virtually any manager, no matter how careful, could not fulfill all planned tasks, as is illustrated by an NKVD report of November 6, 1938:

In the factory territory there are 160 rail cars of finished products. Up to 20 rail cars contain defective products that have not been removed from the factory. Part of the products have been in the factory several years. In one section of the factory there are about 35 tons of a highly explosive acid. One hundred tons of P-12 are improperly stored, which in the case of explosion threatens not only the local population but also Moscow.[23]

It is unclear how a manager faced with increased coercion improves performance. The threat of punishment could be better neutralized not by improving performance (whatever that means), but by setting up scapegoats or cultivating protectors.

Even if the producer could fulfill the plan, the plan changed. By design and intent, the plans that producers were legally obligated to fulfill could be altered at any time in the normal process of plan corrections (see Chapter 8). The dictator could walk away from any plan at any moment, leaving the producer scrambling to fulfill a revised plan. Producers felt

---

[23] Simonov, *Voenno-Promyshlenny*, 111.

entirely justified in protecting themselves from arbitrary changes by issuing their own internal plans, delaying information necessary to prepare
preliminary plans, hiding capacity, and by overdemanding inputs. Planners had no idea what inputs were necessary when confronted with the
usual avalanche of requests.

If the hands of producers had been tied by detailed and closely monitored plans, producer misbehavior would be a less serious problem. But
the Politburo planned only a few products; Gosplan issued only general
plans to avoid responsibility. Most planned tasks originated in the ministry
or a main administration of the ministry; only the most important were
approved by the dictator. Hence, most economic decisions were made by
the managers of production themselves, a disturbing fact to a dictator
well aware of massive managerial opportunism. During periods of lesser
coercion, dictators had implicit contracts with producers: If you failed
to fulfill the plan, you could either designate a scapegoat or you would
be punished, but your punishment would be mild and reversible. During
periods of peak coercion, even the most distinguished of managers could
be imprisoned or executed. Punishment for plan failure was of symbolic
importance because plans, supposedly issued by the dictator, were by definition perfect. Failure, therefore, could be due only to human failure.

This basic principal–agent conflict set the stage for the discussion of
economic reform, which was allowed by the party starting in the mid-
1950s. Producers argued for increased freedom and reduced petty tutelage. Planners argued that producers must be kept under control by coercive means because they produced too little, demanded too much, charged
too high prices, and skimped on quality. It was easy to understand the
producers' position. They were held responsible, plagued by ill-conceived
plans and, even worse, by moving targets. The producer's lament remained
the same from 1930 to 1985. Orzhonikidze (1930): "From the decrees that
are being received I guess the impression is that we are idiots. They give
us every day decree upon decree, each successive one is stronger than the
previous and without foundation."[24] A chief defense contractor (speaking more than fifty years later) echoed Ordzhonikidze: "They would stick
their heads into every single issue. They would say: 'This must be so and
so.' We told them they were wrong, but they would demand that things
be done they way they said it should be done."[25] Producers complained

---

[24] Quoted in Khlevnyuk, *Stalin i Ordzhonikidze*, 32.
[25] Statement of deputy chairman of military industrial complex about the interference by
the Central Committee, in Ellman and Kontorovich, *Destruction*, 47.

that superiors gave orders but bore no responsibility. Ordzhonikidze (in an outburst in a Politburo meeting of August 1931): "You want to play the role of bureaucrat, but when my factories fall apart, it is I who must answer not those of you who engage in such 'serious discussions' here."[26] The deputy chairman of the military industrial plant echoed these sentiments some fifty years later: "They [the defense branch department of the Central Committee] would inquire why the plan isn't being fulfilled, they acted like they were another Council of Ministers. But they had more authority and none of the responsibilities."[27] Ministry officials as both recipients and issuers of orders, like Ordzhonikidze, could characterize their own orders as "beautiful," whereas the orders they received were without foundation.

The producers' remedy to unfounded orders from above was increased autonomy. Ordzhonikidze, already in 1931, offered to make heavy industry self-financing if he could make his own decisions. The same idea resurfaced with the Liberman proposals of 1961, and was partially implemented in 1964. Until the enterprise law of 1987, producer demands for greater independence were put off. Both sides had valid arguments. Producers, if left to their own devices, would underproduce and overdemand resources. Producers pointed to stupid, contradictory, and changing orders and excessive meddling preventing them from running their enterprises efficiently. This fifty-five–year stalemate ended with the enterprise law of 1987, which terminated ministry control of enterprises. In 1987 (the enterprise law) and in 1988 (the divorce of party from the economy), Gorbachev brought the Soviet Union to a watershed similar to 1929, when a quite different dictator, Stalin, concluded that a new system was needed. Gorbachev's reform-economy soothsayers (much like Stalin's Preobrazhensky) promised growth acceleration if enterprises were freed and the economy were opened to the outside world. Other pillars of the system, such as state ownership and the party's leading role, need not be touched. Clearly, a Stalin or a Politburo of the 1950s or 1960s would not have sacrificed key pillars of the system – planning and the party intervention. When Ordzhonikidze's 1931 reform proposal was sternly rebuffed, he had to fire scapegoats whom he blamed for such heretical ideas. Similar reform proposals in the 1960s received a more sympathetic hearing, but they were only given lip service. The Gorbachev reforms of 1987 and 1988 were for real.

[26] Khlevnyuk et al., *Stalin i Kaganovich. Perepiski*, 55.
[27] Ellman and Konotorovich, *Destruction*, 46.

The reform stalemate persisted for more than a half century for good reason. A state-owned enterprise left to its own devices would operate like a complex vehicle without a steering mechanism. It would be owned by everyone and hence by no one. In whose interests should it be operated? There were no organized markets in which to buy inputs and sell outputs. There were no scarcity prices to indicate what is cheap and what is expensive. For such an enterprise to function effectively, it had to operate in an entirely new institutional setting in which property rights were clearly defined, resources were allocated by markets, and the institutions of a market economy present. In other words, the Soviet economy would have to be transformed into a market economy. Barring such a transformation, it was unclear whether the economy would function better with coercion or as an independent unit. The Soviet Union, in fact, had a preview of the effect of reduced coercion. When planning targets were deliberately moderated in 1976 to encourage managers to use their resources more efficiently, output growth contracted but the efficiency of resource use did not improve.[28] The system's founders, coming off the experience of a quasimarket economy in the NEP, clearly understood more than fifty years earlier that enterprises must be coerced if resources are allocated administratively. The system had to wait more than fifty-five years for a dictator to come along who did not understand this basic principle. When coercion was dropped in 1987 and 1988, the result was the collapse of output and the eventual path away from reform toward transition.

The timing of Gorbachev's leap of faith is a puzzle. His predecessors had lived with slow rates of growth for more than a decade and a half. Two factors may have played a role: First, Gorbachev may have concluded that the USSR could not maintain its status as a military superpower without radical reform, particularly under pressure from a more belligerent U.S. President whose economy was recovering rapidly. Second, Gorbachev may have concluded that the economic problem was not one of growth but of efficiency. Virtually all our evidence speaks to the fact that the administrative-command system was geared for growth of physical outputs, not to the efficiency of their production. Soviet economists had promised since the mid-1960s that if enormous hidden reserves could be tapped, production could be raised by as much as 50 percent. True, the Soviet economy did have untapped reserves, but they were not to be unleashed through simple measures that did not require an end of the

[28] Gertrude Schroeder, "The Slowdown in Soviet Industry, 1976–1982," *Soviet Economy 1*, no. 1 (January–March 1985), 42–74.

administrative-command system. Gorbachev and his advisors lacked this rather basic insight.

Incentives and Effort Primitive capital accumulation was an overriding economic goal of the first Soviet dictator. A vast program of capital construction would lift the Soviet Union out of its relative backwardness and protect it from its encircling enemies. Stalin and his allies feared that capital accumulation would be held hostage by peasants, whose demands for a high standard of living would reduce national savings insofar as consumption is what is left of output after investment and other nonconsumption spending. If investment is to rise dramatically, consumption must fall. The burden of capital accumulation was to be placed directly on the peasantry. Industrial and construction workers were to be spared; their living standards could be maintained or even grow due to the sacrifices of the countryside. Insofar as peasants would not voluntarily "pay" for accumulation, extreme coercive power, concentrated in the dictator's hands, had to be applied. To ensure that priority workers received satisfactory real wages, Stalin personally devised a rationing system that would administratively direct limited consumer goods to "those who work for industrialization" (see Chapter 4). The hope was that all Soviet citizens would be buoyed by the prospect of a brighter future and would be transformed into "new Soviet men" willing to sacrifice for the good of society. The five-year plan should serve as a vision of the future, to provide the inspiration for the new Soviet man.

The brief experience with the militarization of labor during War Communism taught the Soviet leadership that workers must be offered carrots, or material rewards, if they are to work hard. People, unlike machines, bricks, and vehicles, care where and under what conditions they work, and they must feel that their rewards are commensurate with their efforts. If work conditions are unsatisfactory, workers will either find ways to change their place of work or, more simply, reduce their work effort. They will reduce their work effort if they are paid less than their fair wage, as defined in terms of social norms. The dictator's recognition of these economic laws of the workplace is seen in his use of the considerable investigative resources of the secret police to gather information on the mood of factory workers and farmers, not potentially valuable independent information on producers (see Chapter 4).

The effort to shift the burden of primitive accumulation to the peasants failed. As peasant real wages fell, so did labor effort and farm output. Even Stalin had to commence a campaign to ship manufactured consumer goods to the countryside and personally raised agricultural procurement prices. General foods shortages created a lucrative private market for agricultural goods that shifted income from the city to the countryside. Peasants destroyed their livestock, the prime source of tractive power, before entering the collective farm, and industry had to replace animal power with farm machinery. Stalin's hope of high rates of capital accumulation without industrial workers being paid less than their fair wage was not realized. The rapid rate of capital formation was accompanied by stagnant or declining living standards of all workers. Hence, the tradeoff between high investment and low consumption and its effects on effort had to be addressed.

Whereas Stalin had feared that peasants would hold his industrialization program hostage, it was the industrial workers who ended up, ironically, with this power. Chapter 4 showed that the extraordinary rates of capital accumulation between 1929 and 1932 pushed industrial workers below their fair wage, causing them to punish their employers with excessive turnover, absenteeism, and generally poor labor effort. The economy's capacity to produce investment goods dropped and the dictator, whose primary goal was the building of new plants and equipment, twice had to cut back on investment. The two investment downturns of the 1930s, during the very period of "building socialism," show the degree to which the nearly 100 million Soviet workers could dictate the pace of industrialization. A dictator who had accumulated history's most coercive political machine was helpless to counter the resistance of the entire work force.

To a dictator with considerable coercive power, the application of force to the factory floor was a tempting prospect. Perhaps workers could be forced to expend effort independently of economic rewards. Direct coercion of labor via imprisonment in the gulag was limited to less than 3 percent of the labor force.[29] Although the gulag system lasted more than two decades, it was eventually abandoned when the costs of coercion proved excessive relative to its benefits.[30] Shortly after the second investment downturn (1937), Draconian measures were applied to the general work force, and these measures remained on the books until the mid-1950s. Laws passed in December 1938 and January 1939 forced

---

[29] Alexei Tikhonov, "Gulag Structure and Size," in *The Economics of Forced Labor: The Soviet Gulag*, eds. P. Gregory and V. Lazarev (Stanford, Calif.: Hoover Institution Press, 2003).

[30] Paul Gregory and Alexei Tikhonov, "The End of the Gulag," in *The Economics of Forced Labor: The Soviet Gulag*, eds. P. Gregory and V. Lazarev (Stanford, Calif.: Hoover Institution Press, 2003).

workers to stay on their current jobs and treated tardiness and laziness as criminal offenses. Punitive laws are effective, however, only if they have a deterrent effect. During the peak enforcement of harsh labor laws (in 1940 and 1941), more than a half million workers were imprisoned and more than 3 million were punished by severe sanctions.[31] A country that was already short on labor could ill afford so many workers immobilized; thereafter, punitive laws were not enforced, and they were dropped from the books in March 1955.

Relations between the dictator and the work force were regulated in the postwar period by what David Granick termed a "job rights economy."[32] Carrots replaced sticks. Job rights represented an implicit contract that workers would not be fired or punished for bad work, and would automatically receive social benefits from the employer. If real wages did not rise, workers were free to follow the popular motto: "You pretend to pay us and we pretend to work." Although managers could still be held responsible for plan failures, workers were no longer threatened with charges of wrecking or sabotage. Considerable emphasis was placed on the "worker collective" as a means of attaching workers to their place of employment. Medical care, child care, vacations, and even consumer goods were provided by the "collective."

The dictator (the Khrushchev collective leadership) installed the job rights economy in the mid-1950s during a period of optimism that growth would be rapid. Increases in real wages would spur work effort, and the resulting economic growth could accommodate both rising investment and consumption. It should be noted that defense could throw a monkey wrench into this plan. With a rising share of defense spending, either investment or consumption would have to be sacrificed.

Figure 10.4 summarizes the relationship between consumption and investment from 1928 to Gorbachev's accession in March 1985. It shows that the doubling of the investment rate, which took place between 1928 and 1937, was financed at the expense of consumption and presumably effort. After the severe sacrifices of both consumption and investment during World War II, both consumption and investment grew rapidly between 1950 and 1960; however, as economic growth began to decline in the late 1960s, both consumption and investment growth dropped. The

---

[31] A. K. Sokolov, "The Period of Forced Labor in Soviet Industry: The End of the 1930s to the Mid-1950s," in *The Economics of Forced Labor: The Soviet Gulag*, eds. P. Gregory and V. Lazarev (Stanford, Calif.: Hoover Institution Press, forthcoming 2003).

[32] Granick, *Job Rights in the Soviet Union*, 1–8.

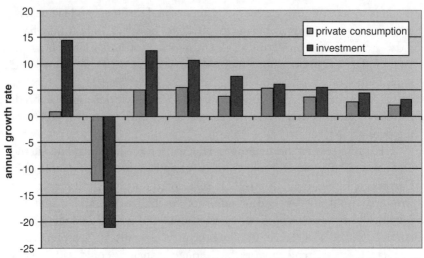

FIGURE 10.4. Relative growth rates of consumption and investment.

decline in investment growth, however, was more severe (from in excess of 10 percent to below 5 percent) than the decline in consumption growth (from 5 to 3 percent).

The dictator faced declining growth deprived of the weapon of coercion – the ability to demand sacrifice from the population. Although workers were "pretending to work," the dictator could not revive the punitive measures that had failed before. Various "new Socialist man" schemes, such as Stakhanovism, had been tried and failed. Gulags had proven too costly. There was no way to release the hidden reserves promised by reform economists. The one remaining option was to annul the implicit "job rights" contract. An experiment was begun in 1967 (called the Shchekino experiment) that allowed the worker collective to fire redundant workers and divide the saved labor costs among themselves. The experiment was ultimately abandoned because it threatened to generate unemployment and because of bureaucratic opposition.[33] The specter of unemployment was frightening to the Soviet leadership up to the very end. The Soviet military, for example, had to accept military ships built without guns because if they were rejected, the workers could not be paid their wages.[34]

---

[33] Ibid., 238–9.
[34] Ellman and Konotorovich, *Destruction*, 48.

The Soviet leadership, over the years, equated lack of labor discipline with labor turnover. Labor turnover was regarded as an *economic "bad"* because work experience specific to the job was lost when workers changed jobs. During the initial industrialization drive, industrial workers changed jobs on average between 1.2 and 1.5 times per year. In physically demanding occupations, like coal mining, they changed jobs between two and three times per year.[35] We lack labor turnover data for the remainder of the 1930s, but we do know that labor turnover peaked again in 1947 during the midst of Draconian laws against changing of jobs.[36] The installation of the job-rights economy apparently had the desired effect of lowering labor turnover to rates equivalent to Western Europe and slightly lower than in the United States.[37] The high turnover rates during periods of extreme restrictions show the inability of even the most highly coercive regime to control an entire labor force. The fact that Soviet labor turnover equivalent to that of Europe continued into the job-rights era shows the dictatorial regime's helplessness. "Planning from the achieved level" had frozen the economy into a fixed allocation of resources. There was no need for the labor force to reallocate itself, but it continued to do so.

Vested Interests The principal–agent conflict split the Soviet leadership into two camps – those that represented industrial or regional interests and those that represented the national interest. The latter were not held responsible for concrete results, although theoretically they could be removed by coup. Stalin and his allies, for example, feared removal during the crises of the first two years of forced industrialization and collectivization. Those representing narrow interests were held responsible for concrete results. If a ministry or a regional authority failed to meet its plan, the "one-man manager" would be held responsible.

Chapters 3 and 6 discussed governance. At least half of Stalin's Politburos represented industrial or regional interests. Ordzhonikidze represented heavy industry, Mikoian represented trade, Kaganovich represented transportation, republican party bosses represented the republic, and party bosses of major cities, such as Moscow and Leningrad, represented the city. Relatively few Politburo members were left to represent

---

[35] Davies, *Crisis and Progress*, 543; Davies, *The Soviet Economy in Turmoil*, 531.

[36] Sokolov, "The Period of Forced Labor." During this period, labor turnover was 64 percent in coal mining, 46 percent in the oil industry, and 34 percent in light industry. This high turnover is also associated with the famine of that period.

[37] Granick, *Job Rights in the Soviet Union*, 15.

encompassing interests. If the Politburo had truly been a collegial body in the 1930s, vested interests could have dominated the agenda through logrolling and vote trading. Stalin's stubborn opposition to lobbying within the Politburo – for lower outputs, more inputs, reduced grain deliveries, and the like – provided the backbone of support for encompassing interests, or at least Stalin's own version of national interests. As quoted in Chapter 6, Stalin admonished the Politburo that it is "disgusting if we begin to deceive each other" and berated colleagues who "could not stand up to the bureaucratic pressure of the minister of heavy industry. If you educate cadres in such a manner, we will not have one faithful party member left." As quoted in Chapter 3, he reminded the Politburo that they must "press on the economic bureaucracy and protect the interests of the state" and that "funds must be discussed in the interests of the state as a whole," not only in the interests of one Politburo member. The ease with which Politburo members organized majority votes for their own programs in Stalin's absence shows the potential for logrolling in the absence of a strong dictator. When the justice ministry issued a reprimand to the Ministry of Heavy Industry for low-quality production, its minister was able to muster a condemnation from the Politburo before an outraged Stalin intervened (see Chapter 3).

In the nested Soviet dictatorship, the conflict between encompassing and narrow interests proceeded at each level. The minister had to remind subordinates that they must deliver to all units within the ministry, not just to their own factories. The Minister of Heavy Industry had to rail against a "rotten and shady" supply official in his own organization whose only answer to customers was "We don't have anything. We can't give anything." The Minister of Light Industry had to call upon his various units "not to go separately to the inspection commissions or elsewhere, but going through the minister and together with the minister." Throughout the entire system, narrow interests looked after themselves, ignoring encompassing interests.

Mancur Olson argued that stationary bandits are transitory figures. Either through infirmity, death, or the gradual erosion of power, vested interests will eventually gain the upper hand.[38] In the Politburo, representatives of narrow interests will eventually compromise with each other to render decisions that are not in the national interest. Ministers and regional authorities will use their economic power to gain concessions. Weaker industrial ministers will be unable to resist the pressures of their

[38] Olson, "The Devolution of Power," 31–40.

subordinates. It is only a matter of time before growth and productivity are forgotten as industrial and regional groups battle for society's economic rents.[39]

The Soviet Union was indeed governed by collective leaderships after Stalin. Although there were a few strong leaders, such as A. Kosygin, who appeared to represent encompassing interests, the typical post-Stalin Politburo consisted of a mix of those representing encompassing and narrow interests. For example, the Brezhnev Politburo of 1976 included four party leaders of republics or large cities, and most of the candidate members were republican leaders.[40] Moreover, as the Central Committee became more complex and developed massive sectoral departments, the leaders of those departments – such as Gorbachev, the head of the agricultural department, or the head of the military-industrial complex – became lobbyists for their industries. The stronger their economic branch, the stronger their economic power.[41] The lobbying actions of giant department monopolies became compelling, as stated by one observer in the 1980s, not only failed to carry out the will of the center, but also increasingly imposed their own interests on the center. The more powerful the ministry (e.g., medium machine building, which united the whole nuclear industry), the more the government danced to its tune.[42]

Stalin's legacy of the all-powerful General Secretary remained intact throughout the Soviet period. The General Secretary continued to have the final say, and it was this tradition that saved the Soviet Union from chaos. However, this legacy created problems when the General Secretary was infirm or senile (e.g., during the final years of Brezhnev and throughout all of Chernenko's term), and it did allow Gorbachev to unleash measures unpopular with the Politburo that destroyed the system itself.

Vested industrial and regional interests are better kept at bay in a strict vertical hierarchy (see Chapter 1). If they do not engage in horizontal transactions and are vertically loyal, they have little power independent of the dictator. They receive materials through vertical orders; as loyal subjects, they deliver their output to users designated by the center. The dictator can retain his highly centralized coercive system simply by

---

[39] Boettke, *Calculation and Coordination*, 176–90; Boettke and Anderson, "Soviet Venality," 37–53.

[40] Paul Cook, "The Political Setting," Joint Economic Committee, Soviet Economy in a New Perspective (Washington, D.C.: U.S. Government Printing Office, October 1976), appendix.

[41] Ellman and Konotorovich, *Destruction*, 46–8, 88.

[42] Y. Yasin, "Getting the Details Wrong," in *The Destruction of the Soviet Economic System* (Armonk, N.Y.: Sharpe, 1998), 149.

enforcing vertical loyalty. A key message of this book is that the highly centralized system carried with it the seeds of its own destruction. The more highly centralized the decision-making process, such as centrally set supply and delivery plans, the more unreliable the official system. Confronted with unfulfillable plans and unreliable supplies, producers had to turn to unofficial transactions. Horizontal unofficial networks developed as alternate sources of power and provided a base for vested interest coalitions. Although the dictator should have fought against horizontal transactions, they were actually encouraged. The Politburo expected ministers to get things done by any means possible. Ministers told enterprise managers that good managers "know how to organize things and produce the required results" irrespective of the official obstacles (see Chapter 7) and that the plan must be fulfilled "at any price." Thus, the dictator was tacitly encouraging the very behavior that would destroy centralized power. Stalin and the Politburo encouraged ministers to work things out themselves and discouraged administrative solutions (see Chapter 7). The minister would tell managers who did not receive official supplies: "You are placing the blame on others when you yourself are to blame" (see Chapter 7). The ministry recognized that "for all practical purposes, the enterprises with their large staffs of supply agents determine the allocation of resources" (see Chapter 7). All of these actions were implicit instructions to engage in horizontal transactions.

Like the continued high turnover of workers during periods of Draconian labor laws, the disobedience of direct orders by managers of production revealed the dictator's impotence. Important producers ignored direct orders and usually got away with it. They, as the producer of vital resources, could always plead that the dictator's order or rule would spoil production. Direct orders to financial authorities to limit credits were not implemented because horizontal transactions created obligations that a lender of last resort could not avoid. On the production side, the problem was presented starkly as "obey the rule and lose production." On the financial side, the choice was presented as bankruptcy (and more efficiency in the long run) versus the immediate loss of the bankrupt enterprise's production (see Chapter 9). Despite a highly centralized and coercive system, the producer appeared to have the upper hand.

It is tempting to join the chorus that the move from the stationary bandit to corporate dictatorship is to blame for declining Soviet growth and performance. Of the three feasible models of dictatorship – we have excluded scientific planning as infeasible – only the stationary bandit model is postulated to produce good economic performance. The power-maximizing dictator and the vested-interest model both yield poor performance. In the selfish-dictator model, political decision making dominates. The corporate model's goal is the distribution of economic rents, not growth and development.

The rapid Soviet growth of the 1930s has been too readily attributed to the stationary bandit. Merely asserting that a stationary bandit directs economic activity does little to explain how such a "miracle" occurs – how a few party elders or a party congress can cause thousands of enterprises to produce and deliver millions of products according to their dictates. Mises explained how markets, through their knowledge of time and place, perform this miracle, but no Soviet text explains how a ten-person Politburo, supported by fewer than three hundred employees (not counting the nine hundred-person Gosplan), could pull off this miracle throughout the 1930s.

Clearly, in the absence of a market, an administrative-planned economy requires some purpose other than political power or rent distribution. Stalin's decision making, although often improvisational, provided consistent purpose in three areas. First, there was consistent opposition to alternative sources of power, especially from powerful production units. Throughout the period, ministries and their main administrations were split up into smaller and smaller independent units, and even petty attempts at empire building were rebuffed. Second, the stationary bandit and his successors were consistent in their priorities, largely unwritten but understood by all. Heavy industry was more important than light industry and, within heavy industry, defense had the highest priority. Priorities played a vital role in bringing some sense of order to the widespread ad hoc interventions. The third source of consistency was the stationary bandit's drive for capital accumulation, discussed previously.

How well an economy coordinated by a stationary bandit works depends on the quality of the stationary bandit's decision making. Economic systems require rational economic decision making, such as not undertaking activities whose costs exceed their benefits. In market economies, private enterprises seek to maximize profits or shareholder value. The stationary bandit's decision-making criteria are more difficult to identify. He should set the optimal investment rate and distribute investment to projects that promote economic development. Producers should be forced to produce the maximum quantities of outputs with the minimum expenditure of resources, such as optimal grain-collection targets that extract maximum grain without starving too many people, creating too much political unrest, or requiring the shipment of scarce tractors.

For the stationary bandit to make rational decisions, he requires enormous information and reasonable decision-making criteria. Our previous discussion of investment choice pointed out that the dictator's choice of investment projects was often bad and politically motivated, although we cannot draw overall conclusions as to their rationality. We do know that the stationary bandit's information came directly from opportunistic agents in low volumes and in distorted forms. In reality, the stationary bandit, like everyone else, operated behind a thick veil of ignorance. Enterprises met production targets with half the materials they swore were essential. Materials were allocated by intuition and feel rather than scientific methods.

Once the stationary bandit's (hopefully rational) decisions are made, they must be imposed on reluctant and opportunistic producers, who may have entirely different agendas. As quoted in Chapter 7, Stalin intensely feared that "the center's directives will remain completely on paper" or that key agencies "will not learn about the Politburo's decision, and it will get bogged down in the bowels" of the bureaucracy. The most powerful industrial-minister dictator had to "curse" and "act like an animal" and "drive to hysterics" the ones who have to carry out the directive in order to get things done by subordinates (see Chapter 7). Stalin dreamed in vain of a "Commission of Fulfillment" that would force fulfillment of orders. Orders had to be issued through a vertical hierarchy after preparation by agents, such as the State Planning Commission, which was not responsible for bad plans (i.e., those that could not be fulfilled). If the dictator was wildly optimistic, the planner had to be equally optimistic, even if the plan was clearly unfulfillable. A basic message of this book is that the real resource allocation was carried out by the producers themselves. The output and supply balances were prepared by the ministries and their branch administrations. Even in the case of highly centralized goods, such as vehicles, the power of the producer was surprisingly great. Decisions were formally made at a centralized level, but the actual producers had the flexibility to make most of society's key resource-allocation decisions themselves. If resource-allocation decisions are being made by the producers in the absence of market allocation, it is hard to conceive of a reasonable result.

During periods of greatest economic tension, such as the Great Break-Through, agents were forced to do things against their will – such as peasants delivering grain at low prices to the state, industrial workers working for less than fair wages, and enterprises being confronted with excessively taut plans. Presumably, at these moments of extreme tension, opportunistic behavior would be most rampant. Under these conditions, it is unclear whether even the most directed, dedicated, and centered stationary bandit would be able to impose his will on reluctant agents. For this reason, it is not clear that a stationary bandit can produce better performance than other economically "inferior" models of dictatorship.

The Dictator Has No Clothes! The Great Break-Through began with great enthusiasm. Party leaders, the rank and file of the party, many managers, and even more workers believed in the cause, which was being directed by an all-knowing party. As they became involved in the process, they began to question the wisdom of party actions. Workers writing on factory walls – "The USSR is a generous country. It sends grain abroad, but is itself hungry" – could not understand why Stalin would export grain when they were hungry (see Chapter 4). Although Lenin had argued that the party make only the most important decisions, Stalin spent as much time worrying about streets and monuments in Moscow, whether a highway should have two or four lanes, or the price of bread as about basic economic and foreign policy. By reserving the right to change any decision, no matter how trivial, all decisions ultimately ended up on his desk. The ridiculousness of this situation must have been apparent to the dictator's immediate circle and to an ever-larger circle of observers.

The myth of party omniscience could not survive the hard reality of arbitrary, incompetent, and petty decision making. The fact that the party allowed itself to remain in the quagmire of petty decision making suggests either a lack of understanding or a complete understanding that their power to make even the most trivial of decisions was indeed their true source of legitimacy. It is no wonder that ideology ceased to play a real role in Soviet society after Stalin, although the rituals of ideology remained intact. One must consider the damage to an administrative-command system of the loss of an ideological foundation.

The administrative-command system was installed, in the first place, because the Soviet leadership, from Lenin in 1917 to Gorbachev in 1985, believed that enlightened decision making by a dedicated, small group of individuals would be superior to the "anarchy of the market." Force and coercion were justified to impose a rational resource allocation. This force was imposed so that Stalin could decide that 40 to 50 rather than 35 to 40 tons of flax should be produced or that factory X should send 10 tons of steel to factory Y, or that a party official in Georgia should get a Buick. Real questions had to be asked about the system's legitimacy.

I I

Conclusions

We began with Joseph Berliner's question: Did the Soviet administrative-command economy fail because of poor leaders (the jockey) or because of the system itself (the horse)? In the past ten chapters, we examined the working arrangements of the Soviet administrative-command economy using its own records from the formerly secret state and party archives. We examined the system in its first two decades. If the jockey was the problem, we would have to conclude that the system could have survived and perhaps prospered with a better jockey. Lenin was incapacitated in December 1922, well before the blueprints for the new system were drawn. Stalin and his team was the first jockey because the system was created under their direction.

If Stalin were the sole jockey, then it could be argued that the system would have worked quite differently and its excesses avoided. We reject such a Stalinocentric interpretation, although we do not deny that Stalin was the principal architect. The Bolshevik Party, whose claim on authority was not challenged after the civil war, had no choice but a totalitarian system. Its core values called for planning, state ownership, and primitive accumulation. We accept the Hayekian proposition that an administrative system based on these core values inevitably breeds a Stalin-like figure. Perhaps this Stalin alter ego would have refrained from excessive terror and purges, but the economy would probably not have been managed much differently. Hence, the system would have been operated in essentially the same way under a Trotsky or a Lenin who survived to an active old age.

Although Stalin was first the "first among equals" and then without equal, he could not manage the system on his own. Stalin could not have achieved his political victories without his allies. After the expulsion of

Trotsky (whose unpopularity made this easy), Stalin required the support of the other Politburo members to oust his remaining opponents. Stalin had to wait another seven years before he could move against his own team and, by that time, the system was clearly in place. During this "period of creation," Stalin relied heavily on his allies; Stalin's policy recommendations could still be voted down occasionally; and he insisted on at least the appearance of collegial decision making.

The growing concentration of political power in Stalin's hands also would have occurred with a Stalin alter ego. Party democracy could not be trusted in a system that required coordinated direction, as the excesses of local party officials during the 1929 to 1930 purges demonstrated. Moreover, the grassroots constituted the ultimate threat to the dictator. Stalin and the Politburo derived their legitimacy as "representatives of the working class" from acquiescence by the rank and file of the party. Hence, they reacted with fear and panic to any move to take issues directly to party members. Moreover, a strong leader was required to create the impression of a united front. The legitimacy of Politburo decisions could only be preserved if they were unanimous. The earlier principle of party discipline, which permitted internal debate and then a rallying around the majority opinion, was abandoned because it allowed opponents of Politburo policies to execute them. "True" Bolsheviks could not be indifferent. A strong leader was required to resolve conflicts and break ties within the ruling elite, a role that Stalin's colleagues turned over to him.

The Soviet administrative-command system had many jockeys, not just one. The jockey was not simply Stalin or the Politburo, but the hundreds or thousands of "smaller Stalins" that populated the "nested dictatorship." The superior at each level behaved as a despot relative to subordinates as did the superior's own "dictator." The administrative-command system consisted of layer upon layer of dictators, each harassing subordinates. Nested dictatorship is a genetic consequence of the need to delegate authority, differences in objectives, and the unequal distribution of information between superiors and subordinates. Each superior faces an uncooperative and untruthful subordinate who can only be moved to positive action by force. One dictator alone could bring little force to bear. Each dictator requires minidictators under him to coerce action at the next level. If the top person disappears from the scene, he is replaced by a clone well versed in the art of coercion. The position within an organization determined the behavior of individuals, not the reverse. As officials were shuffled from one position to another, they shifted gears to represent the interests of the new organization. Rapid industrialization

270   *The Political Economy of Stalinism*

fanatics became immediate proponents of moderation as they moved from encompassing positions, such as control commissions, to positions that served narrow interests, such as industrial ministers. In the 1930s, there were four chairpersons of Gosplan and three ministers of heavy industry. Although the personalities and backgrounds of these high officials were quite different, changes in leadership had no noticeable effect on the way the institution functioned.

This book has shown that Stalin or the Politburo could make pitifully few decisions. The Politburo personally made and executed three types of decisions consistently in the 1930s – the investment budget, the distribution of foreign exchange, and grain collections. Other decisions were made by subordinates. Even the most immediate subordinates, such as Gosplan, made relatively few decisions – at most ten thousand of the millions of resource-allocation decisions made annually. The vast majority of resource-allocation decisions were pushed down to lower levels, where they were made by opportunistic agents. The nested dictatorship was thus a battlefield between superiors and subordinates, where the superior (dictator) imposed force and coercion on his agent to limit opportunistic behavior. The dictators (note: plural) imposed coercive orders on their subordinates based on incomplete and inaccurate information, and the subordinate was confronted with a mass of confusing, ill-devised, and apparently arbitrary instructions for which he was personally responsible.

The administrative-command system was run by three different regimes prior to 1985 – by Stalin, Khrushchev, and the Brezhnev-Andropov-Chernenko dynasty. Despite a greater willingness to experiment with minor changes, the administrative-command system continued to function in almost exactly the same way after Stalin. Although the administrative-command system was assembled in great haste and by trial and error, it was remarkably durable and immutable. The inconsequentiality of the jockey is reflected in the fact that Stalin's successors did not change the administrative-command economic system. Aware of the system's many defects, they placed themselves on an uncomfortable treadmill of reforms, which questioned the system's viability without offering the prospect of real improvement. The Great Purges of 1937 to 1938 liquidated virtually all of the old Bolsheviks, who were replaced by a new generation of younger leaders. The Communist Party, which had been led by old Bolsheviks in their fifties and sixties, was now headed by those in their thirties and forties. The new generation's first real opportunity to exercise power was the Nineteenth Party Congress of 1952 – a congress noted for its ratification of the status quo.

Stalin's successors did not change the administrative-command system because there was no solution to the principal–agent problem between the dictators and the agents. Producer–agents could rightly argue that they were inundated with arbitrary and destructive orders; if only they could be left to make their own decisions, the vast hidden reserves of the economy could be released. Their dictators, on the other hand, could point out that the agents were opportunistic and they lied, cheated, and operated their enterprises in their own interests. Both were correct. A totally independent Soviet enterprise would have operated without direction either by command or from a nonexistent market. The enterprise dictators could not improve the quality of their decision making because they would continue to lack accurate information and they would lack rational criteria on which to base their decisions. The administrative-command system did not allow a solution to the principal–agent problem.

The result was a low-level equilibrium. Virtually all economic instructions were based on the principle that this year's activity would be last year's plus a minor adjustment. The massive imbalances were resolved by arbitrary interventions by the thousands of "dictators" empowered to intervene. There could be no general rules because they would have interfered with the authority of officials to intervene. The only remaining glue to the system was an implicit system of priorities that provided some degree of order. In effect, the economy was frozen in place as the other world economies progressed.

The Soviet administrative-command system emphasized rituals such as May Day parades on Red Square, five-year plans promising a better future, party congresses, and the myth of party omniscience up to its last days. Producers were more likely to obey orders they regarded as legitimate; workers were more likely to sacrifice if they believed the vision of a better future. The Great Break-Through began with enthusiasm. Party leaders, the rank and file of the party, many managers, and even more workers believed in the cause that was being directed by an all-knowing party. As they saw the process in action, however, they would naturally question its wisdom. Workers could not understand why Stalin would export grain when they were hungry. Managers would wonder why they had to fulfill contradictory orders. Party leaders would puzzle over why Stalin spent as much time worrying about streets and monuments in Moscow, whether a highway should have two or four lanes, or the price of bread as about basic economic and foreign policy. By reserving the right to change any decision, no matter how trivial, all decisions ultimately ended up on the desks of dictators such as Stalin, the Politburo, the minister, or the regional party official. The absurdity of this situation must have been apparent to the dictator's immediate circle and to an ever-larger circle of observers. The fact that the party allowed itself to remain in the quagmire of petty decision making suggests either a lack of understanding or a complete understanding that the power to make even the most trivial of decisions was indeed their true source of power.

The leaders of the administrative-command system, from Lenin in 1917 to Gorbachev in 1985, preferred administrative decisions to the "anarchy of the market." In the early years of building socialism, coercive power was perhaps easier to justify as citizens saw new factories, canals, and railways being completed. Totalitarian decision making became more difficult to justify when the system settled into a routine. Although the totalitarian foundation of the system survived Stalin, its ideological basis did not. The true challenge did not come from a potential political rival; rather, its alternative had been from the very beginning a completely different economic system – a system in which markets, not politicians, allocate resources. Gorbachev unwittingly brought to life the beginnings of this alternative system in 1987 and 1988, when he freed enterprises from state and party intervention.

Appendix A: Archival Sources

Our primary archival resources consist of the following collections: First, the secret "Red Files" (*Liternye opisi*, GARF fond 5446 – or "lettered files") of the chancellery of the highest state body, the Council of People's Commissars, shed considerable light on the actual workings of the Soviet political and economic system of the 1930s. The relatively compact Red Files contain only documents classified as secret at the time of registration. The general criterion was to include all documents containing any mention of party, army, or police. Because local, regional, and national party leaders were typically involved in decision making, the Red Files cover the most sensitive issues of the period – monetary policy and finance, hard currency and reserve funds, foreign trade and foreign relations, the activities of Soviet representatives abroad, military affairs, the secret police (OGPU/NKVD), gulag operations, resettlement of ethnic minorities, catastrophes, and strategic commodities, including armaments and dual-use commodities like fuels and vehicles. From 1938 onward, the volume of Red Files increases because of increased demand for secrecy.

Second, the files of various industrial ministries and of their main industrial administrations located primarily in RGAE were used to study industrial ministries and their dealings with central authorities. Given that large collections exist for every ministry, we focused on the two dominant ministries: the Ministry of Heavy Industry and the Ministry of Light Industry. Given that the industrial departments of each ministry (twenty-six departments for heavy industry and eighteen departments for light industry) maintained separate archives, often larger than the ministry's own archive, we limited our investigation to one heavy-industry department, metals, and to several light industry departments.

The third key collection consists of the archives of the Party Control Commission, which was empowered to investigate wrongdoing by party members. This collection contains files on thousands of investigations that shed light on the informal workings of the Soviet system, including black markets, informal networking, corruption, and other illicit activities that were supposed not to exist in a socialist society.

The fourth collection is the archive of the Ministry of Interior, denoted by the infamous acronyms OGPU, NKVD, or MVD, including its main administration for labor camps, gulag. These massive archives cover virtually all aspects of penal labor, imprisonments, and other forms of punishment. They include gulag production and construction targets, production and cost statistics, the hiring out of penal labor, camp mortality statistics, escape reports, and so on. These files include a number of internal assessments of the workings of the gulag and internal plans for major reforms, leading up to the 1953 amnesty.

We also used the archival fond of the Central Committee of the Communist Party of the Soviet Union (CPSU), which includes materials related to party congresses and conferences; statistics on the evolution of the party and the political elite, including the party censuses of 1921 and 1927; documents of Central Committee back offices including finance; propaganda, and ideology mostly from the late Stalin era (1939–1953).

Other collections used include the personal funds of prominent party and industrial leaders and smaller collections, such as the Nineteenth Party Conference file, which contains all documents related to the 1952 congress.

Appendix B: The Structure of the State

Organization of Ministries

NKTP and NKLP, like their superior SNK, were divided into branch and functional departments managed by a central administration under the minister. Starting with thirteen glavks in 1932, NKTP had, by 1938, thirty-four glavks to manage specific sectors, such as metals or coal, machinery of different types, defense products, and shipbuilding. The number of NKTP's functional departments rose from thirteen in 1932 to twenty-four in 1938 (Table B.1). Judging from employment figures, the main business of NKTP was *managing production*, not setting prices or monitoring financial results. In 1938, NKTP's average glavk employed 153 persons for a total of 5,195 employees; the average functional sector employed 62 persons for a total of 1,488 employees. The two largest glavks were Coal Administration (Glavugol'), employing 339 persons, and Metals Administration (Gump), employing 287 persons. NKTP's central office employed only 35 persons. NKTP was a major producer of military goods and had a large "special sector" of around five hundred persons to manage defense and other secret production.[1] In all, NKTP employed 7,375 persons: 5,592 in glavks and 1,137 in functional sectors.

Unlike NKTP, NKLP was a union-republican ministry with headquarters in both Moscow and in the republics. In 1933, NKLP directly employed 2,547 persons, 1,737 of whom were in the Moscow office and 810 were in its republican branches (Tables B.2a and B.2b). NKLP also lists

---

[1] It is difficult to break out the "special sector" from a residual category of 599 employees. We assume that most of this residual worked in the special sector.

TABLE B.I. *Staff of NKTP, 1930s*

	April 1932	November 1932	January 1934	1938
Number of Branch Glavks	13	14	29	34
Number of Functional Sectors	13	12	18	24
Number of Employees in Branch Glavks	2,955	2,938	3,120	5,195
Number of Employees in Functional Sectors	1,096	816	1,012	1,488
Average Number of Employees in One Branch Subdivision	227	210	108	153
Average Number of Employees in One Functional Subdivision	84	68	56	62

Note: In some cases, such division into functional and branch subdivisions is ambiguous (title, glavk, or sector does not always reflect the purpose of subdivision).

employment figures for "Greater NKLP," including the administrations of all-union trusts (3,989)[2] and trading and procurement organizations (1,932). The trading and procurement administrations employed forty-seven thousand persons. Thus, NKLP was half as large as NKTP using the most narrow definition; about as large as NKTP, including top managers of trusts and supply organizations; and it eclipsed NKTP if all trading and procurement employees were included.

The ministry glavks mirrored the structure of the ministry. NKTP's metal administration (Gump) was divided into seven branch administrations, which managed specific types of products, and seventeen functional sectors that managed planning, personnel, finance, capital construction, and prices. Unlike the ministry, most employees of glavks were in functional and not branch departments. In March 1937, Gump employed 15 persons in its central administration, 164 persons in its seven branch administrations (e.g., metals, ores, fired bricks), and 352 persons in its seventeen functional departments (Table B.3). The preponderance of employment in functional activities is explained by the fact that the glavks carried out market functions, such as supply, transport, and production allocation. Some 55 percent of functional employees were active in such quasimarket activities.[3]

[2] These all-union trusts apparently were converted into glavks by the second half of the 1930s, because they have the same designations as the later glavks, such as cotton textiles, linen, wool, silk, and artifical leather.
[3] In the 1930s, the industrial ministries were responsible for construction; there was no

TABLE B.2A. *NKLP Staff, First Half Year–1933*

	Average Number of Workers for the Quarter		
	1st Quarter	2nd Quarter	Total for the 1st Half Year
NKLP Personnel	2,757	2,520	2,547
NKLP USSR	1,705	1,668	1,737
Republican NKLPs	1,052	852	810
Trusts	3,865	4,062	3,989
Industrial Personnel	3,244	3,445	3,370
Construction and Construction Supply Personnel	621	617	619
Sales and Supply Enterprises	48,183	51,102	49,642
Central Personnel	1,947	1,917	1,932
Sales and Supply Network	46,236	49,185	47,710
Other Enterprises	12,161	12,298	12,229
Enterprises Subordinated to NKLP	181	212	210
Total	67,147	70,194	68,617

In 1937, Gump had 595 employees to oversee the production of 27 million tons of pig iron, 18 million tons of steel ingots, 13 million tons of rolled steel, 3 million tons of nickel, and so on.[4] Organizing the production and distribution of the hundreds of factories that produced these products with fewer than six hundred employees appeared to be a forbidding task.

Table B.4 shows that Gump was staffed mostly by engineers, planners, and economists, who accounted for more than half of Gump's staff. Accountants, bookkeepers, and lawyers accounted for less than 15 percent of employment. Tables B.5a, B.5b, B.6a, and B.6b show the organization of two NKLP glavks in the second half of the 1930s: the Main Administration for Leather Footwear and the Main Administration for Knitting Industry. NKLP glavks were smaller than NKTP glavks. Leather footwear, one of its larger glavks, employed at its peak 217, and knitting employed at its peak 115. In those years in which supply and delivery

separate ministry of construction. Capital construction was supervised by the Administration of Capital Construction (called UKS), whereas construction was carried out by construction departments within glavks. The director of construction was usually the deputy director of the glavk. The special status of capital construction is evidenced by the fact that, in 1933, one third of Gump's personnel was in capital construction.

[4] Zaleskii, *Stalinist Planning*, 551. These figures are for 1937.

TABLE B.2B. *Wage Bill of NKLP, First Half of 1933 (Rubles)*

	1st Quarter			2nd Quarter			Total, First Half Year		
	According to the Plan	Actual	% of Plan	According to the Plan	Actual	% of Plan	According to the Plan	Actual	% of Plan
Personnel of NKLP	2,887	2,863	99.2	2,611	2,522	96.6	5,257	5,158	98.1
NKLP USSR	1,740	1,753	100.7	1,747	1,711	98.0	3,487	3,465	99.4
Republican NKLPs	1,146	1,110	97.6	864	811	94.1	1,769	1,693	95.6
Personnel of Trusts	3,367	3,226	95.8	3,177	3,292	103.6	6,545	6,520	99.6
Industrial Personnel	2,678	2,668	99.6	2,530	2,670	105.5	5,210	5,340	102.5
Construction and Construction Material Personnel	688	558	81.1	646	621	96.1	1,335	1,180	88.4
Sales and Supply Enterprises	28,273	25,486	90.1	28,193	26,090	92.5	56,466	51,577	91.3
Central Personnel	1,898	1,817	95.7	1,777	1,783	100.3	3,676	3,600	97.9
Sales and Supply Network	26,375	23,669	89.7	26,415	24,307	92.0	52,790	47,976	90.9

| Other Enterprises | 8,332 | 8,263 | 97.3 | 8,678 | 8,504 | 96.9 | 17,010 | 16,767 | 97.0 |
| Enterprises Subordinated to NKLP | 139 | 127 | 87.7 | 141 | 135 | 92.9 | 281 | 262 | 89.8 |

Source: RGAE, 7604.1.1166, 107–10, "Data about quantity and expenditure for total wage bill in people's commissariats trusts, sales and supply, and other enterprises of NKLP of the USSR for the first half year of 1933."

Notes: Republican ministries – NKLP of Russian SSR, NKLP of Ukrainian SSR, NKLP of Turkmenian SSR, NKLP of Georgia, NKLP of Armenia, NKLP of Azerbaijan. There are no data for NKLP of Uzbek SSR.

Industrial trusts – cotton, linen, woolen, silk, hemp-jute, leather-ersatz, trust "Dubitel," trust "Kotonin," trust "Podsobnih Predpriatiy," trust "Trikiglavmashina," trust "Detal'mashina." The data of personnel of the cotton industry trust are not complete for the first quarter, which encompasses 66% and in second quarter encompasses 79% of planned trusts. The data of silk trusts are available only for Soiuzshelkotrest without Sredazshelk. Trust "Trikiglavmashina" was organized only in the second quarter of 1933. There are no data for trust "Uchpolittekhoborudovanie."

Sales and supply enterprises – Soiuzkhlopkosbyt, Soiuzkhlopkotekhsnab, L'nosnabsbyt, Soiuzsherst'sbyt, Soiuzzagotsherst', Sherst'tekhsnab, Shelksnabsbyt, Trikotazhsnabsbyt, Kozhsnabsbyt, Soiuzzagotkozh, Zagotdubitel', Spichsnab, Spicheksport, Steklofarforsnabsbyt, Soiuzshveysbyt, Pen'kosnabsbyt, Soiuzutil', Steklofarforsyr'e. There are no data for Soiuzkhlopkosyr'e; Pen'kosnabsbyt was organized on January 4, 1933, Steklofarforsyr'e was organized on January 4, 1933.

Other enterprises – workshop of Kozhsnabsbyt, workshop of Soiuzkhlopkosbyt, Kul'tpromproekt, Proektmashlegprom, Gosproektstroylegprom, Orgtekstil', NISes, VUZes and technical schools, *Legkaia Industriia* newspaper, NTS of construction industry. There are no data for Orgkozha; coverage of NISes includes 76% in the first quarter, VUZes and technical schools – 63% in the first, and 66% in the second quarter.

Enterprises subordinated to NKLP – Avtobaza, Canteen No. 1, Canteen LIT "A," shoe workshop, administration of NKLP building construction.

279

TABLE B.3. *The Staff and Structure of Gump, March 1937*

Subdivision	Staff	%
Central		
Management	8.0	1.3
Apparat	7.0	1.2
Industry Branch		
Metallurgy department	21.0	3.5
Pipe department	29.0	4.9
Coke-chemical department	54.0	9.1
Refractory department	39.0	6.6
Nonmetal mineral department	6.0	1.0
Consumer goods department	5.0	0.8
Functional Department		
Iron-ore department	10.0	1.7
Planning department	18.0	3.0
Finance department	12.0	2.0
Accounting department	18.0	3.0
Equipment department	22.0	3.7
Supply department	38.0	6.4
Metal sales department	121.0	20.3
Pricing department	3.0	0.5
Labor department	10.0	1.7
Personnel department	6.0	1.0
Special department	6.0	1.0
Department of transportation	10.0	1.7
Department for internal transfers of metal products	9.0	1.5
Power and fuel department	13.0	2.2
Mechanization department	7.0	1.2
AKhO	39.0	6.6
Secret service department	15.0	2.5
Chief engineer office	5.0	0.8
Administration of Capital Construction (UKS)	35.0	5.9
Maintenance staff	29.0	4.9
Total	595.0	100.0
Total branch glavks and sectors	7.0	
Total functional sectors	17.0	
Total number of employees in branch glavks and sectors	164.0	
Total number of employees in functional sectors	352.0	
Average number of employees in one branch subdivision	23.4	
Average number of employees in one functional subdivision	20.7	

TABLE B.4. *Gump's Employees and Their Distribution by Profession,*
March 1937

Profession	Employees	%
Managers	7	1.2
Engineers	123	20.7
Planners	80	13.4
Economists	80	13.4
Financiers	21	3.5
Accountants	59	9.9
Commodity Experts	66	11.1
Secretaries	76	12.8
Officials	56	9.4
Maintenance Staff	22	3.7
Lawyers	5	0.8
Total	595	100.0

Note: The classification of professions in some cases is ambiguous. The most disputable is attribution to planning department employees of sales, supply, and equipment departments.

departments were included in glavk employment, they constituted a large percentage of total glavk employment. In 1937, for example, the supply and delivery department constituted more than half of the employment in the leather footwear glavk. Throughout the 1930s, supply and delivery departments were reshuffled. At times, they were independent ministerial organizations; at other times, they were subordinated to the glavk.

A vast amount of human resources was devoted to supplies and to deliveries. The supply department (*snabzhenie*) was responsible for obtaining materials and equipment. The delivery department (*sbyt*) was responsible for the allocation of output among various users. In both Gump and in the leather footwear glavk, more than half of personnel worked on supply and deliveries. NKLP's central administration of trade and supply organizations employed as many people as the main Moscow office. We do not know how many enterprise employees worked in supply and distribution, but the number must have been large.[5] It is exactly these resources that replaced the market in an administrative-command system.

[5] Berliner, *Factory and Manager*; Granick, *Management of Industrial Firms.*

TABLE B.5A. *Staff of Leather Footwear Administration of NKLP, 1935–1939*

	1935	1937	1939
Management			
Managers	3	6	3
Supervisors			7
Out of branches	2		
Industry Branch			
Leather branch	13	11	
Footwear branch	12	10	
Manufacturing-administrative department of footwear enterprises			7
Technical department			11
Maintenance team			5
Department of republican and local industry			6
Functional Department			
Planning department	19	19	19
Financial and accounts department	8	16	13
Personnel department	6	7	3
Labor and wage department		4	10
Fuel and energy group	4	3	
Transportation department			2
Sales department		59	39
Supply department		49	23
Support department	9	9	13
Special sector	4	6	6
Capital construction department		12	9
Total	80	217	176

TABLE B.5B. *Staff of Leather Footwear Administration by Branch and Functional Divisions*

	1935	1937	1939
Total of branch subdivisions	2	2	4
Total of functional subdivisions	6	10	10
Branch subdivision staff	25	21	29
Functional subdivision staff	50	184	137
Average number of workers in branch subdivision	12.5	10.5	7.3
Average number of workers in functional subdivision	8.3	18.4	13.7

Note: Calculated using 1935 – RGAE, 7604.9.145, 80–3; 1937 – RGAE, 7604.9.155, 57–66; 1939 – RGAE, 7604.9.168, 60–5.

TABLE B.6A. *Staff of Knitting Industry Glavk, 1935–1939*

	1935	1937	1939
Management			
Managers	3	7	7
Support workers			8
Workers out of sector and group	3		
Industry Branch			
Manufacturing-administrative department			7
Technical department			10
Department of republican industry			4
Managerial sector of machine-building plants			4
Planning-manufacturing sector	22	12	
Functional Department			
Planning sector			14
Financial sector	2	7	4
Accounts department			10
Personnel department	3		2
Labor and wage department			8
Maintenance department			8
Supply and sales team		7	
Supply department			10
Sales department			4
Organization of capital construction		7	11
Special sector			4
Total	38	40	115

TABLE B.6B. *Staff of Knitting Administration by Branch and Functional Divisions*

	1935	1937	1939
	Absoulte Value		
Total of branch subdivisions	1	1	4
Total of functional subdivisions	2	3	10
Branch subdivision staff	22	12	25
Functional subdivision staff	5	21	75
Average number of workers in branch subdivision	22	12	6.25
Average number of workers in functional subdivision	2.5	7	7.5

Note: Calculated using 1935 – RGAE, 7604.9.145, 80–3; 1937 – RGAE, 7604.9.155, 57–66; 1939 – RGAE, 7604.9.168, 60–5.

TABLE B.7. *Schedule of Staff Downsizing in People's Commissariat and Central Establishments of USSR*

Organization Name	Approved Staff, 1933	Approved Staff, 1934
NKTP (Commissariat of Heavy Industry)	9,266	7,360
Central Apparat	6,771	5,266
Local Bodies	2,495	2,094
NKLP (Commissariat of Light Industry)	1,800	1,450
NKPS (Commissariat of Transportation)	4,296	3,908
NKLes (Commissariat of Timber Industry)	1,426	1,210
Central Apparat	1,101	930
Local Bodies	325	280
NKSovkhoz (Commissariat of State Farms)	1,668	1,090
Central Apparat	1,008	760
Local Bodies	660	330
NKZem (Commissariat of Agriculture)	4,954	4,348
Central Apparat	4,619	4,047
Local Bodies	335	301
NKVneshtorg (Commissariat of Foreign Trade)	1,979	1,813
Central Apparat	484	420
Authorized Apparat	512	470
State Quality Inspection	180	160
Hunting Inspection	53	53
Customs	750	710
NKSnab (Commissariat of Supply)	2,460	200
NKSviazi (Commissariat of Communication)	3,091	3,066
Central Apparat	586	526
Local Bodies	2,505	2,540
Gosplan	750	693
TsUNKhU (Central Statistical Committee)	11,796	11,050
Central Apparat	583	530
Republican UNKhU	1,282	1,120
Regional UNKhU	3,002	2,700
City Inspection	800	800
District Inspection	6,129	5,900
NKF (Commissariat of Finance)	612	583
NKID (Commissariat of Foreign Affaires)	334	330
NKVod (Commissariat of Water Transportation)	863	650
Sudotrans (Ship Transport Association)	322	265
GlUprGrazhVozdFlota (Administration of Merchant Marines)	554	529
Glavsermorput' (Administration of Northern Waterway)	153	216
GUKFP	172	146

(continued)

TABLE B.7. *(continued)*

Organization Name	Approved Staff, 1933	Approved Staff, 1934
Procurement Committee of the Council of People's Commissars	11,375	10,263
Central Apparat	357	305
Authorized Apparat in Republics and Districts	1,615	1,455
District Bodies	9,403	8,503
Committee of Radio Installation and Broadcasting	750	736
Supreme Court	285	285
Central Apparat	65	65
Local Transport Court	220	220
Office of Public Prosecutor	608	625
Central Apparat	238	255
Local Transport Office of Public Prosecutor	370	370
Establishments of the Council of People's Commissars and the State Defense Council	7,940	7,636
Chancellory	230	233
Pricing Committee	7	5
Committee of Producer's Cooperative	15	14
Reserves Committee	52	57
Goods Fund Committee	20	18
Authorized Apparat of Goods Fund Committee	54	54
Fuel Committee	15	16
Transport Committee	14	9
All-Union Migration Committee	38	38
Local Bodies of All-Union Migration Committee	72	85
Invention Committee	29	27
Innovation Bureau	153	153
Scientist Assistance Commission	51	51
Lenin's Department of Scientist Assistance Commission	12	10
Scientific House in Moscow	84	73
Scientific House in Leningrad	33	33
Old Scientific People's House	11	11
Standardization Committee	101	98
Gosarbitrazh (State Arbitration Committee)	59	59
Control Center of Measures and Weights	82	75
Local Bodies of TsUMERVES	836	600
Central Commission of Crop Capacity	40	36
Local Bodies of Commissions of Crop Capacity	1,375	1,375
United Secretariate of Committees	21	35
Medical Department of the Kremlin	1,070	1,105
Dining-room	97	102

(continued)

TABLE B.7. *(continued)*

Organization Name	Approved Staff, 1933	Approved Staff, 1934
Establishments of Medical Department (based on special funds)	158	164
Academy of Science	3,211	3,100
Establishments of Central Executive Committee	3,189	3,148
Secretariat	120	115
Finance Department	45	47
Economic Administration	105	150
Economic Department	63	63
Educational Institutions Committee	31	20
Commission of High Education	96	90
Academic Committee	1,916	1,768
Komzet	8	8
Municipal Economy Council	47	50
Sports Council	61	61
Civil Department of the Kremlin Commandant's Office	600	673
Commandant's Office of Bolshoy Theatre	40	43
Chairman Secretariat	13	16
Fire Station of Bolshoi Theatre	44	44
All-Union Committee of Agricultural Sciences	96	86
Central Department of Hydrometeorological Service	252	217
EKOSO of Central Asia	138	138
Trade Union Apparatus	25,922	24,302
Committee of Soviet Control	8,620	2,714
Central Bodies	620	350
Local Bodies without Serving Staff	8,000	2,364
Total Entire State Apparatus	105,671	90,854

Source: L 113–114 Decree of SNK #810 from 4.11.34 – About downsizing of the staff and management costs on economic and cooperative organizations in 1934.

Exhibit B-1

The Structure of NKTP in 1937

Secretariat of the Minister and his Deputies

Minister's Control Commission

Ministry Administration

Branch Units:

1. Main Administration of Coal Industry
2. Main Administration of Petroleum Industry
3. Main Administration of Divot Industry

4. Main Administration of Energy
5. Main Administration of Ferrous Metallurgy (GUMP)
6. Main Administration of Special Steel
7. Main Administration of Tube-Rolling Industry
8. Main Administration of Ore Industry
9. Main Administration of Coke–Chemical Industry
10. Main Administration of Refractory Industry
11. Main Administration of Copper Industry
12. Main Administration of Zinc and Lead Industry
13. Main Administration of Nickel and Tin Industry
14. Main Administration of Aluminium Industry
15. Main Administration of Gold and Platinum Industry
16. Main Administration of Rare Metal Industry
17. Main Administration of Nitrogen Industry
18. Main Administration of Chemical Industry
19. Main Administration of Dye Industry
20. Main Administration of Synthetic Filament
21. Main Administration of Plastic Industry
22. Main Administration of Gas Industry and Industry of Synthetic Scarce Fuels
23. Main Administration of Building Industry
24. Main Administration of Construction Material Industry
25. Main Administration of Cement
26. Main Administration of Technical Glass Industry
27. Main Administration of Mining and Fuel Machine Building Industry
28. Main Administration of Building Hydroelectric Power Stations
29. Main Administration of Harvesting and Woodworking
30. Main Administration of Geology

Functional Units:
1. Planning Department
2. Personnel Department
3. Finance Department
4. Accounts Department
5. Department of Blue-Collar Workers and Wages
6. Capital Construction Department
7. Sales Department
8. Housing Department
9. Economic-Reporting Department
10. Military Department
11. Bureau of Inventions

12. Bureau of Standardization
13. Legal Department and Arbitration
14. Bureau of Complaints
15. Central Administrative Board of Supply
16. Central Administrative Board of Transportation
17. Central Administrative Board of Education

Other Units
  1. Technical (Science) Council
  2. State Inspection of Mines
  3. Other State Inspection
  4. Administration of Militarized Special Units and Fire Brigades

Source: SNK decree 10.11.1937 – "NKTP Charter."

Exhibit B-2

The Structure of Gump

Management and Secretariat of Glavk

Manufacturing Departments:
  Department of Quality Steel
  Department of Ferrous Metallurgy
  Coke Department
  Iron-Ore Department
  Refractory Department
  Department of Steel Constructions
  Direct Ferrum Recovery Committee

Functional Departments:
  Planning Department
  Finance Department
  Supply Department
  Department of Equipment
  Personnel Department
  Transport Department
  Department of Improvement

Administration of Capital Construction:
  Technical Planning Inspection
  Work Planning Department
  Estimate and Controlling Group
  Department of Equipment

Bibliography

Archival Material and Bibliographies of Archival Material

References to archival material are given in the following notation: Archive Fond.Register.File: Page.

GARF – Gosudarstvenny Arkhiv Rosiskoi Federatsii (State Archive of the Russian Federation).

RGAE – Gosudarstvenny Arkhiv Ekonomiki (Russian State Archive for the Economy).

RtsKhINDI – Rosiiskii Tsentr Khraneniia i Izucheniia Dokumentov Noveiishei Istorii (Russian Center for the Preservation and Study of Documents of Contemporary History) renamed **RGASPI** (Russian State Archive of Social and Political History).

KPK files – Kommissia Partiinogo Kontrolia. (Documents of the Party Control Commission).

Kratkiy Putevoditel': Fondy i Kollektsii Sobrannye Tsentral'nym Partiinym Arkhivom (Gosudarstvennaia Arkhivnaia Sluzhba Rossiiskoi Federatsii. Moscow: Blagovest, 1993.

State Archival Service of the Russian Federation, a Research Guide: I. Guide to Collections. Edited by William Chase and Jeffrey Burds. Moscow: Blagovest, 1994.

Sobranie Zakonov SSSR. 1931, 1932.

Svod Zakonov i Postanovlenii Raboche-Krest'ianskogo Pravitel'stva. 1937, 1938.

Za Industrializatsiu, 1933.

Ekonomicheskaia Zhizn' (EZ), no. 8., 1933; no. 24, 1933; no. 36, 1933.

Vestnik Pravleniia Gosbanka (VPG), 1930, no. 8, 15–16, 30, 31.

Biulletin Gosarbitrazha, no. 4, 8–9.

Denezhnoe Obraschenie i Kredit v SSSR, 1938.

Encyclopedia of Russia and the Soviet Union. New York: McGraw Hill, 1961.

Mezhdunarodny Fond Demokratii Aleksandra Iakovleva. Available at: *http://www.idf.ru*

Published Material

Akerloff, George, "Gift Exchange and Efficiency Wages: Four Views," *American Economic Review* 74, no. 2 (May 1984).

Akerloff, George, and Janet Yellen. "The Fair Wage–Effort Hypothesis and Unemployment," *Quarterly Journal of Economics* 105, no. 2 (May 1990).

Arnold, A. *Banks, Credit, and Money in Soviet Russia*. New York: Columbia University Press, 1937.

Arrow, Kenneth J. "Little's Critique of Welfare Economics," *American Economic Review* 41 (December 1951).

Atlas, M. S. *Razvitie Gosudarsvennogo Banka SSSR*. Moscow: Gosfinizdat, 1958.

Averianov, D. V. *Funktsii i Organizatsionnaia Struktura Organov Gosudarsatvennogo Upravleniia*. Kiev: Nauka, 1979.

Bajt, Alexander. "Investment Cycles in European Socialist Economies: A Review Article," *Journal of Economic Literature* 9, no. 1 (March 1971).

Barnett, Vincent. "The People's Commissariat of Supply and the People's Commissariat of Internal Trade." In *Decision Making in the Stalinist Command Economy, 1932–37.* Edited by E. A. Rees. London: MacMillan, 1997.

Batyrev, V. M., and V. K. Sitnin. *Planovaia Kreditnaia Sistema SSSR*. Moscow: Ogiz, 1945.

Beliik, Y. "Changes in the Central Committee Apparatus." In *The Destruction of the Soviet Economic System*. Armonk, N.Y.: Sharpe, 1998.

Belova, Eugenia. "Economic Crime and Punishment." In *Behind the Façade of Stalin's Command Economy*. Edited by Paul Gregory. Stanford, Calif.: Hoover Institution Press, 2001.

Belova, Eugenia, and Paul Gregory. "Dictators, Loyal and Opportunistic Agents: The Soviet Archives on Creating the Soviet Economic System," *Public Choice*, 113, no. 3–4 (December 2002), 265–86.

Berelovich, A., and B. Danilov. *Sovetskaia Derevnia Glazami VChK-OGPU-NKVD*. Vol. 1. 1918–1922. Moscow: Rosspen, 1998.

———. *Sovetskaia Derevnia Glazami VChK-OGPU-NKVD*. Vol. 2. 1923–1929. Moscow: Rosspen, 2000.

Bergson, Abram. *The Real National Income of Soviet Russia Since 1928*. Cambridge, Mass.: Harvard University Press, 1961.

———. *The Economics of Soviet Planning*. New Haven: Yale University Press, 1964.

Berliner, Joseph. *Factory and Manager in the USSR*. Cambridge, Mass.: Harvard University Press, 1957.

———. "Soviet Initial Conditions: How They Have Affected Russian Transition." Paper presented at the International Conference, Moscow University, Harvard Davies Center and University of Houston International Economics Program, "Soviet Economy in the 1930s–1970s," Zvenigorod, Russia; June 22–24, 2001.

———. "The Contribution of the Soviet Archives." In *Behind the Facade of Stalin's Command Economy*. Edited by Paul Gregory. Stanford, Calif.: Hoover Institution Press, 2001.

———. *The Innovation Decision in Soviet Industry*. Cambridge: The MIT Press, 1976.

Bleaney, Michael. "Investment Cycles in Socialist Economies: A Reconsideration," *Oxford Economic Papers* 43, no. 3, 1991.

Boettke, P. J. *Calculation and Coordination: Essays on Socialism and Transitional Political Economy*. London: Routledge, 2001.

———. *Why Perestroika Failed: The Politics and Economics of Socialist Transformation*. New York: Routledge, 1993.

Boettke P. J., and G. Anderson, "Soviet Venality: A Rent-Seeking Model of the Communist State." *Public Choice* 93, 1997.

Bogolepov, M. N. *Sovetskaia Finasovaia Sistema*. Moscow: Gosfinizdat, 1947.

———. *Finansovy Plan piatiletia*. Moscow: n.p., 1929.

Bolshaia Sovetskaia Entsiklopedia, vol. 7. Moscow: Sovetskaia Entsiklopedia, 1975.

Bogomolova, E. V. *Upravlenie Sovetskoi Ekonomiki v 20-e gg: Opyt Regulirovaniia I Samoorganizatsii*. Moscow: INION RAN, 1993.

Boldin, Valery. *Ten Years That Shook the World: The Gorbachev Era as Witnessed by his Chief of Staff*. New York: Basic Books, 1994.

Carr, E. H. *The Bolshevik Revolution 1917–1923*, vol. 2. New York: MacMillan, 1951.

Carr, E. H., and R. W. Davies. *Foundations of a Planned Economy, 1926–1929*, vol. 1. London: MacMillan, 1969.

Chuev, F. I. *Sto Sorok Besed s Molotovym*. Moscow: Terra, 1991.

———. *Tak Govoril Kaganovich*. Moscow: Otechestvo, 1992.

Coase, Ronald. "The New Institutional Economics," *American Economic Review* 88, no. 2 (May 1998).

Conyngham, William J. *The Modernization of Soviet Industrial Management*. Cambridge: Cambridge University Press, 1982.

Cook, Paul. "The Political Setting," Joint Economic Committee, Soviet Economy in a New Perspective. Washington, D.C.: U.S. Government Printing Office, October 1976.

Danilov, V. P. *Rural Russia under the New Regime*. Bloomington: Indiana University Press, 1988.

Davies, R. W. *Crisis and Progress in the Soviet Economy, 1931–1933*. Basingstoke, England: MacMillan, 1996.

———. "Making Economic Policy." In *Behind the Façade of Stalin's Command Economy*. Edited by Paul Gregory. Stanford, Calif.: Hoover Institution Press, 2001.

———. *The Development of the Soviet Budgetary System*. Cambridge: Cambridge University Press, 1958.

———. *The Socialist Offensive: The Collectivization of Agriculture*, vol. 1. Cambridge, Mass.: Harvard University Press, 1980.

———. *The Soviet Collective Farm, 1929–1930*. Cambridge, Mass.: Harvard University Press, 1980.

———. *The Soviet Economy in Turmoil, 1929–1930*. Cambridge, Mass.: Harvard University Press, 1989.

———. "Short-Term Credit in the USSR: Some Post-War Problems." *Soviet Studies 5*, no. 1 (1953/54).

———. "Why Was There a Soviet Investment Cycle in 1933–37?" "Information and Decision Making in the Soviet Economic Bureaucracy," University of Warwick Summer Workshop, July 16, 1999.

Davies, R. W., and O. Khlevnyuk. "Gosplan." In *Decision Making in the Stalinist Command Economy, 1932–37.* Edited by E. A. Rees. London: MacMillan, 1997.

———. "Stakhanovism, the Politburo and the Soviet Economy." Paper presented at conference on "Stalin's Politburo, 1928–1953," European University Institute, Florence; March 30–31, 2000.

Desai, Padma, and Todd Idson. *Work without Wages: Russia's Nonpayment Crisis.* Cambridge, Mass.: MIT Press, 2000.

Directorate of Intelligence, *Handbook of Economic Statistics, 1991.* CPAS 91–10001, September 1991.

Dobb, Maurice. *Soviet Economic Development Since 1917,* 5th ed. London: Routledge & Kegan Paul, 1960.

Domar, Evsey. "A Soviet Model of Growth." In *Essays in the Theory of Economic Growth.* New York: Oxford University Press, 1957.

Dyker, David. *The Future of Soviet Economic Planning.* Beckenham, Kent, England: Croon Helm, 1985.

Ekonomicheskaia Entsiklopedia: Promyshlennost' i Stroitel'stvo. Moscow: Gosudarstvennoe Nauchnoe Izdatel'stvo, 1962.

Ellman, Michael. "Did the Agricultural Surplus Provide the Resources for the Increase in Investment in the USSR During the First Five-Year Plan?" *Economic Journal 85*, no. 4 (December 1975).

Ellman, Michael, and Vladimir Kontorovich. *The Destruction of the Soviet Economic System.* Armonk, N.Y.: Sharpe, 1998.

Erlich, Alexander. *The Soviet Industrialization Debate, 1924–28.* Cambridge, Mass.: Harvard University Press, 1960.

Fortescue, Stephen. "The Technical Administration of Industrial Ministries." Soviet Industry Science and Technology Work Group, Centre for Soviet and East European Studies, University of Birmingham, England; February 1986.

Franchetti, Mark. "Stalin Drew Cartoons of His Victims' Fate," *London Sunday Times,* July 8, 2001.

Gaddy, C., and B. Ickes. "Russia's Virtual Economy," *Foreign Affairs* (September–October 1998).

Gerschenkron, Alexander. *Economic Backwardness in Historical Perspective* (Cambridge, Mass.: Harvard University Press, 1962).

Getty, J. Arch. *Origins of the Great Purges.* Cambridge: Cambridge University Press, 1985.

Getty, J. Arch, and Oleg Naumov. *The Road to Terror: Stalin and the Self-Destruction of the Bolsheviks, 1932–1939.* New Haven: Yale University Press, 1999.

Gorlin, Alice C. "The Power of Industrial Ministries," *Soviet Studies 37*, no. 3 (1985).

Gorlin, Alice, and D. P. Doane. "Plan Fulfillment and Growth in Soviet Ministries," *Journal of Comparative Economics* 4, no. 3 (1983).

Gosplan USSR, Metodicheskie Ukazania k Rasrabotke Gosudarstvennykh Planov Ekonomicheskogo i Sotsial'nogo Razvitiia SSSR. Moscow: Economika, 1980.

Granick, David. *Job Rights in the Soviet Union: Their Consequences.* Cambridge: Cambridge University Press, 1987.

———. *Management of Industrial Firms in the USSR.* New York: Columbia University Press, 1954.

———. *Soviet Metal Fabricating and Economic Development.* Madison: University of Wisconsin Press, 1967.

———. "The Ministry as the Maximizing Unit in Soviet Industry," *Journal of Comparative Economics* 4, no. 3 (1980).

Gregory, Paul. *Before Command: An Economic History of Russia from Emancipation to the First Five-Year Plan.* Princeton, N.J.: Princeton University Press, 1994.

———. *Russian National Income, 1885–1913.* New York: Cambridge University Press, 1982.

———. "Russia and Europe: Lessons of the Pre-Command Era." In *European Economic Integration as a Challenge to Industry and Government.* Edited by R. Tilly and P. Welfens. Berlin: Springer, 1996.

———. *Restructuring the Soviet Economic Bureaucracy.* Cambridge: Cambridge University Press, 1990.

———. *Socialist and Nonsocialist Industrialization Patterns.* New York: Praeger, 1970.

———. "Soviet Defense Puzzles: Archives, Strategy, and Under-Fulfillment," *Europe–Asia Studeis* 55, no. 61 (September 2003).

Gregory, Paul, and Robert Stuart. *Russian and Soviet Economic Structure and Performance,* 6th ed. Reading, Mass.: Addison Wesley, 1998.

———. *Russian and Soviet Economic Structure and Performance,* 7th ed. Boston: Addison Wesley, 2001.

———. *Soviet and Post-Soviet Economic Structure and Performance,* 5th ed. New York: Harper Collins, 1994.

———. *Soviet Economic Structure and Performance,* 2nd ed. New York: Harper and Row, 1981.

———. *Soviet Economic Structure and Performance,* 4th ed. New York: Harper & Row, 1990.

Gregory, Paul, and Andrei Markevich. "Creating Soviet Industry: The House That Stalin Built," *Slavic Review,* 61 (Winter 2002), 787–814.

Gregory, Paul, and Alexei Tikhonov. "The End of the Gulag." In *The Economics of Forced Labor: The Soviet Gulag.* Edited by Paul Gregory and Valery Lazarev. Stanford, Calif.: Hoover Institution Press, forthcoming.

Grossman, Gregory. "Scarce Capital and Soviet Doctrine," *Quarterly Journal of Economics* 67, no. 3 (August 1953).

———. "The Second Economy of the USSR," *Problems of Communism* 26 (September–October, 1977).

Harberger, Arnold. "Evaluating Development Experiences in Latin America and East Asia," Third Senior Policy Forum, East West Center; Honolulu, Hawaii; May 1997.

Harris, J. R. *The Great Urals: Regionalism and the Evolution of the Soviet System.* Ithaca, N.Y.: Cornell University Press, 1999.

Harrison, Mark. "National Income." In *The Economic Transformation of the Soviet Union, 1913–1945.* Edited by R. W. Davies, Mark Harrison, and S. G. Wheatcroft. Cambridge: Cambridge University Press, 1994.

———. "The Peasantry and Industrialization." In *From Tsarism to the New Economic Policy.* Edited by R. W. Davies. Houndsmills, England: MacMillan, 1990.

Harrison, M., and B. Y. Kim. "Plan, Siphoning, and Corruption in the Soviet Command Economy." Warwick Economic Research Paper Series, no. 606, 2001.

Harrison, M., and N. Simonov. "Voenpriemka: Prices, Costs, and Quality Assessment in Defence Industries." In *The Soviet Defence-Industry Complex from Stalin to Khrushchev.* Edited by J. Barber and M. Harrison. London: MacMillan, 1998.

Hayek, F. A. "Socialist Calculation: The Competitive Solution." *Economica*, n.s., 7 (May 1940).

———. *The Road to Serfdom.* Chicago: Chicago University Press, 1944.

———. *The Road to Serfdom,* 50th Anniversary ed. Chicago: Chicago University Press, 1994.

———. "The Use of Knowledge in Society." *American Economic Review* 35 (1945).

Hewett, E. A., *Reforming the Soviet Economy: Equality Versus Efficiency.* Washington, D.C.: Brookings Institution, 1988.

Hollander, Paul. "Which God Has Failed," *The New Criterion on line* (cited April 15, 2002). Available at *www.newcriterion.com.*

Holzman, Franklyn. "Foreign Trade." In *Economic Trends in the Soviet Union.* Edited by Abram Bergson and Simon Kuznets. Cambridge, Mass.: Harvard University Press, 1963.

———. "Financing Soviet Economic Development." In *Capital Formation and Economic Growth.* Edited by Moses Abramovitz. Princeton, N.J.: Princeton University Press, 1955.

———. "Soviet Inflationary Pressures, 1928–1957," *Causes and Cures, Quarterly Journal of Economics* 74, no. 2 (1960).

Howitt, Peter. "Looking Inside the Labor Market: A Review Article," *Journal of Economic Literature* 40, no. 1 (March 2002).

Hunter, Holland. "Optimal Tautness in Developmental Planning," *Economic Development and Cultural Change* 9, no. 4 (July 1961).

Hunter, Holland, and Janusz Szyrmer. *Faulty Foundations: Soviet Economic Policies, 1928–1940.* Princeton N.J.: Princeton University Press, 1992.

Inkeles, Alex, and Raymond Bauer. *The Soviet Citizen.* Cambridge, Mass.: Harvard University Press, 1959.

Istoriia Kommunisticheskoi Partii Sovetsogo Soiuza. Moscow: Polizdat, 1959.

Joskow, Paul. "Contract Duration in Long-Term Contracts: Empirical Evidence from Coal Markets." In *Case Studies in Contracting and Organization*. Edited by Scott Masten. New York: Oxford University Press, 1967.

Joyce, Christopher. "The Karelian Gulag." In *The Economics of Forced Labor: The Soviet Gulag*. Edited by Paul Gregory and Valery Lazarev. Stanford, Calif: Hoover Institution Press, forthcoming.

Junker, James. *Socialism Revised and Modernized: The Case for Pragmatic Market Socialism*. New York: Praeger, 1992.

Kantorovich, V. I. *Sovetskie Sindikaty*. Moscow: n.p., 1928.

Karcz, J. "Thoughts on the Grain Problem," *Soviet Studies 18*, no. 4 (April 1967).

Katz, Lawrence. "Efficiency Wages Theories: A Partial Evolution." In *NBER Macroeconomics Annual 1986*. Edited by Stanley Fischer. Cambridge: MIT Press, 1986.

Keren, Michael. "The Ministry, Plan Changes, and the Ratchet Effect in Planning," *Journal of Comparative Economics 6*, no. 4 (1982).

Khanin, G. *Sovetsky Ekonomichesky Rost: Analiz Zapadnykh Otsenok*. Novosibirsk: Eko, 1993.

Khlevnyuk, O. V. *Politburo: Mekhanizmy Politicheskoi Vlasti v 1930-e gody*. Moscow: Rosspen, 1996.

———. "Sovetskaia Ekonomicheskaia Politika na Rubezhe 40-50 Godov i Delo Gosplana," working paper; Florence, Italy; March 2000.

———. *Stalin i Ordzhonikidze: Konflikty v Politburo v 30-e gody*. Moscow: Izdatel'skiy Tsentr Rosiia Molodaia, 1993.

———. "The Economy of the Gulag." In *Behind the Façade of Stalin's Command Economy*. Edited by Paul Gregory. Palo Alto, Calif.: Hoover Institution Press, 2001.

———. "The People's Commissariat of Heavy Industry." In *Decision Making in the Stalinist Command Economy, 1932–37*. Edited by E. A. Rees. London: MacMillan, 1997.

Khlevnyuk, O. V., and R. Davies. "The End of Rationing in the Soviet Union 1934–1935," *Europe-Asia Studies 51*, no. 4, 1999.

Khlevnyuk, O. V., R. Davies, L. P. Kosheleva, E. A. Ris, and L. A. Rogovaia. *Stalin i Kaganovich. Perepiski. 1931–1936 gg*. Moscow: Rosspen, 2001.

Khlevnyuk, O. V., A. V. Kvashonkin, L. P. Kosheleva, and L. A. Rogovaia. *Stalinskoe Politburo v 30-e gody*. Moscow: AIRO-XX, 1995.

Knight, F. "Lippmann's the Good Society," *Journal of Political Economy*, December 1936, cited by Boettke, *Calculation and Coordination: Essays on Socialism and Transitional Political Economy*. London: Routledge, 2001.

Kornai, Janos. *Economics of Shortage*. Amsterdam-New-York-Oxford: North-Holland Publishing Company, 1980.

Kratkaia Istoria SSSR. Moscow: Nauka, 1972.

Krueger, Gary, and Marek Ciolko. "A Note on Initial Conditions and Liberalization During Transition," *Journal of Comparative Economics 1*, no. 4 (December 1998).

Kuznets, Simon. "A Comparative Appraisal." In *Economic Trends in the Soviet Union*. Edited by Abram Bergson and Simon Kuznets. Cambridge: Harvard University Press, 1963.

———. *Modern Economic Growth*. New Haven: Yale University Press, 1966.

Lazarev, Valery. "Evolution of the Soviet Elite and Its Post-Communist Trans-formation." Conference "Initial Conditions and the Transition Economy in Russia," University of Houston; Houston, Texas; April 19–21, 2001.

Lazarev, Valery, and Paul Gregory. "Commissars and Cars: The Political Economy of Dictatorship," *Journal of Comparative Economics* 31, no. 1, 2003.

———. "The Wheels of Command," *Economic History Review* 55, 2 (May 2002).

Lenin, V. I. *The Development of Capitalism in Russia*. Moscow: Progress, 1977.

———. "Report on Concessions at a Meeting of the Communist Group of the All-Russia Central Council of Trade Unions, April 11, 1921." In *Collected Works*, 4th English Edition, vol. 32. Moscow: Progress Publishers, 1965.

Levine, Herbert. "The Centralized Planning of Supply in Soviet Industry." In *Comparisons of the United States and Soviet Economies*. Washington, D.C.: U.S. Government Printing Office, 1959.

Lewin, Moshe. *Russian Peasants and Soviet Power*. London: Allen & Unwin, 1968.

Lih, Lars, Oleg Naumov, and Oleg Khlevnyuk. *Stalin's Letters to Molotov, 1925–1936*. Yale University Press, 1995.

Linz, Susan, and Robert Martin. "Soviet Enterprise Behavior Under Uncertainty," *Journal of Comparative Economics* 6, no. 1, 1982.

Malle, Silvana. *The Economic Organization of War Communism, 1918–1921*. Cambridge: Cambridge University Press, 1985.

Markevich, Andrei. [In Russian] "Was the Soviet Economy Planned? Planning in the People's Commissariats in the 1930," PERSA Working Paper No. 25 (Version 23, January 2003), University of Warwick, England; Department of Economics.

Markevich, Andrei, and Paul Gregory. "Was the Soviet Economy a Planned Economy? Answer of the Soviet Archives of the 1930s." Zvenigorod International Conference; Zvenigorod, Russia; June 2001.

McKay, John. *Pioneers for Profit: Foreign Entrepreneurship and Russian Industrialization, 1885–1913*. Chicago: University of Chicago Press, 1970.

Merl, Stephan. *Der Agrarmarkt und die Neue Ökonomische Politik*. Munich: Oldenbourg, 1981.

Mesa-Lago, Carmelo. *Market Socialist and Mixed Economies: Comparative Policy and Performance, Chile, Cuba, and Costa Rica*. Baltimore: The Johns Hopkins Press, 2000.

Mihalyi, Peter. *Socialist Investment Cycles Analysis in Retrospect*. Amsterdam: Kluwer Academic Publishers, 1992.

Mikoian, A. I. *Tak Bylo. Razmyshleniia o Minuvshem*. Moscow: Vagrius, 1999.

Millar, James (ed.). *Politics, Work and Daily Life in the USSR: A Survey of Former Citizens*. Cambridge: Cambridge University Press, 1987.

———. "Soviet Rapid Development and the Agricultural Surplus Hypothesis," *Soviet Studies* 22, no. 1 (July 1970).

———. "The Importance of Initial Conditions in Economic Transitions: An Evaluation of Economic Reform Progress in Russia," *Journal of Socio-Economics* 26, no. 4, 1997.

Mises, Ludwig. *Socialism: An Economic and Sociological Analysis*. Translated by J. Kahane. London: Jonathyn Cape Ltd., 1936.

Mokhtari, Manouchehr, and Paul Gregory. "State Grain Purchases, Relative Prices, and the Soviet Grain Procurement Crisis," *Explorations in Economic History 30* (1993).

Montias, Michael. "Planning with Material Balances in Soviet-Type Economies," *American Economic Review 49*, no. 5 (December 1959).

Moryukov, M. Y. "Penal Labor and the Economics of the White Sea Canal." In *The Economics of Forced Labor: The Soviet Gulag*. Edited by Paul Gregory and Valery Lazarev. Stanford, Calif.: Hoover Institution Press, 2003.

Murrell, Peter, and Mancur Olson. "The Devolution of Centrally Planned Economies," *Journal of Comparative Economics 15*, no. 2 (June 1991).

Niskanen, William A. *Bureaucracy and Public Economics*. Aldershot, England: Edward Elgar, 1994.

———. *Public Analysis and Public Choice*. Cheltenham, England: Edward Elgar, 1998.

Narodnoe Khoziaistvo SSSR za 70 Let. Moscow: Finansy i Statistika, 1987.

North, D. C. "Institutions and Economic Performance," In U. Maki, B. Gustafsson, and C. Knudsen (eds.), *Rationality, Institutions, and "Economic Methodology."* London: Routledge, 1993.

Nove, Alec. "The Problem of Success Indicators in Soviet Industry," *Economica 25*, no. 97 (1985).

Nove, Alec. *The Soviet Economic System*. London: Allen & Unwin, 1977.

Nutter, G. W. "The Soviet Economy: Retrospect and Prospect." In *Political, Military, and Economic Strategies in the Decade Ahead*. New York: Praeger, 1963.

Ofer, Gur. *The Service Sector in Soviet Economic Growth*. Cambridge: Harvard University Press, 1973.

Olsevich, Yury, and Paul Gregory. *Planovoia Sistema v Retrospektive: Analiz i Intervui s Rukovoditeliami Planirovaniia SSSR*. Moscow: Teis, 2000.

Olson, Mancur. "The Devolution of Power in Post-Communist Societies." In *Russia's Stormy Path to Reform*. Edited by Robert Skidelsky. London: The Social Market Foundation, 1995.

———. *The Logic of Collective Action: Public Goods and the Theory of Groups*. Cambridge, Mass.: Harvard University Press, 1971.

———. *The Rise and Decline of Nations: Economic Growth, Stagflation, and Social Rigidities*. New Haven, Conn.: Yale University Press, 1982.

Osokina, Elena. *Za Fasadom Stalinskogo Izobiliia*. Moscow: Rosspen, 1998.

Owen, Thomas. *The Corporation Under Russian Law, 1800–1917*. Cambridge: Cambridge University Press, 1991.

Powell, Raymond. "Plan Execution and the Workability of Soviet Planning," *Journal of Comparative Economics 1*, no. 1 (March 1977).

Preobrazhensky, E. A. *The New Economics*. Translated by Brian Pierce. Oxford: Oxford University Press, 1964.

Rees, E. A. (ed.). *Decision Making in the Stalinist Command Economy, 1932–37*. London: MacMillan, 1997.

———. "Leaders and Their Institutions." In *Behind the Facade of Stalin's Command Economy*. Edited by Paul Gregory. Stanford, Calif.: Hoover Institution Press, 2001.

———. "The People's Commissariat of Timber Industry." In *Decision Making in the Stalinist Command Economy, 1932–37*. Edited by E. A. Rees. London: MacMillan, 1997.

———. "The People's Commissariat of Transport (Railroad)." In *Decision Making in the Stalinist Command Economy, 1932–37*. Edited by E. A. Rees. London: MacMillan, 1997.

Rees, E. A., and D. H. Watson. "Politburo and Sovnarkom." In *Decision Making in the Stalinist Command Economy, 1932–37*. Edited by E. A. Rees. London: MacMillan, 1997.

Roberts, Paul Craig. *Alienation and the Soviet Economy*. Albuquerque: University New Mexico Press, 1971.

Rutland, Peter. *The Myth of the Plan*. LaSalle, Ill.: Open Court, 1985.

Schrettl, Wolfram. "Anspruchsdenken, Leistungsbereitschaft, and Wirtschaftzyklen," In *Wachstumsverlangsamung und Konjunkturzyklen in Underschiedlichen Wirtschaftssystemen*. Edited by Armin Bohnert et al. Berlin: Duncker & Humblot, 1984.

———. "Konsum und Arbeitsproduktivitat." *Beck'sche Schwarze Reihe, Band* 271. Munich: C. H. Beck, 1984.

———. "On the Volume of Soviet Investment and Some Implications," *Forschungsbericht* (1974).

Schrettl, Wolfram, and Paul Gregory. "Fair Wages and Unfair Dictators." DIW Working Paper, Summer 2002.

Schroeder, Gertrude. "The Soviet Economy on a Treadmill of Reforms." In U.S. Congress Joint Economic Committee, *Soviet Economy in a Time of Change*. Washington, D.C., 1979.

———. "The Slowdown in Soviet Industry, 1976–1982," *Soviet Economy 1*, no. 1 (January–March 1985).

Schumpter, Joseph. *Capitalism, Socialism and Democracy*. Cambridge: Harvard University Press, 1934.

Shleifer, Andrei, and Robert Vishny. "Pervasive Shortages Under Socialism," *Rand Journal of Economics 23*, no. 2 (Summer 1993).

Simonov, N. *Voenno-Promyshlenny Kompleks v 1920-1950-e gody*. Moscow: Rosspen, 1995.

Sitnin, V. K. *Debitorsko-Kreditorskaia Zadolzhennost' v 1935 Gody*, Report of Ministry of Finance in RGAE, 7733.14.900.

———. *Kontrol Rublem v Sotsialisticheskom Obschestve*. Moscow: Gosfinizdat, 1956.

———. "Payments in Ferrous Metallurgy," *Ekonomicheskaya Zhizn'*, no. 69, 1933.

———. *Vospominaniia Finansista*. Moscow: Luch, 1993.

Sokolov, A. K. "Period Prinuzhdeniia k Trudu v Sovetskoi Promyshlennosti i Ego Krizis," Institute of Russian History, Russian Academy of Sciences, August 2002.

———. "The Period of Forced Labor in Soviet Industry: The End of the 1930s to the Mid-1950s" In *The Economics of Forced Labor: The Soviet Gulag.* Edited by P. Gregory and V. Lazarev (Stanford, Calif.: Hoover Institution Press, 2003).

Spulber, Nicholas. *Soviet Strategy for Economic Growth.* Bloomington: Indiana University Press, 1964.

Stalin, I. V., *Voprosy Leninizma,* 10th ed. Moscow, 1937.

Strumilin, S. G. *Na Planovom Fronte 1920–1930 gg.* Moscow: Gospolizdat, 1958.

———. *Ocherki Sovetskoi Ekonomiki. Resursy i Perspektivy.* Moscow: Nauka, 1928.

Stuart, Robert, and Christina Panayotopouolos. "Decline and Recovery in Transition Economies: The Impact of Initial Conditions," *Post-Soviet Geography and Economics* 40, no. 4, 1999.

Sutton, Anthony C. *Western Technology and Soviet Economic Development, 1917–1930.* Stanford: Hoover Institution Press, 1971.

The International Bureau of the Revolutionary Party, http://www.geocities.com/ leftcom.html

Tikhonov, Alexei. "The End of the Gulag." In *The Economics of Forced Labor: The Soviet Gulag.* Edited by P. Gregory and V. Lazarev. Stanford: Hoover Institution Press, 2003.

Tikhonov, A., and P. Gregory. "Central Planning and Unintended Consequences: Creating the Soviet Financial System, 1930–1939," *Journal of Economic History* 60, no. 4 (2000).

———. "Stalin's Last Plan," In *Behind the Façade of Stalin's Command Economy.* Edited by Paul Gregory. Stanford: Hoover Institution Press, 2001.

Treisman, D. *After the Deluge: Regional Crises and Political Consolidation in Russia.* Ann Arbor: University of Michigan Press, 1999.

Treml, Vlad. "Production and Consumption of Alcoholic Beverages in the USSR: A Statistical Study," *Journal of Studies on Alcohol* 36 (March 1975).

Tsentralnoe Statisticheskoe Upravlenie, *Statisticheskii Spravochnik 1928* (Moscow: Izdatel'st vo Ts.S.u, 1929).

Ts.S.U. SSSR, Narodnoe Khoziaistvo SSSR v 1977 g. Moscow: Statistika, 1978.

Tsipkin, I. N. *Sovetskiy Kredit.* Moscow: n.p., 1933.

Vainshtein, A. L. "Dinamika Narodnogo Dokhoda i Ego Osnovnykh Komponentov," *Ekonomicheskie i Matematicheskie Metody* 3, no. 1 (January–February 1967).

Vickrey, William. *Microstatics.* New York: Harcourt, Brace and World, 1964.

Vincentz, Volkhart. "Wachstumsschwankungen der Sowjetischen Wirtschaft: Ausmass, Auswirkungen, and Urssachen," *Bericht des Bundesinstituts für Ostwissenschaftliche und Internationale Studien,* no. 15, March 1979.

Volin, Lazar. *A Century of Russian Agriculture.* Cambridge: Harvard University Press, 1970.

Vyas, A. "Primary Accumulation in the USSR Revisited," *Cambridge Journal of Economics* 3, no. 3, 1979.

Vyshniakov, V. G. *Struktura i Shtaty Sovetshogo Gosudarstva i Upravleniia.* Moscow: Nauka, 1972.

Weitzman, Martin. "Soviet Postwar Growth and Capital-Labor Substitution," *American Economic Review* 60, no. 4 (September 1970).

Wheatcroft, S. G., and R. W. Davies (eds.). *Materials for a Balance of the Soviet National Economy, 1928–1930.* Cambridge: Cambridge University Press, 1985.

Who Was Who in the USSR. Metuchen, N.J.: Scarecrow Press, 1972.

Wilhelm, J. "Does the Soviet Union Have a Planned Economy?" *Soviet Studies* 21 (April 1979).

Williamson, Oliver. "The Institutions of Governance," *American Economic Review* 88, no. 2 (May 1998).

Williamson, O. E., and S. G. Winter (eds.) *The Nature of the Firm.* Oxford: Oxford University Press, 1993.

Wintrobe, Ronald. *The Political Economy of Dictatorship.* Cambridge: Cambridge University Press, 1998.

Yasin, Y. "Getting the Details Wrong." In *The Destruction of the Soviet Economic System.* Armonk, N.Y.: Sharpe, 1998.

Zaleskii, Eugene. *Stalinist Planning for Economic Growth 1933–1952.* Chapel Hill: University of North Carolina Press, 1980.

Zaleskii, K. A. *Imperiia Stalina. Biograpficheckii Entsiklopedicechekii Slovar'.* Moscow: Beche, 2000.

Zoteev, G. "The View from Gosplan." In *The Destruction of the Soviet Economic System.* Armonk, N.Y.: Sharpe, 1998.

Index

administrative-command system
  collapse of, 243
  as creation of Stalin, 15
  early history of, 7–8
  evolves into single-person dictatorship,
    64
  Gorbachev on, 2
  money and credit in, 217–18
  planners' preferences in, 76
  planners and producers in, 127
  after Stalin, 271
  supply chains in, 179
agriculture
  capital accumulation for, 30–1
  collective farms in, 40–4
  collectivization of, 23, 47–8
  grain collection crises in, 31–40
  under New Economic Policy, 28–9
  during War Communism, 28
Anderson, G., 190
Andreev, A.A., 136, 162
Arrow, Kenneth, 64
Arrow Impossibility Theorem, 64
automobiles, 147–8, 248

Baibakov, N.K., 7n
banking, 215, 223
  socialist theory of, 217–18
  State Bank (Gosbank) for, 150
Barsov, A.A., 47
Bergson, Abram, 46, 76
Beria, L.P., 67

Berliner, Joseph, 4, 21, 268
Boettke, Peter, 140, 190
Bolshevik Party, see Communist Party of
    the Soviet Union
Bolsheviks, 16, 26–7
Brezhnev, Leonid, 245, 263
Briukhanov, Nikolai, 18–19n
Bukharin, Nikolai, 17, 18, 27
  in Politburo, 50, 54
  in power struggle with Stalin, 51, 52

capital,
  domestic, 236–40
  imported, 235–6
capital accumulation, 29–31, 249, 252,
    257, 258
Carr, E.H., 41
Central Committee
  conflicting interests within, 65–66
  regional leaders on, 80
  staff of, 112, 128
  on Stakhanovism, 106
  Stalin on members of, 66–7
Central Planning Board, 10, 68
Chernenko, 263
chervonets, 28
China, 1n, 243
civil war (Russia), 27
collectivization of agriculture, 23, 39–40
  collective farms, 40–4
commercial credit, 226–8
communism, 4

decision making by, 267
economic dictatorship of, 9
economic policies of, 2
on enforcement of directives, 165
on First Five-Year Plan, 120, 122
on five-year plans, 205
foreign exchange commission headed by,
235
government decrees rejected by, 58
grain collection crises under, 32,
34–40
Great Break-Through policy of, 22–3
Great Terror of, 182
on Grin'ko, 214
inevitability of, 15, 20
on interventions in plans, 211
investment decisions made by, 250–1
on Kuibyshev, 185
on Mikoian, 169–70
models of dictatorship of, 11–15
on money supply, 239–40
on narrow interests of Politburo
members, 136, 262
as old Bolshevik, 27
on Ordzhonikidze, 155, 235–6
on other Politburo members, 64–5
party discipline under, 54–6
personnel matters decided by, 161–2
on planning, 183
in post-Lenin power struggle in CPSU,
50–2
price of grain raised by, 47–8
as referee of disputes, 67–8
regional interests and, 80–1
routine decisions made by, 71–2
on Rukhimovich, 153, 163
Rykov removed from power by, 56–7
Soviet economy inherited by, 93
Soviet Union after death of, 75
on state budgets, 237
on state spending, 239
Trotsky feared by, 62
vacations of, 113*n*, 114
State Arbitration Commission, 220
State Archive of the Russian Federation
(GARF), 8–9
State Bank (Gosbank), 150, 218–19,
241–42
automatic crediting by, 223–24
commercial credit issued by, 226–27

as lender of last resort, 228–31
reform of 1931 and, 224–6
state budgets, 234–40
State Planning Commission (Gosplan), 2,
69–70, 151–2, 192
on abuse of discretion, 144–5
decisions made by, 270
dispute between Heavy Industry ministry
and, 149–50
on dual planning, 144
five-year plans and, 120–2
generalized, nonconcrete, plans of, 143
heads of, 184–6
Heavy Industry Ministry and, 142
industrial orders from, 165
information from, 116
lack of power of, 132
loyal agents on, 137–8
in operational planning process, 193–4
planning by, 138–9
purges of (1929), 184
regional interests and, 80
staff of, 128
"stationary bandit" model, 11–12, 45, 63,
68, 186–7, 262, 264–7
Strumilin, S.G., 120, 152
Syrtsov, S.I., 49
Szyrmer, J., 171

Tal', 219
Third Five-Year Plan (1938–43), 118,
121
Tomsky, M.P., 50, 52, 54, 81
Trotsky, Leon, 19, 27, 29–31, 51, 183, 269
on control of resources, 154
expulsion from Politburo of, 53
on Gosplan, 152
peasant support for, 41
in Politburo, 54
on power of CPSU, 56
Stalin versus, 62

Union of Soviet Socialist Republics (USSR)
decline in economic growth in, 246–7
division of power between CPSU and,
52–3
economic growth in, 243–5
replaced by Russian Federation, 1
after Stalin's death, 75
see also government

Vainshtein, A.L., 83
vehicles, 146–8, 248
vested interests, 261–5
Voroshilov, K.E., 7n, 17, 52, 170
  in Politburo, 50, 81
vouchers (money surrogates), 233
Voznesensky, N.A., 19
Vyshinsky, A., 146

wages, 84–91
  arrears in, 232
  Stakhanovism and, 102–6
  see also fair-wage theory
War Communism, 2, 24, 27–8, 240, 257
Wintrobe, Ronald, 14

Worker-Peasant Inspection (Party Control Commission), 131, 221, 223–4
World War II, 121

Yakovlev, Y.A., 44
Yenukidze, A.S., 17, 167

Zaleski, Eugene, 183
  on delegation in planning, 188
  on economic policy and plans, 123–4
  on five-year plans, 118, 119
  on resource management, 122, 151–2, 180
  on Soviet planning, 189, 191
Zhdanov, A.A., 37, 112, 237–8
Zolotorev, 160